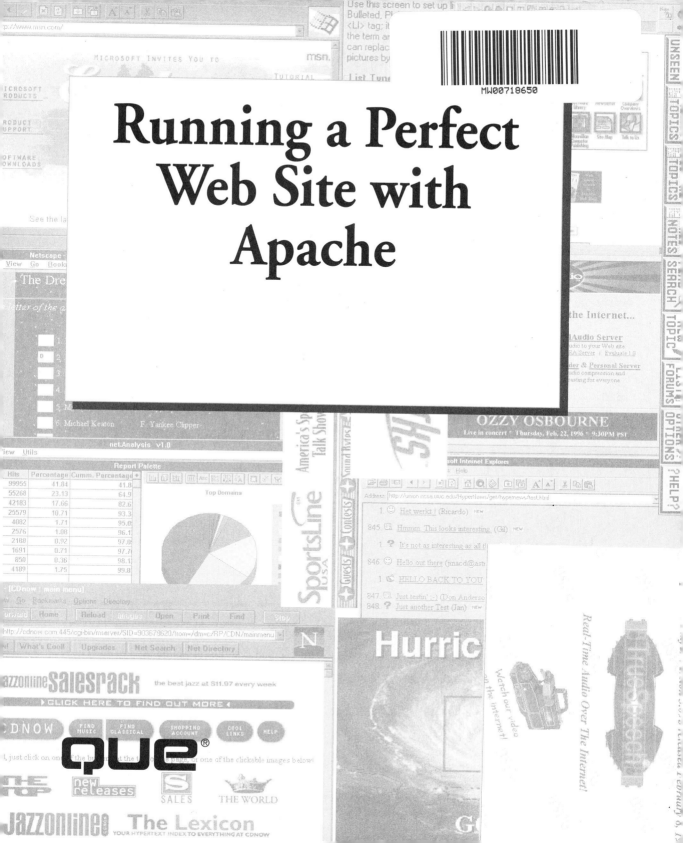

Running a Perfect Web Site with Apache

Check out Que® Books on the World Wide Web
http://www.mcp.com/que

As the biggest software release in computer history, Windows 95 continues to redefine the computer industry. Click here for the latest info on our Windows 95 books

Make computing quick and easy with these products designed exclusively for new and casual users

Examine the latest releases in word processing, spreadsheets, operating systems, and suites

The Internet, The World Wide Web, CompuServe®, America Online®, Prodigy®—it's a world of ever-changing information. Don't get left behind!

Find out about new additions to our site, new bestsellers and hot topics

In-depth information on high-end topics: find the best reference books for databases, programming, networking, and client/server technologies

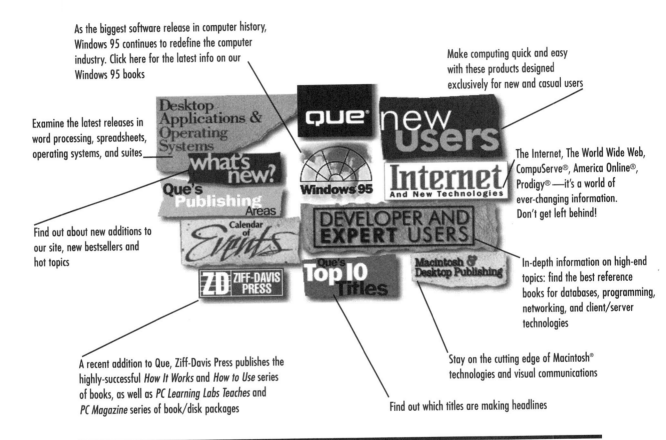

A recent addition to Que, Ziff-Davis Press publishes the highly-successful *How It Works* and *How to Use* series of books, as well as *PC Learning Labs Teaches* and *PC Magazine* series of book/disk packages

Stay on the cutting edge of Macintosh® technologies and visual communications

Find out which titles are making headlines

With 6 separate publishing groups, Que develops products for many specific market segments and areas of computer technology. Explore our Web Site and you'll find information on best-selling titles, newly published titles, upcoming products, authors, and much more.

- Stay informed on the latest industry trends and products available
- Visit our online bookstore for the latest information and editions
- Download software from Que's library of the best shareware and freeware

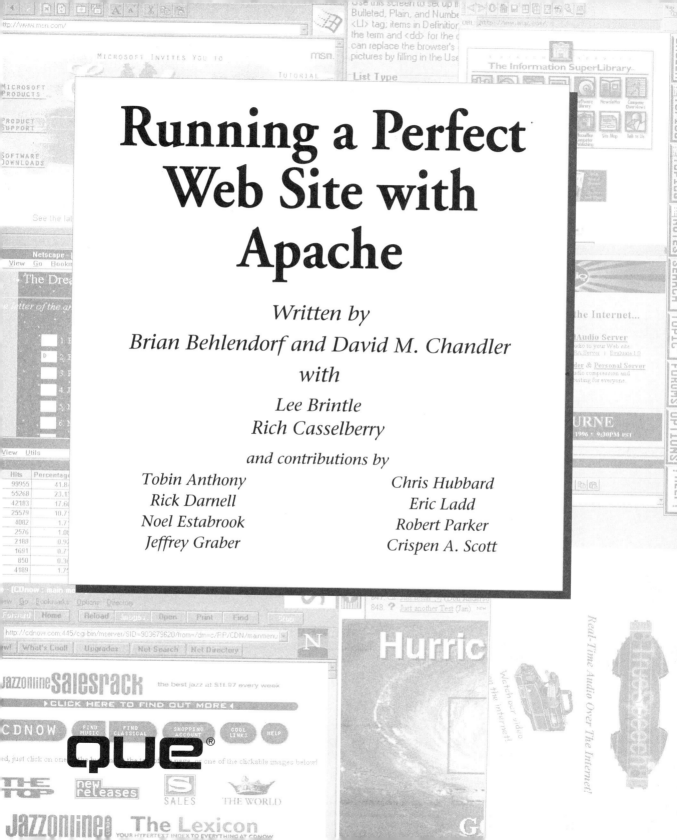

Running a Perfect Web Site with Apache

Written by

Brian Behlendorf and David M. Chandler

with

Lee Brintle
Rich Casselberry

and contributions by

Tobin Anthony
Rick Darnell
Noel Estabrook
Jeffrey Graber

Chris Hubbard
Eric Ladd
Robert Parker
Crispen A. Scott

que®

Running a Perfect Web Site with Apache

Copyright©1996 by Que® Corporation.

Library of Congress Catalog No.: 96-68043

ISBN: 0-7897-0745-4

98 97 96   6 5 4 3 2 1

Interpretation of the printing code: the rightmost double-digit number is the year of the book's printing; the rightmost single-digit number, the number of the book's printing. For example, a printing code of 96-1 shows that the first printing of the book occurred in 1996.

All terms mentioned in this book that are known to be trademarks or service marks have been appropriately capitalized. Que cannot attest to the accuracy of this information. Use of a term in this book should not be regarded as affecting the validity of any trademark or service mark.

Screen reproductions in this book were created using Collage Plus from Inner Media, Inc., Hollis, NH.

Composed in *Stone Serif* and *MCPdigital* by Que Corporation

Credits

President
Roland Elgey

Publisher
Joseph B. Wikert

Editorial Services Director
Elizabeth Keaffaber

Managing Editor
Sandy Doell

Director of Marketing
Lynn E. Zingraf

Title Manager
Jim Minatel

Acquisitions Manager
Cheryl D. Willoughby

Acquisitions Editor
Doshia Stewart

Product Director
Benjamin Milstead

Production Editor
Danielle Bird

Editors
Elizabeth A. Bruns
Noelle Gasco
Patrick Kanouse
Mike La Bonne
Susan Ross Moore
Kelly Oliver
Brook Thaler

Product Marketing Manager
Kim Margolius

Technical Editors
Kyle Amon
Todd Brown
Paul Ehteridge
Faisal Jawdat
Greg Newman
Paolo Papalardo
Mark Surfas

Technical Specialist
Nadeem Muhammed

Acquisitions Coordinator
Jane Brownlow

Operations Coordinator
Patricia J. Brooks

Editorial Assistant
Andrea Duvall

Book Designer
Ruth Harvey

Cover Designer
Dan Armstrong

Production Team
Stephen Adams, Jason Carr,
Anne Dickerson, Joan Evan,
Jessica Ford, Trey Frank, Jason Hand,
Daniel Harris, Damon Jordan,
Daryl Kessler, Clint Lahnen,
Bob LaRoche, Michelle Lee,
Julie Quinn, Laura Robbins,
Bobbi Satterfield, Jody York

Indexer
Tim Tate

About the Authors

Brian Behlendorf is a technologist and entrepreneur. As Chief Technology Officer at Organic Online, he directs the investigation and implementation of new functionality for Organic clients, and plays a strong role in the Internet public standards and software development communities. Predestined for the computer age when his parents met as employees at IBM, Behlendorf studied computer science at Berkeley where his interest in the Internet was piqued in 1991. His interests in music and dance culture led to the establishment of one of the first nonacademic Web sites in early 1993, a site which has since grown into a collaborative publishing effort known as Hyperreal. In the fall of 1993 he set up a Web server for *Wired Magazine*, at first served by a 486/66 over a 14.4 connection. This served as the prototype for *HotWired*, where Behlendorf served as Chief Engineer. Behlendorf left in April 1995 to work for Organic Online, a startup he co-founded and had been moonlighting at since the fall of 1993. Behlendorf is also a co-founder and maintainer of the "www-vrml" mailing list, which served as the basis for the VRML public development effort, and he hosts, administrates, and contributes to the Apache development effort.

David M. Chandler is a World Wide Web enthusiast in Cedar Rapids, Iowa. He currently runs Internet At Work, a Midwestern consulting firm specializing in network security, Intranet development, and advanced Web applications. Chandler previously managed Web servers for the Collins Avionics & Communications Division of Rockwell International. He has programmed computers since 1982 when he received a TI-99/4A as a gift. Chandler holds a degree in Electrical Engineering from the University of Kansas. When he's not at his computer, he enjoys the mountains and flying as a private pilot. You can reach Chandler via e-mail at **chandler@iwork.net** or on the Web at **http://www.iwork.net/~chandler**.

Lee Brintle is the president and founder of Leepfrog Technologies, Inc. (**http://www.leepfrog.com**), located in Iowa City which specializes in custom database programming for the Web and providing direct access to the Internet. He has written a variety of Web browsers and servers, including a cable television Web browser. Lee has developed a trusted third-party user authentication security system for use on the Web, and also has tinkered with parallel processing and distributed databases. He was introduced to the distributed security and database arena by a too-healthy dose of the original MUDs. In that laughingly brief period he calls "free time," he plays Wally-Ball, helps administrate the ISCABBS (**telnet://bbs.isca.uiowa.edu**), enjoys role-playing, and the too-infrequent late-night card game. Lee received a BS in Computer Science from the University of Iowa, and can be reached at **lbrintle@leepfrog.com**. Drop him a line; he enjoys social e-mail.

Rich Casselberry is currently working as the Network Manager for Current Technology in Durham NH (**http://www.curtech.com/**). He lives in Southern Maine with his fiancée Kandi, two cats (Mitz and Zeb) and a minia-ture dachshund (Prince). Prior to working at Current Technology, Rich worked as a UNIX System Specialist for Cabletron Systems for four and a half years. It was here that he first learned about the Internet and networking. Rich graduated from New Hampshire Technical College in 1992 with an Associates degree in Computer Engineering Technology.

Tobin Anthony holds a Ph.D. in aerospace engineering, but has been tinker-ing with computers for over 18 years specializing in the UNIX and MacOS environments. A strict vegetarian, devout Roman Catholic, and lapsed private pilot, Anthony spends what little spare time he has with his wife Sharon and three children, Michelle, Austin, and Evan. Anthony works as a spacecraft control systems engineer at NASA's Goddard Space Flight Center in Greenbelt, MD. E-mail and Web stops are welcome at **tobin@pobox.com** and **http://pobox.com/~tobin**.

Rick Darnell is a midwest native who now lives with his wife and two daughters in Missoula, MT. He began his career in print at a small weekly newspaper after graduating from Kansas State University with a degree in broadcasting. While spending time as a freelance journalist and writer, Rick has seen the full gamut of personal computers since starting out with a Radio Shack Model I in the late 1970s. Darnell serves as a volunteer firefighter and member of a regional hazardous materials response team.

Noel Estabrook is currently a faculty member of the College of Education at Michigan State University after having obtained degrees in Psychology, Edu-cation, and Instructional Technology. He is heavily involved in delivering Internet Training and technical support to educators, professionals and lay-men. In addition to writing, he also runs his own training business part-time.

Most recently, Estabrook has been involved in authoring on the Web and co-authored Que's *Using UseNet Newsgroups* and *Using FTP*. His e-mail address is **noele@msu.edu**.

Jeffrey Graber is a technical consultant for Compuware Corp. at their Washington, DC branch. There, Graber is responsible for the management and development of Internet services and business. In addition, he manages a major client Internet site at the National Science Foundation. Graber has been involved in Web development almost since it began. He has developed several sites for other government agencies. Graber has spoken on the topic of the WWW at the 2nd and 4th International WWW conferences (sponsored by the official W3.org) as well as MecklerMedia's WebDev Conference. He is also founder and chair of the DC area Internet Developers Association (**http: //www.shirenet.com/dcida/**). Over the years, Graber has taught numerous computer science courses and given presentation at numerous conferences.

Chris Hubbard is an Internet veteran and technical supervisor with Questar Microsystems, responsible for documentation, testing, and implementation of WebQuest products. His broad professional experience and a wide range of outside interests uniquely qualify him to discuss the World Wide Web in general, and WebQuest in particular. A member of the HTML Writers Guild, Hubbard has consulted and built HTML pages for numerous high-profile clients. For recreation, Hubbard surfs the Web discovering and correcting defective Web pages. You can e-mail him at **chris.hubbard@questar.com**.

Eric Ladd is a "math teacher turned Internet teacher" and currently works as Internet training coordinator for Walcoff and Associates, Inc., a communications and technology firm in Fairfax, VA. He holds B.S. and M.S. degrees in Mathematics from Rensselaer Polytechnic Institute in Troy, New York, where he also taught calculus, linear algebra, and differential equations for six years. Rensselaer also taught Ladd a thing or two about running a newspaper, engineering late-night angst radio shows, and managing a bar. Away from work and writing, he enjoys running, ice hockey, and spending far too much time playing with his new computer.

Robert Parker first caught the writing bug in the machine room of the Yale Computer Science Facility, tending mainframe systems equipped with an awesome 256K of core memory. He has crafted technical publications for such firms as Compu-Teach, DAK Industries, and most recently Quarterdeck

Corporation; scripted and narrated educational videotapes, radio theater, and commercials; and is currently on the faculty at Glendale College, where both he and his father teach courses in the same division. Parker is currently completing his doctorate in conducting, and hopes someday to retire from a successful career as a beloved professor of music.

Crispen A. Scott is an independent hardware and software engineering consultant who lists among his accomplishments such varied projects as the digital anti-skid braking system for the B-2 Stealth Bomber, various Windows drivers and applications, and embedded control systems for the medical and industrial control fields. Scott is currently developing home pages, CGI applications, and establishing Web sites for Chicago-based customers of his Commercial, Residential and Institutional Software Corporation. In addition, Scott also lectures, conducts seminars, and presents training reviews nationally. Scott is a continuing, lifelong student who barely remembers graduation from the University of Tennesee, and ardently follows his favorite sports: football and lacrosse. In his "spare" time, Scott is continuing to polish his writing skills in both the poetry and science fiction genres. Scott can currently be reached at **crisin19@starnetinc.com**, and, in the near future, at his Web site. Search for "Chicago Developments" using your favorite search engine.

We'd Like To Hear From You!

As part of our continuing effort to produce books of the highest possible quality, Que would like to hear your comments. To stay competitive, we *really* want you, as a computer book reader and user, to let us know what you like or dislike most about this book or other Que products.

You can mail comments, ideas, or suggestions for improving future editions to the address below, or send us a fax at (317) 581-4663. For the online inclined, Macmillan Computer Publishing has a forum on CompuServe (type **GO QUEBOOKS** at any prompt) through which our staff and authors are available for questions and comments. The address of our Internet site is **http://www.mcp.com** (World Wide Web).

In addition to exploring our forum, please feel free to contact me personally to discuss your opinions of this book: I'm **102121,1324** on CompuServe, and **bmilstead.que.mcp.com** on the Internet.

Thanks in advance—your comments will help us to continue publishing the best books available on computer topics in today's market.

Benjamin Milstead
Product Director
Que Corporation
201 W. 103rd Street
Indianapolis, Indiana 46290
USA

Contents at a Glance

Contents

7 Creating and Managing an Intranet   **115**

III Doing HTML   157

8 Basic HTML: Understanding Hypertext   159

9 HTML 2.0, HTML 3.0, and Extensions   193

10 HTML Editors and Tools 233

14 More Scripting Options 355

15 Search Engines and Annotation Systems 379

17 Database Access and Applications Integration   429

18 Financial Transactions   445

Introduction

In the spring of 1995, I was copied on a piece of e-mail from a fellow Webmaster in France to three others who, along with myself, had spent some time modifying the Web server that had been released by the National Center for Supercomputing Applications (NCSA). We had each submitted our "patches" to NCSA, but because of a team exodus to a certain start-up software company in Mountain View, NCSA had few resources to continue development of what was then, by far, the most popular Web server out there. Thus, the five of us decided we had the time and interest to start our own Web server development effort, branching off from the development paths taken by the NCSA team. Since most of us were Webmasters for content providers or educational or research institutions, we had no desire or time to make this a commercial venture. Instead, we realized we had nothing to lose by helping each other. I suggested the name "Apache," which was a code name for my own vaporware server project, and only later realized what a great pun it made ("A patchy Web server"). And from that, the project was born.

The Apache development team quickly grew to well over 40 people, with a core development team of roughly 12 people. At one point, in the summer of 1995, the internals of the server were significantly reorganized by Rob Thau, a graduate student at the Massachusetts Institute of Technology, which produced not only a tremendous improvement in speed, but also a highly generalized API (Application Programming Interface) to the internals of the server. This API has made it possible to enhance functionality in a very modular way—not only can you add features without having to modify existing files, but third party developers can create new modules without requiring that they be "officially" rolled into the Apache releases.

Today (as of the April 1st Netcraft Survey, at **http://www.netcraft.co.uk/ Survey/Reports/**) Apache is the single most-used Web server on the Internet, with more installations than all other commercial web servers combined. Public support exists on the UseNet newsgroup **comp. infosystems.www.servers.unix**, and several companies provide commercial support for Apache.

The Apache project has also spawned some parallel efforts. The Apache-SSL project is an integration of the Secure Sockets Layer specification. SSL is the security protocol that Netscape's browsers and servers implement for secure communications. It is also supported by Microsoft's Internet Explorer and numerous other browsers. Both are covered in this book.

What This Book Is

This book is designed for those who are new to setting up a Web server on a UNIX platform. The featured Web server is Apache, though many of the subjects covered are applicable to other Web servers. The basics of constructing a Web site are also covered—authoring HTML (including HTML extensions), CGI scripting, integrating new media types, installing and running a search engine, usage statistics analysis programs, database interfaces, and more. Finally, it includes a CD-ROM with the Apache server source code and binaries for a variety of platforms.

These chapters include:

- Chapter 1, "The State of the World Wide Web." This chapter examines where the Web came from, how the Web is changing today, and why you should have a presence on it.

- Chapter 2, "Introduction to Web Servers." The basic terminology of Web serving is discussed; details about the HyperText Transfer Protocol (HTTP) and the types of data one can put on a Web server are also discussed.

- Chapter 3, "Setting Up a Web Presence." In this chapter, you will learn about hosting a site on your own machine versus leasing a site on another server, how to choose a hardware and software combination for your server, and what sort of Internet connectivity you should get.

- Chapter 4, "Getting Started with Apache." This chapter takes you through the basic steps of compiling, installing, and configuring the Web server.

■ Chapter 5, "Apache Configuration." This chapter covers all the aspects of complete Apache configuration, such as MIME type assignment, directory indexing, server side includes, internal imagemap handling, cookies, configurable logging, content negotiation, access control, virtual hosts, and custom error messages.

■ Chapter 6, "Managing an Internet Web Server." Real nuts-and-bolts issues regarding server performance and security are covered here. Included within are tips for using Apache on very heavily loaded Web servers.

■ Chapter 7, "Creating and Managing an Intranet." This chapter describes how to maximize the effectiveness of your internal server. It explains how you can manage server content, provide useful features, and protect your internal network from hostile access.

■ Chapter 8, "Basic HTML: Understanding Hypertext." In this chapter, you will learn the basics of authoring HTML. This includes distinguishing between logical and presentational tags, and how to embed images and hyperlinks on a page.

■ Chapter 9, "HTML 2.0, HTML 3.0, and Extensions." This chapter covers the complete HTML 2.0 specification, plus other extensions which have been proposed for standardization, and also some browser-specific extensions.

■ Chapter 10, "HTML Editors and Tools." This chapter covers authoring tools for both Windows and UNIX, and includes sections on HTML filters and other types of algorithmic HTML generation, as well as HTML validation programs.

■ Chapter 11, "Graphics and Imagemaps." This chapter covers the basics of using images on your Web sites, including pointers to various image manipulation tools. This chapter includes discussion of both client-side and server-side imagemaps, as well as tools to create them on Windows and UNIX.

■ Chapter 12, "HTML Forms." The essentials of HTML form programming are covered, with descriptions of the different types of form widgets, an explanation of the two types of form data submission, and more.

■ Chapter 13, "CGI Scripts and Server APIs." This chapter explains in detail how to use each of these three features to create dynamic, compelling Web sites.

■ Chapter 14, "More Scripting Options." This chapter explores JavaScript and Visual Basic Script, two new client-side scripting languages for dramatically extending the impact of Web pages.

- Chapter 15, "Search Engines and Annotation Systems." This chapter goes over the basics of setting up simple, shareware search engines for your pages, as well as systems for Web-based collaboration and annotation.

- Chapter 16, "Usage Statistics and Maintaining HTML." This chapter tells you the best way to handle your voluminous logfile data, with pointers to logfile analysis programs. Also included are pointers to programs which help ensure the integrity of your collection of documents.

- Chapter 17, "Database Access and Applications Integration." This chapter discussed in general terms the models for integrating databases with the Web. Sample applications are given, as are lots of tips on creating such applications.

- Chapter 18, "Financial Transactions." This chapter briefly covers the history of online commerce, security protocols, digital cash, and how to become a merchant on the Web.

- Chapter 19, "Interactive and Live Applications." Discussion about integrating audio, video and virtual reality into your Web site is covered in this chapter.

What This Book Is Not

While this book covers a lot of basics regarding setting up a Web server, both from a software/configuration perspective and from a content/HTML perspective, this book is not a UNIX tutorial book. This book presumes a basic knowlege of UNIX, including UNIX terminology such as what "cron" is or how UNIX "daemons" work.

Conventions Used in This Book

Certain conventions are used in *Running a Perfect Web Site with Apache* to help you absorb the ideas easily.

> **Tip**
>
> Tips suggest easier or alternate methods of executing a procedure or approaching a task.

New terms are introduced in *italics* and text you type appears in **boldface**. World Wide Web URLs (essentially document addresses) are also presented in **boldface**.

Note

This paragraph format indicates additional information that might help you avoid problems, or that might be considered when using the described features.

Caution

This paragraph format warns you of hazardous procedures.

▶ See "Section Title," p. xx

Running a Perfect Web Site with Apache uses marginal cross references so you can quickly find related information in the book. These are listed by section or chapter title and page number for convenience.

▶ See "Chapter Title," p. xx

Throughout the book, you'll also see the WebmasterCD icon (shown beside this paragraph) in the margins. Where you see this icon, the text is discussing software or a document on the WebmasterCD that is included with this book.

Part I

Planning Your Web Server

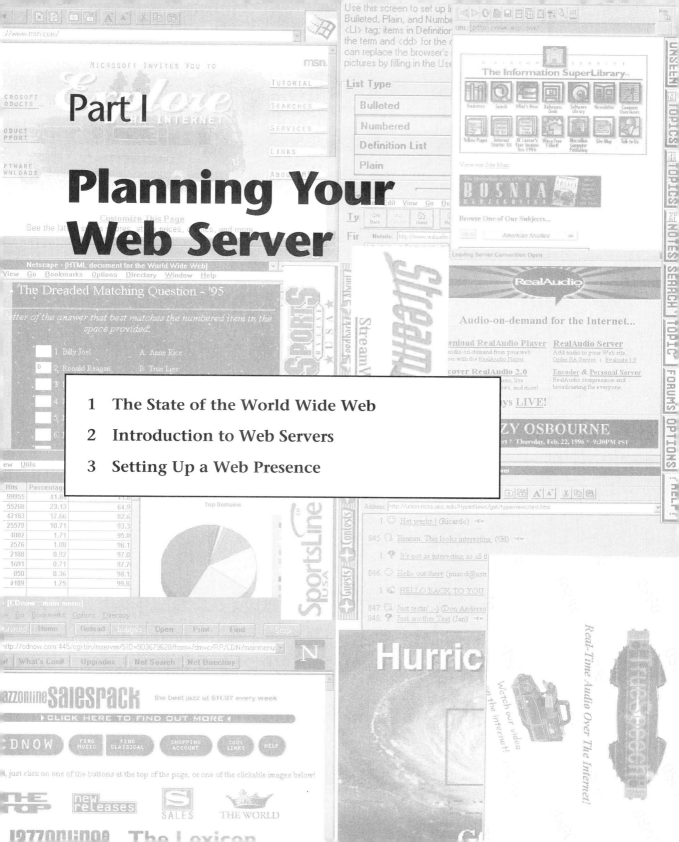

## CHAPTER 1

The State of the World Wide Web

In the six years since Tim Berners-Lee unleashed his graphical NeXT application, "WWW.app," upon an unsuspecting public, the World Wide Web has grown into *the* standard networked information infrastructure. (See **http://www.w3.org/pub/WWW/History.html**.) Its graphical interface and hypertext capabilities have caught the fancy of individuals and the media like no other Internet tool in history. Businesses, schools, government and non-profit organizations, and millions of individuals are flocking to the Web to promote themselves and their products in front of an audience spanning the entire planet. Millions more are using the Web on a daily basis as a tool to conduct business, get informed, be entertained, and even form virtual communities.

It's difficult to watch a sporting event, a commercial, or even the news without seeing that increasingly familiar *http://*— telling us of yet another enterprise on the Web. Because of the Web's popularity and its cost-effectiveness as a marketing tool, the World Wide Web is quickly becoming the electronic marketplace of the decade.

In this chapter, you learn:

- Where the Web has been
- How Web usage is changing
- How you might do business on the Web
- Where the Web is going

The Scope of the World Wide Web

The Web is now accessible in over 200 countries on all seven continents, and its information and services range from the esoteric to the absurd. As of this writing, the Alta Vista search engine reports that its robot has indexed 21 million Web pages, and the Netcraft Web Server Survey reports 135,000 different Web servers in its database. Web sites are maintained by universities, companies, public institutions, states, cities, and even high schools. Even McMurdo Station in Antarctica has a Web site. A number of powerful search engines (like Alta Vista) and catalog sites (like Yahoo) allow rapid information location and retrieval, making the Web the ultimate tool for research, interactive entertainment, and even advertising. For more information, see **http://www.w3.org/pub/WWW/History.html**, **http://www.altavista.digital.com**, **http://www.netcraft.co.uk/Survey/Reports,** and **http://www.mcmurdo.gov/**.

One of several reasons why the World Wide Web rose to such prominence was because the underlying technology, HyperText Transfer Protocol (HTTP) and the Hypertext Markup Language (HTML), were "free." (See **http://www.w3.org/pub/WWW/Protocols/** and **http://www.w3.org/pub/WWW/MarkUp/**.) Anyone could write an HTML viewer or HTTP application without having to pay anyone royalties or licensing fees. This also made it easy for the Web to be platform independent—a Microsoft Windows Web browser has no problem talking to a UNIX Web server, and a Windows Web browser can display the HTML pages exactly the same as a Macintosh Web browser or UNIX Web browser does.

Furthermore, because HTML describes documents at a structural level rather than a "pretty picture" level, HTML is extremely portable between platforms of different capabilities. In other words, it is possible to write a well-formed HTML page that looks equally attractive on a graphical Web browser like Mosaic as it does on a text-only browser like Lynx. In fact, some companies are building audio-only Web browsers for the visually impaired, and HTML's structural markup makes this not only possible, but quite elegant.

Note
The Web is not free from forward compatibility problems—HTML has lacked a formal evolutionary strategy, and the one in HTTP (content negotiation) has not been widely implemented. Thus, many companies use new HTML tags, some of which cause older browsers to act inelegantly. This means you will often see sites that say "You must use Browser X to view these pages," which is more often a statement on the page author's capabilities than your browser's capabilities, since a site designed with care can be elegant for all browsers. Web standards coordination is the responsibility of the World Wide Web Consortium. See **http://www.w3.org/**.

> **Note**
>
> There are many good sources for Internet usage statistics. One is located at Matrix Information and Directory Service (**http://www.mids.org/**). There are still statistics available at NSFNet (**http://nis.nsf.net/nsfnet/statistics/**), though the project was dismantled in April 1995.

The Web's Phenomenal Growth

In January 1993, there were only 50 known Web servers in existence. Today, the Web has become the largest source of traffic on the Internet. Table 1.1 and figure 1.1 show the growth of the Web relative to other Internet services on the Internet. You can find more details about the data shown in figure 1.1 at **http://www.nielsenmedia.com/demo.htm**. As was mentioned earlier, Web servers are in almost every developed country in the world.

> **Note**
>
> If you're interested, a list of all registered servers is available from **http://www.w3.org/hypertext/DataSources/WWW/Servers.html**.

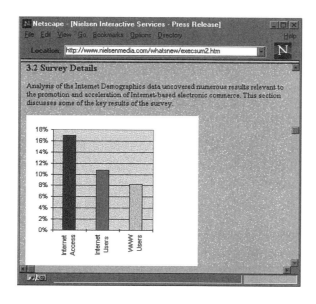

Fig. 1.1
This data was taken by a Nielsen survey conducted on Web usage.

Table 1.1   Growth of World Wide Web Traffic Percentage of Total Byte Traffic Change on the NSF Backbone in a Four-Month Period

Service Name	Port	Rank %	Pkts	Rank %	Bytes
Beginning of Four-Month Period					
ftp-data	20	1	18.758	1	30.251
www	80	2	13.122	2	17.693
telnet	23	3	10.357	6	3.715
End of Four-Month Period					
www	80	1	21.443	1	26.250
ftp-data	20	2	14.023	2	21.535
nntp	119	3	8.119	3	8.657

As table 1.1 illustrates, the World Wide Web already comprises more traffic than any other Internet function. Despite the fact that the Web has been in operation for several years now, it is still able to grow at a rate of almost 20 percent a year.

Note

The World Wide Web traffic in table 1.1 reflects only connections to World Wide Web servers. Web browsers can also connect to FTP (File Transfer Protocol), Gopher, and other types of servers.

But do we know anything else about who is actually on the Web? The Nielsen study mentioned in figure 1.1 tells us quite a bit about who is on the Net. Among the findings:

- 56 percent of WWW users were between 25-44 years old.
- 64.5 percent of users were male.
- 88 percent had at least some college education.

The Proliferation of Web Server Software

One of the barometers of the growth of the Web is the incredible number of different products out there, particularly in the Web server field. Two years ago, there were roughly half a dozen Web servers, all products of research groups or experimentation. Now there are dozens and dozens of different

Web server products out there. Many are commercial, but the free Web servers (like Apache) continue to be developed, supported, and very widely used. The chart available from WebCompare shows over 45 actively supported Web servers. For more information, see **http://www.webcompare.com/ server-main.html**.

Why You Want To Be on the WWW

There is little doubt that there are some huge benefits to being on the Web today. In business, numbers speak volumes. There is no doubt that the Web has them. Web users are generally educated, professional, middle to upper-middle class people who want to use the Web for information, research, fun, and even for purchasing products.

Like every new major medium that has come before, the Web has distinct, inherent, and unique advantages to other media. Instant access to information resources—also known as the "pull" model compared to television's "push" model—is one of the most significant advantages. Many commercial sites report thousands of visitors within the first days of operation. Electronic malls are appearing everywhere, and financial transactions are becoming safer all the time.

The best thing about the Web, of course, is that it isn't going to go away. It's only going to get bigger and bigger. Connections will get faster, computers will get better, programming will get slicker, and access will get better. Most importantly, more people will getting online.

So, you're convinced. The Web is the greatest thing since tail fins, right? Well, almost. There are definitely a lot of advantages to doing business on the Net (as well as some pitfalls), and it will definitely be helpful to know about some of them. Who's out there? What are they like? Are they ready to buy your product? Who's doing business on the Web?

Some of those questions are easy to answer. We know that there are a lot of educated professionals on the Internet. We also know that many of them are involved in education, research, and industry. It's time to dig a little deeper and find out a little bit about how the Web can serve businesses and consumers of all kinds.

More Than a High-Tech Billboard: Your Name on the Web

The Web has proven that people will come—in droves—to the Internet if it's easy to use and accessible. For those in business for profit, being on the Web, referred to as "having a presence on the Web," usually serves two main purposes.

One reason many business get on the Web is to sell their product. Many companies, such as CD-Now, are focused on marketing a specific product or class of products (see fig. 1.2). They are not as concerned about establishing a brand identity or giving information away. They offer a product, and hope people will buy it. For more information about CD-Now, see **http://www.cdnow.com/**.

Fig. 1.2
CD-Now is a Web-based company that sells music on the Internet.

Another big motivation for businesses to get on the Net is for advertising purposes. These companies want to further the equity they have established with their name brand, whether it be local, statewide, or national (see figures 1.3 and 1.4).

Companies who use the Web for this purpose are often service-based businesses, such as Global Information Services & Design in Michigan. Still others offer products that are just very difficult to sell over the Web and for whom product familiarity is of utmost importance. Again, these types of companies are generally national in nature or are service providers of some sort.

Table 1.2 shows what businesses reported when asked what they used the Web for. As you can see, many of the functions already being employed through other media are being utilized on the Web even today.

Fig. 1.3
GISD is a Michigan company that provides Internet training and other services.

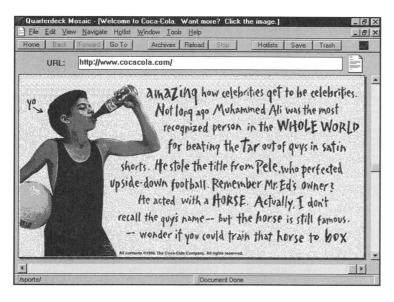

Fig. 1.4
Even Coca-Cola, known the world around, advertises on the Web.

Table 1.2 Business Usage of the Web	
Percent of WWW Business Users Who Have Used It to...	
Collaborate with others	54%
Publish information	33%

(continues)

Table 1.2 Continued	
Percent of WWW Business Users Who Have Used It to...	
Gather information	77%
Research competitors	46%
Sell products or services	13%
Purchase products or services	23%
Provide customer service and support	38%
Communicate internally	44%
Provide vendor support and communications	50%

Web Demographics: Who Is Your Audience?

It's time to talk about a few specifics about who exactly is on the Internet, and whether they actually buy what a business has to sell. We're going to return to the Nielsen survey mentioned in figure 1.1 for some more statistics that were gathered from 280,000 telephone interviews nationwide.

If you're interested in getting a copy of the full report, The Final Report is available for purchase from CommerceNet (phone: 415-617-8790; e-mail: **survey@commerce.net**) and Nielsen Media Research (phone: 813-738-3125; e-mail: **interactive@nielsenmedia.com**). You can also find summary information on the Web at **http://www.nielsenmedia.com/demo.htm**.

So what did the Nielsen survey find? Well, over 2.5 million Americans have purchased products and services over the WWW. Again, as with all other numbers, these too will continue to grow. Earlier in the chapter, you were given a glimpse of some general demographics of users. The survey showed specific results important for businesses.

- 25 percent of WWW users had incomes over $80,000 a year.
- 55 percent of users have used the Web to research products or services and 14 percent have actually purchased them.
- There was a user base of 18 million Web users in the United States and Canada
- Total time spent on the Internet in the U.S. and Canada was actually equivalent to the total time spent watching rented video-tapes!

Cautionary Note

As rosy a picture as the Web paints, there are some downsides. The biggest is that any Internet survey or usage statistics fail to take into account the still large majority of people who do not access the Internet. Even with 18 million users using the Web on a regular basis according to the Nielsen report, that still leaves over 250 million people in the U.S. and Canada who still aren't on, not to mention the billions of people around the world who have yet to get online, where the rate of Internet penetration is even less. See **http:// www.census.gov/** and **http://www.statcan.ca/Documents/ English/Faq/Pop/pop.htm**.

The Internet is not yet (nor will it likely ever be) a panacea for everyone's advertising and marketing woes. It's another tool that can, and should, be utilized along with other more traditional media.

What Will the Web Be Like Tomorrow? Next Week?

Now that you have a better idea of where the Web has been and where it is, wouldn't you like to know where it's going? Wouldn't we all? A popular TV commercial shows all sorts of fanciful futuristic gadgets as being "the future." The commercial ends with the conclusion that each possibility is likely and it's sheer guess-work as to what the future will actually hold. To an extent, that commercial is right, but we can make some educated guesses.

We know that many advances are being made in technology that are now used on the cutting edge. Although we can't know exactly what everything will be like later, we can attempt to point out some directions the Web appears to be moving in, and what in particular you should be thinking about.

Problems with Today's Web Technology

There's no doubt the Web's popularity has benefited in no small part from increased public awareness and the availability of dial-up Internet connections. But, let's face it, if any of you have tried to look at a complicated Web site using a 28.8 kbps modem, you know that we've still got a long way to go.

Not only are there problems with access speed, but, as was mentioned in the last section, a large segment of the population remains untapped. The culture of the Internet is also changing—as more people get online, the demographics shift from those primarily in the computer and academic industry, to something that reflects more of the mainstream American and worldwide culture. This is on the whole a very good thing, but it can lead to some transitional problems, as we will later see.

Finally, a big roadblock to online commerce is the lack, or perceived lack, of security on the Internet. This problem is partially technological and partially psychological. There are protocols that can encrypt and validate transactions, such as Netscape's "Secure Sockets Layer" protocol or TERISA system's "S-HTTP" protocol. (See **http://home.netscape.com/newsref/std/ SSL.html** and **http://www.terisa.com/shttp/intro.html**.) But many users are concerned about giving, say, their credit card to an entity they only know about through the Internet. A few well-publicized Internet hacking incidents have also discouraged trust. This will be solved, but not by technology alone.

Breaking the Speed Limits

In the past, getting a full connection to the Internet required a high-speed leased telephone line and expensive networking hardware. As a result, only businesses and large institutions could afford Internet access. This limited the Internet's usefulness for commercial purposes. However, the introduction of high-speed modems and dial-up Internet Service Providers (ISPs) has made WWW access from home both possible and practical.

The Serial Line Internet Protocol and Point-to-Point Protocol (SLIP and PPP) are two commonly used schemes for transferring Internet data to a home computer over the regular phone system. These protocols allow home users to obtain full Internet connections without having to purchase a leased line or expensive connecting hardware. This means that SLIP and PPP users can do everything that users with faster leased-line connections can do, albeit quite a bit slower.

Note

"SL/IP" is equivalent to "SLIP." Both refer to Serial Line Internet Protocol; this book uses SLIP.

But as services get bigger and more complicated, even high-speed modems often don't do the job. The use of ISDN (Integrated Services Digital Network) lines has recently become more popular, but even this solution brings up the problem of needing specialized add-on cards and protocols. ISDN is also quite expensive and is not available in many areas. As an example, a typical ISDN line in North Carolina now costs over $200 for installation and will cost an additional $75 per month to maintain (for more on ISDN, go to **http:// alumni.caltech.edu/~dank/isdn/**).

Two areas that seem to hold a lot of promise for solving the bandwidth problems are cable modem access and satellite delivery. Satellite delivery is probably farther away, but some cable companies in the United States are already offering Internet access through the same line through which you receive your TV stations. One example is TCI in East Lansing, which already offers 10Mbps/sec (Ethernet speed) Internet connections for under $50 a month. It's expected that these types of connections will only get cheaper and more widespread in the future.

As more and more schools, libraries, community colleges and other public institutions get connected, those who use these facilities will also become Internet users. In addition, ISP rates will continue to fall and, as Internet Service becomes available through more accessible and accepted means (such as cable modems), people's fear of technology will also continue to decrease.

One of the last factors involved in increased usage will stem from a not-so-obvious source. In the past, if you wanted Internet service, you had to contact the provider, install the software, make the connection, and basically go through a lot of trouble to get online. However, with the breakout of Windows 95, OS/2 Warp, and other "Internet-Ready" operating systems, the Internet is now built-in (see fig. 1.5). When Internet access becomes as easy as buying your computer, plugging it in, and getting online, a large barrier to access will be removed.

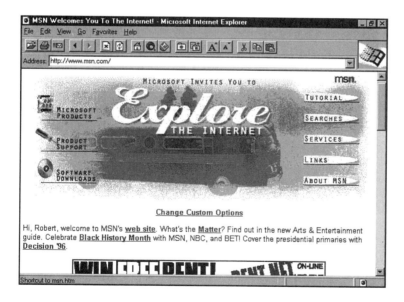

Fig. 1.5
Microsoft's Internet Explorer incorporates the same functionality as Netscape right out of the box.

New Technologies

Web site developers and Web content creators are now getting faced with a dizzying array of new technologies: Java, VRML, Shockwave, MPEG audio and video, and more. (See **http://java.sun.com/, http://www.vrml.org/,** and **http://www.macromedia.com/**.) The Web has always been multi-media, but until recently that has been limited to inlined GIF and JPEG images, and externally-played sound and movie files. As the state of browser technology has advanced, so too have the types of media that can be supported. Newer browsers that support a plug-in architecture can now support an arbitrary number of new media types, so we can expect to see an explosion of new types as companies start building these plug-ins.

Java and VRML are not covered in this book too deeply; they are both complex enough and powerful enough to merit their own books, and there are plenty of those out there. But well-prepared Webmasters should be aware of their existence, when they are appropriate, and how to integrate them into the server.

What Looks Good About the Web's Future

The future really is bright. We've already looked at many of the things that are available or soon will be that will make using the Web more efficient, profitable, and sensible. Perhaps one of the biggest benefits of all these changes is in the opportunity presented to small organizations without a lot of computer expertise or a lot of money to establish a presence on the Web.

Running a Web server, as this book will hopefully prove, can be not only a pretty rewarding experience, but also a pretty inexpensive endeavor. The software provided with this book is free. The software and hardware for a UNIX operating system can be pretty cheap if you purchase a 486 or Pentium and install Linux on it, and bandwidth is getting less expensive all the time. One reason for the success of the Web has been that it has been very easy to set up and add content to a server, and thus there were no restrictions as to who could do it or what they could say. Even as "the big boys" come to play in this sandbox, that liberating capability is not likely to disappear.

As an example of this, the Windows 95 Web site (developed by a company other than Microsoft, by the way), at **http://www.windows95.com/**, runs BSDI on a Pentium with Apache (the same software provided with this book) and handles approximately 2 million hits on a busy weekday. The total hardware and software cost is somewhere around $5000, so don't let anyone fool you into thinking you need big expensive iron to put out a "real" Web site.

The Web has experienced terrific growth in the first several years of existence. Fueled by applications in business, government, education, and research, and turbo-charged by dramatic improvements in browser and server technology, the Web is poised to become *the* electronic marketplace and information source of the century. ❖

CHAPTER 2

Introduction to Web Servers

The World Wide Web is an evolving paradigm. The Web sports a different look today than it did at its inception only a few short years ago. This chapter describes some Web nomenclature; also, some types of data you can convey via the Web are discussed. There is almost no limit to the types of data you can provide to your Web users.

You'll want to provide Web services that are both innovative and useful. You can accomplish this by first understanding some of the terminology associated with the Web; furthermore, you will develop an appreciation for the type of material available through the Web by visiting some popular sites. This chapter provides:

- Definitions of terms associated with the World Wide Web
- An introduction to the HyperText Transport Protocol
- A discussion of some of the Internet protocols that predate the World Wide Web
- The types of data that you can serve via the World Wide Web
- Methods used to secure Web servers

Web Tech Terminology

Before covering the types of services you can offer through the Web, this section covers some of the terminology that is used in this book. In addition, it describes some of the underlying protocols that make data transfer using the World Wide Web possible.

Definitions

The *World Wide Web* describes a cross-platform, interactive network of Internet sites that offer hypertext document access. Also known as *the WWW* or simply *the Web,* the World Wide Web supports a variety of data formats.

HyperText Transport Protocol, more commonly known as *HTTP*, is the Internet protocol that allows data transfer through the World Wide Web. It's a stateless protocol similar to Gopher; connections are opened and closed as data is transferred between hosts. FTP connections differ because they are held open at the users' discretion.

A *Web browser* is an application that allows users to view documents within a hypertext context. Web browsers allow text and graphics to be viewed and formatted beside each other. The Web supports transfer of many different data types; when a Web browser encounters a data format that it cannot natively display, it launches relevant applications to display those files.

A *Web server* is a program that responds to requests from Web browsers via HTTP. Servers transfer HTML files, corresponding graphics, and other content via HTTP to remote computers that are running Web browsers.

HyperText Markup Language, or *HTML*, is the de facto document format of the World Wide Web. Text and graphics are formatted in WWW documents using HTML; Web browsers process these documents transferring the HTML commands into the desired format in the Web browser display window.

Helper applications are those applications defined within Web browsers that display file formats that the browser itself can not "inline." Browsers such as Netscape and Mosaic can display inline text and graphics. However, file formats as MPEG, audio files, and PostScript are not supported within most Web browsers. Therefore, the browser hands the file off to the requisite helper application so that the user can view the file.

The Client-Server Model

As with most other enterprise systems, the World Wide Web works within a *client-server* paradigm. The Web operates through exchange of data between Web clients, or browsers, and Web servers. These servers field requests from Web browsers for certain files that can be comprised of almost an unlimited number of data types.

Figure 2.1 details a schematic of how Web browsers interact with a single Web server. Several browsers can simultaneously request files from a single server. This server, depending on its processing and networking resources, processes these requests and returns requisite files to the browsers.

Web Protocols

The HyperText Transport Protocol (HTTP) is the most common method of transporting data between WWW browsers and servers. The protocol was developed in 1989 for the purpose of transporting documents along the

Internet via a hypertext interface. In contrast to FTP, an HTTP connection between computers requires few resources. The protocol was designed to very nimbly recover text and other data from HTTP servers with very little overhead required from the browser or server computers.

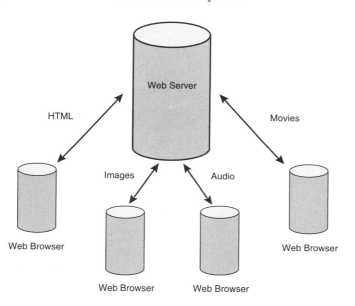

I

Planning Your Web Server

Fig. 2.1
World Wide Web servers interact with requests from various Web browsers. Servers can transmit any arbitrary number of content types to the client.

The HTTP specifications undergo periodic review by a committee of Internet specialists. The current standard is HTTP/1.0, which supersedes the original HTTP/0.9. Further versions of HTTP are under review; they will provide greater capabilities to Web browsers in the areas of performance and security. For more information, see **http://www.ics.uci.edu/pub/ietf/http/**.

An HTTP connection between a Web client and server can be separated into four separate actions:

- *Connection Launch*   The HTTP server constantly listens on a certain IP port for a request from a Web browser. This port is usually specified as port 80, but nonstandard ports can be included in the URL.

- *Client Request*   After a connection is established, the browser sends a request to the server. In addition to querying the server regarding a CGI script or a certain image, sound, or HTML file, the browser sends a little information about itself, such as what content types it understands, the name of the browser, and more.

- *Server Response*   The server, having digested the request from the browser, sends an HTTP message to the browser. This server tells the browser what level of HTTP is being supported, a bunch of meta-information about the object requested (such as its last-modified date), and the response itself.

- ■ *Connection Close*   Having sent the message, the connection is terminated by either the client or server. In HTTP/1.1, connections may stay open at this point to wait for another request, and thus repeat the cycle.

As you can see, as opposed to FTP or Telnet connections, the HTTP connection does not stay open. As a result, a server can maintain many more HTTP connections for a given length of time than it can support remote logins.

Tip

For more specific information on HTTP, visit the World Wide Web Consortium HTTP specification at **http://www.w3.org/pub/WWW/Protocols/**.

Understanding MIME

The Multimedia Internet Mail Exchange (MIME) message representation protocol is a means of conveying information about a file that is being sent through the Internet. This protocol conveys information about the message through MIME headers but leaves the message content or body in the form of plain text. For this reason, MIME is an excellent means of transferring files between different platforms. For example, you can use the e-mail program Eudora to send a graphics file from your Macintosh to a PC user. If the PC user is also running Eudora, or any other MIME-capable mail reader, the program will read the MIME header and attach the relevant tag to the file to make it readable by the correct application.

Much like HTTP, MIME content headers are under a standards process. The key information in the header is the MIME type and subtype that identify the type of message content. The MIME type will usually consist of one of the types listed in table 4.1.

Table 4.1   Common MIME Types

Type	Function
application	Defines client applications
audio	Defines audio formats
image	Defines image formats
message	Used for electronic mail messages

Type	Function
multipart	Used for transmission with multiple parts
text	Defines text formats
video	Defines video formats
x-"string"	Denotes an experimental MIME type not recognized as a standard

The content header is comprised of a type and subtype. The subtype specifically defines the message content within the context of the MIME type. For example, an HTTP server will send the following MIME type/subtype in response to a Web client query

```
text/html
```

This header information tells the browser to expect some text and specifically some HTML text. Web browsers, as opposed to other applications, understand that MIME types need to be interpreted as HTML and displayed accordingly. Similarly, a MIME header containing the information

```
image/gif
```

would tell the browser the following ASCII text is actually a GIF image. The browser then displays the GIF within the window or launches a GIF-viewing application.

There are a variety of MIME subtypes defined for each type. The HTTP server needs to correlate the type of information it's serving to a certain MIME type. For example, if it's serving a JPEG file as part of a Web page, the server needs to somehow know that

- the file is a JPEG formatted-file
- image/jpeg is the standard MIME classification for that file

The Web server needs to have some means of identifying files and the relevant MIME types in order to tell the browsers what to expect.

Pre-WWW Protocols

One reason for the success of the WWW is the ability of Web browsers to transfer data using protocols other than HTTP. Hence, Web clients such as Mosaic and Netscape Navigator can serve as FTP and Gopher clients in addition to interpreting HTTP. Modern Web clients have positioned themselves as all-in-one Internet tools. There are more uses for an Internet server than just serving Web pages.

There are many Internet protocols built on top of TCP/IP and, while HTTP is the 800-lb gorilla of the bunch, there are other useful capabilities that you may want to offer on your server. The File Transfer Protocol is useful for quickly transferring large amounts of data. Many shareware and freeware applications are available on Internet servers through FTP connections. Gopher offers an even more intuitive and flexible means of transferring files. Furthermore, you may want to set up your Internet site as an e-mail server for your organization. In this manner, users will be able to send and exchange mail with one another as well as with other users on the Internet. Finally, you may want to offer UseNet newsgroup access to your organization. In addition to offering UseNet groups, many large organizations, such as corporations and universities, often establish newsgroups of local interest to the organization.

Content Delivery

As mentioned earlier in this chapter, a variety of file formats can be served via the World Wide Web. This section covers some of the content types that modern Web browsers support.

Text

Tim Berners-Lee conceived of the World Wide Web as a means of displaying documents with hypertext links to other documents, particularly documents of other content types. These hypertext links allow users to refer to documents that are located throughout the Internet. This "Web" of documents extends throughout the Net. While many formats are either displayed within Web browsers or viewed with helper applications, most of the information on Web pages is displayed as text.

Web servers use HTML to store text files for the purpose of formatting text and graphics within a Web browser. Figure 2.2 shows how text and graphics can be formatted to appear within a Web browser window. The use of HTML allows Web designers to apply a variety of styles and formatting to the text within a browser window.

Graphics

Figure 2.2 shows how text and graphics can be displayed in the same browser window. Displaying graphics is one of the most appealing features of using the Web. Photographs, clip art, and cartoons can be easily downloaded by Web users. Using various features of HTML allows you to display graphics and text in a manner not unlike printed media. This is one reason why the Web is competing with more conventional media for the public's attention.

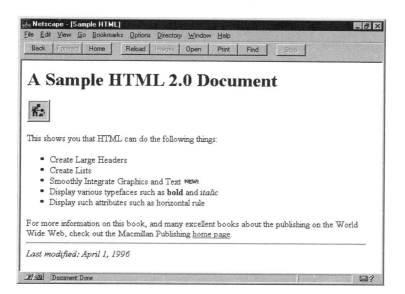

In the early days of the Web, the Mosaic browser could only display files using the *Graphic Interchange Format* (*GIF*). This format allows accurate display of simple images such as clip art, cartoons, or text. With the advent of Netscape, an additional graphic format was supported for inline imaging. The *Joint Photographic Expert Group* (*JPEG*) format is useful for displaying complicated images, such as photographs and intricate line art, more accurately and in smaller files than can GIF.

Tip

For more information on the pros and cons of using JPEG and GIF images, consult the JPEG FAQ at **http://www.cis.ohio-state.edu/hypertext/faq/usenet/jpeg-faq/top.html**

Audio

The capability to download audio files using the World Wide Web adds an exciting new dimension to the Internet. Any computer with a sound card and the appropriate software can download sound files from sites that publish them. High-fidelity sound files, such as those sampled from an audio CD, can be quite large even for a few seconds recording. Some home pages publish greetings from the Webmaster or even the head of the sponsoring organization.

Not all browsers support sounds; helper applications are needed to play the sound files. Sun Microsystems' AU format is a popular format, as are MPEG audio and the proprietary RealAudio format. For more information, see **http://www.iis.fhg.de/departs/amm/layer3/** and **http://www.realaudio.com/**.

Video

Much like sound, downloading video files through the Web is an exciting means of transferring information. However, like sound files, video files take an enormous amount of space and require a long time to transmit over even high-speed network connections. Downloading movies over a modem connection is nothing short of a tortuous exercise in patience.

Most browsers cannot display movies within the browser; an appropriate helper application is required. Two common formats are the *Motion Pictures Expert Group* (MPEG) and *QuickTime*. For more information, see **http://www.cis.ohio-state.edu/hypertext/faq/usenet/mpeg-faq/** and **http://quicktime.apple.com/**. More often than not, movie files served via the Web take up a small portion of the desktop so as to conserve file size. Figure 2.3 shows an example of how movie files can be served via the Web. In this example, movies of the same sequence are stored in a variety of formats.

Fig. 2.3
Sites containing weather-related movie files are popular with many Web users. Note the large size of some movie files.

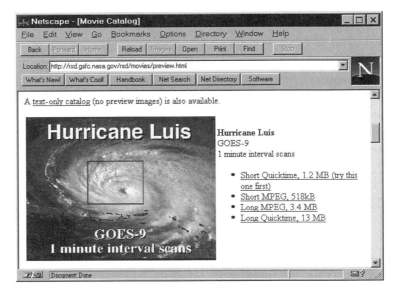

Forms

Soon after the introduction of Mosaic, the HTML standard was extended by the NCSA developers to include several new capabilities. The capability to develop interactive forms on a Web page is one of those. Figure 2.4 shows the types of objects that you can use on a Web page to retrieve information from Web users. Users can enter text in text fields and can select options using radio buttons and check boxes. These devices are available as familiar graphical user interface features on many Windows applications.

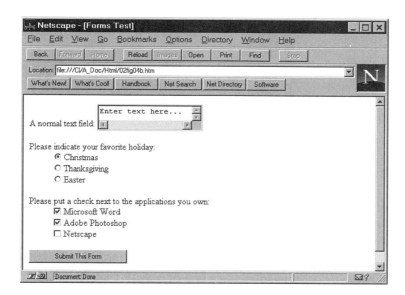

Fig. 2.4
There are several types of HTML forms you can use to retrieve information from Web users.

These forms do not process any of the information they contain. They merely act as a conduit for conveying information to a third-party application on the server. These scripts adhere to the Common Gateway Interface standard and represent a means of processing information retrieved from HTML forms. CGI scripts can be written in almost any language with Perl, C/C++, and UNIX shell being prevalent on UNIX-based WWW servers, and C/C++ and Visual Basic being heavily used as scripting languages under Windows-based Web servers.

Using information gleaned from a page containing HTML forms, CGI scripts can send e-mail, search databases, or even create HTML pages to present to the user. You can see these functions on the Web in a variety of implementations.

Virtual Reality

One alternative to HTML is the *Virtual Reality Modeling Language* (*VRML*— rhymes with *thermal*). VRML is a standard language for representing three-dimensional data. HTML allows you to construct a two-dimensional publishing metaphor for graphics and text, but VRML is a totally separate language designed to extend the metaphor to a third dimension. With Netscape and HTML, you meander across a page and click on links and graphics as you see fit. A VRML browser allows you to travel through a third dimension as well. Instead of two-dimensional imagemaps, VRML "worlds" can have hallways that you can traverse. You can display information from a variety of three-dimensional perspectives rather than from the rigid display defined by a two-dimensional Web browser.

Whereas you jump from page to page using HTML, VRML users jump between "worlds." These worlds can be created with various VRML editors, or in very simple cases, by hand. Loading a world over the Internet does not require much more time than a large graphic does using HTML.

Programming in VRML is analogous to programming in HTML. The three-dimensional interface leads to new possibilities in information publishing. If you have ever played Doom or another 3-D action game, you have seen some of the applications of three-dimensional graphics under Windows. As you explore other VRML worlds, you can think of ways that you can use the three-dimensional metaphor to present information to your users. Examples of this metaphor can include a VR implementation of a library where users can navigate through virtual stacks to browse some of the libraries selections.

Custom Web Scripts

As mentioned above, CGI scripts stand together with HTML and HTTP as the three major components of the World Wide Web. Using CGI scripts, you can customize the type of information you serve to users. Data is passed from the browser to the script residing on your server. The script receives the data, parses the commands into a comprehensible format, and then returns the results in the form of a Web page. Many powerful search engines and other popular devices found on the Web are constructed using CGI scripts.

Security

Possibly no other aspect of your WWW server requires more attention than security. Depending on whether you wish to provide secure communication through your server or to protect certain areas of your server from individuals within your organization, securing your server requires a great deal of planning and forethought. There are hardware options for ensuring secure access to your server, but the measures discussed here are implemented in software.

Securing your server transactions allows you to provide a variety of transactions. For example, you can conduct online business by allowing transmission of financial data such as credit card numbers. You can also protect various documents for viewing by authorized personnel within your organization.

The security schemes described in this section are new and not yet widely implemented throughout the Web. For this reason, financial transactions over the Web are not occurring in a widespread fashion. Implementation of these schemes will enable a burgeoning world of commerce to develop.

Tip

For a look at how some online transactions are conducted, visit First Virtual at **http://www.fv.com**.

The WWW Security Model

You have several options with which to restrict access to your server. You may wish to restrict access to certain documents to certain users. You may also want to enable access to groups of users. The following sections discuss these options.

Domain Restrictions

By restricting access to your server by domain, you can enable or deny access to large groups of people. For example, if your organization has the Internet address "anywhere.com," you can enable access to your server only to those computers within the "anywhere.com" domain. Users with computers outside this domain could be restricted from accessing your server.

User Authentication

If you desire to further restrict access to your server to smaller groups of users, you can employ some means of authentication. Much like a remote Telnet session, you can require users to enter an account name and password upon accessing certain documents on the server. You can store and access sensitive documents in this manner.

Data Encryption

One way of securing the data on your server is not to alter the data but to encrypt the communication between your server and various Web browsers. The algorithms discussed in this section are used to encrypt HTTP transactions using a variety of methods. Not only does your server need to support these methods but Web browsers must adhere to these standards.

The Secure Sockets Layer Protocol

The *Secure Sockets Layer* (*SSL*) *Protocol*, proposed by Netscape, is designed to provide accurate and secure communication between two applications such as your Web server and a Web browser. Implemented by several servers such as WebSite and the Netscape Commerce Server, SSL allows secure communication of financial transactions or a variety of other connection types. SSL is an open protocol and has been recently proposed to the Internet Engineering Task Force.

The SSL protocol is composed of two layers: the SSL Record Protocol and the SSL Handshake Protocol. The *SSL Record Protocol* is used for encapsulation of various higher level protocols. One such encapsulated protocol, the *SSL Handshake Protocol,* allows the WWW server and client to authenticate each other and to negotiate an encryption algorithm and cryptographic keys before the application protocol transmits or receives its first byte of secure data. The advantage of SSL is that it is application-protocol independent. A higher level protocol can layer on top of the SSL Protocol transparently.

The SSL protocol provides connection security with three basic properties:

- The transmission is private because encryption is used after an initial handshake to define a secret key

- The connection can be authenticated using popular cryptographic schemes such as RSA or DSS

- The connection is reliable—a message integrity check is included with the transmission

The advantage of using SSL is that it's a layered protocol. For your Web site, you may want to use SSL to secure your Web connections. However, you could also use SSL to secure UseNet transactions via *Network News Transmission Protocol* (*NNTP*). Furthermore, you could use SSL to secure e-mail traffic via *Simple Mail Transfer Protocol* (*SMTP*), or file transfer via FTP. However, both client and server must implement SSL to do this.

Secure-HTTP

Secure-HTTP, or *S-HTTP*, is an encryption standard designed solely for the purpose of securing HTTP transactions. S-HTTP acts to secure Web connections in three chief ways: signature, encryption, and authentication. You can attach digital signatures to documents using a CGI script. You can encrypt messages using a variety of encryption algorithms, including the very popular PGP. However, one advantage of S-HTTP is that encryption can occur between a server and a client without necessarily requiring a predetermined encryption key. In contrast to a less comprehensive password authentication scheme, S-HTTP authentication requires the unique identifier upon request. Such an authentication scheme might be employed to complete financial transactions.

Both S-HTTP and SSL are based on public-key cryptography, where the parties involved have a pair of keys, one that is private and never revealed, and one that is public. The infrastructure for supporting the distribution of keys is known as "X509," and will be deployed over the coming year. However, SSL and S-HTTP transactions can be used today. ❖

## CHAPTER 3

Setting Up a Web Presence

This chapter discusses the first steps you need to take to create a presence on the Web: getting the connection to the Internet itself, and selecting a system to host your presence. You can follow two basic paths to put your site on the Internet: The first part of this chapter discusses the benefits and costs of each; the second part of the chapter discusses the choices you'll need to make when building the Web server itself. Even if you're setting up an internal Web server with no connection to the Internet, take a look through the section about building the perfect Web server.

Setting up an Internet Web server can be quite a complex undertaking, and the detailed knowledge required would fill far more than just a single book. This chapter describes important parts of the process and outlines the choices you need to make.

In this chapter, you learn:

- The advantages and disadvantages of hosting your own site or leasing space from a provider
- What kind of Internet connections are available and the hardware they require
- How to select the operating system and hardware for your Web server

Establishing a Presence

There are two basic ways to create a presence on the Web: hosting the site on an Internet service provider's machine or somewhere outside your machine, or hosting it on your own machine and managing the bandwidth and hardware/software issues yourself. Each method has its own benefits and costs; the method you choose depends on your needs.

Key Considerations

Putting information on the Web requires HTTP server software (as provided on the CD accompanying this book) and a system to host that information. The first choice you need to make is whether to support that system yourself—including tending the hardware, configuring and monitoring the server, and installing all the information or services you want to provide to the world—or to lease Web space from your Internet provider and let your provider do all the nitty-gritty of running the server. It may sound like a simple choice—after all, why not just sit back and let someone else do all the dirty work? But actually, the choice is a little more complex. The main trade-offs you make when you decide whether to have your provider host your Web site or whether you host the site yourself are *cost* and *control*.

Reviewing and Comparing the Alternatives

When your provider hosts your Web site, the provider takes care of obtaining the hardware, maintaining the system, worrying about security, and may even be able to design and produce your Web pages. Depending on the complexity of your Web site, creating a Web site can be a considerable effort, especially if you need to integrate it with an existing network. Having your provider do all the work can certainly be very convenient. It can, however, also be costly, depending on the number of conveniences you require and the rates your provider charges for his services. There are really no standards when it comes to Web site hosting, so costs and services vary wildly. This isn't to say there aren't some really good groups out there doing commercial Web hosting services in a very professional manner, however. When you rely totally on the provider, aside from the content of the information you supply for the Web, you often have less control over your Web site. Your provider may not allow things such as access counters (the "you are visitor number so-and-so" that appears at the bottom of many Web pages) or other on-the-fly page customizations because of system concerns or capabilities. Your provider takes care of all the hardware, including a high-speed 24-hour-a-day connection to the Internet, but if your provider's system goes "off the air," there's nothing you can do about restoring your Web presence.

When you host your own Web site, you have total control over all aspects of your site; its features, its services, its hours of operation. You also have total responsibility for its operation (or lack thereof if you run into problems). The highest costs are in setting up the server and the network connection; once the server is up and running, all you'll need to pay will be your Internet connection charge and whatever fees are involved in making the physical connection between your system and the Internet. Your initial cost can be very low—after all, your most crucial software, including the Web server itself, is included on the CD-ROM with this book—or quite high, if you have complex security requirements.

There are a few other factors to consider. If you already have a full-time Internet connection for other purposes (such as FTP or e-mail), you should host your own Web site—most of the hard work of integrating the Internet and your internal network will already have been done. If your needs are very simple—for example, if you just want to host a few pages, want to run the Web server only for limited hours, or if you don't want to connect your Web server to an internal network—you're also a good candidate for your own Web site. Once you have a connection established, setting up the Web server itself is simple.

Finally, you need to consider what kind of information your server might gather as well as what kind it will distribute. If you want to collect sensitive or confidential information (for example, credit card numbers or customer names and addresses), your provider must support secure Web transactions. More importantly, you must be able to trust your provider to keep your confidential information secret. If you don't want to trust your provider with your secrets, you'll need to operate the secure server yourself, which is not a small undertaking.

Here's a summary of the advantages and disadvantages to hosting your own Web site.

Issue	Your Own Server	Leased Space
Cost	Low to moderate, depending on bandwidth needs	Varies widely
Control	You have total control	Control is an option
Features	Your site has any features you want	Your site only has features they allow
Security	You must configure	They do it for you
Setting up the server software	Simple to moderately difficult	They do it for you
Setting up the hardware	Can be *very* complicated, especially the Internet connection	They do it for you

---

Note

There are a couple happy mediums between having your provider do *all* the work at his own server and setting up a Web site by yourself. Some providers (or other specialists) can assist in the initial setup of the server, including designing Web pages. You can then take over server operations. Alternately, some Internet access providers will let you locate your machine at their machine room for a monthly fee, essentially giving you as much bandwidth as they themselves have without having to deliver that bandwidth to your door. You can still control everything on that server, hardware, and software, it's just sitting in a locked cage somewhere else. This is called *server co-location*.

The next few sections cover some of the details involved in getting the Internet connection. Leasing space from a provider is explained more fully, and the hardware you'll need to make the connection to the Internet yourself is described.

Leasing Space

Leasing space is a popular, easy way to get your presence on the Web quickly. The greatest appeal of leased space is that your provider gives you a high-speed Internet connection—all day, every day. However, your provider's charge for this service may be as much as, or more than, what it would cost you to provide a satisfactory Internet connection, but with the added flexibility that your own server provides.

Working with Leased Space

When you have a leased Web site, you either tell your provider how you want your pages set up, or you create them yourself and send them to your provider, most frequently via FTP.

As was mentioned earlier, a leased Web site can only provide those services that your provider allows. Will your provider allow you to use the forms and scripts you want to use to collect information or provide services? Some don't, for security reasons. Will your provider allow you to use programs (called *server-side includes*) or implement new content types like Java or VRML?

Finding a Provider

Finding a provider today is extremely simple, just by using the Internet itself. A search of the Yahoo Web site for "Internet Providers" yields a dizzying array of Internet access providers, Web page designers, and network specialty firms, in every locale and every price range. Some firms provide browser forms for price quotes, or just descriptions of services; others provide full pricing schedules.

Table 3.1   WWW Service Providers

H=HTML Authoring/Web Application Development

C=CGI Script Processing

S=WAIS or other search capabilities offered

P=Prebuilt applications

Speed=Speed of service provider's connection to the Internet

Area=Area code(s) served in part or in whole by local dial-up access. If no area code is listed, provider either offers national dial-up access or none at all.

Name and URL	Services	Speed	Area
Computer Solutions by Hawkinson **http://www.mhv.net/**	HP	T1	914
Telerama Public Access Internet **http://www.lm.com/**	HCSP	T1	412
Quantum Networking Solutions **http://www.gcr.com**	HC	14K	
Internet Presence & Publishing, Inc. **http://www.ip.net/**	HCSP	T1	804
Computing Engineers, Inc. **http://www.wwa.com/**	HCSP	56K	312, 708
South Valley Internet **http://www.garlic.com**	CS	56K	408
Branch Information Services **http://branch.com**	HCSP	T1	313
APK, Public Access UNI*. **http://www.wariat.org**	HS	216	
Internet Distribution Services, Inc. **http://www.service.com/**	HCSP	T1	415
Cyberspace Development, Inc. **http://marketplace.com**	HS	T1	

(continues)

Table 3.1 Continued			
Name and URL	**Services**	**Speed**	**Area**
BEDROCK Information Solutions, Inc. **http://www.bedrock.com/**	HCS	T1	
Electric Press, Inc. **http://www.elpress.com**	HCSP	T1	
Quadralay Corporation **http://www.quadralay .com/home.html**	HCSP	T1	
Downtown Anywhere, Inc. **http://www.awa.com/**	HCSP	frac. T1	
Internet Marketing, Inc. **http://cybersight.com/ cgi-bin/imi/s?main.gmml**	HCS	T1	
The New York Web **http://nyweb.com**	HCSP	T1	
The Sphere Information Services **http://www.thesphere.com**	HC	56K	
The Computing Support Team, Inc. **http://www.gems.com/**	HCS	T1	
The Internet Group **http://www.tig.com/**	HCS	T1	
Lighthouse Productions **http://netcenter.com**	HP	115K	
Catalog.Com Internet Services **http://www.catalog.com**	T1		
Great Basin Internet Services **http://www.greatbasin.net/**	HCSP	56K	702
Net+Effects **http://www.net.effects.com**	HCSP	14K	
XOR Network Engineering **http://plaza.xor.com/**	HCS		
BizNet Technologies **http://www.biznet.com .blacksburg.va.us/**	HCSP	T1	
Sell-it on the WWW **http://www.electriciti.com/**	H	T1	
RTD Systems & Networking, Inc. **http://www.rtd.com/**	HCP	T1	602
Atlantic Computing Technology Corporation **http://www.atlantic.com/**	HCSP	56K	

Name and URL	Services	Speed	Area
InterNex Information Services, Inc. **http://www.internex.net/**	HCS	T1	510, 415, 408
Teleport, Inc. **http://www.teleport.com**		56k	503, 206
QuakeNet **http://www.quake.net/**	H	T1	415
Internet Information Services, Inc. **http://www.iis.com**	HCSP	T1	301, 410, 703
CyberBeach Publishing **http://www.gate.net/**	HCSP	T1	305, 407, 813, 904
Primenet **http://www.primenet.com/**	HCP	T1	602
TAG Systems, Inc. **http://www.tagsys.com/**	HC	56K	
Internet Information Systems **http://www.internet-is.com/**	HCS	frac. T1	
Stelcom, Inc. **http://www.webscope.com**	HC	frac. T1	
Coolware, Inc. **http://none.coolware.com/**	HCS	56K	
IDS World Network Internet Access Services **http://www.ids.net**	HCSP	T1	401, 305, 407, 914
SenseMedia Publishing **http://www.picosof.com**	H	T1	408
Home Pages, Inc. **http://www.homepages.com**	HCSP	128K	
TeleVisions, Inc. **http://www.tvisions.com**	H	T1	
Internet Services Corporation **http://www.netservices.com/**	HCSP	T1	
EarthLink Network, Inc. **http://www.earthlink.net**	HC	T1	213, 310, 818
New Jersey Computer Connection **http://www.njcc.com**	H	56K	609
CTS Network Services **http://www.cts.com**	HCSP	T1	619
The Tenagra Corporation **http://arganet.tenagra.com/ Tenagra/tenagra.html**	HCS	T1	

Costs

The recent competition for Internet services, and the (relatively) low cost of the necessary technology, has lowered the prices and raised the quality of Internet service in general, but prices and services vary widely from provider to provider. For example, one provider offers a wide range of prices, from an extremely low rate for very small businesses (a little over $200 setup charge and around $30 per month) to a high rate for large, high-volume sites (almost $6,000 setup and nearly $2,000 per month). Some providers have fixed rates; others charge by the number of pages accessed or by the amount of data the server transmits. Providers also have a range of "package deals" with varying degrees of flexibility and services, ranging from a simple "you upload it, we publish it" to page design and application programming.

Tip

It definitely pays to shop around for Internet services, even for simple personal access. A savings of even $20 per month adds up quickly. And don't be afraid to look outside your geographical area for low-cost services. Remember, it's the *World Wide* Web, and if you have local Internet access yourself, you can FTP your pages to a provider's server in another state as easily as you can to one across the street.

Concerns and Advantages

Leasing your presence on a provider's Web server provides an easy way to establish your presence on the Web, but one with many constraints and one that may not be cost-effective for your needs. If you don't want to hassle with network connections, server security, and system maintenance, and don't mind giving up control of your Web presence, this is definitely the way to go. If you already have the Internet connection, or can't find a provider package that suits your needs or your budget, consider running your own server.

Connecting Your Own Web Server

If you decide to host your own Internet server, you will need to provide your own Internet connection. Again, this is something that is best done by professionals, and a good Internet access provider will be able to do most of the dirty work for you. This section is intended to give you an overview of some of your choices.

All Internet connections have several costs, all of which add up alarmingly quickly:

- The hardware required to make the connection itself—ranging from a simple plug-in modem to multiple routers and other network connectivity devices
- The provider's setup cost (sometimes includes the service charge for installing equipment at your site, sometimes doesn't)
- The cost of the Internet service itself
- The price of the physical connection to the Internet—ranging from an ordinary phone line to special data lines

Of course, the faster and the more complex the connection, the more expensive it will be.

Connection Types: Switched versus Leased

There are two basic types of Internet connection: *switched connections,* which use some sort of intermediary technology between your system and the Internet, and *leased lines,* a direct network connection to the Internet itself.

Leased lines are the method of choice for anyone needing full-time high-speed connections. Leased lines are the fastest type of Internet connection; they are also the most expensive. Connecting a high-speed leased line to your system is probably the single, most complicated operation in the entire Web server setup process, and you will need to budget plenty of time and money to make that connection.

A slow leased line (56 kbps, about twice as fast as a standard 28.8 kbps modem) provides more than enough bandwidth for e-mail and news, but is not much faster than a regular home dial-up connection when transmitting heavy graphics.

The most common leased-line connection is a T1, which has a very respectable data rate of 1,544 kbps (more than 50 times faster than a 28.8 kbps modem). T1s provide enough bandwidth for dozens of Web servers, so several users can each use only a part of the T1, sharing the bandwidth as well as the cost. A full T1 connection costs between $1,000 and $3,000 per month, not including the cost of the leased line (which can be as much again as the Internet access charge). Many providers offer fractional T1 lines in 256 kbps increments. Even higher up the bandwidth food chain are T3 connections (also sometimes called OC3 connections), which are a very respectable 45 megabits per second speed. Typically, these are reserved for sites with very heavy loads—unless you are planning on being one of the top 50 Web sites in terms of traffic, this is probably overkill for you. T3 line and Internet access charges can be as high as $25,000 per month.

Leased lines can't just be plugged into a network card on the back of your computer; they require additional hardware, the most important being a *router*, a device that controls the flow of data between the Internet and your local network or system. Cost for routers (not always including installation and support) range from $1,000 to $4,000. Routers can be crucial components in your network security system, and the more protection your internal network requires, the more important your routers become.

Leased lines also require a *Channel Service Unit/Data Service Unit* (CSU/DSU or just CSU) installed between the leased line and the router. CSUs run from around $300 to around $3,000, depending on the speed you require. T3 DSUs and routers can run you well into $80,000 before you're done.

> **Tip**
>
> Leave a little "room to grow" when you purchase your router and CSU; you can often save upgrade costs later by spending a little more up front for higher speed equipment.

If you want to run a high-volume server with heavy graphics, you will probably need a leased line of some kind. However, in addition to these traditional solutions, there are several alternative technologies that you might explore if you don't require leased lines' ultra-high speeds (or can't afford leased lines' high costs).

Table 3.2   Leased Line Providers in the United States

The following information is taken from the InterNIC Leased Line Providers List that is published by the InterNIC, a project of the National Science Foundation, and is reprinted here with permission. Some of the entries have been modified to reflect new information and addresses.

```
=============================================================
InterNIC Information Services       E-mail: info@internic.net
General Atomics (GA)                Phone: (619) 455-4600
P.O. Box #85608                     Fax: (619) 455-4640
San Diego, CA 92186-9784


=============================================================

InterNIC Internet Service Providers List: Leased Line Only (United States)

-------------------------------------------------------------------------------

Permission for noncommercial distributions is granted, provided that this file is
distributed intact, including the acknowledgment, disclaimer, and copyright notice
found at the end of this document.

*******************************************************************************
```

Adhesive Media, Inc.
Eden Matrix Online Service
John Herzer
adhesive-media@eden.com

Texas
(512) 478-9900 x200 (PHONE)
(512) 478-9934 (FAX)

AlterNet
alternet-info@uunet.uu.net

US and International
(800) 4UUNET3 (PHONE)

American Information Systems
Josh Schneider
schneid@ais.net

Illinois
(708) 413-8400 (PHONE)
(708) 413-8401 (FAX)

ANS
Sales and Information
info@ans.net
http://www.ans.net

US and International
(800) 456-8267 (PHONE)
(703) 758-7717 (FAX)

APK Public Access
Zbigniew Tyrlik
support@wariat.org

Ohio
(216) 481-9428 (PHONE)

BBN BARRNet, Inc.
John Toth
info@barrnet.net

California, Nevada
(415) 528-7111 (PHONE)
(415) 934-2665 (FAX)

Beckemeyer Development
Sales
info@bdt.com

California
(510) 530-9637 (PHONE)
(510) 530-0451 (FAX)

CCnet Communications
Information
info@ccnet.com

California
(510) 988-0680 (PHONE)
(510) 988-0689 (FAX)

CERFnet
CERFnet Hotline
sales@cerf.net

Western US and International
(800) 876-2373 (PHONE)
(619) 455-3990 (FAX)

CICnet
Marketing and Sales Dept.
info@cic.net

Midwestern United States
(800) 947-4754
(313) 998-6703 (PHONE)
(313) 998-6105 (FAX)

Clark Internet Services
ClarkNet Office
info@clark.net

Northeastern United States
(800) 735-2258
(410) 254-3900 (PHONE)
(410) 730-9765 (FAX)

Cloud 9 Internet
Scott Drassinower
scottd@cloud9.net

New York
(914) 682-0626 (PHONE)
(914) 682-0506 (FAX)

Supernet, Inc.
Anthony Rael
info@csn.net
www.csn.net

Colorado
(303) 296-8202 x124 (PHONE)
(303) 296-8224(FAX)

Connix
Jim Hogue
office@connix.com

Connecticut
(860) 349-7059 (PHONE)

CRL Network Services
Sales
sales@crl.com
info@crl.com

California
(415) 837-5300 (PHONE)

Planning Your Web Server

(continues)

Table 3.2   Continued

CTS Network Services Sales **support@cts.com**	California (619) 637-3637 (PHONE) (619) 637-3630 (FAX)
CyberGate, Inc. Dan Sullivan **sales@gate.net**	Florida (305) 428-4283 (PHONE) (305) 428-7977 (FAX)
DFW Internet Services, Inc. Jack Beech **sales@dfw.net**	Texas (817) 332-5116 (PHONE) (817) 870-1501 (FAX)
DIGEX Sales **sales@ digex.net**	United States/International (800) 99DIGIX (PHONE) (301) 847-5215 (FAX)
EarthLink Network, Inc. Sky Dayton **info@earthlink.net**	California (213) 644-9500 (PHONE) (213) 644-9510 (FAX)
Edge Internet Services Tim Choate **info@edge.net** **tchoate@edge.net**	Tennessee (615) 726-8700 (PHONE) (615) 726-0665 (FAX)
Escape (Kazan Corp) Sales **info@escape.com**	New York (212) 888-8780 (PHONE) (212) 832-0344 (FAX)
Evergreen Internet Phil Broadbent **sales@libre.com**	Arizona (602) 230-9330 (PHONE) (602) 230-9773 (FAX)
Florida Online Jerry Russell **jerry@digital.net**	Florida (407) 635-8888 (PHONE) (407) 635-9050 (FAX)
HoloNet HoloNet Staff **support@holonet.net**	North America (510) 704-0160 (PHONE) (510) 704-8019 (FAX)
Global Internet Network Services Network Information Center **info@gi.net**	(800) 682-5550 (PHONE) (402) 436-3030 (FAX)
Global Enterprise Services Sergio Heker, President **market@jvnc.net**	US and International (800) 35-TIGER (PHONE) (609) 897-7310 (FAX)
IACNet Devon Sean McCullough **info@iac.net**	Ohio (513) 887-8877 (PHONE)
ICNet Ivars Upatnieks **info@ic.net**	Michigan, Ohio (313) 998-0090 (PHONE)
IDS World Network Information **info@ids.net**	Northeastern US (800) IDS-1680 (PHONE)

Innovative Data Services
Sales
info@id.net

Michigan
(810) 478-3554 (PHONE)
(810) 478-2950

INTAC Access Corporation
Sales
info@intac.com

New Jersey
(201) 944-1417 (PHONE)
(201) 944-1434 (FAX)

InterAccess
Lev Kaye
info@interaccess.com

Illinois
(800) 967-1580 (PHONE)
(708) 498-3289 (FAX)

The Internet Access Company
Sales
info@tiac.net

Massachusetts
(617) 276-7200 (PHONE)
(617) 275-2224 (FAX)

Internet Atlanta
Dorn Hetzel
info@atlanta.com

Georgia
(404) 410-9000 (PHONE)
(404) 410-9005 (FAX)

Internet Channel, Inc.
Tony Walters
sales@internet-channel.net

U.S./Worldwide
(803) 722-7900 (PHONE)
(803) 722-4488 (FAX)

Internet Express
Customer Service
service@usa.net

Colorado
(800) 592-1240 (PHONE)
(719) 592-1201 (FAX)

Internet On-Ramp, Inc.
Sales
sales@on-ramp.ior.com

Washington
(509) 624-RAMP (PHONE)
(509) 323-0116 (FAX)

Internetworks
Internetworks, Inc.
info@i.net
ftp.i.net:/pub/internetworks

United States and Pacific Rim
(503) 233-4774 (PHONE)
(503) 614-0344 (FAX)

Interport Communications Corp
Sales and Information
info@interport.net
http://www.interport.net

New York
(212) 989-1128 (PHONE)

IQuest Network Services
Robert Hoquim
info@iquest.net

Indiana
(800) 844-UNIX
(317) 259-5050 (PHONE)
(317) 259-7289 (FAX)

Kaiwan Corp
Rachel Hwang
sales@kaiwan.com

California
(714) 638-2139 (PHONE)
(714) 638-0455 (FAX)

LI Net, Inc.
Michael Reilly
questions@li.net

New York
(516) 265-0997 x101 (PHONE)

Lightside, Inc.
Fred Condo
lightside@lightside.com
http://www.lightside.net/

California
(818) 858-9261 (PHONE)
(818) 858-8982 (FAX)

Los Nettos
Joe Kemp
los-nettos-info@isi.edu
http://www.isi.edu/ln

Southern California
(310) 822-1511 (PHONE)
(310) 823-6714 (FAX)

(continues)

Planning Your Web Server

Table 3.2 Continued

netMAINE, Inc. Andy Robinson **sales@maine.net**	Maine (207) 780-6381 (PHONE) (207) 780-6301 (FAX)
MCSNet Karl Denninger **info@mcs.net**	Illinois (312) 248-8649 (PHONE) (312) 248-9865 (FAX)
MichNet/Merit Recruiting Staff **info@merit.edu**	Michigan (800) 682-5550 (PHONE) (313) 764-9430 (313) 747-3185 (FAX)
Minnesota Regional Network (MRNet) Dennis Fazio **info@mr.net**	Minnesota (612) 342-2570 (PHONE) (612) 342-2873 (FAX)
MSEN Owen S. Medd **info@msen.com**	Michigan (313) 998-4562 (PHONE) (313) 998-4563 (FAX)
MV Communications Sales **info@mv.mv.com**	New Hampshire (603) 429-2223 (PHONE)
NEARNET NEARNET Information Hotline **nearnet-join@near.net**	Northeastern U.S. (617) 873-8730 (PHONE) (617) 873-5620 (FAX)
NetAxis Luis Hernandez **luis@eliza.netaxis.com**	Connecticut (203) 969-0618 (PHONE) (203) 921-1544 (FAX)
NETCOM On-line Communications Services Business or Personal Sales **info@netcom.com**	United States (800) 353-6600 (PHONE) (408) 983-5950 (PHONE) (408) 241-9145 (FAX)
netILLINOIS Peter Roll **info@illinois.net**	Illinois (708) 866-1804 (PHONE) (708) 866-1857 (FAX)
Network Intensive Sales and Information **info@ni.net** **http://www.ni.net/**	California and New Mexico (714) 450-8400 (PHONE) (800) 273-5600 (PHONE) (714) 450-8410 (FAX)
New Mexico Technet, Inc. Marianne Granoff **granoff@technet.nm.org**	New Mexico and Navajo Reservation (incl: AZ, UT, CO Reservations) (505) 345-6555 (PHONE) (505) 345-6559 (FAX)
New York Net Bob Tinkelman **sales@new-york.net**	New York (718) 776-6811 (PHONE) (718) 217-9407 (FAX)
Northcoast Internet **support@northcoast.com**	California (707) 443-8696 (PHONE) (707) 441-0321 (FAX)

NorthWest CommLink
Garlend Tyacke
gtyacke@nwcl.net

Washington
(206) 336-0103 (PHONE)
(206) 336-2339 (FAX)

Northwest Nexus, Inc.
Information
info@nwnexus.wa.com
support@halcyon.com

Washington
(206) 455-3505 (PHONE)
(206) 455-4672 (FAX)

NorthwestNet
Member Relations
info@nwnet.net

Northwestern US
(206) 562-3000 (PHONE)
(206) 562-4822 (FAX)

NYSERNet
Sales
info@nysernet.org

New York
(315) 453-2912 (PHONE)
(315) 453-3052 (FAX)

OARnet
Larry L. Buell
info@oar.net

Ohio
(614) 728-8100 (PHONE)
(614) 728-8110 (FAX)

Old Colorado City Communications
L.S. Fox
thefox@oldcolo.com

Colorado
(719) 528-5849 (PHONE)
(719) 528-5869 (FAX)

Panix
New User Staff
info-person@panix.com

New York City, Nassau Cty
in Long Island, Jersey City,
New Jersey
(212) 741-4400 (PHONE)
(212) 741-5311 (FAX)

Ping
Brett Koller
bdk@ping.com

Georgia
(404) 399-1670 (PHONE)
(404) 399-1671 (FAX)

Pioneer Global
Craig Komins or Brian Breen
sales@pn.com
http://www.pn.com

Massachusetts
(617) 375-0200 (PHONE)
(617) 375-0201 (FAX)

Planet Access Networks
Fred Laparo
fred@planet.net
http://www.planet.net

New Jersey
(201) 691-4704 (PHONE)
(201) 691-7588 (FAX)

PREPnet
nic@prep.net

Pennsylvania
(412) 268-7870 (PHONE)
(412) 268-7875

Primenet
Clay Johnston
info@primenet.com

Arizona
(602) 870-1010 x109 (PHONE)
(602) 870-1010 (FAX)

PSINet
PSI, Inc.
info@psi.com

United States and International
(800) 82PSI82
(703) 709-0300 (PHONE)
(800) FAXPSI1 (FAX)

QuakeNet
Sales
info@quake.net

California
(415) 655-6607 (PHONE)
(415) 377-0635 (FAX)

(continues)

Planning Your Web Server

Table 3.2   Continued

The Rabbit Network, Inc. Customer Liaison Services **info@rabbit.net**	Michigan (800) 456-0094 (PHONE) (810) 790-0156 (FAX)
Red River Net Craig Lien **lien@rrnet.com**	Minnesota, North and South Dakota (701) 232-2227 (PHONE)
Rocky Mountain Internet, Inc. Rick Mount **info@rmii.com**	Colorado (800) 900-RMII (PHONE) (719) 576-0301 (FAX)
Scruz-Net Matthew Kaufman **info@scruz.net**	California (800) 319-5555 (PHONE) (408) 457-5050 (PHONE) (408) 457-1020 (FAX)
SeaNet Igor Klimenko **igor@seanet.com**	Seattle (206) 343-7828 (PHONE) (206) 628-0722 (FAX)
Sibylline, Inc. Dan Faules **info@sibylline.com**	Arkansas (501) 521-4660 (PHONE) (501) 521-4659 (FAX)
SIMS, Inc. Natalie Carrigan **info@sims.net**	South Carolina (803) 853-4333 (PHONE) (803) 722-4488 (FAX)
South Coast Computing Services, Inc. Sales **sales@sccsi.com**	Texas (713) 917-5000 (PHONE) (713) 917-5005 (FAX)
SprintLink SprintLink **info@sprintlink.net**	US and International (800) 817-7755 (PHONE) (703) 904-2680 (FAX)
SURAnet Kimberly Donaldson **kdonalds@sura.net**	Southeastern US, South America, Puerto Rico (301) 982-4600 (PHONE) (301) 982-4605 (FAX)
Synergy Communications Sales Department **info@synergy.net**	United States (402) 346-4638 (PHONE) (402) 346-0208 (FAX)
Telerama Public Access Peter Berger **sysop@telerama.lm.com**	Pennsylvania (412) 481-3505 (PHONE) (412) 481-8568 (FAX)
THEnet (Connectivity for Education and Government in Texas) Frank Sayre **f.sayre@utexas.edu**	Texas (512) 471-2444 (PHONE) (512) 471-2449 (FAX)
ThoughtPort Authority, Inc. David Bartlett **info@thoughtport.com**	National (314) 474-6870 (PHONE) (800) ISP-6870 (PHONE) (314) 474-4122 (FAX)

UltraNet Communications, Inc.
Sales
info@ultranet.com

Massachusetts
(508) 229-8400 (PHONE)
(800) 763-8111 (PHONE)
(508) 229-2375 (FAX)

US Net, Inc.
Services
info@us.net

Eastern United States
(301) 572-5926 (PHONE)
(301) 572-5201 (FAX)

VERnet
James Jokl
net-info@ver.net

Virginia
(804) 924-0616 (PHONE)
(804) 982-4715 (FAX)

ViaNet Communications
Joe McGuckin
info@via.net

California (PHONE)
(415) 903-2242 (PHONE)
(415) 903-2241 (FAX)

VNET Internet Access, Inc.
PO Box 31474
Charlotte, NC 28231
info@vnet.net

National
(800) 377-3282 (PHONE)

WestNet
Lillian or Chris
staff@westnet.com

Western United States
(914) 967-7816 (PHONE)

WiscNet
Network Information Center
wn-info@nic.wiscnet.net

Wisconsin
(608) 262-4241 (PHONE)
(608) 262-4679 (FAX)

WLN
Rushton Brandis

info@wln.com

Washington
(800) DIAL-WLN (PHONE)
(206) 923-4000 (PHONE)
(306) 923-4009 (FAX)

WorldWide Access
Kathleen Vrona
support@wwa.com

Illinois
(708) 367-1870 (PHONE)
(708) 367-1872 (FAX)

XMission
Support
support@xmission.com

Utah
(801) 539-0852 (PHONE)
(801) 539-0853 (FAX)

Acknowledgment and Disclaimer

This material is based on work sponsored by the National Science Foundation under Cooperative Agreement No. NCR-9218749. The Government has certain rights in this material. Any opinions, findings, and conclusions or recommendations expressed in this material are those of the author(s) and do not necessarily reflect the views of the National Science Foundation, General Atomics, AT&T, or Network Solutions, Inc.

Frame Relay

Frame relay is an interesting new technology that attempts to maximize the way systems use communications bandwidth. Here's an extremely simplified example of how frame relay works. Imagine a typical telephone conversation: at some point in the conversation, you pause a moment to collect your thoughts. While you're *not* speaking, the phone line is still dedicated to your conversation; while you're silent, your telephone is still sending data (it's just silent data, if you will).

In a frame relay system, while you were pausing to think, the system "loans" your phone line to another conversation, and restores your connection as soon as you began talking again. This way, the phone circuits can be kept busy, even while you're not using them. Now imagine that instead of waiting for a long pause in the conversation, the frame relay system was able to "borrow" the phone line between the sentences, even the words, of your conversation. By switching rapidly during the pauses between several conversations, the same phone line can carry several conversations at once, while maintaining the integrity of each conversation.

Frame Relay systems are fast and efficient, and can run between 56 kbps and 512 kbps (equivalent to about half a T1). Some of its proponents claim that frame relay can support speeds up to 50 Mbps, about the same speed as the Internet backbone itself.

> **Tip**
>
> For more information about frame relay technology, see the Frame Relay Forum's Web site at:
>
> **http://frame-relay.indiana.edu/**

Hardware/Software. Frame relay is a cooperative system; not only do you need the appropriate frame relay access equipment, but your provider must be able to support the system. To use a frame relay system, you'll need a router and possibly other hardware. Some routers are frame-relay compliant, as are some network switches. You don't need any additional network software on your server machine besides your Windows network package.

Costs. Costs vary significantly, as do pricing schemes, ranging from fixed price for a particular amount of service, or a per-data-transmitted price. Initial costs can run to more than $5,000; the frame relay connection fee itself can vary from around $200 to $1,000, depending on the provider and the speed of the connection you select—and of course, there's also the cost of the physical frame relay line, which varies from region to region.

Concerns. Frame relay is becoming a stable and reliable alternative to leased-line technology. The major concern working with frame relay is whether your provider supports it, and whether you can support its cost.

ISDN

Unlike the other technologies discussed so far, *ISDN* (Integrated Services Digital Network) is a dial-up service. The technology has been around for years, but it is recently becoming popular, especially for users that need a high-speed on-demand Internet connection. ISDN service provides two channels, each of which can be used for voice or data. By combining both channels, it's possible to achieve a total data rate of 128 kbps (about four times faster than an ordinary 28.8 kbps modem).

Hardware/Software. ISDN requires a special ISDN modem, but not necessarily a special line; usually, an ordinary phone line will work. The ISDN modem replaces the ordinary modem, and plugs right into your system.

Costs. ISDN modems cost significantly less than router systems—you can get ISDN modems for between $200 and $300. There is a monthly charge for the ISDN service, and a charge per minute. Essentially, ISDN service is just an extremely expensive phone call, and is billed as such.

Concerns. ISDN is extremely cost-effective for brief, high-speed connections, but a poor choice for full-time Web servers. A 24-hour ISDN connection would run charges up quickly. At just $2 per hour, ISDN costs $48 per day, $336 per week, $1,344 per month—which turns out to be about as much as the initial set-up charge for some leased-line services. If you want to operate your server for just a few hours a day, ISDN may be a good idea—if you plan to keep the connection open longer than that, you should probably investigate a leased-line solution. ISDN is also not a universally offered service, even by the major providers.

Analog Modem

The analog modem is the workhorse of the typical Web user; fast, inexpensive analog modems have made the wide audience of the Web possible. And, yes indeed, you can run a Web server with just a basic analog modem—but at a price of performance.

Hardware/Software. Modems are extremely inexpensive for their capabilities. Prices being as low as they are, you should get the fastest modem you can: 28.8 kbps. Most UNIX operating systems these days have fairly robust dial-up access packages, Linux and BSDI probably providing the most stable packages.

Costs. Fast analog modems at this writing were available in the $200-300 range, some even down to $140. If you are selecting a modem for a Web server, don't pay extra for voice mail or fax capabilities—you won't be using them.

Given the popularity of the home and home-business Web server, some providers are beginning to offer 24-hour SLIP/PPP access, as low as $50-60 per month. A single dedicated phone line is usually very inexpensive, but you might want to speak to your phone company about whether a special rate is available for 24-hour calls.

Concerns. The single greatest concern of the modem-based server is speed. How many times have you sat watching the download counter on your personal Internet account, wishing that your 28.8 kbps modem was faster? You may be able to run a very simple text-only Web site over a 28.8 kbps modem, but if you intend to offer high graphics or multimedia-like image maps, an ordinary modem is just too slow.

Building the Perfect Server

If you're going to host your own Web site (whether on an internal network or on the Internet), you will need a system to run the server and to store whatever Web pages you want to provide. If you've done any computer shopping recently, you know that getting the "latest and greatest" can run up costs in a hurry. However, with careful shopping—and careful consideration of your needs, you can obtain a more-than-satisfactory system at a very reasonable price.

There are two main considerations in building a server system:

- How much traffic do you expect to support?
- Can your system grow as your needs grow?

The capacity of your system must be matched to the amount of traffic you expect to support. If you're running an Internet server, response to customer's requests is crucial; a slow server makes a poor impression. You must also look at your future needs and select a path you can follow if you need to upgrade to a larger system.

So which platform and operating system should you buy? The answer to that question is so tinged with religion in the UNIX community that making a recommendation here would do nothing but alienate some fraction of readers, if not all of them. By and large there is really no operating system or platform that is a *bad* choice for a Web server, so your choice should be based on considerations like:

- What operating system do you currently use and enjoy?
- What other kinds of software do you want to run—commercial databases?
- What can you afford?

As mentioned earlier, the URL **http://www.windows95.com/** is running on a Pentium with BSDI and handles 2 million hits a day without a problem. Anecdotal evidence from elsewhere suggests Sparc 2's capable of handling 500,000 hits/day without much problem either. You should choose whatever platform you are most comfortable on, that you know the most about and trust the most. Even Linux on a 386 runs more than one moderately busy Web server!

One of the biggest things that can skew the capacity of the server, though, is if you plan on using CGI scripts, particularly computationally intensive CGI scripts. The heavier the script, the more processing power you'll need. This is a tricky thing to try and gauge, but you should be aware of it.

The important considerations in choosing the hardware, though, are:

- *Memory requirements.*   While Apache and other Web servers are pretty easy on the system in terms of CPU (when tuned right), they can be pigs when it comes to memory. A moderately busy Web server running on Intel hardware should be given about 32 megabytes of memory, at least. An equally busy server on a RISC-chip-based platform should be given 64 megabytes. This is all presuming that the only thing this box will be used for is the Web server—if not, then this is the amount of extra memory you should add over and above the amount used for the other processing.

- *Disk speeds.*   Because so much of what a Web server does is related to shoving files around, Web servers are often very demanding on the I/O systems. You should make sure that whatever system you get has the best internal "bandwidth" possible. On Intel platforms, for example, this means making sure you get a PCI motherboard and a PCI SCSI-3 disk controller, with SCSI-3 disks. This internal bandwidth is probably much faster than your bandwidth to the Internet, but servers do a lot of processing internally so that extra headroom is essential.

- *Ethernet cards.*   There is a surprising amount of variance between good and bad EtherNet cards. Don't skimp in this department, or you may find your output to your network to be very poor.

These are the essential considerations. All the UNIX vendors are aware of this; their operating systems were punished over the last year or two by high performance systems, and just about all of them have since made performance tuning a priority. But as noted earlier, for the common case (just dishing out flat files), extremely cheap hardware can go an extremely long way. ❖

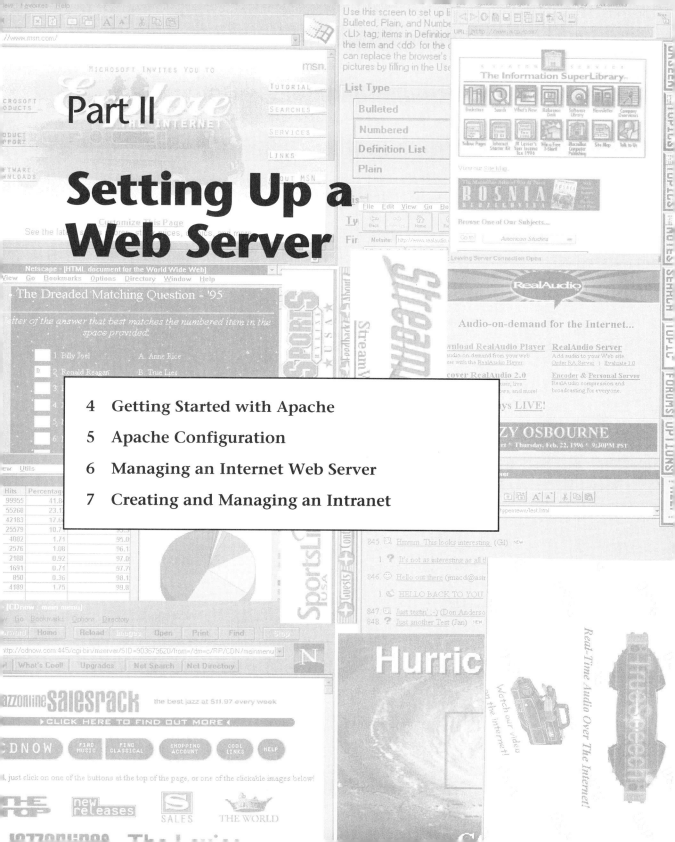

Part II

Setting Up a Web Server

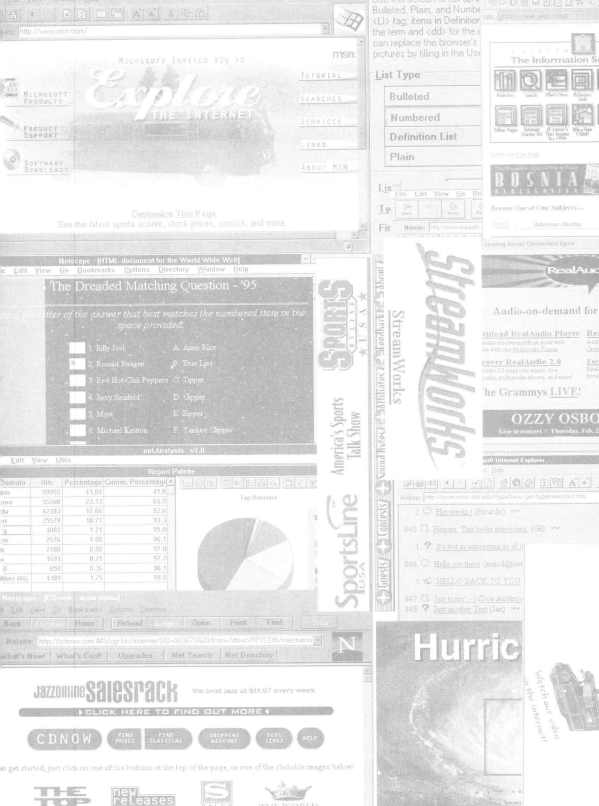

http://www.msn.com/

Use this screen to set up li
Bulleted, Plain, and Numbe
<LI> tag; items in Definition
the term and <dd> for the d
can replace the browser's
pictures by filling in the Use

List Type

| Bulleted |
| Numbered |
| Definition List |
| Plain |

Lis
Ty
Fir

File Edit View Go Bo

Go Home
Back

Netsite: http://www.realaudio.

Leaving Server Connection Open

Netscape - [HTML document for the World Wide Web]

Edit View Go Bookmarks Options Directory Window Help

The Dreaded Matching Question - '95

place the letter of the answer that best matches the numbered item in the space provided.

1. Billy Joel
2. Ronald Reagan
3. Red Hot Chili Peppers
4. Jerry Seinfeld
5. Myst
6. Michael Keaton

A. Anne Rice
B. True Lies
C. Tipper
D. Gipper
E. Zipper
F. Yankee Clipper

net.Analysis v1.0

Edit View Utils

Report Palette

Domain	Hits	Percentage	Cumm. Percentage
m	99955	41.84	41.8
ne	55268	23.13	64.9
fu	42183	17.66	82.6
et	25579	10.71	93.3
g	4082	1.71	95.0
ov	2576	1.08	96.1
a	2188	0.92	97.0
s	1691	0.71	97.7
il	850	0.36	98.1
ther (46)	4189	1.75	99.8

Top Domains

S-Ports ONLINE USA

SportsLine USA

America's Sports Talk Show

StreamWorks

soft Internet Explorer

Help

Address: http://union.ncsa.uiuc.edu/HyperNews/get/hypernews/test.html

1. ☺ Het werkt ! (Ricardo) NEW
845. 🗎 Hmmm. This looks interesting. (Gil) NEW
  1. ❓ It's not as interesting as all th
846. ☺ Hello out there (jmacd@astr
  1. ☺ HELLO BACK TO YOU
847. 🗎 Just testin' ;-) (Don Anderso
848. ❓ Just another Test (Jan) NEW

Netscape - [CDnow : main menu]

Edit View Go Bookmarks Options Directory

Back Forward Home Reload Images Open Print Find Stop

Netsite: http://cdnow.com:445/cgi-bin/mserver/SID=903679620/from=/dm=c/RP/CDN/mainmenu

What's New! | What's Cool! | Upgrades | Net Search | Net Directory

Hurric

Real-Time Audio Over The Internet!

Watch our video on the Internet!

## CHAPTER 4

Getting Started with Apache

Although this chapter, like many others, is specific to the Apache server, the vocabulary is certainly applicable to other Web servers. In particular, the NCSA family of servers has much in common with Apache with respect to configuration files, since Apache was derived originally from the NCSA 1.3 server, and maintaining backwards compatibility with existing NCSA servers was a mandate with the development team.

This chapter deals with all the essential steps between the software on the CD-ROM (or downloaded from the Net) and a running, breathing, living server. If you have installed an Apache or NCSA server before, you can probably safely skip this chapter—perhaps skim it to look for essential differences. This chapter covers:

- The compilation of the source code for the server.
- The elemental parts of the configuration files.
- Some basic "why didn't the Web server come up?" debugging help.
- Obtaining, installing, and launching Apache-SSL.

Compiling Apache

Apache is known to compile on just about every UNIX variant out there: Solaris 2.X, SunOS 4.1.X, Irix 5.X and 6.X, Linux, FreeBSD/NetBSD/BSDI, HPUX, AIX, Ultrix, OSF1, NeXT, Sequent, AUX, SCO, UTS, Apollo Domain/OS, QNX, and probably a few you've never even tried yet. A port to OS/2 has been done, and a Windows NT port is rumored to be in the works. Portability has been a high priority for the development team.

Before you go about compiling Apache, make sure a binary suitable for your platform is not already available on the CD-ROM included with this book. There is a README file on the CD-ROM that explains which system binaries are provided. If there is a suitable binary, you can skip the compilation process and move on to the next section, although if you ever want to add new modules or tweak the functionality provided by Apache, you'll need to know how to compile it.

Copy the source code package to a part of your file system. Depending on which OS you are on, you'll need up to 10 spare megabytes of disk to compile the server. Unpack it and go to the /src subdirectory. A sequence of commands to do this might look like

```
cd /CDROM
cp apache_1.0.3.tar /usr/local/etc/
tar -xvf apache_1.0.3.tar
cd apache_1.0.3/src
```

Step 1: Edit the Configuration File

This file is used by the Configure program to create a Makefile specifically targeted to your platform, with any runtime defines set if necessary, and with the modules you have chosen compiled together. It also creates a modules.c, which contains information about which modules to link together at compilation time.

You must declare which C compiler you are using, and you must uncomment the appropriate setting for AUX_CFLAGS and AUX_LIBS for the platform on which you are compiling. For example, the following is appropriate if you are using the GNU C compiler

```
CC=gcc
```

And if, say, you want to set it to use Solaris instead of the default, which is SunOS, you want to change the section that reads:

```
# For SunOS 4
AUX_CFLAGS= -DSUNOS4
# For Solaris 2.
#AUX_CFLAGS= -DSOLARIS2
#AUX_LIBS= -lsocket -lnsl
```

to the following:

```
# For SunOS 4
#AUX_CFLAGS= -DSUNOS4
# For Solaris 2.
AUX_CFLAGS= -DSOLARIS2
AUX_LIBS= -lsocket -lnsl
```

> **Note**
>
> For the CFLAGS definition: If you want every file with the execute bit set to be parsed for server side includes, set `-DXBITHACK`. If you wish to eliminate the overhead of performing the reverse-DNS lookup when an entry is written to the logfile, set `-DMINIMAL_DNS`.
>
> If, on the other hand, you want to have an even greater sense of confidence in the hostname, you can set `-DMAXIMAL_DNS`. You would set this if you were protecting parts of your site based on hostname. Doing this is optional, and is mostly provided for backwards compatibility with NCSA 1.3.

At the bottom of the file is a list of packaged modules that come with the Apache distribution. Notice that not all of them are compiled in by default. To include a module in the build, uncomment the entry for it. Notice that some modules are mutually exclusive—for example, it would not be wise to compile both the configurable logging module and the common logging module at the same time.

Also, some modules, like mod_auth_dbm, may require linking to an external library, and need an entry added to the EXTRA_LIBS line. You'll learn more about modules in a little bit; for the purposes of getting up and running I'd recommend simply using the defaults as provided.

Step 2: Run the *Configure* Script

This is a simple Bourne shell script that takes the Configuration file and creates a Makefile out of it, as well as modules.c. If you are feeling ambitious, you can look at and edit httpd.h, which sets a lot of defaults for some low-level functionality, most of which is set anyway in the configuration files.

Step 3: Run *make*

This compiles the server. You might see some warnings about data types, particularly if you compiled with `-Wall` set, but none of the errors should be fatal.

If all went well, you should now have an executable program in your /src directory called httpd.

Establishing the File Hierarchy

The next step in the process of setting up a server is to make some fundamental decisions regarding where on the file system different parts of the server

II

Setting Up a Web Server

will reside. Write down your decisions for each of these; they will be needed in the section on "Basic Configuration."

First, there is the *server root*. This is the subdirectory in which you unpacked the server, and from which the conf/ directory, the logs/ subdirectory, the cgi-bin/ subdirectory, and other server-related directories lead. The default suggestion is to have this as /usr/local/etc/httpd. You will be able to have your configuration files and log files in other locations—the server root was designed to be a convenient place to keep everything server-related together. Also, if the server crashes and leaves a core file, it will be found in the server root directory.

Second, there is the *document root*. This is the directory in which all your HTML and other media reside. A file in here called myfile.html would be referenced as http://host.com/myfile.html. It is recommended that this be outside the server root and in its own directory. Since you'll be referring to it frequently, it should be pretty short—for example, /home/www or /www/htdocs. If you are implementing a Web server on top of an FTP server, for example, you might want to point the document root at /home/ftp/pub.

Finally, you need to decide where on your server you will keep your logfiles. This should be a space with a fairly large working area, depending on how busy you estimate your server will be. For a point of reference, a site with 100K hits per day (which would fall under moderate traffic, relatively speaking) can expect to generate 15 MB per day of logfile information.

Later in this book, you'll deal with automated logfile rotation and logfile analysis tools, but for now just be aware of the disk space issue. Furthermore, for performance reasons, it's usually best to have the log directory on a separate disk partition or even a separate disk altogether, because on even a moderately busy server the access log can be written to several times per second.

Basic Configuration

This section covers the minimal set of changes you need to make to the configuration files in order to launch a basic Web site.

▶ See Chapter 6, "Managing an Internet Web Server," for information about advanced configuration.

There are three separate configuration files in Apache. This model goes back to NCSA, and the reasoning is sound: there are largely three main areas of administrative configuration, so setting them up as separate files allows the Web master to give different write permissions to each if he or she so desires.

You will find the configuration files for Apache in the conf/ subdirectory of the server root directory. Each has been provided with a `-dist` appendage; it is recommended that you make a copy without the `-dist` and edit those new files, keeping the `-dist` versions as backups and reference.

The basic format of the configuration files are a combination of a shell-like interface and pseudo-HTML. The elemental unit is the *directive*, which can take a number of arguments. Essentially:

```
Directive argument argument....
```

i.e.

```
Port 80
```

or

```
AddIcon /icons/back.gif ..
```

Directives can also be grouped together inside certain pseudo-HTML tags. Unlike HTML, these tags should be on their own line. For example:

```
<Virtualhost www.myhost.com>
DocumentRoot /www/htdocs/myhost.com
ServerName www.myhost.com
</Virtualhost>
```

httpd.conf

The first configuration file to look at is httpd.conf. This is the file that sets the basic system-level information about the server—what port it binds to, which users it runs under, and so on. If you are not the systems administrator of the site at which you are installing the server, you might want to ask the administrator to help you with these questions.

The essential items in this file to cover are:

```
Port <number>
```

for example,

```
Port 80
```

This is the TCP/IP port number to which the Web server binds. Port 80 is the default port in "http:" URLs; in other words, "http://www.myhost.com/" is equivalent to "http://www.myhost.com:80/."

For a number of reasons, however, you might want to run your server on a different port; for example, there is already a server running on port 80, or this is a server you want to keep secret. (Though if there is sensitive information on this, you should at least do host-based access control, if not password protection.)

```
User <#number or uid>
Group <#number or uid>
```

as in

```
User nobody
Group nogroup
```

This is the UNIX user that the Web server will run as. Apache needs to be launched as root in order to bind to a port lower than 1024—this is a basic security feature of all UNIX implementations. Immediately after grabbing the port, Apache changes its effective user ID to something else, typically as user nobody. This is for security reasons—running your Web servers as root means that any hole in the server (be it through the server itself, or through a CGI script, which is much more likely) could be exploited by an outside user to run a command on your machine. Thus, setting the user to nobody, www, or some other reasonably innocuous user ID is the safest bet. This user ID needs to be able to read files in the document root, as well as have read permission on the configuration files. The argument should be the actual user name— if you want to give the numeric user ID, prepend the number with a pound sign (#). The Group directive is the same issue; decide which group ID you want the server to run with.

```
ServerAdmin <email address>
```

This should be set to the e-mail address of a user who can receive mail related to the actions of the server. In the case of a server error, the message given to the browser visiting your site will include a message to the effect of "please report this problem to user@myhost.com." In the future, Apache may send warning e-mail to this user if it encounters a major systems-related problem.

```
ServerRoot <directory>
```

for example

```
ServerRoot /usr/local/etc/httpd
```

This is the server root decided upon earlier. Give the full path, and don't end it with a slash.

```
ErrorLog <directory/filename>
TransferLog <directory/filename>
```

These two directives specify exactly where to log errors and Web accesses. If the filename given doesn't start with a slash, it is presumed to be relative to the server root directory. It was suggested earlier that the logfiles be sent to a separate directory outside of the server root; this is where you specify that logging directory and the name of the log files within that directory.

```
ServerName <DNS hostname>
```

At times, the Web server will have to *know* the hostname it is being referred to as, which can be different from its real hostname. For example, the name

"www.myhost.com" might actually be a DNS alias for
"gateway.myhost.com." In this case, you don't want the URLs generated by
the server to be "http://gateway.myhost.com/." `ServerName` allows you to set
that precisely.

srm.conf

The second configuration file to cover before launch is srm.conf. The important things to set in that file are:

```
DocumentRoot <directory>
```

As described before, this is the root level of your tree of documents—be that
/usr/local/etc/httpd/htdocs or /www/htdocs. Based on my experience, it's a
very good idea to keep it short and concise. This directory must exist and be
readable by the user the Web server runs as.

```
ScriptAlias <request path alias> <directory>
```

`ScriptAlias` lets you specify that a particular directory *outside* of the document root can be aliased to a path in the request, *and* that objects in that directory are executed instead of simply read from the file system. For example,
the default offering

```
ScriptAlias /cgi-bin/ /usr/local/etc/httpd/cgi-bin/
```

means that a request for http://www.myhost.com/cgi-bin/fortune will
execute the program /usr/local/etc/httpd/cgi-bin/fortune. Apache comes
bundled with a number of useful beginner CGI scripts, simple shell scripts
that illustrate CGI programming. However, you probably don't want to turn
them by default. I recommend commenting this line out until you're sure
you want to use it as your CGI invocation mechanism.

Finally, the directory containing the CGI scripts should *not* be under the
document root—bizarre interactions between the code that handles
`ScriptAlias` and the code that handles request/pathname resolution could
cause problems.

Just as with httpd.conf, there are many extra features that are discussed in
upcoming sections.

access.conf

Access.conf is structured more rigidly than the other configuration files; all
the content is contained within <Directory></Directory> pseudo-HTML tags
that define the scope of the directives listed within. So for example, the directives in between

```
<Directory /www/htdocs>
```

and

```
</Directory>
```

affect everything located under the /www/htdocs directory. Furthermore, wildcards may be used, for example

```
<Directory /www/htdocs/*/archives/>
....
</Directory>
```

applies to /www/htdocs/list1/archives/, /www/htdocs/list2/archives/, and so on. The most important directive to set at this point is Options. Options takes a list of keywords that enable or disable particular functionality.

It's important to establish a conservative set of functionality when the site is first launched. I would recommend using just Indexes at the very beginning. For example:

```
Options Indexes
```

Starting Up Apache

To start Apache, simply run the binary you compiled earlier (or your precompiled binary) with the -f flag pointing to the httpd.conf file also created earlier. For example:

```
/usr/local/etc/httpd/src/httpd -f /usr/local/etc/httpd/conf/
httpd.conf
```

It's probably a good idea at this point to use the UNIX command ps to see if httpd is running, typically something like

```
ps -augwx ¦ grep httpd      (BSD-based systems)
ps -ef ¦ grep httpd         (SVR4-based systems)
```

will suffice. To your surprise you, you will hopefully see a number of simultaneous httpd processes running. What's going on?

The first Web servers, like the CERN and NCSA servers, used the model of one main Web server cloning itself with every single request that came in. The clone would respond to the request, while the original server returned to listening to the port for another request. While certainly a simple and robust design, the act of *cloning* (or in UNIX terms, *fork*) was an expensive operation under UNIX, so loads above a couple hits per second were quite punishing even on the nicest hardware. It was also difficult to implement any sort of *throttling*, reducing the amount of cloning that took place when the number of clones was very high since it was hard for the original server to know how many clones were still around. Thus servers had no easy way to refuse or delay connections based on a lack of resources.

Apache, like NCSA 1.4+, Netscape's Web servers, and a couple of other UNIX-based Web servers, instead uses the model of a group of persistent children running in parallel. The children are coordinated by a parent process, which can tell how many children are alive, spawn new children if necessary, and even terminate old children if there are many idle ones, depending on the situation. *Parent* and *child* are the actual UNIX terms.

Back to the server. Fire up your Web browser and go to **http://www.myhost.com/**. Did it work? If all went well, you should be able to see a directory index listing of everything in the document root directory, or if there's an index.html in that directory, you would see the contents of that file.

Other command line options are shown in the following table:

Option	Result
-d serverroot	Sets the initial value for ServerRoot.
-X	Runs the server in single-process mode; useful for debugging purposes, but don't run the server in this mode for v serving content to the outside world.
-v	Prints the version of the server, and then exits.
-?	Prints the list of available command-line arguments to Apache.

Debugging the Server Start-Up Process

Apache is usually pretty good about giving meaningful error messages, but some are explained in more detail here.

```
httpd: could not open document config file .....
fopen: No such file or directory
```

This is usually the result of giving just a relative path to the -f argument, so Apache looks for it relative to the compiled-in server root (what's set in src/httpd.h) instead of relative to the directory you are in. You must give it either the full path or the path relative to the compiled-in server root.

```
httpd: could not bind to port [X]
bind: Operation not permitted
```

This was most likely caused by attempting to run the server on a port below 1024 without launching it as "root." Most UNIX operating systems prevent people without root access from trying to launch a server—any type of server—on a port less than 1024. If you launch the server as root, the error message should disappear.

```
httpd: could not bind to port
bind: Address already in use
```

This means that there is already something running on your machine at the port you have specified. Do you have another Web server running? There is no standard UNIX mechanism for determining what's running on what ports; on most systems, the file /etc/services can tell you what the most common daemons are, but it's not a complete list. You could also try using the netstat command, with various options such as -a.

```
httpd: bad user name ....
httpd: bad group name ....
```

The user or the group you had set in httpd.conf didn't actually exist on your system. You might see errors telling you that particular files or directories don't exist. If it looks like the files are there, make sure they are readable by the user IDs that the server runs as (i.e., both root and nobody).

Suppose Apache has started up, and according to ps it's actually running. But when you go to the site, you get:

- No connection at all. Make sure that there are no firewalls between you or the server that would filter out packets to the server. Secondly, try using "telnet" to the port you launched the Web server on; for example "telnet myhost.com 80." If you don't get a Connected to myhost.com message back, your connection is not even making it to the server in the first place.

- 403 Access Forbidden. Your document root directory may be unreadable, or you may have something in your access.conf file that prevents access to your site from the machine where your Web browser is.

- 500 Server Error. Is your front page a CGI script? The script may be failing.

These are the most common errors made in initial server start-ups. If you can establish that contact with the server is actually being made, the next best place to look for error information is in the ErrorLog. Future sections describe each new piece of functionality and also discuss the errors that misconfiguration can bring up.

Apache-SSL

At this point, we will take a slight detour and discuss setting up a variant of the Apache Web server, Apache-SSL, which can conduct secure transactions over the Secure Sockets Layer protocol. SSL is an RSA public-key based encryption protocol developed by Netscape Communications for use in the Netscape Navigator browser and Netscape Web servers.

Until recently, the only options for doing SSL transactions on the World Wide Web has been to use a proprietary server, such as the Netscape Commerce server or the OpenMarket Secure server. Strongly encrypting versions of these servers have not been available outside the United States due to export restrictions in the U.S.

Eric Young, author of the widely used libdes package, along with Tim Hudson, wrote a library that implements SSL, eponymously named SSLeay. The SSLeay package has since expanded to become an all purpose cryptography and certificate handling library, while retaining the same name, "SSLeay."

Ben Laurie, a member of the Apache Group, then took the SSLeay library and interfaced it with the Apache server, making his patches available to people on the Net. Sameer Parekh, of Community ConneXion, Inc., (hereafter referred to as C2) then took Ben Laurie's patches and built a package legal for use within the United States.

Because the RSA technology used by SSL in the United States is covered by patents owned by RSA Data Security, Inc. (RSADSI) (**www.rsa.com**), it is not legal to use the SSLeay package "out-of-the-box" within the United States. C2 licensed the RSA technology to make use of the package legal within the United States, using the "RSAREF" package, produced by RSADSI and Consensus Development Corporation (**www.consensus.com**).

Due to export restrictions, it is not legal for someone outside the United States to download and install the C2 Apache-SSL package. In fact, we couldn't even put the SSL patches on the CD-ROM included with this book because the book would suddenly have earned the label "munition" and clearance from the U.S. Government would have been required!

Therefore, the installation process for Apache-SSL differs for those within the United States versus those who live outside the U.S. People within the U.S. can simply download the package from C2, at **http://apachessl.c2.org/**, and install it. Outside the United States, people must separately install SSLeay, and then patch Apache with Ben Laurie's patches from his site.

Within the United States, it is legal to use the version of Apache-SSL available for download from C2 for noncommercial purposes only. In order to use Apache-SSL commercially, people must purchase an Apache-SSL Commerce license from C2. After downloading the package from C2, the installation of the server is rather straightforward.

As with the standard Apache, you must first edit the Configuration file to reflect the system and any custom modules you may want installed. The lines regarding SSL in the Configuration file should be ignored. The installation process automatically deals with them.

Next, you need to configure RSAREF for your system. The noncommercial distribution of Apache-SSL comes with full RSAREF source code, so you must edit the rsaref/install/makefile to reflect your system. There is usually not much that needs to be edited in this file, except for the C compiler that you need to use. The commercial version, however, does not come with RSAREF source code, but with RSAREF object code for a number of platforms. If you have the commercial release of Apache-SSL, you need to copy the proper version of the RSAREF library from rsaref/install/objs and place it in rsaref/install/rsaref.a.

Finally, to finish the configuration, run Configure in the ssl/ directory. Running Configure will give you a list of support platforms for SSLeay. Choose one and run Configure again in order to configure SSLeay properly for the platform of your choice.

To build, type **make** at the top-level.

Once the server is successfully compiled, you run make install, in order to install SSLeay and Apache-SSL into /usr/local/ssl and /usr/local/etc/httpd. The installation installs both an SSL version and a plain non-encrypting version of the Apache server in those locations.

Before you can begin using SSL, however, you need to generate your key/certificate pair for use with SSL. The C2 Apache-SSL distribution comes with the program "genkey" you can use to generate your key and certificate. Run /usr/local/ssl/bin/genkey httpd. This generates a public/private RSA keypair for use with the server, and puts it in /usr/local/ssl/private/httpd.key. It also generates a PKCS #10 Certificate Signing Request, which you send to the Certificate Authority of your choice (for example, Verisign) along with the proper documentation. The script also generates a *test certificate*, so that you can start using the server immediately, without waiting for your Certificate Authority to reply with a signed certificate.

After the key/certificate pair is generated and installed in the proper location, you are ready to start using the server! First, however, familiarize yourself with the SSL-specific configuration directives to Apache-SSL.

```
SSLCertificateFile filename
```

The filename is the location where your server's certificate is stored. It is either relative to /usr/local/ssl/certs, or, if you provide a full pathname, it's the full path to the certificate file. The SSLCertificateFile directive is required.

```
SSLCertificateKeyFile filename
```

The SSLCertificateKeyFile is required, unless the file listed in SSLCertificateFile also contains the key. This file name must be relative to /usr/local/ssl/private. It can't be a full pathname.

```
SSLLogFile filename
```

The SSLLogFile is where Apache-SSL logs specific information regarding SSL for each connection, such as the cipher used, and client-authentication information.

```
SSLVerifyClient   0, 1, or 2
```

SSLVerifyClient determines whether or not the server should use X509 client authentication. 0 means no, 1 means it is optional, and 2 means that a client certificate is required.

```
SSLVerifyDepth depth
```

The SSLVerifyDepth is how far along a certificate chain the server should look for a root Certificate Authority when verifying a given client certificate. If you're not using X509 client certificates, a good default value is probably 1.

```
SSLFakeBasicAuth
```

The SSLFakeBasicAuth directive allows you to use X509 client certificates to provide for Basic HTTP/1.0 authentication for accessing various realms of your Web server's document tree.

Note

SSLFakeBasicAuth must be used with SSLVerifyClient 2. If used with any other SSLVerifyClient setting, it is subject to subversion.

After having installed the certificate and key in /usr/local/ssl/certs/httpd.cert and /usr/local/ssl/private/httpd.key, you can start the server by merely running /usr/local/etc/httpd/start, which starts up the server with some default configuration files, located in conf/httpd.conf and ssl_conf/httpd.conf.

II

Setting Up a Web Server

For people outside the United States, the installation process is more involved. You must obtain the SSLeay package (**ftp://ftp.psy.uq.oz.au/ pub/Crypto/SSL/**) and then install it according to the directions in the package.

Second, you must obtain Ben's patches to Apache from his site, at **http:// www.algroup.co.uk/ApacheSSL/**. The patches must then be installed to your Apache source tree, according to the directions included with the package.

It should be noted that, at publication time, Verisign (**www.verisign.com**, a spin-off from RSA, which was the first Certificate Authority for SSL) had just started signing keys generated for Apache-SSL. Other CA's are expected to crop up—Netscape 2.0 comes with half a dozen others defined and waiting to be recognized. In fact, Netscape 2.0 (and hopefully by the time you read this, other browsers) allow for arbitrary CA's to be used, warning the user that a new CA is being used, but still allowing the encrypted conversation to take place. ❖

## CHAPTER 5

Apache Configuration

By this point you should have a running, minimal Web server. In this chapter, you learn about most of the functionality that comes bundled with the server. This chapter is organized as a series of tutorials, so that new users can get up-to-speed. Toward the end of the chapter, you dive into some experimental Apache modules as well.

By the time you read this chapter, given the rapid pace of development, there will be some significantly new functionality implemented and released. However, the existing functionality is not likely to change much. The Apache Group has had a strong ethic toward backward compatibility.

In this chapter, you will learn how to:

- Configure the MIME types of objects on the server
- Use those MIME types to trigger special actions
- Redirect and alias requests for different parts of your site
- Configure directory indexing
- Set up and use server side includes
- Set up internal imagemap handling
- Use "cookies" to track user sessions
- Set up configurable logging
- Turn on and use content negotiation
- Configure access control based on hostnames and IP numbers, or passwords
- Configure "virtual" hosts
- Customize the server's error messages

In short, this chapter covers most of the major functionality of Apache 1.0.

Configuration Basics

The srm.conf (also known as the ResourceConfig file, which is a directive that can be set in httpd.conf) and access.conf (also known as the AccessConfig file, also a directive in httpd.conf) files are where most of the configuration related to the actual objects on the server takes place. The names are mostly historical—at one point, when the server was still NCSA, the only thing access.conf was good for was setting permissions, restrictions, authentication, and so forth. Then, when directory indexing was added, the cry went out for the capability to control certain characteristics on a directory-by-directory basis. The access.conf file was the only one that had any kind of structure for that: the pseudo-HTML <Directory> container.

With Apache's revamped configuration file parsing routines, most directives can literally appear anywhere. For example, within <Directory> containers in access.conf, within <VirtualHost> containers in httpd.conf, and so on. However, for sanity's sake, you should keep some structure to the configuration files. You should put server-processing-level configuration options in httpd.conf (like Port, <VirtualHost> containers, etc.), put generic server resource information in srm.conf (like Redirect, AddType, directory indexing information, etc.), and per-directory configurations in access.conf.

In addition to the <Directory> container, there is the <Limit> container, which is used within <Directory> containers to specify certain HTTP methods to which particular directives apply. Examples will be given later in this chapter.

Per-Directory Configuration Files

Before you get too deep into the long list of features, take a look at a mechanism that controls most of those features on a directory-by-directory basis by using a file in that directory itself. You can already control subdirectory options in access.conf, as outlined in the previous chapter. However, for a number of reasons, you may want to allow these configurations to be maintained by people other than those who have the power to restart the server (such as people maintaining their home pages), and for that purpose the AccessFileName directive was invented.

The default AccessFileName is .htaccess. If you want to use something else, for example, .acc, you would say the following in the srm.conf file:

```
AccessFileName .acc
```

If looking for this file is enabled, and a request comes in that translates to the file /www/htdocs/path/path2/file, the server will look for /.acc, /www/.acc, /www/htdocs/.acc, /www/htdocs/path/.acc, and /www/htdocs/path/path2/.acc, in that order. Also, it will parse the file if it finds it to see what configuration options apply. Remember that this parsing has to happen with each hit, separately, so this can be a big performance hit. If you turn it off by setting the following in your access config file:

```
<Directory />
AllowOverride None
</Directory>
```

For the sake of brevity and clarity, let's call these files .htaccess files. What options can these files affect? The range of available options is controlled by the AllowOverride directive within the <Directory> container in the AccessConfig file, as mentioned previously. The exact arguments to AllowOverride are as follows:

Argument	Result
AuthConfig	When listed, .htaccess can specify their own authentication directives, such as AuthUserFile, AuthName, AuthType, require, and so on.
FileInfo	When listed, .htaccess can override any settings for metainformation about files, using directives such as AddType, AddEncoding, AddLanguage, and so forth.
Indexes	When listed, .htaccess files can locally set directives that control the rendering of the directory indexing, as implemented in the module mod_dir.c. For example, FancyIndexing, AddIcon, AddDescription, and the like.
Limit	Allow the use of the directives that limit access based on hostname or host IP number (allow, deny, and order).
Options	Allow the use of the Options directive.
All	Allow all of the above to be true.

AllowOverride options are not merged, which means that if the configuration for /path/ is different than the configuration for /, the /path/ one will take precedence because it's deeper.

MIME Types: *AddType* and *AddEncoding*

A fundamental element of the HTTP protocol, and the reason why the Web was so natural as a home for multiple media formats, is that every data object transferred through HTTP had an associated MIME type. What does this mean?

II

Setting Up a Web Server

> **Note**
>
> MIME stands for *Multipurpose Internet Mail Extensions*, and its origins lie in an effort to standardize the transmission of documents of multiple media through e-mail. Part of the MIME specification was that e-mail messages could contain meta-information in the headers—information *about* the information being sent. One type of MIME header is Content-Type, which states the format or data type the object is in. For example, HTML is given the label "text/html," and JPEG images are given the label "image/jpeg". There is a registry of MIME types maintained by the Internet Assigned Numbers Authority at **http://www.isi.edu/div7/iana/**.

When a browser asks a server for an object, the server gives that object to the browser and states what its "Content-Type" is, and the browser can make an intelligent decision about how to render the document. For example, it can send it to an image program, to a postscript viewer, or to a VRML viewer.

What this means to the server maintainer is that every object being served out must have the right MIME type associated with it. Fortunately, there has been a convention of expressing data type through two-, three-, or four-letter suffixes to file name—i.e., foobar.gif is most likely to be a GIF image.

What the server needs is a file to map the suffix to the MIME content type. Fortunately, Apache comes with such a file in its config directory, a file called mime.types. You'll see that the format of this file is simple. The format consists of one record per line, where a record is a MIME type and a list of acceptable suffixes. This is because, while more than one suffix may map to a particular MIME type, you can't have more than one MIME type per suffix. You can use the `TypesConfig` directive to specify an alternative location for the file.

The Internet is evolving so quickly that it would be hard to keep that file completely up-to-date. To overcome that, you can use a special directive called `AddType`, which can be put in an `srm.conf` file like the following:

```
AddType x-world/x-vrml wrl
```

Now, whenever the server is asked to serve a file that ends with ".wrl," it knows to also send a header like the following:

```
Content-type: x-world/x-vrml
```

Thus, you don't have to worry about reconciling future distributions of the `mime.types` file with your private installations and configuration.

As you'll see in future pages, however, `AddType` is also used to specify "special" files that get magically handled by certain features within the server.

A sister to `AddType` is `AddEncoding`. Just as the MIME header `Content-Type` can specify the data format of the object, the header `Content-Encoding` specifies the *encoding* of the object. An encoding is an attribute of the object as it is being transferred or stored; semantically, the browser should know that is has to "decode" whatever it gets based upon the listed encoding. The most common use is with compressed files. For example, if you have

```
AddEncoding x-gzip gz
```

and if you then access a file called "myworld.wrl.gz," the MIME headers sent in response will look like the following:

```
Content-Type: x-world/x-vrml
Content-Encoding: x-gzip
```

And any browser worth its two cents will know "Oh, I have to uncompress the file before handing it off to the VRML viewer."

Alias, ScriptAlias, **and** *Redirect*

These three directives, all denizens of srm.conf, and all three implemented by the module `mod_alias.c`, allow you to have some flexibility with the mapping between "URL-Space" on your server and the actual layout of your file system.

If that last statement sounded cryptic, don't worry. What it basically means is that any URL that looks like "http://myhost.com/x/y/z" does not have to necessarily map to a file named "x/y/z" under the document root of the server:

```
Alias /path/ /some/other/path/
```

The preceding directive will take a request for an object from the mythical subdirectory /path under the document root and map it to another directory somewhere else entirely. For example, a request for

```
http://myhost.com/statistics/
```

might normally go to `document root` /statistics, except that for whatever reason you wanted it to point somewhere else outside of the document root. Say /usr/local/statistics. For that you'd have the following:

```
Alias /statistics/ /usr/local/statistics/
```

To the outside user this would be completely transparent. If you use `Alias`, it's wise not to alias to somewhere else inside of document root. Furthermore, a request like

```
http://myhost.com/statistics/graph.gif
```

would get translated into a request for the file

```
/usr/local/statistics/graph.gif
```

ScriptAlias is just like Alias, with the side-effect of making everything in the subdirectory by default a CGI script. This might sound a bit bizarre, but the early model for building Web sites had all the CGI functionality separated into a directory by itself, and referenced through the Web server as shown in the following:

```
http://myhost.com/cgi-bin/script
```

If you have in your srm.conf

```
ScriptAlias /cgi-bin/ /usr/local/etc/httpd/cgi-bin/
```

then the preceding URL points to the script at "/usr/local/etc/httpd/cgi-bin/script." As you'll see in a page or two, there is another way to specify that a file is a CGI script to be executed.

Redirect does just that—it redirects the request to another resource. That resource could be on the same machine, or somewhere else on the Net. Also, the match will be a substring match, starting from the beginning. For example, if you did:

```
Redirect /newyork http://myhost.com/maps/states/newyork
```

then a request for

```
http://myhost.com/newyork/index.html
```

will get redirected to

```
http://myhost.com/maps/states/newyork/index.html
```

Of course, the second argument to Redirect can be a URL at some other site. Just make sure that you know what you're doing. Also, be wary of creating loops accidentally. For example,

```
Redirect /newyork http://myhost.com/newyork/newyork
```

can have particularly deleterious effects on the server!

A Better Way To Activate CGI Scripts

You read earlier that there is a more elegant way of activating CGI scripts than using ScriptAlias. You can use the AddType directive and a "magic" MIME type, like so:

```
AddType application/x-httpd-cgi cgi
```

When the server gets a request for a CGI file, it maps to that MIME type, and then catches itself and says "Aha! I need to execute this instead of just dish it out like regular files." Thus, you can have CGI files in the same directories as your HTML and GIF and all your other files.

A later chapter will go into more detail about the implementation of CGI in Apache.

Directory Indexing

When Apache is given a URL to a directory, instead of to a particular file, for example

```
http://myhost.com/statistics/
```

Apache first looks for a file specified by the DirectoryIndex directive in srm.conf. In the default configs, this is index.html. You can set a list of files to search for, or even an absolute path to a page or CGI script:

```
DirectoryIndex index.cgi index.html /cgi-bin/go-away
```

The preceding directive says to look for an "index.cgi" in the directory first. If that can't be found, then look for an "index.html" in the directory. If neither can be found, then redirect the request to "/cgi-bin/go-away."

If it all fails to find a match, then Apache will create, completely on-the-fly, an HTML listing of all the files available in the directory:

```
<Give a figure here of the directory listing output>
```

There are quite a few ways to customize the output of the directory indexing functionality. First, you need to ask yourself if you care about seeing things like icons or last-modified times in the reports. If you do, then you want to turn to

```
FancyIndexing On
```

otherwise, you'll just get a simple menu of the available files, which you may want for security or performance reasons.

With that going on, you must ask whether you need to customize it further, and how. The default settings for the directory indexing functionality are already pretty elaborate.

The AddIcon, AddIconByEncoding, and AddIconByType directives customize the selection of icons next to files. AddIcon matches icons at the file name level by using the pattern

```
AddIcon iconfile filename [filename] [filename]...
```

Thus, for example,

```
AddIcon /icons/binary.gif .bin .exe
```

means that any file that ends in .bin or .exe should get the binary.gif icon attached. The file names can also be a wildcard expression, a complete file name, or even one of two "special" names: `^^DIRECTORY^^` for directories and `^^BLANKICON^^` for blank lines. So you can see lines like

```
AddIcon /icons/dir.gif ^^DIRECTORY^^
AddIcon /icons/old.gif *~
```

Finally, the "iconfile" can actually also be a string containing both the iconfile's name and the alternate text to put into the ALT attribute. So, your examples should really be

```
AddIcon (BIN,/icons/binary.gif) .bin .exe
AddIcon (DIR,/icons/dir.gif) ^^DIRECTORY^^
```

The `AddIconByType` directive is actually a little bit more flexible and probably comes more highly recommended in terms of actual use. Instead of tying icons to file name patterns, it ties icons to the MIME type associated with the files. The syntax is very roughly the same:

```
AddIconByType iconfile mime-type [mime-type]…
```

`mime-type` can be either the exact MIME type matching what you have assigned a file, or it can be a pattern match. Thus, you see entries in the default configuration files like the following:

```
AddIconByType (SND,/icons/sound2,gif) audio/*
```

This is a lot more robust than trying to match against file name suffixes.

`AddIconByEncoding` is used mostly to distinguish compressed files from the others. This makes sense only if used in conjunction with `AddEncoding` directives in your srm.conf file. The default srm.conf has these entries:

```
AddEncoding x-gzip gz
AddEncoding x-compress Z
AddIconByEncoding (CMP,/icons/compressed.gif) x-compress x-gzip
```

This will set the icon next to compressed files appropriately.

The `DefaultIcon` directive specifies the icon to use when none of the patterns match a given file when the directory index is generated.

```
DefaultIcon /icons/unknown.gif
```

It is possible to add text to the top and the bottom of the directory index listing. This capability is very useful as it turns the directory indexing capabilities from just a UNIX-like interface into a real dynamic document interface. There are two directives to control this: `HeaderName` and `ReadmeName`, which specify the file names for the content at the top and bottom of the listing, respectively. Thus, as shown in the default srm.conf file:

```
HeaderName HEADER
ReadmeName README
```

When the directory index is being built, Apache will look for "HEADER.html." If it finds it, it'll throw the content into the top of the directory index. If it fails to find that file, it'll look for just "HEADER," and if it finds that it will presume the file is plain text and do things like escape characters such as "<" to "<", and then insert it into the top of the directory index. The same process happens for the file "README," except that the resulting text goes into the bottom of the generated directory index.

In many cases, be it for consistency or just plain old security reasons, you will want to have the directory indexing engine just ignore certain types of files, like Emacs backup files or files beginning with a ".". The IndexIgnore directive addresses this; the default setting is

```
IndexIgnore */.??* *~ *# */HEADER* */README* */RCS
```

This line might look cryptic, but it's basically a space-separated list of patterns. The first pattern matches against any "." file that is longer than three characters. This is so that the link to the higher-up directory (..) can still work. The second (*~) and third (*#) are common patterns for matching old emacs backup files. The next ones are to avoid listing the same files used for HeaderName and ReadmeName as in the preceding. The last (*/RCS) is given because many sites out there use RCS, a software package for revision control maintenance, which stores its extra (rather sensitive) information in RCS directories.

Finally you get to two really interesting directives for controlling the last set of options regarding directory indexing. The first is AddDescription, which works similarly to AddIcon.

```
AddDescription description filename [filename]...
```

That is

```
AddDescription "My cat" /private/cat.gif
```

As elsewhere, filename can actually be a pattern, so you can have

```
AddDescription "An MPEG Movie Just For You!" *.mpg
```

Finally, you have the granddaddy of all options-setting directives, IndexOptions. This is the smorgasbord of functionality control. The syntax is simple:

```
IndexOptions option [option]...
```

The list of available options are listed in the following table:

Option	Explanation
FancyIndexing	This is the same as the separate FancyIndexing directive. Sorry to confuse everyone, but backward compatibility demands bizarre things sometimes!
IconsAreLinks	If this is set the icon will be clickable as a link to whatever resource the entry it is associated with links to. In other words, the icon becomes part of the hyperlink.
ScanHTMLTitles	When given a listing for an HTML file, the server will open the HTML file and parse it to obtain the value of the <TITLE> field in the HTML document, if it exists. This can put a pretty heavy load on the server, since it's a lot of disk accessing and some amount of CPU to extract the title from the HTML, so it's not recommended unless you know you have the capacity.
SuppressDescription, SuppressLastModified, SuppressSize	These will suppress their respective fields in the directory indexing output. Normally each of those (Description, Last Modified, Size) is a field in the output listings.

By default none of these are turned on. The options do not *merge*, which means that when you are setting these on a per-directory basis by using either access.conf or .htaccess files, setting the options for a more specific directory requires resetting the complete options listing. For example, envision the following in your access configuration file:

```
<Directory /pub/docs/>
IndexOptions ScanHTMLTitles
</Directory>
<Directory /pub/docs/others/>
IndexOptions IconsAreLinks
</Directory>
```

Directory listings done in or below the second directory, /pub/docs/others/, would not have ScanHTMLTitles set. Why? Well, you figured administrators would need to be able to disable an option they had set globally in a specific directory, and this was simpler than writing "NOT" logic into the options listings.

If you run into problems getting directory indexing to work, make sure that the settings you have for the Options directive in the access config files allow for directory indexing in that directory. Specifically, the Options directive must include Indexing. Furthermore, if you are using .htaccess files to set things like AddDescription or AddIcon, the AllowOverride directive must include in its list of options FileInfo. This is covered in more depth later in this chapter.

User Directories

Sites with many users sometimes prefer to be able to give their users access to managing their own parts of the Web tree in their own directories, using the URL semantics of

> http://myhost.com/~user/

Where "~user" is actually an alias to a directory in the user's home directory. This is different from the Alias directive, which could only map a particular pseudo-directory into an actual directory. In this case, you want "~user" to map to something like "/home/user/public_html," and because the number of "users" can be very high, some sort of macro is useful here. That macro is the directive UserDir.

With UserDir you specify the subdirectory within the users' home directory where they can put content, which is mapped to the "~user" URL. So in other words, the default

> UserDir public_html

will cause a request for

> http://myhost.com/~eric/index.html

to cause a lookup for the UNIX file

> /home/eric/public_html/index.html

presuming that /home/eric is eric's home directory. The default of public_html is a historical artifact more than anything else. There's no reason why you can't make it "Web_stuff" or something like that.

Note

Apache 1.1's user-directory module will have even more functionality, but at press time the feature set has not been nailed down.

Special Modules

Most of the functionality that distinguishes Apache from the competition has been implemented as modules to the Apache API. This has been extremely useful in allowing functionality to evolve separately from the rest of the server, and for allowing for performance tuning. This section will cover that extra functionality in detail.

Server Side Includes

Server side includes are best described as a preprocessing language for HTML. The "processing" takes place on the server side, such that visitors to your site never need know that you use server side includes, and thus requires no special client software. The format of these includes looks something like the following:

```
<!--#directive attribute="value" -->
```

Sometimes a given "directive" can have more than one attribute at the same time. The funky syntax is due to the desire to hide this functionality within an SGML comment—that way your regular HTML validation tools will work without having to learn new tags or anything. The syntax is important; leaving off the final "--," for example, will result in errors.

#include

This directive is probably the most commonly used directive. It is used to insert another file into the HTML document. The allowed attributes for this directive are `virtual` and `file`. The functionality of the `file` attribute is a subset of that provided by the `virtual` attribute, and it exists mostly for backward compatibility, so its use is not recommended.

The `virtual` attribute instructs the server to treat the value of the attribute as a request for a relative link—meaning that you can use "../" to locate objects above the directory, and that other transforms like `Alias` will apply.

For example:

```
<!--#include virtual="quote.txt" -->
<!--#include virtual="/toolbar/footer.html" -->
<!--#include virtual="../footer.html" -->
```

#exec

This directive is used to run a script on the server side and insert its output into the SSI document being processed. There are two choices: executing a CGI script by using the `cgi` attribute, or executing a shell command by using the `cmd` attribute.

For example:

```
<!--#exec cgi="counter.cgi" -->
```

would take the output of the CGI program `counter.cgi` and insert it into the document. Note that the CGI output still has to include the "text/html" content type header or an error will occur.

Likewise,

```
<!--#exec cmd="ls -l" -->
```

would take the output of a call to `ls -l` in the document's directory and insert it. Like the `file` attribute to the `#include` directive, this is mostly for backward compatibility, because it is something of a security hole in an untrusted environment.

> **Note**
>
> There are definitely security concerns with allowing users access to CGI functionality and even greater concerns with #exec cmd, such as `cmd="cat/etc/passwd"`. If the site administrator wishes to allow people to use server side includes, but not to use the #exec directive, then they can set `IncludesNOEXEC` as an option for the directory in the access configurations.

#echo

This directive has one attribute, `var`, whose value is any CGI environment variable as well as a small list of other variables:

Attribute	Defintion
DATE_GMT	The current date in Greenwich Mean Time.
DATE_LOCAL	The current date in the local time zone.
DOCUMENT_NAME	The file system name of the SSI document, not including the directories below it.
DOCUMENT_URI	In a URL of the format "http://host/path/file." This is the "/path/file" part.
LAST_MODIFIED	The date the SSI document was modified.

Example:

```
<!--#echo var="DATE_LOCAL" -->
```

This will insert something like `Wednesday, 06-Mar-96 10:44:54 GMT` into the document.

#fsize, #flastmod

These two directives print out the size and the last-modified date, respectively, of any object given by the URI listed in the `file` or `virtual` attribute, as in the `#include` directive. For example

```
<!--#fsize file="index.html" -->
```

would return the size of the index.html file in that directory.

#config

You can modify the rendering of certain SSI directives by using this directive.

The `sizefmt` attribute controls the rendering of the #fsize directive with values of `bytes` or `abbrev`. The exact number of bytes is printed when `bytes` is given, whereas an abbreviated version of the size (either in `K` for kilobytes or `M` for megabytes) is given when `abbrev` is set.

Thus, for example, a snippet of SSI HTML like

```
<!--#config sizefmt="bytes" -->
The index.html file is <!--#fsize virtual="index.html" --> bytes
```

would return `The index.html file is 4,522 bytes`. Meanwhile, if

```
<!--#config sizefmt="abbrev" -->
```

was used, "The index.html file is 4K bytes" would be returned. The default is `abbrev`.

The `timefmt` directive controls the rendering of the date in the `DATE_LOCAL`, `DATE_GMT`, and `LAST_MODIFIED` values for the #echo directive. It uses the same format as the `strftime` call (In fact, that's what the server does. It calls `strftime`.) This format consists of variables that begin with %. For example, %H is the hour of the day, in 24-hour format. The list of variables is best found by consulting your system's "man" page by typing **man strftime** for directions as to how to construct a `strftime`-format date string.

An example might be:

```
<!--#config timefmt="%Y/%m/%d-%H:%M:%S" -->
```

and the resulting date string for Jan. 2, 1996 at 12:30 in the afternoon would thus be

```
1996/01/02-12:30:00
```

Finally, the last attribute the `config` directive can take is `errmsg`, which is simply the error to print out if there are any problems parsing the document. For example, the right default is:

```
<!--#config errmsg="An error occurred while processing this
directive" -->
```

Internal Imagemap Capabilities

The default imagemap module supplied with Apache allows you to reference imagemaps without using or needing any CGI programs. This functionality is contained in the `mod_imap` module. First, you add to your srm.conf yet another magic `AddType` directive:

```
AddType application/x-httpd-imap map
```

This now means that any file ending with ".map" will be recognized as an imagemap file. After restarting the server to pick up the change, one can make reference to a .map file directly.

Look at an example: the following document, index.html, has an imagemap on it, where the image is usa.jpg and the mapfile is usa-map.map. The HTML to build that imagemap would look like:

```
<A HREF="usa-map.map"><IMG SRC="usa.jpg" ISMAP></A>
```

Imagemaps are covered in more detail in a later chapter—the only important thing from a configuration standpoint is that the magic content type is activated.

Cookies

HTTP *cookies* are a method for maintaining statefulness in a stateless protocol. What does this mean? In HTTP, a session between a client and a server typically spans many separate actual TCP connections, thus making it difficult to tie together accesses into an application that requires state, such as a shopping cart application. Cookies are a solution to that problem. As implemented by Netscape in their browser and subsequently by many others, servers can assign clients a *cookie*, meaning some sort of opaque string whose meaning is significant only to the server itself, and then the client can give that cookie back to the server on subsequent requests.

The module *mod_cookies* nicely handles the details of assigning unique cookies to every visitor, based on their hostname and a random number. This cookie can be accessed from the CGI environment as the HTTP_COOKIE environment variable, for the same reason that all HTTP headers are accessible to CGI applications. The CGI scripts can use this as a key in a session tracking database, or it can be logged and tallied up to get a good, if undercounted, estimate of the total number of users that visited a site, not just the number of hits or even number of unique domains.

Happily, there are no configuration issues here—simply compile with mod_cookies and away you go. Couldn't be easier.

Configurable Logging

For most folks, the default logfile format (also known as *Common Logfile Format*, or CLF) does not provide enough information when it comes to doing a serious analysis of the efficacy of your Web site. It provides basic numbers in terms of raw hits, pages accessed, hosts accessing, timestamps, etc., but it fails to capture the "referring" URL, the browser being used, and any cookies being used. So, there are two ways to get more data for your logfiles: by using the NCSA-compatibility directives for logging certain bits of info to separate browsers, or using Apache's own totally configurable logfile format.

NCSA Compatibility

For compatibility with the NCSA 1.4 Web server, two modules were added. These modules log the `User-Agent` and `Referer` headers from the HTTP request stream.

`User-Agent` is the header most browsers send that identifies what software the browser is using. Logging of this header can be activated by an `AgentLog` directive in the srm.conf file, or in a virtualhost-specific section. This directive takes one argument, the name of the file to which the user-agents are logged. For example:

```
AgentLog logs/agent_log
```

To use this, you need to ensure that the `mod_log_agent` module has been compiled and linked to the server.

Similarly, the `Referer` header is sent by the browser to indicate the tail end of a link—in other words, when you are on a page with a URL of "A," and there is a link on that page with a URL of "B," and you follow that link, the request for page "B" includes a `Referer` header with the URL of "A." This is very useful for finding what sites out there link to your site, and what proportion of traffic they account for.

The logging of this header is activated by a `RefererLog` directive, which points to the file to which the referers get logged.

```
RefererLog logs/referer_log
```

One other option the `Referer` logging module provides is `RefererIgnore`, a directive that allows you to ignore `Referer` headers, which contain some string. This is useful for weeding out the referers from your own site, if all you are interested in is links to you from other sites. For example, if your site is "www.myhost.com," you might want to use the following:

```
RefererIgnore www.myhost.com
```

Remember that logging of the `Referer` header requires compiling and linking in mod_log_referer.

Totally Configurable Logging

The previous modules were provided, like many Apache features, for backward compatibility. They have some problems, though. Because they don't contain any other information about the request they are logging from, it's nearly impossible to tell which `Referer` fields went to which specific objects on your site. Ideally all the information about a transaction with the server can be logged into one file, extending the `common logfile format` or replacing it altogether. Well, such a beast exists, in the `mod_log_config` module.

This module implements the `LogFormat` directive, which takes as its argument a string, with variables beginning with `%` to indicate different pieces of data from the request. The variables are:

Variable	Definition
%h	Remote host.
%l	Remote `identd` identification.
%u	Remote user, as determined by any user authentication that may take place. Note that if the user was not authenticated, and the status of the request is a 401, this field may be bogus.
%t	The common logfile format for time.
%r	First line of request.
%s	Status. For requests that got internally redirected, this is status of the original request; `%>s` will give the last.
%b	Bytes sent.
%{Foobar}i	The contents of Foobar: header line(s) in the request from the client to the server.
%{Foobar}o	The contents of Foobar: header line(s) in the response from the server to the client.

So, for example, if you wanted to capture in your log just the remote hostname, the object they requested, and the timestamp, you would do the following:

```
LogFormat "%h \"%r\" %t"
```

And that would log things that looked like

```
host.outsider.com "GET / HTTP/1.0" [06/Mar/1996:10:15:17]
```

Note that you really have to use a quote around the request variable—the configurable logging module does not escape the values of the variables. But use a slash-quote, `\"`, to distinguish that from the end of the string.

Say you want to add logging of the `User-Agent` string to that as well—in this case, your log format would become:

```
LogFormat "%h \"%r\" %t \"%{User-Agent}i\""
```

II

Setting Up a Web Server

Because the `User-Agent` field typically has spaces in it, it too should be quoted. Say you want to capture the `Referer` field:

```
LogFormat "%h \"%r\" %t %{Referer}i"
```

You don't need the escaping quotes because `Referer` headers, since they are URL's, don't have spaces in them. However, if you are building a mission-critical application you might as well quote it as well, because the `Referer` header is supplied by the client and thus there are no guarantees about its format.

The default format is the Common Logfile Format (CLF), which in this syntax is expressed as

```
LogFormat "%h %l %u %t \"%r\" %s %b"
```

In fact, most existing logfile analysis tools for CLF will ignore extra fields tacked onto the end, so to capture the most important extra information and yet still be parseable by those tools, you might want to use the format:

```
LogFormat "%h %l %u %t \"%r\" %s %b %{Referer}i \"%{User-
➥Agent}i\""
```

Power users take note: If you want even more control over what gets logged, you can use the configurable logging module to implement a simple conditional test for variables. This way, you can configure it to only log variables when a particular status code is returned, or not returned. The format for this is to insert a comma-separate list of those codes between the % and the letter of the variable, like so:

```
%404,403{Referer}i
```

This means that the `Referer` header will only be logged if the status returned by the server is a `404 Not Found`, or a `403 Access Denied`. All other times just a "-" is logged. This would be useful if all you cared about using `Referer` for was to find out old links that point to resources no longer available.

The negation of that conditional is to put a ! at the beginning of the list of status codes; so for example,

```
%!401u
```

will log the user in any user authentication transaction, unless the authentication failed, in which case you probably don't want to see the name of the bogus user anyway.

Remember that, like many functions, this can be configured per virtual host. Thus, if you want all logs from all virtual hosts on the same server to go to the same log, you might want to do something like

```
LogFormat "hosta ...."
```

in the `<virtualhost>` sections for hosta and

```
LogFormat "hostb ...."
```

in the `<virtualhost>` sections for hostb. More details about virtual hosts will appear later in this chapter.

A key note: You have to compile in `mod_log_config` for this functionality. You must also make sure that the default logging module, `mod_log_common`, is not compiled in, or the server will get confused.

Content Negotiation

Content negotiation is the mechanism by which a Web client can express to the server what data types it knows how to render, and based on that information, the server can give the client the "optimal" version of the resource requested. Content negotiation can happen on a number of different characteristics—the content type of the data (also called the *media type*), the human language the data is in (English, French, etc.), the character set of the document, and its encodings.

Content Type Negotiation

For example, say you want to use inlined JPEG images on your pages. You don't want to alienate people using older browsers, which don't know how to inline JPEG images, so you also make a GIF version of that image. Even though the GIF might be larger or only 8-bit, that's still better than giving the browser something it can't handle, causing a broken link. So, the browser and the server *negotiate* for which data format the server sends to the client.

The specifications for content negotiation have been a part of HTTP since the beginning. Unfortunately, it can't be relied upon as extensively as one would like. For example, current browsers that implement plug-ins, by and large do not express in the connection headers which media types they have plug-ins for. Thus, content-negotiation can't be used to decide whether to send someone a ShockWave file or its Java equivalent, currently. The only safe place to use it currently is to distinguish between inlined JPEG or GIF images on a page. Enough browsers in use today implement content negotiation closely enough to get this functionality.

The `mod_negotiation.c` in Apache 1.0 implements the content negotiation specifications in an older version of the HTTP/1.0 IETF draft, which at the time of this writing is on its way to informational RFC status. It was removed because the specification was not entirely complete, and a document describing it could not be labeled "Best Current Practice," which is what the HTTP/1.0 specification became. Content negotiation is getting significantly enhanced for HTTP/1.1. However, this doesn't mean it can't be safely used now for inlined image selection.

To activate it, you must include the module `mod_negotiation.c` into the server. There are actually two ways to configure content negotiation:

- Using a type-map file describing all the variants of a negotiable resource with specific preference values and content characteristics
- Setting an `Options` value called `MultiViews`.

Since your focus is pragmatic, you will go only into the "MultiViews" functionality. If you are interested in the type-map functionality, the Apache Web site has documentation on it.

In your access.conf file, find the line that sets the options for the part of the site you wish to enable content negotiation within. This may be the whole site, but that's fine. If `MultiViews` is not present in that line, it must be. The `All` value does not, ironically enough, include `MultiViews`. This is again for backward compatibility. So, you might have a line that looks like:

```
Options Indexes Includes Multiviews
```

or

```
Options All MultiViews
```

Once this change is made, restart your server to pick up the new configuration.

With this turned on, you can do the following: place a JPEG image in a directory, say /path/, and call it image.jpg. Now, make an equivalent GIF format image, and place it in the same directory, as image.gif. The URLs for these two objects are

```
http://host/path/image.jpg
```

and

```
http://host/path/image.gif
```

respectively. Now, if you ask your Web browser to fetch,

```
http://host/path/image
```

the server will go into the /path/ directory, see the two image files, and then determine which one to send based on what the client states it can support. In the case where the client says it can accept either JPEG images or GIF images equally, the server will choose the version that is the smallest, and send that to the client. Usually, JPEG images are much smaller than GIF images.

So, if you made your HTML look something like the following:

```
<HTML><HEAD>
<TITLE>Welcome to the Gizmo Home Page!</TITLE>
</HEAD><BODY>
<IMG SRC="/header" ALT="GIZMO Logo">
Welcome to Gizmo!
<IMG SRC="/products" ALT="Products">
<IMG SRC="/services" ALT="Services">
```

then you can have separate GIF and JPEG files for `header`, `products`, and `services`, and the clients will for the most part get what they claim they can support.

Note that, if you have a file called "image" and a file called "image.gif," the file called "image" will be requested no matter if a request is made for just "image." Likewise, a request specifically for "image.gif" would never return "image.jpg" even if the client knew how to render JPEG images.

Human Language Negotiation

If `MultiViews` is enabled, you can also distinguish resources by the language they are in, such as French, English, and Japanese. This is done by adding more entries to the file suffix namespace that map to the languages the server wishes to use, and then giving them a ranking that ties can be broken. Specifically, in the "srm.conf" file, go two new directives, `AddLanguage` and `LanguagePriority`. The formats are as follows:

```
AddLanguage en .en
AddLanguage it .it
AddLanguage fr .fr
AddLanguage jp .jp
LanguagePriority en fr jp it
```

Say you want to use this to negotiate on the file "index.html," which you had available in English, French, Italian, and Japanese. You would create an "index.html.en," "index.html.fr," "index.html.it," and "index.html.jp," respectively, and then reference the document as "index.html." When a multilingual client connects, it should indicate in one of the request headers (`Accept-Language`, to be specific) which languages it prefers, and it expresses that in standard two-letter notation. The server sees what the clients can accept, and gives them "the best one." `LanguagePriority` is what organizes that decision of "the best one." If English is unacceptible to the client, try French, otherwise try Japanese, otherwise try Italian. `LanguagePriority` also states which one should be served if there is no `Accept-Language` header.

Because the language mapping suffixes and the content-type suffixes share the same namespace, you can mix them around. "index.fr.html" is the same as "index.html.f.," Just make sure that you reference it with the correct negotiable resource.

As-Is Files

Often, you might like to request specific HTTP headers in your documents, such as Expires:, but you don't want to make the page a CGI script. The easiest way is to use the `httpd/send-as-is` magic MIME type.

```
AddType httpd/send-as-is asis
```

This means that any file that ends in ".asis" can include its own MIME headers. However, it *must* include *two* carriage returns before the actual body of the content. Actually, it should include two carriage return / line feed combinations, but Apache is forgiving and will insert that for you. So, if you wanted to send a document with a special unique custom MIME type you didn't want registered with the server, you can send:

```
Content-type: text/foobar

This is text in a very special "foobar" MIME type.
```

The most significant application I've run across for this is as an extremely efficient mechanism for doing server-push objects without CGI scripts. The reason a CGI script is needed to create a server-push usually is that the Content-type usually includes the multipart separator (since a server-push is actually a MIME multipart message). For example,

```
Content-type: multipart/x-mixed-replace;boundary=XXXXXXXX

--XXXXXXXX
     Content-type: image/gif

....(GIF data)....
--XXXXXXXX
Content-type: image/gif

....(GIF data)....
--XXXXXXXX
....
```

By making this stream of data a simple file instead of a CGI script, you save yourself potentially a lot of overhead. Just about the only thing you lose is the ability to do timed pushes. For many people, slow internet connection acts as a sufficient time valve.

If you have MultiViews turned on, you can add an ".asis" to the end of a file name and none of your links need to be renamed. For example, "foobar.html" can easily become "foobar.html.asis," while still being able to call it "foobar.html."

One last compelling application of "asis" is being able to do HTTP redirection without needing access to server config files. For example, the following .asis file will redirect people to another location:

```
Status 302 Moved
Location: http://some.other.place.com/path/
Content-type: text/html

<HTML>
<HEAD><TITLE>We've Moved!</TITLE></HEAD>
<BODY>
<H1>We used to be here, but now we're
<A HREF="http://some.other.place.com/path/">over there. </A>
</H1>
</BODY></HTML>
```

The HTML body is there simply for clients who don't understand the 302 response.

Advanced Functionality

Host-Based Access Control

One can control access to the server, or even a subdirectory of the server, based on the hostname, domain, or IP number of the client's machine. This is done by using the directives allow and deny, which can be used together at the same time by using order. allow and deny can take multiple hosts:

```
deny from badguys.com otherbadguys.com
```

Typically, you want to do one of two things: you want to deny access to your server from everyone but a few other machines, or you want to grant access to everyone except a few hosts. The first case is handled as follows:

```
order allow,deny
allow from mydomain.com
deny from all
```

This means, "only grant access to hosts in the domain 'mydomain.com'." This could include "host1.mydomain.com," "ppp.mydomain.com," and "the-boss.mydomain.com."

The order directive above tells the server to evaluate the allow conditions before the deny conditions when determining whether to grant access. Likewise, the "only exclude a couple of sites" case described above can be handled by using:

```
order deny,allow
deny from badguys.com
allow from all
```

order is needed because, again mostly for historical reasons, the order in which directives appear is not significant. Thus, the server needs to know which rule to apply first. The default for order is deny,allow.

II

Setting Up a Web Server

There is a third argument to `order`, called `mutual-failure`, in which a condition has to pass both the `allow` and `deny` rules in order to succeed. In other words, it has to appear on the `allow` list, and it must not appear on the `deny` list. For example,

```
order mutual-failure
allow from mydomain.com
deny from the-boss.mydomain.com
```

In this example, `the-boss.mydomain.com` is prevented from accessing this resource, but every other machine at `mydomain.com` can access it.

It should be mentioned at this point that protecting resources by hostname is dangerous. It is relatively easy for a determined person who control the reverse-DNS mapping for their IP number to spoof any hostname they want. Thus, it is strongly recommended that you use IP numbers to protect anything sensitive. In the same way you can simply list the domain to refer to any machine in that domain, you can also give fragments of IP numbers:

```
allow from 204.62.129
```

This will only allow hosts whose IP numbers match that, such as `204.62.129.1` or `204.62.129.130`.

Typically, these directives are used within a `<Limit>` container, and even that within a `<Directory>` container, usually in an access.conf configuration file. The following example is a good template for most protections; it protects the directory `/www/htdocs/private` from any host except those in the `204.62.129` IP space.

```
<Directory /www/htdocs/private>
Options Includes
AllowOverride None
<Limit GET POST>
order allow,deny
deny from all
allow from 204.62.129
</Limit>
</Directory>
```

User Authentication

When you place a resource under *user authentication*, you restrict access to it by requiring a name and password. This name and password is kept in a database on the server. This database can take many forms; Apache modules have been written to access flat file databases, DBM file databases, Msql databases (a freeware database), Oracle and Sybase databases, and more. This book covers only the flat-file and DBM-format databases.

First, some basic configuration directives. The `AuthName` directive sets the authentication "Realm" for the password-protected pages. The "Realm" is what gets presented to clients when prompted for authentication—"Please enter your name and password for the realm   ."

The `AuthType` directive sets the authentication type for the area. In HTTP/1.0 there is only one authentication type, and that is `Basic`. HTTP/1.1 will have a few more, such as `MD5`.

The `AuthUserFile` directive specifies the file thT contains a list of names and passwords, one pair per line, where the passwords are encrypted by using the simple UNIX `crypt()` routines. For example,

```
joe:D.W2yvlfjaJoo
mark:21slfoUYGksIe
```

The `AuthGroupFile` directive specifies the file which contains a list of groups, and members of those groups, separated by spaces. For example:

```
managers: joe mark
production: mark shelley paul
```

Finally, the `require` directive specifies what conditions need to be met for access to be granted. It can list only a specified list of users who may connect, it can specify a group or list of groups of users who may connect, or it can say any valid user in the database is automatically granted access. For example:

```
require user mark paul
(Only mark and paul may access.)

require group managers
(Only people in group managers may access.)

require valid-user
(Anyone in the AuthUserFile database may access.)
```

The configuration file ends up looking something like this:

```
<Directory /www/htdocs/protected/>
AuthName Protected
AuthType basic
AuthUserFile /usr/local/etc/httpd/conf/users
<Limit GET POST>
require valid-user
</Limit>
</Directory>
```

If you want to protect it to a particular group, the configuration file looks something like the following:

```
<Directory /www/htdocs/protected/>
AuthName Protected
```

```
AuthType basic
AuthUserFile /usr/local/etc/httpd/conf/users
AuthGroupFile /usr/local/etc/httpd/conf/group
<Limit GET POST>
require group managers
</Limit>
</Directory>
```

DBM Authentication

Apache can be configured to also use DBM files for faster password and group-membership lookups. To use this, you must have the mod_auth_dbm module compiled into the server.

DBM files are UNIX file types that implement a fast hashtable lookup, making them ideal for handling large user/password databases. The flat-file systems requires parsing the password file for every access until a match is found, potentially going through the entire file before returning a can't find that user error. Hash tables, on the other hand, know instantly whether a "key" exists in the database, and what its value is.

Some systems use the ndbm libraries; some use the berkeley db libraries. However, the interface through Apache is exactly the same.

To use a DBM file for the database instead of a regular flat file, you use a different directive, AuthDBMUserFile instead of AuthUserFile. Likewise for the group file—AuthDBMGroupFile instead of AuthGroupFile is used.

Take a look at creating the DBM files. There is a program supplied in the support subdirectory of the Web site called "dbmmanage." It is a file for creating and managing DBM files. The basic syntax is as follows:

```
dbmmanage dbmfile command key [value]
```

command can be one of: add, adduser, view, delete

So, to add a value to a DBM file called "users," one would say:

```
dbmmanage users add joe joespassword
```

You have just added a record to the DBM file, with joe as the key and joespassword as the value. To see this you say:

```
dbmmanage users view joe
```

or if you want to see the whole database,

```
dbmmanage users view
```

However, you want to store encrypted passwords, because that's what the server uses for authentication. For that you use the `adduser` command:

```
dbmmanage users adduser joe joespassword
```

Now, if you do a `view` to look at it, `joespassword` will be replaced by a lot of what looks like junk. Don't worry, that's the encrypted password.

Groups are done a little bit differently in DBM files. Instead of making the key of the database the group, the key is the user and the value is a comma-separated list of the groups that user is in. For example:

```
dbmmanage group adduser joe managers,production
```

Wait, you say, there's no file called "users." Why do I see a "users.pag" and "users.dir"?

Well, DBM files are pretty weird. They aren't like regular files; they can't be looked at. Some systems implement the hash table by keeping the index separate from the data, as in this example with the .pag and .dir files. On BSD systems, where Berkeley DB is implemented, DBM files are saved with a ".db" appendix. So, one should get used to the idea that the "name" of a DBM file is actually its file name without the suffix.

The configuration file snippet now looks something like:

```
<Directory /www/htdocs/protected/>
AuthName Protected
AuthType basic
AuthDBMUserFile /usr/local/etc/httpd/conf/users
AuthDBMGroupFile /usr/local/etc/httpd/conf/group
<Limit GET POST>
require group managers
</Limit>
</Directory>
```

Note that `users` and `groups` must be the "name" of the DBM file, as described in the preceding. Pointing to

```
AuthDBMUserFile /usr/local/etc/httpd/conf/users.db
```

would not work.

> **Note**
>
> Make sure that you don't put the user and group databases in the public Web tree, *ever*. Several Web search engines out there have proven themselves to be efficient sources for /etc/passwd files unintentionally put on the site. Don't take that risk.

Virtual Hosts

Apache implements a very clean way of handling *virtual hosts*, which is the name for the mechanism for being able to serve more than one host on a particular machine. Due to a limitation in HTTP, this is accomplished currently by assigning more than one IP number to a machine, and then having Apache bind differently to those different IP numbers. For example, a UNIX box might have 204.122.133.1, 204.122.133.2, and 204.122.133.3 pointing to it, with www.host1.com bound to the first, www.host2.com bound to the second, and www.host3.com bound to the third.

This book will not go into how to configure additional IP addresses for your machine, since that varies completely from platform to platform. Your user manual for the operating system should contain information about configuring additional numbers—this is a standard capability on just about all systems these days.

Virtual hosts are configured using a container in httpd.conf. They look something like this:

```
<VirtualHost www.host1.com>
DocumentRoot /www/htdocs/host1/
TransferLog logs/access.host1
ErrorLog logs/error.host1
</VirtualHost>
```

The attribute in the `VirtualHost` tag is the hostname, which the server looks up to get an IP address. Note that if there is any chance that `www.host1.com` can return more than one number, or if the Web server might have trouble resolving that to an IP number at any point, you might want to use the IP number instead.

Any directives put within the `VirtualHost` container pertain only to requests made to that hostname. The `DocumentRoot` points to a directory which (presumably) contains content specifically for `www.host1.com`.

Each virtual host can have its own access log, its own error log, its own derivative of the other logs out there, its own `Redirect` and `Alias` directives, its own `ServerName` and `ServerAdmin` directives, and more. In fact, the only things it cannot support, out of the core set of directives, are:

```
ServerType, UserId, GroupId, StartServers, MaxSpareServers,
MinSpareServers, MaxRequestsPerChild, BindAddress, PidFile,
TypesConfig, and ServerRoot.
```

If you plan on running Apache with a large number of virtual hosts, you need to be careful to watch the process limits; for example, some UNIX platforms only allow processes to open 64 file descriptors at once. An Apache child will consume one file descriptor per logfile per virtual host, so 32 virtual hosts each with its own transfer and error log would quickly cross that limit. You will notice if you are running into problems of this kind if your error logs start reporting errors like `unable to fork()`, or your access logs aren't getting written to at all. Apache does try and call `setrlimit()` to handle this problem on its own, but the system sometimes prevents it from doing so successfully.

Customized Error Messages

Apache can give customized responses in the event of an error. This is controlled using the `ErrorDocument` directive. The syntax is:

```
ErrorDocument <HTTP response code> <action>
```

Where `HTTP response code` is the event which triggers the `action`. The `action` can be:

- A local URI to which the server is internally redirected.
- An external URL to which the client is redirected.
- A text string, which starts with a `'"'`, and where the `%s` variable contains any extra information if available.

For example:

```
ErrorDocument 500 "Ack! We have a problem here: %s.
ErrorDocument 500 /errors/500.cgi
ErrorDocument 500 http://backup.myhost.com/
ErrorDocument 401 /subscribe.html
ErrorDocument 404 /debug/record-broken-links.cgi
```

Two extra CGI variables will be passed to any redirected resource: `REDIRECT_URL` will contain the original URL requested, and `REDIRECT_STATUS` will give the original status that caused the redirection. This will help the script if its job is to try and figure out what caused the error response.

Assorted httpd.conf Settings

There are a couple last configuration options that fell through the cracks.

BindAddress

At startup, Apache will bind to the port it is specified to bind to, for all IP numbers which the box has available. The `BindAddress` directive can be used to specify only a specific IP address to bind to. Using this, one can run multiple copies of Apache, each serving different virtual hosts, instead of having one daemon which can handle all virtual hosts. This is useful if you want to run two web servers with different system user-id's for security and access control reasons.

For example, let's say you have three IP addresses (1.1.1.1, 1.1.1.2, and 1.1.1.3, with 1.1.1.1 being the primary address for the machine), and you want to run three Web servers, yet you want one of them to run as a different user ID than the other two. One would have two sets of configuration files; one would say something like

```
User web3
BindAddress 1.1.1.3
ServerName www.company3.com
DocumentRoot /www/company3/
```

And the other would have

```
User web1
ServerName www.company1.com
DocumentRoot /www/company1/
<VirtualHost 1.1.1.2>
ServerName www.company2.com
DocumenbtRoot /www/company2/
</VirtualHost>
```

If you launch the first, it will only bind to IP address `1.1.1.3`. The second one, since it has no `BindAddress` directive, will bind to the port on all IP addresses. So, you want to launch a server with the first set of config files, then launch another copy of the server with the second set. There would essentially be two servers running.

PidFile

This is the location of the file containing the process-ID for Apache. This file is useful for being able to automate the shutdown or restart of the web server. By default, this is `logs/httpd.pid`. For example, one could shut down the server by saying:

```
cat /usr/local/etc/httpd/logs/httpd.pid ¦ xargs kill -15
```

You might want to move this out of the logs directory and into something like /var, but it's not necessary.

Timeout

This directive specifies the amount of time that the server will wait in-between packets sent before considering the connection "lost." For example, `1200`, the default, means that the server will wait for 20 minutes after sending a packet before it considers the connection dead if no response comes back. Busy servers may wish to turn this down, at the cost of reduced service to low-bandwidth customers. ❖

## CHAPTER 6

Managing an Internet Web Server

This chapter deals with making your server robust, efficient, automated, and secure.

One of the biggest strengths of the Apache Web server is that it is highly tunable—just about every feature that imposes any sort of extra server load is an option, which means you can sacrifice features for speed if you need to do so. That said, Apache is designed for speed and efficiency, even with all its features enabled; for all but the most CGI intensive sites, you'll probably swamp a full T1 worth of bandwidth before exhausting the resources of a well-constructed Linux/Pentium box.

Apache has also been designed to give site administrators control over where to draw the line between security and functionality. For some sites with many internal users, such as an Internet service provider, being able to control the policies toward what functionality can be used where is important. Meanwhile, a Web design shop might want complete flexibility, even if it means that an errant CGI script could expose a security hole or do damage. In fact, many people feel that CGI in general is one big security risk, but we'll get to that in a bit.

In this chapter, you learn about:

- Server child process control
- Increasing efficiency
- Hardware issues
- Log File Rotation
- Security issues

Make no mistake, this is a somewhat technical chapter. You may want to come back to this chapter later.

Server Child Process Control

As described earlier, Apache employs the concept of a *swarm* of semi-persistent daemons, sometimes called *children*, running and answering queries simultaneously. While the size of that swarm varies, there are limits to how large it can get, and how quickly or slowly it can grow. This is critical; one of the main performance problems with older servers that executed a fork() system call at every request was that there was no way to control the total number of simultaneous daemons, so when the main memory of a machine would get consumed and start swapping, the machine would just become unusable. This was colloquially called *daemon-spamming*.

Some other servers out there let you specify a fixed number of processes, with the "fork for every request" behavior kicking in if all the children are busy when a new request comes in. This is also not the best model—not only do many people set that fixed number too high (having 30 children running when only five need to be, which can hinder performance), but this model also removed the protection against daemon-spamming.

So, the Apache model is to start out with a certain number of persistent processes, and make sure you always keep some number (actually, a range somewhere between a minimum and a maximum) of "spare" processes to handle a wave of simultaneous requests. If you have to launch a few more processes to maintain the minimum number of spares, no problem. If you find yourself with more idle servers than your maximum number of spares, the excess idle ones can be killed. There is a maximum number of processes, beyond which no more will be launched, to protect the machine against daemon-spamming.

This algorithm is configured using the following configuration directives:

```
StartServers   10
MinSpareServers 5
MaxSpareServers 10
MaxClients    150
```

The numbers given above are the defaults. This says that when Apache launches, 10 children (StartServers) are automatically launched, regardless of the request load at start. If all 10 children are swamped, more are forked until all requests can be answered as fast as they are received. This requires at least five (MinSpareServers), but not more than 10 (MaxSpareServers) free servers to deal with *spikes* in requests (i.e., when a sudden burst of requests comes in well within half a second of each other). Incidentally, these spikes are often caused by browsers that open a separate TCP connection for each inline image in a page in an attempt to improve perceived performance to the user, often at the expense of the server and network.

Usually a stable number of simultaneous child processes is reached, but if the requests are just pouring in (you've installed the Pamela Anderson Fan Club page on your site, for example), then you might reach the MaxClients limit. At that point, requests will queue into your kernel's "listen" queue, waiting to get served. If still more pour in, your visitors will eventually see a "connections refused" message. However, this is still preferable to leaving unlimited the number of simultaneous processes, since the server would just launch children with wild abandon and start daemon-spamming, resulting in nobody getting any response from the server at all.

It is recommended that you do not adjust MaxClients, because 150 is a good number for most systems. However, you might be itching to see how many requests you can handle with that multiprocessor Sun Sparc 1000 with a gigabyte of RAM; in that case, setting MaxClients much higher makes sense. On the opposite end of the spectrum, you might be running the Web server on a machine with limited memory or CPU resources, and you might want to make sure that Apache doesn't consume all of resources at the cost of possibly not being able to serve all requests that come to your site. In that context, setting MaxClients lower makes sense.

The Scoreboard File and MMAP

Because this multiprocess model required some decent communication between the parent and child processes, the most cross-platform method of performing that communication was chosen: a *scoreboard file*, where each child had a chunk of space in the file to which it was authorized to write, and the parent httpd process watched that file to get a status report and make decisions about whether to launch more child processes or kill idle processes.

At first, this file was located in the /tmp directory, but after hearing of problems regarding UNIX setups that regularly clear out /tmp directories (causing the server to go haywire), the scoreboard file has since been moved into the log directory. You can configure where this goes exactly with a ScoreBoardFile directive.

There is a program in the /support subdirectory in the Apache distribution called httpd_monitor. It can be run against the scoreboard file to give a picture of the state of all the child processes and whether they are just starting, active, sleeping, or dead. It can give you a good idea of whether your settings for `MaxSpareServers` and `MinSpareServers` are decent. Consider it a close equivalent to the UNIX system command `iostat`.

There is a more efficient mechanism under some UNIX variants for this, however, using the `mmap()` system call. For those platforms that support it, Apache 1.1 now uses this functionality. Unfortunately, it means that there is no longer any scoreboard to run httpd_monitor against. If you want this back, find the #define for HAVE_MMAP in conf.h relevant to your OS, and recompile. Apache 1.1 also implements a similar system for System 5-based UNIX variants using "shared memory."

Apache is in the stages of being instrumented pretty deeply, which will, hopefully, result in some sort of real-time statistics interface through an HTTP query to the server itself.

Increasing Efficiency in the Server Software

There are many ways to increase performance over the standard setup, including smarter ways to configure your resources, features that can be turned off for better performance, and even things at the operating system and hardware level that can be addressed. All of this makes a difference between a regular Web server and a high-performance Web server.

Most non-hardware improvements fall into three categories: those that reduce the load on the CPU, those that reduce the amount of I/O to the disk, and those that reduce the memory requirements.

Server Side Includes

Server side includes can cause both an increased disk access load and an increased CPU load. The CPU penalty comes from having to parse the HTML file looking for the includes; parsing a file is a fair amount more intensive than just reading it and spitting it out to the socket. The disk access penalty comes from having to make two, three, four, or more separate disk accesses to pull together the page to get served. For example, a typical SSI document might need a header and footer pulled into memory to get served. That's three disk accesses to pull the document together, instead of one. If the inlined HTML files were large, the difference would not be as large. Because they are usually small files, the disk access penalty is relatively large. The problem is compounded by any CGI script that might be included as well; if you had an SSI page with two CGI scripts included, you'd probably get at least twice the performance hit than if you had one CGI script that just rendered the whole page in the first place.

.htaccess Files

Searching directories for .htaccess files is fairly painful; since they work hierarchically, when a request is made for /path/path2/dir1/dir2/foo, Apache will look for an .htaccess file in *every* subdirectory. In this case, that's at least five. This is a significant disk access load that's best to avoid if possible.

To solve this, you should put anything controlled via your .htaccess files into the access.conf configuration file or even the srm.conf file. If you have to look for .htaccess files in subdirectories and you can narrow it down to a specific subdirectory, it's possible to have the server only look for .htaccess files in that subdirectory by the use of `AllowOverride`.

For example, suppose your document root was in /www/htdocs, and you want to turn off the searching for .htaccess files, except for in /www/htdocs/dir1/dir2 and everywhere below. You would put something like the following into your access.conf configuration file:

```
<Directory /www/htdocs>
Options All
AllowOverride None
</Directory>
<Directory /www/htdocs/dir1/dir2>
Options All
AllowOverride All
</Directory>
```

It's important that they are listed in that order so that the second `<Directory>` doesn't take precedence over the first.

Using .asis Files for Server-Push Animations

.asis files, as you read about earlier, are distinguished by having their HTTP headers directly embedded in the file itself. They are a useful optimization for certain types of files, like server-push animations, which demand the ability to set their own headers and are usually dished out by CGI scripts. The usual server-push CGI script has the additional overhead of assembling the images on the fly, whereas with an .asis file, the whole stream can be linked into one file, reducing the I/O hit. Using .asis also helps the memory and CPU performance situation.

The only thing one loses is the ability to do `timed pushes`, where there is a lapse of time between frames implemented as a `sleep()`. But because server-push is also bandwidth-limited, many consider that to be a dubious feature.

Quick Tips on Hardware Issues

While this book is mostly about a piece of software, there are definitely some decisions one can make about the hardware setup to support the server, particularly heavily loaded servers.

Separate Disks for Logs and Data

One of the biggest causes of a disk access bottleneck is having your Web logs and data on the same disk. Put your log files on a separate disk—in fact, if you can, put them on a separate SCSI chain all together. If your Web server has a higher load average than you'd like, but there's still idle CPU time, you're probably disk access bound. This situation is fairly easy to correct.

Disk Caching in Memory

In many cases, the biggest hit in servicing an HTTP request comes from physically pulling the file from disk and pumping it to memory and then off to the client. If you have disk caching on, you can dramatically cut the response time for simple, small, non-CGI requests.

Kernel Modifications

Many older UNIX variants, and even some recent ones, have certain basic TCP/IP implementation problems that cause heavily visited sites to take forever to respond to requests, or even just freeze up, even though the actual load on the machine might be very low. Because HTTP/1.0 is not connection-based and a page with 10 inlined images necessitates 11 separate TCP connections (simultaneously, on some browsers), TCP implementations in UNIX kernels really get a workout when used as a heavily loaded Web server. Most were not designed to handle 100 connections per second, though now that is becoming a design requirement.

Because every operating system is different, it doesn't make sense to go into too much depth here. However, some of the things to watch for are:

- SOMAXCONN—usually a kernel option in a configuration file, or for those operating systems that come with source, sometimes a compile-time option. This is the maximum number of socket connections that can be maintained in the listen() queue. On many operating systems, this is set to be somewhere around five, maybe 16. There is no harm and lots of good done to increase this to 64, 128, even 256. You don't want it much larger than that; the data structures can get too big and take up more memory than they should, but 128 is a good number for moderate to heavy sites.

■ Network mbufs—again, this is usually either a compile-time or runtime option for most operating systems. Increasing this will cause the run-time memory requirements of the kernel to increase slightly, but will allow for better network throughput.

The Apache Project maintains a page on specific details about tuning for different platforms at **http://www.apache.org/docs/perf.html**.

Log File Rotation

Certainly one goal for the site administrator should be to automate the rotation of access and error logs. Even a lightly loaded server will generate a couple megabytes of log activity per day. Left unchecked, your disk space could dry up fast.

The most basic element of log file rotation is to get the Web server to stop writing to the old log and start writing to another without disrupting service to the outside users. The most straightforward way to accomplish this is by renaming the log just slightly, and sending a HUP signal to the parent process. "Just slightly" means, renaming it to "access_log.0" or something similar on the same hard disk, on the same partition. Why? Each child has a file descriptor open to the log file. When you rename the file, the file descriptor will still point to the same actual log right up until the time the child receives an "echo" of the SIGHUP from the parent process. When that happens, the file descriptor is closed, a new one is obtained, and the new access_log gets created. This is pretty much the only way to guarantee not losing traffic reports while rotating logs.

Here is an example script that performs such a rotation:

```
#!/bin/sh
logdir="/usr/local/etc/httpd/logs"    # name of the log directory
acclog="access_log"                   # name of the access log
errlog="error_log"                    # name of the error log
pidfile="$logdir/httpd.pid"           # file that stores the
                                         parent's # process ID

mv $logdir/$acclog $logdir/$acclog.0
mv $logdir/$errlog $logdir/$errlog.0
kill -HUP 'cat $pidfile'
```

This needs to be run as the same user that launched the HTTP daemon originally, for example, "root." You may want to write additional scripts to place these ".0" files into an archive of some sort; my favorite one is to use the year and month as subdirectories, such that the logs for January 1, 1996, go into a file named "1996/01/01" somewhere off a directory with a lot of room. That way, it's easy to archive off somewhere else (to DAT tape, to CD-ROM, or even to remove it) by moving a directory.

Security Issues

The security of your server is, no doubt, one of your biggest concerns as a Web site administrator. Running a Web server is, by its nature, a security risk. For that matter, so is plugging your machine into a network at all. However, there is a lot that can be done to make your Web server more secure, both from external forces (people trying to break into your site) and internal forces (your own Web site users either mistakenly or willingly opening up holes).

CGI Issues

The biggest cause for concern about protecting your site from external threats are CGI scripts. Most CGI scripts are shell-based, using either PERL or C-shell interpreted programs rather than compiled programs. Thus, many attacks have occurred by exploiting "features" in this system. CGI Security is covered in the CGI section of this book, so this section won't go into too much detail about how to make CGI scripts themselves safe. There are a couple important things you should know, however, as an administrator.

A CGI script runs with the user-ID of the server child process. In the default case, this is "nobody." To adequately protect yourself, you may want to consider the "nobody" user an untrustworthy user on your site, making sure that user does not have read permission to files you want to keep private and does not have write permission anywhere sensitive. Certain CGI scripts will demand write access to certain files (for example, for a guestbook application). So if you want to enable those types of applications, it's best to specify a directory to which CGI scripts can write without worrying about a malicious or misdirected script overwriting data that it shouldn't.

Furthermore, site administrators can limit the use of CGI to specific directories using the `ScriptAlias` directive. Alternatively, if one has turned on .cgi as a file extension for CGI scripts, one can use the `Options ExecCGI` directive in access.conf to further control its use.

An example of this follows. If you want to allow for CGI to be used everywhere on the site (with a document root of /home/htdocs) except for the "users" subdirectory because you don't trust your users with CGI scripts, your access.conf should look something like the following:

```
<Directory /home/htdocs/>
Options Indexes FollowSymLinks Includes Multiviews ExecCGI
AllowOverride None
</Directory>

<Directory /home/htdocs/users/>
Options Indexes SymLinksIfOwnerMatch IncludesNOEXEC Multiviews
AllowOverride None
</Directory>
```

Because ExecCGI isn't in the `Options` list for the second directory, no one can use CGI scripts there.

Unfortunately, there really is no middle ground between allowing CGI scripts and disallowing them. Currently, most languages used for CGI programs do not have security concepts built into them, so applying rules like "don't touch the hard disk" or "don't send the /etc/passwd file in e-mail to an outside user" need to be dealt with in the same manner as if you had an actual UNIX user who needed the same restrictions applied to him or her. Maybe this will change when Sun's Java language gets more use on the server side, or when people use raw interpreted languages less and higher-level programming tools more often.

Server Side Includes

As you can see from the previous example, there was another change between the *trusted* part of the server and the *untrusted* part: the `Includes` argument to `Options` was changed to `IncludesNOEXEC`. This allows your untrusted users to use server side includes without allowing the `#include` of CGI scripts or the `#exec` command to be run. The `#exec` command is particular by troublesome in an untrusted environment because it basically gives shell-level access to an HTML author.

Symbolic Links

In an untrusted environment, UNIX symbolic links also are a concern for the Web site administrator. A malicious user could very easily create a symbolic link from a directory where he has write permission to an object or resource, even outside the document root, to which all he needs is read permission. For example, one could create a link to the /etc/passwd file, and then release that onto the Web, exposing your site to potential crack attempts, particularly if your operating system does not use shadow passwords.

> **Note**
>
> There was a recent incident involving the Alta Vista search engine (**www.altavista.digital.com**), in which a search for words common to password files (bin, root, ftp, and so on) turned up references to actual password files that had, intentionally or not, been left public. These included a few with the encrypted pass-words, which were easy enough to break with a few hours of CPU time on most workstations.

To protect against this, the site administrator has two options: to only allow symbolic linking if the owner of the link and the owner of the linked-to resource are the same by using `SymLinksIfOwnerMatch`, or to disallow symbolic links altogether by not specifying `FollowSymLinks` or `SymLinksIfOwnerMatch`.

Also note that both `<Directory>` segments in the previous example included `AllowOverride None`. That is the most conservative setting; if you want to allow certain things to be tunable in those directories using .htaccess files, you can specify them with the `AllowOverride` directive. However, stating `none` is the safest policy.

Publicly Writeable Spaces

The last security threat that is specific to Web servers is that of allowing pub-licly writeable spaces to be served up via HTTP. For example, many sites out there allow their FTP "incoming" directory to be accessed via the Web di-rectly. This can be a security hole if someone were to place a malicious CGI script there or a server side include file which calls `#exec` to do some damage. If you decide you need to take the risk of providing this service, there are some things you can do to protect yourself.

First, the most conservative setting you should set for the `Options` direc-tive is:

```
Options Indexes
```

You could use `None`, but `Indexes` really doesn't introduce any additional secu-rity problems, as long as you're comfortable with others being able to down-load anything that has been submitted. In the light of recent legislation by the U.S. government regarding "indecent" materials, you may not want to take this risk either.

Second, make sure you set `AllowOverride None` so that people can't upload an .htaccess file into your directory and modify all your settings and security policies.

Third, make sure that the FTP daemon you are using does not allow the execute bit to be set. By preventing that, you prevent the execution of uploaded CGI scripts. If you are using XBitHack to activate your server side includes, then you can prevent those from being run as well. This is mainly a backup for setting the Options as above, which should protect you against these threats anyway.

These same laws apply if you have CGI scripts that generate their own uniquely addressable HTML or CGI files. For example, if the guestbook.cgi program constantly appends the submitted personal information to a guestbook.html file, all the same rules apply; the contents of that HTML file must be considered unsafe. This can be improved if the CGI script double-checks what's getting written and removes "dangerous" code, such as server side includes. ❖

## CHAPTER 7

Creating and Managing an Intranet

No matter what a company's business, employee information-sharing methods, as well as the criteria which determine to whom such accessibility is granted, will always be top priorities. From company newsletter-type gossip, to high-level proprietary engineering data, the power of HTML and Apache can help to make the search for such material less expensive, less time-consuming, and just easier all around.

Nevertheless, it can be confusing and, initially, complicated to set up an enterprise-wide Web site. This chapter will demonstrate how to set up Apache in your company, as well as how to secure it from use by unauthorized outsiders; following that is a discussion that explains how to maintain your new Web space and add some useful features.

In this chapter, you learn:

- ■ Why your company should have an internal Web server
- ■ What kind of hardware and software will be needed
- ■ Which browser(s) are best to standardize on
- ■ How to relocate your existing documents and format new ones
- ■ How to add documents to your Web space without losing organization
- ■ How to add some useful features to you internal Web server
- ■ How to analyze and address security concerns
- ■ How to safely share your information with other companies

Benefits of an Intranet

Every company already has in place some kind of method for distributing information among its employees: from bulletin boards in the cafeteria, to the sending of overly numerous memoranda (resulting in automatic placement in the so-called "circular file" more often than not), to old-fashioned weekly (or even several-times-a-day) meetings which, by definition, cannot be held at the absolutely most-convenient time for all in attendance. Some have attempted to utilize their networking software to ease this burden, but it is either too simplistic for such purposes, or not compatible across platforms.

Software companies have made great strides in the past few years; a lot of vendors are claiming to have incorporated "Workgroup Technology, " "Groupware, or "Document Sharing." Upon closer examination, however, one quickly determines that these systems are proprietary by nature, the result being that one needs an expensive server, in addition to clients for each machine and, of course, not all platforms are supported by every client. Some packages require fundamental network changes in addition to added software and hardware requirements.

Fortunately, along came the World Wide Web, originally designed to be an easy way for scientists to share ideas. It is based on a simple and open data format (HTML) and a common network protocol (TCP/IP). This means it is easy to set up and operate and, due to the open data format, there is a plethora of clientele. An *Intranet* is basically an internal Web site, though the term is also used to describe other supporting programs such as e-mail or UseNet news.

Using Apache (and any WWW browser), you can easily set up many effective ways to share information, communicate ideas, and exchange tips. We will cover a few ways in which developing an internal Web server can help.

Bulletin Boards

One of the more popular uses for internal Web servers is as a bulletin board system. This, much like the traditional corkboard, allows people to add notices and information for everyone's use. Unlike the older paper system, though, the HTML bulletin board can be set up to be searchable, which, of course, puts much more data at one's nearly instantaneous disposal.

Using CGI scripts or writable documents, it is easy to create an attractive, friendly bulletin-board system which can be used by the whole company. Another advantage the electronic bulletin has is that it can be shared over the network. Users can be in the same building or in a different country; as long as they have network access, they can see your notices.

Information Center

An internal Web server also functions well as an information clearinghouse. Most organizations have many documents that need to be available to

employees, such as employee handbooks, phone listings and documents setting out company policies. This is usually done by printing out the information and delivering it separately to each individual employee in the company
or group. This is expensive and time-consuming, and is easily replaced by a
series of HTML documents. This saves time because the documents no longer
need to be individually distributed and, since the documents remain in electronic form, the company will save money on printing costs. Using HTML
also allows searching and hypertext-referencing and can easily be changed
with a simple text editor.

In addition to policies and handbooks, HTML can be used to distribute company information or industry news. A company newsletter can be as simple
as a single HTML page, or it can have multiple pages and contain references
to information stored across the Internet. It can have back issues archived
and completely searchable. Industry news can also be as simple or as complex
as deemed necessary.

It is also possible to have an electronic phone or e-mail list containing all the
names, addresses and extensions; users would then search using the browser's
search feature, or it may include a form to query a search engine.

Documents To Add to the Information Center

Employee handbooks

Policies and procedures

Phone or e-mail lists

Company newsletter

Industry news

Common Forms

Common business forms can also be added to the Web server. This allows the
owner of the document to modify it and make changes instantly available to
form users. It also makes it easier for employees to find the form for which
they are looking.

In some cases, the form can be handled automatically by using CGI scripts, or
forwarded to the correct people, directly from the client's browser.

► For more infor-
mation on CGI
scripts and CGI
security see
Chapter 13,
"CGI Scripts
and Server
APIs," p. 339

Caution

Automating scripts can be a time-saver, as well as a security problem. Think carefully
before automating a form request. Scripts that don't carefully check what they are
doing can cause damage by executing commands improperly.

Forms To Add to the Web Server

Equipment request form

Vacation request form

Network change requests

New user account forms

Support desk trouble ticket forms

Software or hardware bug reports

Workgroup Server

As previously mentioned, the Web was originally designed to help share information among different research groups located within various organizations. It can also be used to share information between or among workgroups.

Workgroups can use the power of the Web to list current projects, past activities, and planned proposals. This allows different groups to contact people who may have already discovered how to avoid a certain problem, or found a better way of doing something.

Team members can set up a central area for all the documentation necessary to a project, and then make allowances for easily adding individual comments. This could be very helpful when designing a new project— for example, each designer could add his or her input to the design as it goes along. This would allow discussions about the document to take place in the body of the document itself and be recorded, along with the document, for others to see.

This documentation can also include any notes, memoranda, reports and studies related to a particular area. The HTML could be searchable, making it easy for engineers to have a wealth of information right at their fingertips when encountering a new situation. This would be helpful for the novice employee, as well as the veteran engineer.

Workgroups can also use a Web server to track project status. The lead developer could create a page showing when things are expected to be done, other developers could add comments to such a file, and everyone would always be up-to-date with scheduling changes.

Workgroup servers can also be used to introduce new team members and help them to become more comfortable in their new positions. It can also help establish friendly working relationships between disparate groups by serving as an introduction center.

Workgroup Uses

List past, present, and future projects

Store related documentation for each project

Store discussions on documents or specifications

Track project status

Create a friendly working environment

Ease the introduction of new group members

Discussion Forum

You can also use the World Wide Web in conjunction with a news server. News servers fit in nicely with Web servers and allow easy discussion between users. Some browsers allow reading and posting news articles without the need for a separate program. Other browsers may require a separate program for posting news. Browsers are covered in more detail later in this chapter.

Internal newsgroups allow open discussion on many topics. Human Resources can answer questions about insurance benefits or vacation time; engineers can discuss current problems or new products. A local newsgroup dedicated to specific software can eliminate hundreds of hours of needless labor, since users can help each other out and avoid the need to call the support desk. The newly hired can get the feel of the company and its tools by reading and posting questions.

Newsgroups are set up in hierarchical form on the Internet; the same can be true for internal use. For example, one may want to set up a news hierarchy.

Sample News Hierarchy

local.eng	Discussion of engineering topics
local.Windows	Discussion of Microsoft Windows
local.outages	Notification of outages
local.specs	Discussions about various company specifications
local.policy	Discussion about corporate policy
local.misc	General discussion

You might want to set up a simple news hierarchy at first, and then expand as groups get filled up. For example, if "local.eng" were getting a lot of messages covering hardware and software issues, one could split the group into "local.eng.hw" and "local.eng.sw". Further division into "local.eng.hw.proj1" and "local.eng.hw.proj2" might later be to everyone's advantage.

News-server software can be downloaded and used without charge from many Internet sites, and can be set up on the same machine as Apache. Larger sites may need to separate the Apache server from the news server for more efficacious performance.

Uses for an Internal News Server

Forum to discuss software packages

Forum to ask policy questions

Notification of upgrades or downtime

Hardware and software discussion

Workgroup discussions

Support line

Note

There are several free news servers available on the UNIX platform. Some of the more common ones are Bnews, Cnews and the more popular INN (Internet News). If you are setting up a new news server, you will probably want to use INN. You can ftp it from various sites such as **ftp.uu.net** in the **/networking/news/nntp/inn** directory.

Monitoring Tool

The World Wide Web can also be used to allow users to see how things are running. Using Apache and Server Side Includes (SSI), or CGI scripts, you can create dynamic pages. These pages can be used in a variety of ways, such as a print queue or network status monitor.

You can create a page to allow users to check the status of their print jobs from their Web browsers. While most operating systems allow a user to check a print queue, setting up an HTML page makes it easy for everyone's use, as well as eliminating the necessity of having different commands for different machines.

In a large network environment, parts of the network might be having problems which can cause abnormal behavior. Rather than having each and every user call the support desk, you can set up a page for checking various parts of the network and assessing status.

Using the Web for Monitoring

Print queues

Network status

Who is logged in

Which machines are in use and busy

Available file systems

HTML as a User Environment

There are cases in which one would want to create a hypertext front end to system software. These might include word processing, database querying, data entry, and order processing.

Many companies are starting to migrate their software to be HTML-compatible; with Java and CGI, almost any application can have such an interface. This will require users to learn only one interface, regardless of the underlying system.

Note

SATAN is a network security-testing package that received a lot of attention in 1995. It allows users to test for known weaknesses in the software used by Internet machines. One of the things that the developers did was to create an HTML interface. Using any browser, you could check or configure the tests, or check the status of a test.

There is also work going on in developing a low-cost (under $500) machine consisting only of a network interface, a keyboard, the CPU, and graphics display. This machine would download HTML or Java applets and display them on the screen. This would allow network managers to standardize on a common interface (HTML) for all the company's computing needs. It would also allow companies to replace overpriced PC's with the newer, more affordable "Net computer."

Choosing the Network

Apache is designed to run over a TCP/IP network — whether this network is the Internet, or a private network, makes no difference to the server; however, some clients may not understand this networking protocol and, will need additional software to work properly with Apache.

> **Tip**
>
> It is possible to view simple HTML files without a network or a server. Most browsers allow you to open a local file and view it. This allows you to follow links and view the page, but it does not allow some of the more advanced features, such as CGI scripts or SSI programs.

About TCP/IP

TCP/IP is actually two layered networking protocols: TCP and IP. IP stands for Internet Protocol and, as the name implies, is the protocol used by the Internet. TCP, the Transmission Control Protocol, runs on top of IP and handles the sending of data between the machine and the network. IP can also run on top of PPP for dial-in access (in which case it would be TCP/PPP), but is still commonly referred to as TCP/IP.

You have probably used TCP/IP before and not been aware of it. Applications such as FTP (the File Transfer Protocol) and Telnet use TCP/IP, although it is user-transparent. You might also be familiar with the Domain Name System (DNS) or Network File System (NFS); these, too, work over IP, using UDP instead of TCP.

> **Tip**
>
> TCP is a reliable stream protocol. This means packets are guaranteed to have been received correctly and in proper order. UDP, on the other hand, simply sends packets. The software using UDP must make sure that the data gets to its destination intact.

One of the main advantages TCP/IP has over other networking protocols is its interconnectivity. It was designed to be used with almost any type of cabling; for example, fiber optic, twisted pair, coaxial cable, or even wireless networks are possible. Additionally, it can be used by any networking topologies, including Ethernet, Token Ring and FDDI. This makes it possible to use TCP/IP in practically any networking environment.

TCP/IP is also machine-independent. UNIX machines can talk to other computers, printers or network devices, just as long as they all understand TCP/IP. The other machine doesn't need to be using the same OS and it needn't be the same type. This has helped to make TCP/IP one of the most popular networking choices around.

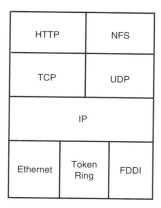

Fig. 7.1
TCP/IP is a layered protocol.

TCP/IP is an open networking protocol which has allowed many vendors to develop applications and systems that incorporate TCP/IP in them. UNIX vendors have been incorporating TCP/IP for years and it is hard to find a UNIX machine without it. It is not, however, as common on the Macintosh or PC platform, and additional software may be required to set it up. Windows 95, Windows NT, and Macintosh System 7.5 all include TCP/IP networking without third-party applications.

TCP/IP Terminology

IP address is the machine address. It consists of four numbers, ranging from 1 to 254. These numbers are called *octets,* and the entire address is referred to as a *dotted quad.* As an example, let's use 10.32.21.199. This number actually consists of two parts: the network number and the host number. The network number is usually the first 2 or 3 octets in the IP address, and the machine number is the remainder.

Netmask determines how much of the IP is the network address and how much is the host address. For example, the netmask of 255.255.0.0 tells us that the first 2 octets are network numbers, and the last 2 octets are host numbers. Sometimes, the netmask is referred to as the "subnet mask."

Networks are conventionally split into 3 classes, A, B, and C. A Class A network has a single octet for a network portion and three octets for the machine portion. Class B networks have two octets for both the machine and network portion, and Class C have three octets for the network and one for the host. The previous example uses a Class B network.

Broadcast address goes along with the netmask. It tells the machine how to talk to everyone on the local network. It is usually the inverse of the netmask plus the network number. For example, if our IP address is 10.32.21.199, and our netmask is 255.255.0.0, then our broadcast address would be 10.32.255.255.

(continues)

(continued)

Gateways or Routers are alternative paths to a different network. They are required if going to a network other than the one in your IP address. In complex networks, there may be many gateways; in most networks, there is a default gateway. This default gateway gets all traffic not destined for the local network.

Using TCP/IP Software

Configuring TCP/IP is not any harder then configuring any other network protocol, such as Novell Netware's IPX, or Microsoft's Netbios. In fact, once a few essentials are understood, it may be that TCP/IP is easier to configure and, if one is experiencing any difficulty, there are many consultants or administrators available who are familiar with TCP/IP.

If you need TCP/IP software you may want to look at some of the commercial Internet Suites in the next section. Most of these suites contain all the software needed to start using the network, including e-mail, FTP, a Web browser and a Telnet package.

There are also shareware and freeware versions available on the Internet and various bulletin boards. Gathering all the networking software and clients for each protocol (Web, mail, FTP) can be time-consuming; sometimes it turns out to be less expensive to go with a commercial package.

Another nice thing about the commercial packages is the support. If you are having a problem with a public domain or shareware product, it is usually possible to get an answer from someone, but requires much more dedication and patience than with supported software. With commercial software, of course, it is much easier to get the answers.

There are two ways to add TCP/IP to a machine: either use TCP/IP as the only protocol, or use multiple protocols on the same machine. It is generally much easier to use just one protocol, but if you are already using networking software that may not be an option.

Note

If your current networking software allows it, you may be able to encapsulate your existing network in an IP packet. This makes it easier to configure your networking software. Check the documentation to see if this is possible.

Setting up TCP/IP on a Windows machine will require a WINSOCK.DLL file to be installed and configured. If this is the only networking protocol, then that is all that is needed. If running different networks from this machine (such as Microsoft networking or NetWare), some experimenting will be necessary in order to get both protocols to work side-by-side. Your networking software documentation should "walk you" through setting up multiple protocols.

If you purchase a commercial suite of products, they will include a WINSOCK.DLL. Using a browser separately will require a Winsock package such as Trumpet Winsock or else a commercial TCP/IP stack.

> ### Note
>
> The WINSOCK.DLL file is the TCP/IP stack on Windows.

Trumpet Winsock

The most widely used shareware Winsock package is Trumpet Winsock. It is available from many FTP sites but only for the Windows environment. Although lacking the TCP/IP clients, it does incorporate support for TCP/IP over a network using a packet driver, or over a modem via PPP or SLIP. Instructions for downloading a packet driver are distributed with Trumpet. If you use a separate browser such as Mosaic or Netscape, this ought to come in handy.

> ### Tip
>
> A packet driver is a software driver for a network board which allows networking software to work "as- is" with any network board or topology. It usually requires a line added to your AUTOEXEC.BAT file.
>
> If using other network products, such as NDIS or ODI, it is still possible to use a packet-driver package by downloading the ODIPKT or NDIS_PKT packages. These packages are called "shims" and allow making your ODI or NDIS software look like a packet driver.

NetManage

NetManage makes a series of TCP/IP applications, ranging from Newt, a TCP/IP stack, to the Chameleon Desktop, a full-fledged Internet suite which includes NFS client and server, X Windows emulation, and almost any Internet application conceivable.

NetManage's TCP/IP stack has support for LANs, and modems using SLIP, CSLIP or PPP. The software runs under Windows 3.1, Windows 95, and Windows NT.

NetManage also has many different packages, so one is only required to pay for what one needs.

FTP Software

FTP software also has many different application suites, ranging from PC/TCP, a TCP/IP stack and some basic applications, to OnNet, a full Internet package, including NFS client and server, e-mail, UseNet, and WWW.

PC/TCP runs on Windows 95, NT, 3.1, and Windows for Workgroups. It also allows DOS applications to have access to TCP/IP. The TCP/IP stack can be used over LANS as well as modems.

MacTCP

If on a Macintosh and looking for a TCP/IP stack, you will probably use MacTCP. MacTCP is a commercial product and contains many clients such as Telnet and FTP. The later versions are very stable, though early versions were known to have problems.

Other TCP/IP packages

There are many other companies making TCP/IP software for PC and Macintosh clients. Look around and find one that has just the utilities necessary. When purchasing a TCP/IP stack for Windows, make sure you are getting a TCP/IP stack that is Winsock- compliant.

Configuring TCP/IP

Configuring TCP/IP either on a Macintosh or on a Windows machine requires a few parameters to be entered, including IP address, netmask or subnetmask, broadcast address, and gateway or router. Some installations might also ask for DNS server, which is used to allow you to use machine names, instead of having to remember their IP address.

Caution

If you aren't sure of the answers in the configuration, check with your network manager. Incorrectly setting these not only causes your machine to communicate improperly, but can also prevent other machines on the network from properly working.

Choosing a Browser

Among the benefits of an Intranet over an Internet is the fact that the company can standardize on a browser. This allows the Web designer to take advantage of some advanced features, such as Java, Frames or special data formats.

Since the browser is visible to all users, it is important to choose one that has the necessary features and, at the same time, will run on all the available platforms. In the following section, we will cover the more popular browsers such as Mosaic, Netscape, and Lynx, as well as browsers from some of the TCP/IP bundles.

> **Tip**
>
> If you don't get one of the bundled packages and instead get just the browser, you will need to get a separate TCP/IP stack.

Current Web browsers support many different things, including form support, different image formats, Frames, Java, Imagemaps, client-side imagemaps, various HTML tags and many other protocols. Fortunately, not every company needs all these features. Some of the more helpful features are:

1. *Forms.*   Forms are required to submit data. Most, if not all, current browsers support forms, though some may display them differently than others.

2. *Image formats.*   Different formats include GIF, JPEG, PCX and XBM. GIF is supported in almost every browser, with JPEG running a close second. There are also interlaced GIF and JPEG formats, which start out blurry, but get clearer as the image comes in. Interlaced images are nice, but are by no means the most important feature. XBM and PCX files are used mostly on UNIX machines and PC's, respectively.

3. *HTML tags.*   Some companies have added their own extensions to their browsers to make up for a lack of features in the HTML specification. Some of the new tags allow centering of text, blinking, or changing colors of fonts or backgrounds.

4. *Frames* are a new feature currently added to Netscape browsers. These allow the Web designer to split the browser display screen into smaller sections. These smaller sections are called frames. If used properly, frames can make navigating the Web much easier, but if used improperly, they clutter the screen and make it unusable.

5. *Java* is a new language designed by Sun Microsystems Inc. It allows the Web designer to add "executable content" to a Web page. Java can be used to offload some of the CPU load off of the main server, and is much more sophisticated than mere CGI scripts.

6. *UseNet news and e-mail access* allow a user to send and receive e-mail and news articles from within the browser. Some browsers allow reading news and posting e-mail, but not posting news and reading e-mail. Others allow both.

7. *Imagemaps and client-side imagemaps* allow the Web designer to have a graphical navigation tool. They can be used to display a floor plan and allow the user to click an area, such as an office, and obtain information about the group or person who uses it. Client-side imagemaps are imagemaps that do the processing on the client side instead of the server, thus reducing the load on the server.

> **Note**
>
> The browser market changes very quickly. Before deciding on a browser, recheck the market for new browsers or enhancements to existing browsers.

The Mosaic Browser

Mosaic was the first graphical WWW browser and handles the common platforms (Windows, Macintosh and UNIX), so they shall be discussed first.

Mosaic was developed at the National Center for Supercomputing Applications (NCSA) at the University of Illinois in order to handle the recently created WWW. Mosaic was the first browser to include images, sound, and text in a browser environment (see fig. 7.2).

The latest version has a built in e-mail sender, hotlist manager, and news reader. It also has support for forms, imagemaps, and most HTML tags. It does not, however, allow posting of news or reading of e-mail. It includes support for inline viewing of GIF, JPEG and XBM. Mosaic must download the entire page before it is displayed and, therefore, has no support for interlaced images. The newer Windows versions require a 32-bit version of Windows such as Win95 or NT. You can download a 32-bit DLL for earlier versions of Windows from Microsoft.

Netscape's Navigator

Netscape Navigator is considered to be the leading browser and now claims over 70 percent of the browser market. It has versions for Windows,

Macintosh and UNIX (like Mosaic) but the current versions are no longer free. The last free version was 0.9 and could be used for noncommercial uses only. Navigator 2.0 has many new features, such as Java, Frames, extended HTML tags, client-side imagemaps and interlaced images. See figure 7.3.

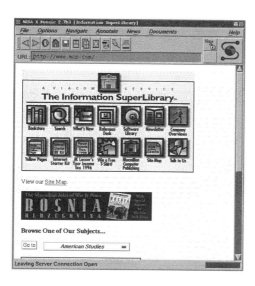

Fig. 7.2
Mosaic captured most of the early browser market.

> **Note**
>
> Netscape has added some extra tags to allow for more formatting options. These include tags to center text, change text size or color, cause sections of text to blink and also allow background images. These are called Netscape extensions.

Netscape has support for a complete e-mail system and can filter mail by subject, date, sender, or size. It allows the user to do almost anything that can be done in a dedicated e-mail package and allows hypertext to be followed with a click of the button (see fig. 7.4).

In addition to the e-mail system, there is also a built-in news system. It allows both reading and posting and can be sorted by subject, date and sender. The news system also allows hypertext linking. This hypertext linking helps make Navigator one of the easiest-to-use Internet systems around.

Another nice feature of Navigator is incremental loading, which means that as the page is downloaded, it is displayed. This allows the user to start reading the text before the entire page is read in. On a fast LAN connection, this may not be as important, but on an internal network made up of slow WAN links, this will most certainly be advantageous.

Fig. 7.3
Macmillan Computer Publishing's site viewed with Netscape.

Fig. 7.4
Netscape's e-mail system.

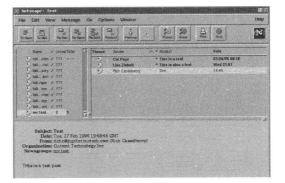

Lynx Text Browser

Lynx is a fast text-only browser, developed at the University of Kansas. Lynx is very useful in environments that use dumb terminals without the ability to display graphics (see fig. 7.5). Lynx is also useful over slow links, since it does not have to download the graphics. See figure 7.5.

Lynx has support for forms but cannot display inline graphics or imagemaps. Lynx can download the graphic and view it with an external viewer; however, the terminal being used must be able to display graphics, and the viewer must be configured separately.

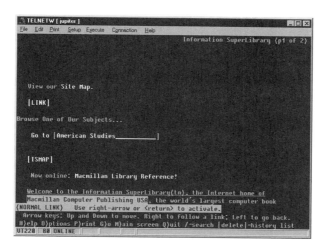

Fig. 7.5
Accessing the
Macmillan site
with Lynx.

Lynx allows the reading of news and the sending of e-mail, but is not a full-fledged news or e-mail system like Navigator. For sites with dumb terminals, Lynx is one of the few existing alternatives.

Microsoft's Internet Explorer

Microsoft's WWW browser is an impressive browser. It supports forms, imagemaps and supports almost all the HTML tags that Netscape does. These include centering, changing font color, backgrounds and font sizing. See figure 7.6.

Explorer also supports GIF and JPEG images and audio sounds. Microsoft has decided to license the Java language from Sun Microsystems and future browsers are expected to have support for it.

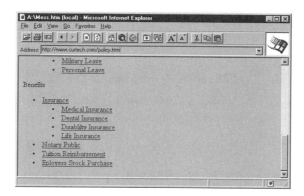

Fig. 7.6
This is what
Microsoft Internet
Explorer looks like.

II

Setting Up a Web Server

Explorer has limited table support but has problems with some tables that Netscape can display. If standardized on Explorer, though, it is easy to work around this.

Microsoft has also announced a version of Explorer for the Macintosh platform.

Chameleon's WebSurfer

The browser that ships with the Chameleon software has all the basic support, such as GIF images, and most HTML tags. It does not however, contain support for Java.

Fig. 7.7
Macmillan's site viewed using WebSurfer.

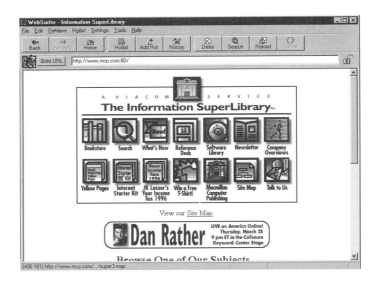

WebSurfer also incorporates a news reader and supports sending of e-mail from the browser.

Network Topology and Speed

Most LANs (Local Area Networks) can transfer at least 4 MB of information a second, which is plenty fast enough for transferring the largest text files. If the network is made up of WAN (Wide Area Networks) links, some network bottlenecks may occur when transferring pages over them.

If using large graphic or audio files, you will experience delays on all but the fastest LAN technologies. Large files will also take more space on the server and place a strain on the client and server machines.

WAN links are generally much slower then LAN connections, usually no more than 1.5 MB and commonly only 56 kbps. Some dial-up links are only 14.4 kbps or 28.8 kbps. If there are many such connections, it is important to be careful about page size.

Even if you have a fast network, and aren't separated by WAN links, it makes sense to place the Apache server as close to the center of the network (or backbone) as possible. This will make the speed even faster and will also increase overall network performance (see fig. 8.8).

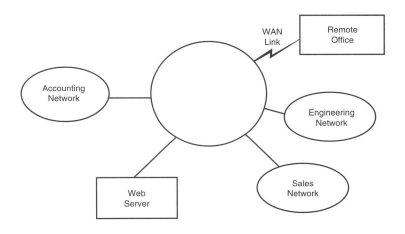

Fig. 7.8
The server should be in the center of the network.

If many groups are using parts of the Web server, one can separate the Web space into multiple servers to increase performance (see fig. 7.9). This allows placing the Web server as close to the main users as possible.

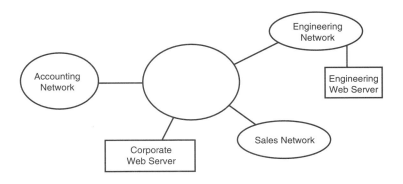

Fig. 7.9
You might want to split your Web server.

Disk Space

If you are only using HTML files, then very little disk space is needed. HTML files are simply ASCII files and don't take up much room.

II

Setting Up a Web Server

Once graphic or audio files are incorporated, the requirement for disk space expands accordingly. An average graphic file can take several megabytes, and some file formats can take over 30 MB per file. Audio files take several megabytes of space for each minute of sound. Using these type of formats will require not only more space, but also more network bandwidth, as discussed in the previous section.

When indexing your Web space, don't forget to consider the space required for the index database. This file can be as much as half the size of the documents combined within. Log files can also take up a lot of space. Log files up to 10 MB a month are not uncommon.

Document Formats

Most companies are made up of different departments and different machine types. Marketing groups may have Macintosh machines, Engineering might have UNIX machines, and there is almost sure to be a wide array of PCs in use.

There are also different formats used on each machine. PC users are likely to be using WordPerfect or Microsoft Word to create files. UNIX users may use text editors or Framemaker to create memoranda, while Macintosh users may use other formats.

Deciding on a common data format is not easy and, in some cases, not possible. Next, we shall take a look at the various formats and their associated benefits.

HTML

HTML was designed to overcome the cross-platform issue, but it is limited in the formatting that can be done to documents. Netscape and others have added specific tags to help, but using these tags requires using specific viewers to properly see them.

► These converters and tools are covered in Chapter 10, "HTML Editors and Tools," p. 233

Many word-processing companies have developed (or are developing) ways to save their documents as HTML documents. Microsoft, Framemaker, Corel and others have filters or templates that you can use to create HTML files using their software.

There are also conversion utilities that will convert from many formats to HTML. Not all documents can be converted easily, though, and sometimes it is easier to recreate a document than to try to convert it.

Microsoft Word

Microsoft Word is a very popular word processor, having the advantage of being available on both the Mac and PC platforms. It allows graphics and various fonts and is very user friendly.

Microsoft Word files, however, are different between versions, and the early versions can't read the newer versions' files. Microsoft has made a Word viewer which is not available on UNIX machines. Still, Word remains a good choice for those owners of Windows or Macintosh machines exclusively.

Postscript

Postscript is a very powerful document language. It is also very popular, and Postscript viewers are available for the major platforms. Almost all the word-processing and drawing packages can save as a Postscript file, making Postscript seem like a good choice.

Postscript files tend to be quite large, especially if they contain many images. While they are quick on high-end machines, Postscript viewers can be slow to load on some others. In spite of this, Postscript is another very good alternative for documents that need more formatting than HTML allows.

Adobe PDF

Adobe Acrobat files allow extensive formatting and also are available on all the popular platforms, such as PC, Mac and UNIX. PDF viewers are available free of charge over the Internet.

Like Postscript, however, PDF files tend to be large and load slowly.

Images

It is also possible to save all documents as an image format such as GIF or JPEG. This would allow easy viewing on the various platforms, except for dumb terminals.

Image files are, unfortunately, very large and would use much more space and network bandwidth than other formats. Also, since image files don't contain ASCII text, they cannot be indexed or searched.

A Combination of Formats

The best alternative is to use a combination of formats to achieve the required result. Any text that does not need specific formatting (such as memoranda or notes) can be done in HTML or converted to HTML. Documents that require specific formatting can be stored in Postscript or image formats to keep their look intact.

Whenever possible, keep the number of formats to a minimum. If your company only uses PC's, then stick to HTML and Word files. If everyone has a fast UNIX machine, use Postscript and HTML.

Setting Up the Web Documents

This section will cover setting up your access-control mechanism and also go over some guidelines to help you set up some of the applications that will make your Web server even more useful.

Managing Content

When setting up documents, one will need to consider how to structure them in order to make their management easier. It often makes sense to group documents according to department. Even though Apache uses hypertext links to create an organized hierarchy of documents, one should still try to maintain a close correspondence between hypertext links and directory layout.

It is also crucial to decide who will be able to change files and create new topics. Will anyone be able to add a new topic? Who should be allowed to change pages? Do all files need to be approved? These questions must be answered in advance of starting to add files to the server.

◀ Chapter 5, "Apache Configuration," gives more information about this directive. See p. 73

Organizing Hierarchy

Apache doesn't have a document control feature, but you can take advantage of the `DirectoryIndex` directive. Using `DirectoryIndex` will make it easier for you to find documents when not in a Web browser; for instance, when editing (see fig. 7.10).

Fig. 7.10
Setting up a directory hierarchy.

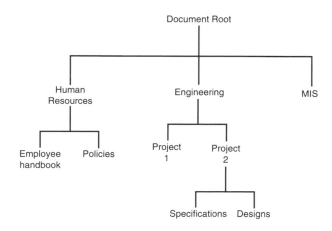

One of the best ways to organize a Web site is to set up directories for each major topic in its DocumentRoot. Using the `DirectoryIndex` directive will set up an "index page" for each topic. That page then references other files stored in that directory, or points to a subdirectory which contains another "index page". Using this file hierarchy makes it easy to organize and maintain the Web server's content.

Getting Files on the Server

If already using NFS, there is an easy way to get your documents on to your Web server. Set up the export list on the Web server to allow developers to mount DocumentRoot to their machines.

NFS may not be desirable in a high-security environment, due to its lack of authentication. PC and Macintosh users can pretend to be any user. Most UNIX users, however, don't allow pretending to be root, but care must still be taken when exporting via NFS.

◀ See Chapter 5, "Apache Configuration," p. 73

> **Caution**
>
> Exporting a file system must be done with care. If an unauthorized user can access DocumentRoot via NFS or FTP, then any server-access control is circumvented.

If you can't use NFS, then FTP is another logical choice. FTP will allow the user to cd to the DocumentRoot directory and also to put the files in place. Using FTP is more secure than NFS, since it asks for a login and password. It does, however, send the login name and password unencrypted across the network, which may be unacceptable in some companies. Security is covered in more detail later in this chapter.

> **Note**
>
> Both of these methods require the UNIX permissions to allow write access to the directory.

Access Control Methods

The first thing you need to do is decide on who will be able to change various documents. There are three types of access control that you can use for your Web server: Open, Distributed and Centralized. We will look at each one in detail later. First, we shall discuss a little about UNIX protections.

II

Setting Up a Web Server

UNIX File Permissions

UNIX file permissions control who can do what to a file or directory. This is the only way to protect documents on your Web server, so it is important to discuss them in some detail.

UNIX permissions have three different levels of access to define who can do what to a file or directory:

- The owner of the file (User)
- A group of users who have access (Group)
- Everyone else (Other)

There are also three different things a user can do to a file:

- View the contents of a file (Read)
- Change the contents of a file (Write)
- Run the file or program (eXecute)

When the permissions are applied to a directory they have slightly different meanings:

- List the contents of a directory (Read)
- Create new files in the directory (Write)
- Access files in the directory (eXecute)

The different levels of access can be defined by a number. Read is 4, Write is 2 and eXecute is 1. To determine the permissions add up the numbers. For example to set Read and Write access would be 6 (4+2).

◀ See Chapter 5, "Apache Configuration," p. 73, for more details about this directive.

The UNIX command to change permissions on a file or directory is chmod ugo <file>. u is the access for the User, g is for the group and o is everyone else. To set a directory up for the user and group to be able to access and add files to a directory, called "hr" and everyone else to be able to get files from the directory we would do "**chmod 771 hr**" . To set up a file, say "policy1", for the user to be able to change and the group and everyone else to be able to read would require "chmod 644 policy1". We could also use "**chmod 755 policy1**" — in the case of HTML files, the execute doesn't matter, unless using the XbitHack directive.

Note

The XBitHack directive is used to tell Apache that an HTML file includes Server Side Includes, and can also be used to send a last-modified header.

Tip

Different versions of UNIX act slightly different. If you are having problems, consult your UNIX documentation.

Now let's apply UNIX permissions to our DocumentRoot to set up different access policies.

Open Access

This type of access control is the easiest to setup and maintain. It allows anyone to change any file in your DocumentRoot. To set this up, simply change the permissions on all the files and directories in the DocumentRoot directory tree. In SunOS4.1, you can cd to DocumentRoot (DocumentRoot is defined in the srm.conf file), and "**chmod -R 777**." The chmod command we have seen before the -R option tells UNIX to perform this recursively.

Caution

Setting permissions so that anyone can read, write or delete any file makes adding documents very easy. However, it can lead to problems if unauthorized users can get access to your file system. With the open access model, these users could change or remove any file on your Web server.

Using the open-access model makes adding documents easy. Unfortunately it also tends to get very confusing, since there is no central authority helping to organize where information is found.

Distributed Access

Distributed management is a scenario where several developers jointly manage content of their area, or a single developer manages a particular area. The server administrator would delegate various permissions to lead developers of a project, while maintaining control of the home page and other areas of the server. The lead developer could then further delegate responsibilities to other developers.

Using distributed access allows the server to maintain structure and also allows users to add documents through responsible developers.

To set up a directory to be administered by a single developer requires the server administrator to change ownership of the directory to him or her. This can be done by using the chown command like "**chown richc hr-docs**."

The directory permissions should be set to 711 to allow the server user (defined by the User directive in httpd.conf) to get files from the directory.

If the directory is to be managed by more than one developer, it becomes necessary to create a group with the users that can control this area and set the permissions to be 771.

Any files created can be set so that only the owner can change them (chmod 644) or so that someone in the same group can change them (chmod 664). This will depend on how your policy is defined. The important thing is to make sure that the server-user has at least read permissions on the files, otherwise they will not show up in your Web tree.

Centralized Access

Centralized access requires any changes to documents to go through the server administrator, or a central authority.

Using this access policy allows structure to constantly be maintained throughout the Web. However, since only one person can make changes, it sometimes can make it hard to add documents as well as being difficult to administer.

Directory permissions for centralized control are simple. All the files and directories under DocumentRoot are owned by one person and set so that only that person has write permissions. All files should be 644 and all directories need to be 711.

Using Multiple Access Methods

Often it is desirable to have different sections under different access permissions. It is normal to have the top-level pages under centralized control, and then have each department maintain their own Web documents. It is a good idea to set up an area for anyone to create files.

To enable users to be able to control specific files, but not to be able to add new files, one would set the directory to 711 (owned by the administrator) and have the files underneath it owned by specific users with permissions set to 644. Administrators can then create the file and use the chown command to give the file away.

Tip

Some UNIX systems don't allow the transfer of ownership to other users, unless logged in as root.

Adding Useful Features

Earlier in this chapter, we discussed some features to add to an internal Web server to make it more useful. In this section, we will discuss strategies for their implementation.

Bulletin Boards

A bulletin board can be as simple as a writable HTML page. Users can edit the file and add notices, and view the page in their browser to read them. Most browsers allow searching the current page for keywords.

A better way would be to create a fill-out form and use a CGI to add a link to the main bulletin board page, and also create a separate page for the notice. The main page should have a list of notices and a subject, and also a search page. The search page should allow users to search by subject, date, author, or full text. See figure 7.11.

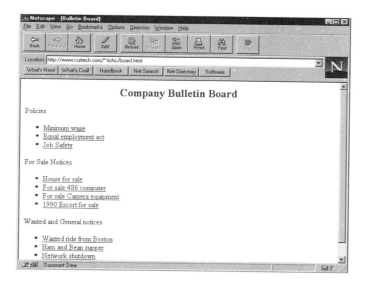

Fig. 7.11
A Bulletin board page.

Handbooks and Newsletters

Creating or converting an employee handbook can be a good way to save money. It allows changes to be made easily and whenever needed, instead of waiting until the next reprint. Using search capabilities can help save employees time by allowing the computer to search through the text.

First, create the Table of Contents page with links to the other pages. Each chapter should be in a separate directory and each section should be a separate page. Use the DirectoryIndex directive to make things easier to understand. See figure 7.12.

Fig. 7.12
A sample table of contents.

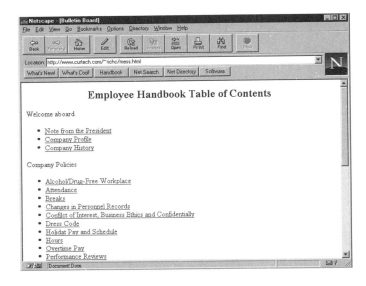

▶ For more information about search capabilities, see Chapter 15, "Search Engines and Annotation Systems," p. 379

▶ See Chapter 17, "Database Access and Applications Integration," p. 429

If your company is using Frames, you can create a special frame for the table of contents so users can easily navigate through the manual.

Create a search page to make it easy to find references to specific topics.

Adding Business Forms

Adding business forms is just like adding any other type of form. Try to make the electronic version look like the paper version so people won't get confused.

It is also possible in some cases to create a CGI script to automate the handling of the form. This can be as simple as e-mailing someone the information on the form or as complex as adding a record to a database.

> **Caution**
>
> Take care when having your CGI make changes — it is possible to have an incorrect script remove records or make unintended changes. It might also be a security problem if users can make changes to which they should not be entitled.

Workgroup Pages

Setting up an area for a specific department can make the WWW a very powerful tool. Different departments might have different ideas on what they will use their area for, but a few common uses are: to track project status, to store documentation (knowledge base) and to introduce the members.

Tracking project status can be done by creating a page with deadlines on it. There should be a form for developers to submit changes such as missing a deadline or finishing part of the project early.

Having all the documentation, notes, meeting minutes and memoranda for a project in a central area makes communication easier.

Setting a directory aside for each project and creating a search capability for it will allow employees to spend more time working on a project and less time searching for relevant information.

A Web page is also a good place to put pages about each team member and what that person's specialty is. Contact information such as phone numbers or e-mail addresses is also helpful.

Discussion Forums

There are several ways to get a discussion area created. The first and easiest way is to create a writable page and have users add comments to it. This, however, is not very interactive or easy to use.

A better way is to use UseNet news groups to allow discussion. Setting up a news server is easy and allows many different discussions to be going on at once.

Tip

Most browsers allow you to read news by using a special URL. news:local.eng.sw would generate a list of news articles in the group local.eng.sw.

Some browsers also allow posting from inside the browsers. Others only allow reading. If your browser allows sending e-mail, but not posting news, you can get a news-to-email gateway and still use newsgroups for discussion.

> **Note**
>
> Mailing list software often has a news gateway. One of these is listproc. Listproc can be downloaded from **ftp://cs-ftp.bu.edu/pub/listserv**.
>
> There is also a PERL script called mail2news which can be found at **ftp://relay.cs.toronto.edu/pub/moraes**.

Monitoring Tools

▶ For more information about SSIs, see Chapter 13, p. 339, "CGI Scripts and Server APIs."

It is often desirable to be able to check on the status of a print job from a Web browser. Using CGI scripts or SSI (and a little creativity), this can be easily done. See figure 7.13.

Create a network status page that contains a list of printers along with how many print jobs they have in them. You could also list who owns the print jobs. Under SunOS, use the `lpc` and `lpq` commands to get this information. Other versions of UNIX may use other commands.

Fig. 7.13
Pages can show the status of all the print queues.

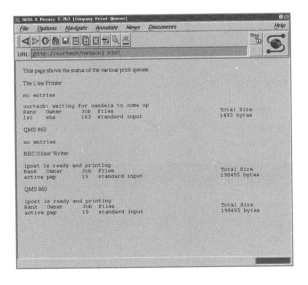

Listing 7.1 is a simple script to list who is using the printers. It is to be used as a Server Side Include.

Listing 7.1   Showing the Status of Print Queues

```
#!/bin/sh
# This script is an example. It is to be used as a SSI.
```

```
#
# Cycle through the printers and get the printer name and number of
jobs
# This next line gets all of our printer names from /etc/printcap.
This way the script
#     is always current.
for name in 'lpc stat all ¦ grep : ¦ sed 's/://g''
        do
# In our printcap we have short names and longer names these are from
our printcap file
# NiceName is the third name.
#lp¦line¦ The Line Printer:\
#ls¦ lascii¦ QMS 860:\
#lw¦lpost¦ NEC Silent Writer:\
#lf¦lproff¦ QMS 860:\
     NiceName='grep "^$name" /etc/printcap ¦ awk -F\¦ ' { print $3 }'
¦ awk -F: ' { print $1 }''
        echo  $NiceName '<p>'
        echo '<PRE>'
        lpq -P$name
        echo '</PRE>'
        done
```

In your network status page, it is good to include a list of machines on the network— placing a green dot if the machine is accessible, for example, or a red dot if it isn't. Using the ping command, one can check to see if the machine is alive or not.

Listing 7.2 is a simple SSI that can be used to test to see if a machine is running or not. It needs a graphic called reddot.gif and greendot.gif. These will be used to show if a machine is reachable on the network or not.

Listing 7.2 Testing Machine Response

```
#!/bin/sh
# Ping each machine and see if they answer
#
# ping might be in a different spot on other UNIX versions. This is
OK for SUNOS
PING=/usr/etc/ping
# Time to wait in seconds before deciding a machine is really down.
If TIMEOUT is
# too long your SSI will take a long time to load.
TIMEOUT=2
for name in machine1 machine2 machine3
        do
        if [ '$PING $name $TIMEOUT ¦ awk ' { print $3 } ' ' = "alive"
]
        then
        echo '<img src="/images/greendot.gif" alt="Alive">
'$name'<BR>'
```

(continues)

Setting Up a Web Server

Listing 7.2 Continued

```
    else
    echo '<img src="/images/reddot.gif" alt="Down"> '$name'<BR>'
    fi
    done
```

Tip

Ping checks the network connection to a machine. It does not check to see if the machine is really working properly. Most versions of ping allow a time-out value. This is important since ping normally waits many seconds before realizing a machine is down. This would cause your page to load very slowly.

It is possible, using SSI and CGI programs, to make almost any UNIX command into a useful page. These examples are just possibilities, and not a definitive list of what is possible.

Protecting Your Data from Outside Access

Once you decide to develop an internal Web site, you need to make sure outsiders have no access it. This should be one of your top concerns. This section will cover the various ways in which one may protect data.

Security Through Obscurity

One of the easiest ways to reduce the risk of someone getting your internal data is simply to fail to inform them it is there. This is called "security through obscurity" and is the least effective method. If it is important to keep out anyone except the most casual browser, use better security.

The first way to try to hide your server is to give it an unusual name. Most companies call their Web server www.company.com, and that is the first place any determined cracker will look.

Caution

If trying to hide the server name, it is important not to post news, send e-mail, or run a Web browser from it. This may cause your machine name to show up in other system's logs. These logs can be set up to get automatically indexed by a search robot.

The second way to make your server less likely to be found is to run it on a nonstandard port. Ports can range from 0 to 65,535, so there is a wide range to choose from. Generally, the first 1024 are considered reserved ports. Make sure the server isn't running on a port that is already in use. The `Port` directive (in your httpd.conf file) defines what port you are running on if you are not running from inetd. If you are running your server from inetd, this is defined in your inetd.conf file.

◀ For more information about the inetd.conf file, see Chapter 5, "Apache Configuration," p. 73

> **Note**
>
> The term *reserved port* means that only root is allowed to run a server on it. It does not mean that the port is in use. Reserved ports have no meaning on a PC or Macintosh, since anyone can run on any port with those platforms.

> **Caution**
>
> Hiding the server will not stop anyone determined to access your data. There is software available that can find any server, regardless of how obscure its name, by searching every possible IP address to which it is assigned. Running on a port other than 80 will slow people down, but there also exists software that will scan all 65,535 ports in a few minutes.

Using the Software To Restrict Access

Chapter 5 covered different security features, including the `Limit` directive. This directive can be restricted to serving only documents within specific IP address ranges.

To use the limit directive as such server-access restriction, set the Limit directive to only allow gets or posts from your IP address range. For example, if your network is 10.32.21.0, then your limit directive should say "allow from 10.32.21.*" and "deny from all".

> **Caution**
>
> Using the Apache server to protect access only stops attacks against your Web server. It does not prevent people from getting your data through other methods, such as FTP or NFS.

It is possible for intruders to trick your Web server into thinking it is part of your network by using IP spoofing. IP spoofing is a means to make a remote machine appear to be from the trusted local network.

Another software product that will help to protect a server is called *TCP wrappers*. It can be downloaded from the Internet and is available free of charge. The wrappers allow defining of who can connect to various ports and also offers some protection against IP spoofing. They also offer logging, and can be used to send different messages to different IP addresses. TCP wrappers can only be used if you are running from inetd.

Firewalling the Internet

Firewalls are the best defense from the Internet. There are different types of firewalls and each has its advantages and disadvantages. We will cover the basic design philosophies and how to use them.

> ### Caution
>
> The Internet can be a source of unauthorized access, but it is not the only way intruders can get in. Modems on people's machines can unintentionally be set up to allow crackers to get into the network.

Screening Routers

Using routers to block access to all machines and ports is one of the more common ways to protect your internal network. You can use a deny-all policy or an allow-all policy.

The deny-all policy says, in effect, not to let anything in except what services are necessary. This is the most secure method, since one can be fairly confident of what gets into your network. For example, if it is desirable to allow e-mail to get into the network, allow port 25 (smtp). See figure 7.14.

Fig. 7.14
Screening routers can be used to allow some protocols to pass while refusing others. Http can pass, Telnet cannot.

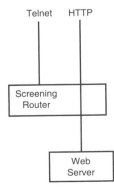

The allow-all policy defines certain services that won't be allowed. For example, to prevent people from logging in, one would deny Telnet and rlogin services. This is not as safe as deny-all, because some services may be overlooked, leaving a backdoor open.

Using screening routers, it is possible to restrict certain types of traffic to certain specific machines; for example, allowing e-mail to every machine may not be necessary, in which case, one would limit e-mail access to only the one machine.

It may also be desirable to limit who can access the Internet from inside the company. It would be possible for employees to, knowingly or not, transfer information outside of the company. Blocking access to the Internet is discussed in a later section.

> **Tip**
>
> Always limit as much as possible, to reduce your risk. Only allow the minimum services through your router that are absolutely necessary and, then, only to the machines that must have them.

Application Gateways

Instead of using a router to pass or deny traffic, it is possible to have programs that decide whether or not to allow specific commands. These are commonly called application gateways, since they are specific to the application they are running (see fig. 7.15).

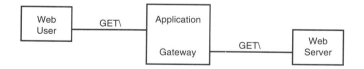

Fig. 7.15
Traffic is kept separate using application gateways.

An example of an application gateway would be a proxy server. Proxy servers allow connections on each side of a network to communicate to each other, but the traffic can be analyzed and limited. For example, using a proxy Web gateway, one might allow GET access but not POST access.

Application gateways often have performance problems, since each network transaction must be checked to be sure it is not doing anything inappropriate. Some application gateways may require slightly different commands than the ones to which users have become accustomed.

Application gateways are, however, very good at auditing and logging accesses, and often are used in conjunction with a screening router.

One of the main problems with an application gateway is the fact that a single compromise makes the entire network vulnerable. Once an account on the gateway machine is broken, it can be used to attack the internal network as a whole.

Using a Combination of Security

Most sites that are connected to the Internet use a combination of these security tools. A common firewall setup would involve one or two screening routers surrounding an application gateway. This offers some protection to the gateway host, as well as reducing risks to the internal network, if a gateway-host compromise occurs. See figure 7.16.

Fig. 7.16
Many sites use multiple protections.

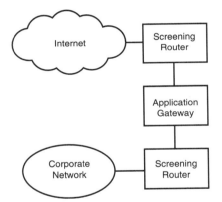

Allowing Users To Safely Access the Internet

To really take advantage of the Internet, users must be able to retrieve information from it. Many people think of the Internet as all fun and games, but there is a wealth of useful business information available as well. This section will discuss ways to allow users to access such information from the Internet safely.

Internet Threats

There are two main threats when allowing users to access the Internet. They are: viruses, and information leaks. The risks from both can be reduced by a few simple technical solutions and by educating prospective users.

Viruses

Viruses are programs that replicate themselves to other files on the same machine and also to other machines. They may or may not be destructive, but they are most certainly always a nuisance.

Viruses can only be controlled by having users scan files on their local machines before using them. Even though all traffic may go through a firewall, it is still not possible to check all the information for viruses.

> **Caution**
>
> Even if it were possible to have your firewall scan for viruses, if people transfer files via other means (such as floppies or tapes) they are still vulnerable.

There are many different type of virus software available both free and commercially. Choose one that is most suitable and make a definite practice of running it.

> **Note**
>
> Virus software must be current to be effective. New viruses are found every day; some can't be found with older virus scanners. Always get the latest version available and keep upgrades current.

Information Leaks

There are many ways for outsiders to break into your network and it is important to reduce the risk if they do. By limiting ease of access to information from within the company, confidential data is protected in the event your site is compromised.

One of the most popular ways to limit information leakage is by using a firewall to limit who can send out information. Information can be sent many different ways, however, and can't be eliminated without disconnecting from the Internet entirely.

The easiest way to limit exposure is to limit what information can get out to the Internet. This is done by blocking direct access out of the company at the router. To allow people to get out to the Internet, install either a proxy server or SOCKS.

Proxy servers are transparent to the user and are available for many different protocols. However, each protocol must have a separate proxy server.

SOCKS, on the other hand, is a more generic tool which can be used with any protocol; however, SOCKS necessitates some changes to the client software. Such software is considered to be *SOCKSified*.

Sharing Your Private Server

There may be times when your private server needs to be accessed from other companies. You may do this via dial-up connections, dedicated network links, or over the Internet.

Using Dial-Up Connections

If users need only access the Web server infrequently, it might make sense to install a dial-in modem. This connection can be running PPP software to allow full network access, or could just be used as a dumb terminal to allow simple access via lynx.

Dial-up connections can be password-protected to eliminate unauthorized use. Using Caller ID (CID) can reduce the risk even more, by enabling one to restrict telephone answering to certain authorized numbers.

Dial-up lines are the most secure way of allowing access into your network, but are usually too slow for simultaneous multiple-party use.

Using a Dedicated Link

If sharing data among sites, you may want to consider a dedicated high-speed link. These links can be ISDN, Frame Relay, or a T1 link.

Dedicated links are only as secure as the network you are connecting to. If the other network can be broken into, so can yours. Therefore, it makes sense to protect yourself from this link, just as you would do so from the Internet in general (see fig. 7.17).

Fig. 7.17
Treat any connection outside your company as hostile.

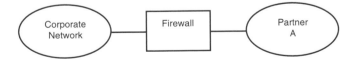

Using Router Access Lists

If you are using the Internet to allow other users to access your company server, or a dedicated line to another company, it might be a good idea to set up an access list on your router.

Setting up an access list which restricts access to your Web server to a specific machine, or list of machines, is a good way to reduce the risk incurred when

connecting. Such risk may be further reduced by allowing only the most remote sites to connect to the port on which your server is running (check the
Port directive or the inetd.conf file).

This will help to protect from access via other means, such as NFS or FTP.

Password Protection

If there is no router to aid in protection, you should at least use the Apache
password protection. This will require valid user names and passwords to
access via the Web server.

Passwords are set up using the Auth and Limit directives in the access.conf
file. This is covered in detail in Chapter 5, "Apache Configuration".

> **Caution**
>
> Using the Web server password protection will protect you from attacks through the
> Web server software. It will not protect you from access by other means such as NFS
> or FTP.

Encryption

Passwords and access lists will provide limited protection but all of your
information is still sent "in the clear". This means anyone on a network
through which your traffic passes can still read the contents.

The only way to keep your information private is by using encryption. Encryption is a means of converting your data to code. For example a simple
way to hide your data would be to UUEncode it. UUEncode is a program that
convert files from 8-bit (binary) data to 7-bit data. This makes it unreadable
unless someone has the UUDecode program.

> **Caution**
>
> UUEncoding a file is not really a secure means of encryption, since all that is needed
> is the UUDecode program. This program is freely available from most FTP sites and is
> also distributed with all UNIX machines.

Using UUEncode will keep casual snoopers from seeing your information, but
a dedicated cracker can save all your information and then run it through
UUDecode in order to read it. A better alternative would be to use an encryption product such as PGP (Pretty Good Privacy) or RSA.

These packages require you to encrypt the data separately and then send it. It is not transparent, so if transparency is important, hardware encryption will be required.

Hardware encryption requires a separate device to be attached, either between you and your network, or between the two networks. An example would be an encrypting router, which will automatically scramble your network data so it will be unreadable. By setting up two encrypting devices at opposite sides of the network, you can have transparent encryption (see fig. 7.18).

Fig. 7.18
Using hardware encryption makes it transparent.

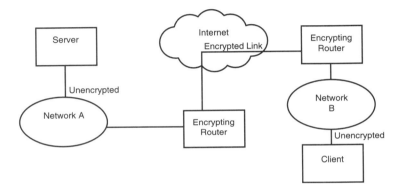

Running Internal and External Servers

Most companies will want to run two Web servers, one for public viewing and one for private use. There are different strategies available to keep these separate.

One Server, Two Directory Trees

◀ For more information about the directives covered in this section, see Chapter 5, "Apache Configuration," p. 73

The simplest way to have separate internal and external areas is to set up different directory areas on a single Web server. You can then use the Limit directive in the access.conf file to allow internal IP addresses access only to the private tree.

> **Caution**
>
> You must define restrictions for all directories, not just DocumentRoot. This includes alias and script directories. This is done by using the directives Limit and AllowOverides.

To set up the directory trees do the following:

1. Create two directories. One for internal and one for external access. They must not be subdirectories of each other.

2. Use the `Limit` directive to only allow internal IP addresses to get to the internal directory.

3. Disable per-directory overrides to make sure your `Limit` directive stays enforced. You can do this by using the `AllowOverides` directive. Set this to none.

Using the same server is the cheapest solution and can be used if there are no alternatives or your internal data is not that important. If the server is compromised, not only is your external data in danger, but your internal data is compromised as well.

One Machine, Two Servers

This strategy also only uses one machine and allows security for the cost-conscious. It offers slightly more protection than the previous example but is not the most secure option available.

Using this technique, you create two separate http configurations, including configuration files and DocumentRoots. This allows you to run separate server processes for internal and external accesses. You will probably want to run your external server on port 80 since that is where most people will look for it. Your internal serve can then run on any unused port.

Running separate servers allow you to configure your internal server to be more or less restrictive then your external server.

The following is how one sets up multiple servers on one machine:

1. Create two separate server directories, including configuration and document directories.

2. Configure your external server as you normally would, but configure your internal one with the same restrictions as the previous procedure. (Use the `Limit` and `AllowOverrides` directives.)

3. Configure your Internal server to use the non-standard port. This is done in either the httpd.conf file, using the `Port` directive, or in the inetd.conf file.

4. When you start your httpd server, you may need to use the `-d` or `-f` flags to point to the right configuration files.

◀ For detailed instructions on setting up Apache see Chapter 4, "Getting Started with Apache," p. 59

Two Machines, One Network

A better alternative to using one machine is to use two machines: one that serves the external pages, and one for internal access.

Using two machines protects your data, so long as unauthorized access remains restricted to only the one machine, your internal and external Web pages will never both be placed in jeopardy.

> **Caution**
>
> If any machine on your network has been compromised, it is possible that all of them have been. Crackers can install sniffer programs to watch the network for passwords and store them in a file or e-mail them to the cracker. The only way to get around this is to always encrypt your traffic.
>
> UNIX machines also can be set up to trust one another, either by creating a "/etc/hosts.equiv" file or by putting a ".rhosts" file in your home directory. Trusting a machine that has been compromised is a sure way to get broken into. Never trust your external Web server.

If one of your servers is compromised, that machine can be used to break into other machines on your network, either by installing a sniffer or taking advantage of host trust.

Two Machines, Two Networks

Having your two machines on the same network, as in the previous scenario, can be a problem if one of them is compromised.

An even better alternative is to separate the two machines by a firewall. This firewall can be as simple as a screening router or a series of routers and application gateways. See figure 7.19.

Fig. 7.19
Set up your external Web server outside your firewall.

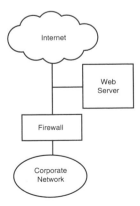

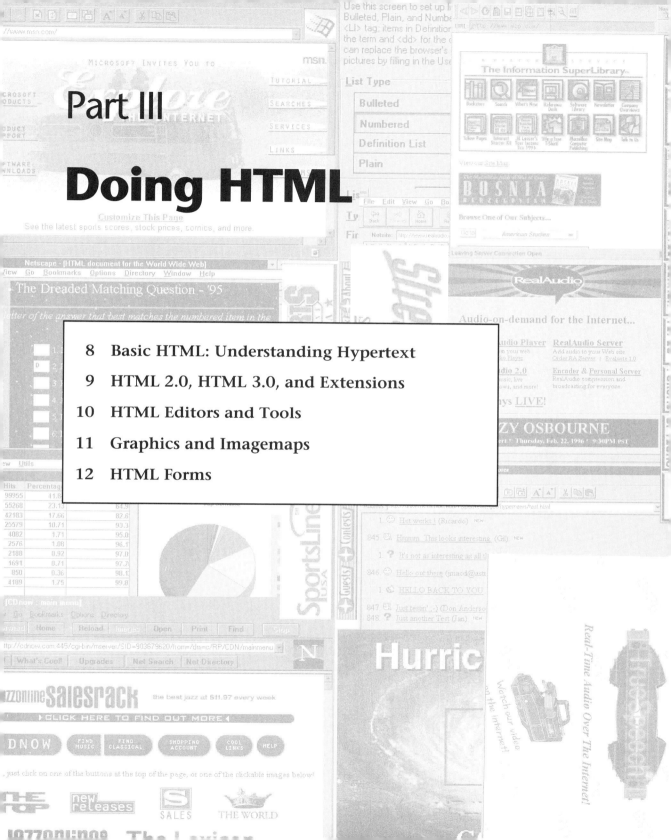

Part III

Doing HTML

## CHAPTER 8

Basic HTML: Understanding Hypertext

The whole point of setting up a Web site is so that users can access the information you place on the site. Publishing documents on the Web requires them to be prepared in *HyperText Markup Language (HTML)*, a page description language with provisions for linking related documents together. It is a simple, text-based language that you can view in a variety of fonts on any platform. You can use it with text-only clients, such as Lynx, on a VT220 terminal or with fully graphical clients, such as Mosaic, on advanced graphical workstations.

The present version of HTML, otherwise known as *HTML 2.0*, is the most commonly used version. Most clients support HTML 2.0, but a few, such as Netscape Navigator and Microsoft Internet Explorer, support additional features, such as blinking text or background sounds, that are not in any HTML specification. Most of this chapter covers standard HTML. Future standards for HTML will include features such as style sheets, tables, support for embedding objects, and possibly a framework for implementing experimental features. The future of HTML promises to make strides toward a universal document format that is both compact and rich in formatting.

In this chapter, you will learn the basics of HTML, including:

- The basic structure of an HTML document
- How to format text into headings, paragraphs, and lists
- The difference between physical and logical styles and how to apply these styles in your documents
- The GIF and JPEG graphical formats
- How to place inline images in a document
- How to set up hypertext and hypergraphic links to other documents

HTML Fundamentals

Before charging right into the HTML tutorial, it is helpful to review some introductory remarks on HTML to give you a sense of what it is, where it came from, and where it is heading.

History of HTML

HTML is an application of the Standard Generalized Markup Language (SGML). SGML arose out of the international standards community to meet the need for "structured" content, which could be validated algorithmically. In other words, SGML is an open, standards-based (ISO8879) language for describing document languages, and describes what their structure is (what "tags" can go in other "tags"). This definition occurs in a Document Type Definition, otherwise known as a DTD. When Tim Berners-Lee first started using HTML, it was not defined using a DTD, but thanks to the work of Dan Connolly and many others, its syntax and format were regularized and a DTD was created. Oftentimes, keeping HTML pure to its SGML background can be a challenge, but the benefits of this to the publishing community are too large to ignore.

> **Note**
>
> Refer to Que's *Special Edition Using SGML* for more information.

The first version of HTML, HTML 0, was developed at CERN in 1990 and is largely out of use today. HTML 1.0 incorporated inline images and text styles (highlighting) and was the version of HTML used by most of the initial Web browsers. HTML 2.0 is the current standard. The future of HTML is being decided by vendor-sponsored groups like the World Wide Web Consortium (**http://www.w3.org/**), or in volunteer standards groups like the IETF (**http://www.ietf.org/**).

HTML Tags

An HTML document is simply the informational text of the document with structural *tags* embedded in the text. These tags are character sequences that begin with a less-than sign (<) and end with a greater-than sign (>). Tags can be used to, among other things, apply a style to text, insert a line break, or place an image in the document. To the "purist," a tag signifies a structure—you're not just saying "make this phrase really big by putting an <H1> around it," you're saying "this is a first-level heading in my document." The idea is similar to older word processors and page layout systems that require insertion of formatting tags to specify bold, underlined, or italicized type. Newer word processors use the same premise, but usually hide these tags from the user. Some word processors, however, allow you to display the formatting tags—WordPerfect, for example, provides you with the Reveal Codes menu option.

For a look at some HTML, first consult figure 8.1, which shows the World Wide Web (W3) Consortium's home page (**http://www.w3.org/**). Choose the Document Source option from Netscape Navigator's View menu to activate a window with the HTML source loaded. The HTML source corresponding to figure 8.1 is shown in figure 8.2.

Inline image   Title   Level 1 heading

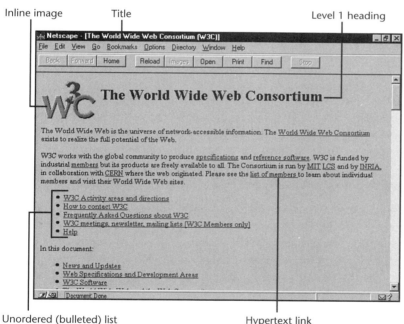

Unordered (bulleted) list   Hypertext link

Fig. 8.1
The W3C home page as displayed by the Netscape Navigator.

III

Doing HTML

Level 1 heading · Title · Inline image

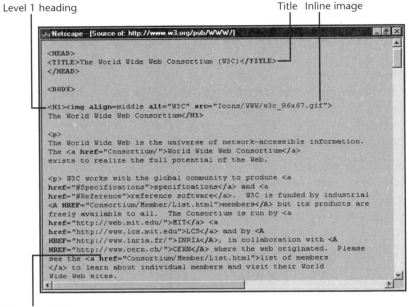

Fig. 8.2
Netscape allows you to view the HTML source of the document in the browser window.

Hypertext link

Viewing the source code of a document is a great way to learn HTML, but you should be aware that not all browsers have this feature. In addition to differences in features, you should also know that different browsers often display the same page in different ways. Figure 8.3 shows the W3C home page in Lynx, a text-only browser. Notice how the elements pointed out in figures 8.1 and 8.2 are rendered differently in Lynx.

You should also be extremely cautious about simply learning by example; while sometimes someone is able to get an interesting effect with a particular tag combination, sometimes this combination is illegal by the specifications. Even though it might look all right in the browser you are using, other browsers may not be able to handle it at all, even if they completely conform to the spec. When in doubt, consult the specs.

The differences in browser rendering are not a significant problem with the basic HTML formatting tags, but they can be an issue when your documents contain more advanced HTML, particularly those tags that are extensions to HTML supported by only a few browsers. This points to an important challenge in creating Web documents: how to incorporate the advanced features while not breaking browsers that can't render those features. As you read this chapter and the next, note the suggestions for writing browser-friendly HTML. Following these suggestions will make your documents accessible to the largest audience possible.

Hypertext link   Inline image   Title   Alternative text for Image

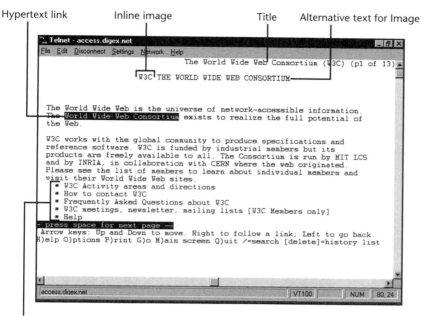

Fig. 8.3
The W3C home page
as displayed by
Lynx.

Unordered (bulleted) list

Platform Independent

Most of HTML's formatting features specify logical rather than physical styles. For example, the heading tags, which normally indicate larger font sizes, do not specify which size to use. Instead, a browser chooses a size for the heading that is larger than its default text size. This allows Macs to view files written on PCs and served by UNIX boxes. This also allows clients like Lynx to render the important text in all caps, if it can't handle changing the font size or color. Even though you can't control the exact font and size with logical structures, it's best to leave it up to the client to handle that logical-to-presentational formatting, since only the client best understands its own rendering limitations.

Three Basic Rules

In spite of the differences between them, Web browsers do consistently follow three rules when parsing HTML. These are:

- White space is ignored
- Tags are not case-sensitive
- Most tags occur in pairs

III

Doing HTML

White Space Ignored

The fact that browsers ignore white space is often a source of frustration for the beginning HTML author. Consider the following HTML:

```
<TITLE>Our Mailing Address</TITLE>
Que Corporation
201 West 103rd Street
Indianapolis, IN  46290-1097
```

The address looks fine on the page, but notice how NSCA Mosaic renders it in figure 8.4.

Fig. 8.4
Carriage returns in the HTML source code don't translate to carriage returns on the browser screen.

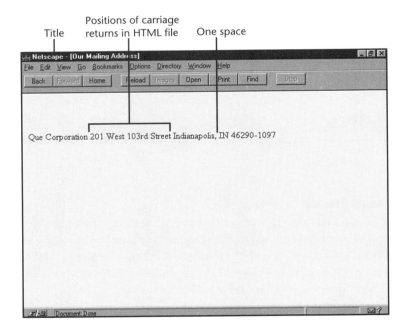

Mosaic tries to display the address all on one line! The carriage returns in the file, which make the address look fine in an editor or on a printout, are ignored by the browser. The same is true of other white space characters like tabs and extra spaces. In the HTML above, there are two spaces between IN and 46290-1097, but only one space between them in the browser window. The second space character is ignored.

Formatting Tags Are Not Case-Sensitive

You can write all HTML formatting tags in upper-, lower-, or mixed case. For example, browsers interpret <TITLE>, <title>, and <Title> the same way.

Most Formatting Tags Occur in Pairs

With only a few exceptions, HTML formatting tags occur in pairs in which the beginning tag activates an effect and the ending tag turns off the effect. Tag pairs are often called *container tags,* since the effects they turn on and off are applied to the text they contain. For example, to specify that a line of text appears in bold, you write:

```
<B>This text will appear in bold.</B>
```

The ending tag in the pair is always preceded by a slash. Among the basic HTML tags, those that do not have a companion ending tag include: <BASE> (base information),
 (line break), <HR> (horizontal rule), and <IMG> (image).

Uniform Resource Locators (URLs)

While not directly related to HTML, *Uniform Resource Locators* (*URLs*) are an important part of HTML documents used in many different tags. For this reason, a quick primer on URLs is in order.

A URL is basically the address of a document on the World Wide Web. The URL is a way of compactly identifying any document on any type of Web-compatible server anywhere in the world. The URL consists of four parts: an "access scheme," Internet address, port, and object. With the exception of the "news" and "mailto" access schemes, the general format for a URL is as follows:

access-scheme://internet_address:port/object

In addition, you can optionally specify search or query information after the object when sending data to a search or script. This is covered in Chapter 12, "HTML Forms."

Access Scheme

The *access scheme* indicates what type of Internet application is requested. Usually an "access scheme" maps directly to an Internet protocol, as is the case with "http," but not always. NNTP for example has both "nntp" and "news" schemes. In order to use a given protocol, both the client (browser) and Internet server must be able to speak that protocol. The most common protocol in Web documents is "http" (HyperText Transfer Protocol), which is spoken by all Web servers and clients. In addition, almost all browsers support FTP, Gopher, Telnet, and News. Some also support WAIS. Some fictional examples of URLs using these protocols follow:

http://webwise.walcoff.com/frontier/pick.html

ftp://ftp.fedworld.gov/pub/irs-pdf/form1040.pdf

III

Doing HTML

gopher://gopher.government.gov/reports/census.txt

telnet://loc.gov

news:sci.psychology.clinical

mailto:info@netscape.com

Note

The news URL is substantially different than the others because it does not specify an Internet address or file name. Instead, it simply names a newsgroup. The name of the news server must be made known to the browser when you initially configure the browser.

Where To Get News

To read Internet news through a Web browser, you have to be able to connect to a news server, which continually receives messages over the Internet and stores them locally for a short time (usually about two weeks). Newsfeeds cost money, and for this reason, no news servers are publicly available on the Internet. If your site wishes to take full advantage of Internet news, you must obtain a newsfeed from your Internet service provider or obtain authorization to connect to your provider's news server.

The mailto: URL allows you to send electronic mail to the specified address directly from your browser. The mailto: URL is supported by Netscape, Lynx, and others, but it isn't supported by all browsers.

Address

The address portion of a URL is simply the hostname or IP (Internet Protocol) number of an Internet server. This address can be either the familiar named dot notation (like **ftp.ncsa.uiuc.edu**) or a number sequence (like **127.0.0.1**).

Port

The port is an optional URL element. If the port is omitted, the default port for the specified protocol is assumed. In the case of HTTP, this is 80.

File Name

The document path, or *file name,* is the same as that used by DOS and UNIX systems alike, although the slash is forward (/) rather than backward (\) for

DOS users. Each slash goes down to the next subdirectory having the speci-fied name, and the path ends in a file name with an extension (such as TXT or HTML). It is also possible to specify a path to an entire directory simply by ending with the directory name and a trailing slash (/). For example, to see the contents of the fruits directory on an FTP server, you can use:

ftp://ftp.healthy.com/fruits/

A URL that specifies a protocol, Internet address, and file name is said to be an *absolute URL*. In some cases, it is also possible to specify one URL relative to another, resulting in a *relative* URL. For example, suppose your base URL is **http://www.healthy.com/fruits/citrus/tarty_fruits.html** and you need to specify the URL of the file intro.html located in the fruits directory (one directory level up from citrus). You can do this with the absolute **URL http://www.healthy.com/fruits/intro.html**, but it can also be appro-priate to give the URL relative to the base URL. In this case, the relative URL would be "../intro.html." The two dots followed by a forward slash (../) are an indicator to move up one directory level. If you need to specify the URL of the file "lemonade.html" in the lemons directory (a subdirectory of the citrus directory), you can use the relative URL "lemons/lemonade.html."

Note

The base URL for a document is specified in the <BASE HREF="*base_url*"> tag. If this tag is not present, then the base is determined by the browser by whatever URL it used to access the document. <BASE> tags are not mandatory. This tag is discussed in the Document Structure portion of the next section.

General HTML Style

While you are generally free to write HTML any way you want, there are a few issues of style to keep in mind. If you're just starting out, take these style issues to heart and develop good authoring habits from the onset. If you've been writing HTML for a while and have perhaps "forgotten" about some of the aspects of good style, this is a great time to remind yourself of them and work them back into your documents.

Uppercase Tags

While it is true that HTML tags are not case-sensitive, it is a good idea to always make them all uppercase. Remember that tags are embedded in other text and this can make them difficult to read when writing or editing HTML. Tags that are all uppercase stand out much better in a sea of text.

Remember, though, that URL's *are* case sensitive.

Document Structure

It used to be that a discussion of HTML document structure would be right at the beginning of an HTML tutorial. However, since most browsers can still parse an HTML file without the structure-defining tags, many authors have fallen out of the habit of including these tags in their documents and their inclusion becomes an issue of style. Good HTML style suggests that you always include tags to define the major parts of your documents. The three major parts are:

- The HTML declaration
- The document head
- The document body

The HTML Declaration

The HTML declaration is simply accomplished by making the <HTML> tag the first thing in your file and making the </HTML> tag the last thing in your file. These container tags say "Everything between us is HTML code."

The Document Head

The document head should immediately follow the <HTML> tag and is contained in the <HEAD> ... </HEAD> tag pair. The document head contains information about the document that is typically transparent to the user. While many informational items can be specified in the document head, the two that you should always include are the title and the base URL of the document.

The document's title is designated with the <TITLE> ... </TITLE> tag pair. You should make your titles descriptive, while still keeping them fairly short. A forty character title is a good rule of thumb. Document titles typically appear at the top of the browser window (refer to fig. 8.1). They are also used in bookmark files.

The base URL of the document is given in the <BASE HREF="*base_url*"> tag. You really only need to set this if you anticipate someone arriving at your page through a URL other than the one on which you wish to base relative URL links.

The Document Body

The document body immediately follows the head and is enclosed in the <BODY> and </BODY> tags. The body contains all of the information that will be presented to the user and the tags used to format that information.

Putting these three parts of the document together, you create a basic template for an HTML document (see listing 8.1)

Listing 8.1   HTML Document Template

```
<HTML>
<HEAD>
<TITLE>Document Title</TITLE>
</HEAD>
<BODY>
Information and formatting commands
</BODY>
</HTML>
```

Many HTML editing programs make this basic template available to you when you create a new document. If you're using a word processor or a simple text editor to write HTML, you can probably create and store this template easily. In either case, there's no reason not to include the structure-defining tags.

Getting Started

To start writing HTML, all you really need is an editor that allows you to save files in ASCII format and a browser to test your documents. If you plan to include images in your documents, you'll need a graphics program as well.

III

Doing HTML

Editor

On UNIX, many people will claim that the best editors are the same editors people on UNIX have been using for a long time, namely, *Emacs* and *vi*. vi is a very simple text editor. Crafted for an era of low memory requirements and small feature sets, "vi" is relatively easy to use but not incredibly full-featured. Emacs, on the other hand, is a very full-featured application. It has a built-in LISP interpreter; one particularly relevant Emacs-LISP module that has been created is the "HTML-Mode" module. Not only will it automatically give you all the default elements of an HTML document when you edit a new file named ".html," it also colors different tags and structural elements, making it very easy to see the difference between an <H1> tag section and an <A> section. More information on these will be provided later.

Browser

You only really need one browser to test your documents, but it's a good idea to look at your HTML files in two or three browsers to make sure your code is as browser-friendly as possible. It's easy to get a copy of the popular browsers. NCSA Mosaic 2.0 and Netscape Navigator 2.0 are available for public download on Mosaic (**ftp://ftp.ncsa.uiuc.edu/Mosaic/**) and Netscape's FTP (**ftp://ftp.netscape.com/**) sites. A browser that actually implements more of the future HTML features is Arena (**http://www.w3.org/pub/WWW/Arena/**), an experimental browser developed and maintained as a reference software piece by the W3C. It should be noted that UNIX only accounts for about 15 percent of the browser market as of this writing, so to really test your pages, it would be wise to check them out on Windows and Mac browsers as well.

HTML Tutorial

With the preliminaries covered, you're now ready to learn the basic HTML tags. All of the tags discussed in this section are found in the document body (between the <BODY> and </BODY> tags) and fall into several categories:

- Paragraphs and line breaks
- Heading styles
- Physical styles
- Logical styles
- Lists
- Special characters
- Horizontal lines

- Images
- Hypertext and hypergraphics

Paragraphs and Line Breaks

The <P> tag is used to indicate the start of a new paragraph. Paragraphs are separated by a blank line. To start a new paragraph without the extra line of separation or to just move to the next line, use the <BR> tag (line break). Line breaks were needed back in figure 8.4 to render an address properly. Figure 8.5 shows the difference between paragraphs and line breaks. Listing 8.2 shows the corresponding HTML.

Listing 8.2   HTML for Figure 8.5

```
<P>Que is the premiere publisher of Internet-related books.
Be sure to visit our Web site at http://www.mcp.com/que/
for more information.
<P>Our mailing address is:
<P>Que Corporation<BR>
201 West 103rd Street<BR>
Indianapolis, IN  46290-1097
```

Paragraph breaks   Title   Line breaks

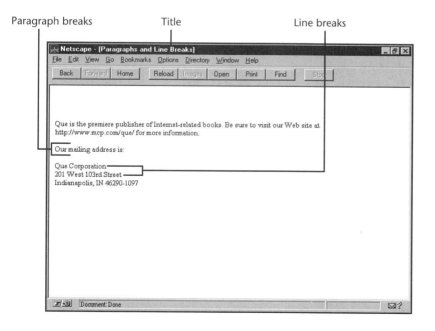

Fig. 8.5
Paragraphs and line breaks help to offset sections of a document.

III

Doing HTML

Heading Styles

HTML supports six heading styles, which are used to make text stand out by varying degrees. These are numbered one through six, with one being the largest. To format text in a heading style, enclose it in the <H*n*> and </H*n*> tags, where *n* is the number of the heading style you want to apply. Figure 8.6 shows how the six heading styles are rendered in Microsoft Internet Explorer by default. The corresponding HTML is shown in listing 8.3.

Listing 8.3   HTML for Figure 8.6

```
<H6>Heading Style 6</H6>
<H5>Heading Style 5</H5>
<H4>Heading Style 4</H4>
<H3>Heading Style 3</H3>
<H2>Heading Style 2</H2>
<H1>Heading Style 1</H1>
```

Fig. 8.6
Headings are used to name and separate sections of a document.

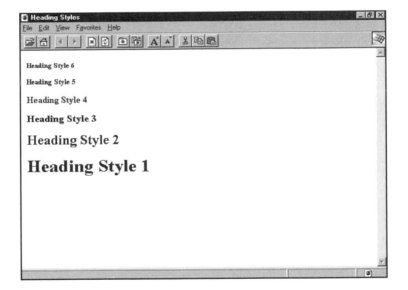

Note

In addition to changing the size of the text and making it boldface, applying a heading style adds some white space above and below the line containing the heading.

Physical Styles

Physical styles are actual attributes of a font, such as bold or italic. HTML supports the four physical styles shown in table 8.1. To apply a physical style, simply place the text to be formatted between the appropriate tag pair shown in the table.

Table 8.1 Physical Styles in HTML	
Name	**Tag**
Bold	`<B>...</B>`
Italics	`<I>...</I>`
Underline	`<U>...</U>`
Typewriter (fixed-width)	`<TT>...</TT>`

> **Note**
>
> According to the HTML specification, browsers are not required to support any text styles. Do not assume that any given style is available in all browsers. In many browsers, for example, the underline style is reserved for displaying hyperlinks. These browsers will ignore the `<U>` and `</U>` tags, as shown in figure 8.7.

Underline style ignored

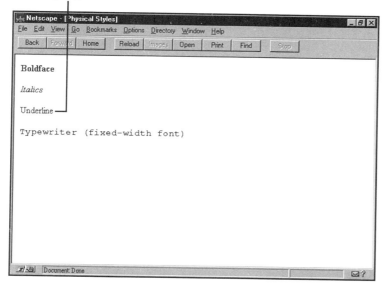

Fig. 8.7
Physical styles are used to render text in boldface, italics, or a fixed width. The underline style is frequently not supported.

> **Note**
>
> The HTML specification allows nesting of physical text styles, though not all browsers support this. For example, "<B>Hello, <I>brown</I> cow</B>" makes sense, but be careful, because something like "<B>Hello, <I>brown</B> cow</I>" does not, and may cause some browsers to crash.

Logical Styles

Logical styles indicate the meaning of the text they mark in the context of the document. Since they are not related to font attributes, logical styles can be rendered differently on different browsers. Table 8.2 lists the common logical styles and their meanings and typical renderings. Closing tags are required for all logical styles, but have been omitted in the table to save space. To create a closing tag, just add a slash before the tag name, like </ADDRESS>.

Table 8.2 Logical Styles in HTML

Style Name	Tag	Typical Rendering
Address	<ADDRESS>	Italics
Block quote	<BLOCKQUOTE>	Left and right indent
Citation	<CITE>	Italics
Code	<CODE>	Fixed-width font
Definition	<DFN>	Bold or bold italics
Emphasis	<EM>	Italics
Keyboard	<KBD>	Fixed-width font
Sample	<SAMP>	Fixed-width font
Strong	<STRONG>	Bold
Variable	<VAR>	Italics

Figure 8.8 shows how Netscape renders many of the logical styles. Listing 8.4 shows the corresponding HTML.

Listing 8.4   HTML for Figure 8.8

```
<H1>Logical Styles</H1>
According to <CITE>Corporate Manual of Style</CITE>,
you <EM>must</EM> include your
<VAR>e-mail address</VAR> below the signature block
of your business letters. Specifically:
<BLOCKQUOTE>Employees with electronic mail addresses
<STRONG>must</STRONG> include them in the signature block.
For example:<BR>
Mary Simpson<BR>
Account Representative<BR>
<ADDRESS>msimpson@abc_corp.com</ADDRESS>
</BLOCKQUOTE>
```

Blockquote   Citation   Emphasis   Variable

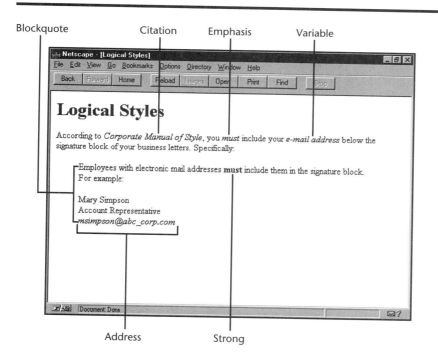

Fig. 8.8
The logical styles,
shown here in
Netscape, describe
the meaning of
marked up text as
it relates to the
document.

Address   Strong

Note

While some browsers allow it, nesting logical styles often does not make sense. For
example, why would you ever put a block quote inside keyboard input?

III

Doing HTML

Physical versus Logical Styles

As you look at the typical renderings in table 8.3, you probably noticed that you can accomplish almost all of them by using the physical styles. If you did notice, you're likely asking "Why should I use the logical styles?" An "official" answer is: to give a contextual meaning to the text that you're marking up. Formatting doesn't really matter with the logical styles; it's the meaning they impart that is important. Such an official answer would come from a person who subscribes to the school of thought that HTML is a page-description language only.

Authors who use HTML as a design tool are likely to cast aside such official responses and just use the physical styles to get the same effect. After all, it is easier to type <I>info@abc_corp.com</I> than it is to type <ADDRESS>info@abc_corp.com</ADDRESS>.

The decision to use physical styles, logical styles, or both ultimately rests with each author, based on his or her take on whether HTML is for page description or page design.

Preformatted Text

Text tagged with the <PRE> and </PRE> tags is treated as *preformatted text* and rendered in a fixed-width font. Since each character in a fixed-width font has the same width, it is easy to line up text into columns and produce a table. Listing 8.5 produces the table you see in figure 8.9.

Listing 8.5   HTML for Figure 8.9

```
<H1>Preformatted Text</H1>
<PRE>
User Name               Login ID        Disk Space
- - - - - - - - - - - -  - - - - - - -   - - - - - - - - -
Terri Johnson           tjohnson           15 MB
Fred Hansen             fredh              15 MB
Pat Norton              pnorton            20 MB
</PRE>
```

Note

Extra spaces, tabs, and carriage returns inside the <PRE> and </PRE> tags are *not* ignored.

Preformatted text

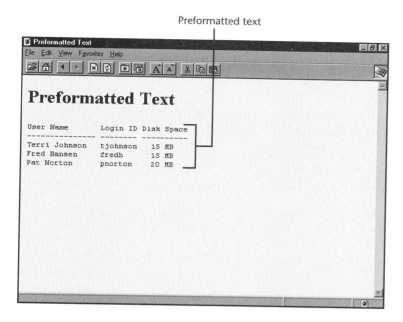

Fig. 8.9
Preformatted text is rendered in a fixed-width font and includes extra white space characters, making it easy to create tables.

Tip

Before you make all of your tables with preformatted text, you should look into the table tags proposed for future versions of HTML. Many browsers, such as Netscape and Mosaic, already support these tags.

Lists

HTML lists provide an easy and attractive way to present information in your documents. All lists require a pair of tags for the type of list and for each list item. Table 8.3 lists three types of formatted lists.

Table 8.3   Formatted Lists in HTML

Type	List Tag	Item Tag(s)
Ordered	<OL>...</OL>	<LI>...</LI>
Unordered	<UL>...</UL>	<LI>...</LI>
Description	<DL>...</DL>	<DD>...</DD>,<DT>...</DT>

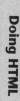

III

Doing HTML

Items in an ordered list are automatically numbered by the browser, starting with the number one. The automatic numbering is convenient, because it spares you from having to do it if you rearrange list items. Unordered list items are bulleted rather than numbered. Description lists allow you to present a term, followed by a description below and indented under the term.

Note

Description lists are sometimes called *definition lists* since they are useful in presenting the term/definition structure of a glossary.

List items in all three list types are indented from the left margin, making it easy to distinguish them from the rest of the body text.

Figure 8.10 shows examples of unordered, ordered, and description lists as produced by listing 8.6.

Listing 8.6   HTML for Figure 8.10

```
<H2>Unordered Lists</H2>
<UL>
<LI>Bulleted list items</LI>
<LI>List items are indented</LI>
</UL>
<H2>Ordered Lists</H2>
<OL>
<LI>Numbered list items</LI>
<LI>List items are indented</LI>
</OL>
<H2>Description Lists</H2>
<DL>
<DT>First term</DT>
<DD>Description of first term</DD>
<DT>Second term</DT>
<DD>Description of second term</DD>
</DL>
```

Caution

Many browsers will "forgive" you if you leave off the </LI> tag at the end of a list item. The next <LI> tag is enough to tell the browser to end the current list item and start a new one. However, browsers *won't* forgive you if you leave off a </DT> or a </DD> tag, so don't forget them.

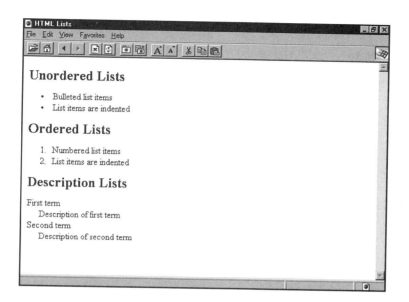

Fig. 8.10
Unordered, ordered, and description lists provide an easy way to break out information.

You can nest lists inside of other lists, as shown in figure 8.11. Listing 8.7 shows the HTML to produce this figure.

Listing 8.7   HTML for Figure 8.11

```
<H1>Nested Lists</H1>
<UL>
<LI>Basic HTML</LI>
<OL>
<LI>Text formatting</LI>
<LI>Graphics</LI>
<LI>Hyperlinks</LI>
</OL>
<LI>Advanced HTML</LI>
<OL>
<LI>HTML 2.0</LI>
<LI>HTML 3.0</LI>
<LI>Netscape Extensions</LI>
</OL>
</UL>
```

III

Doing HTML

Unordered list items   Nested ordered lists

Fig. 8.11
Nesting ordered
lists inside an
unordered list lets
you create an
outline structure.

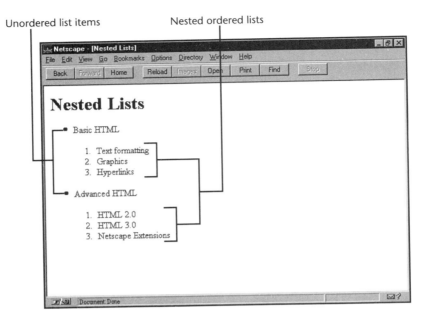

Special Characters

Because many characters have special meanings in HTML, it is necessary to
use special character sequences when you want special characters to show up
as themselves. You can also use special character sequences to produce foreign language characters and symbols. These are referred to as *SGML entities*.

Reserved Characters

Because the less than (<), greater than (>), and quotation mark (") characters
are used in HTML formatting tags, the characters themselves must be represented by special character sequences. The ampersand (&) is used in these
special sequences, so it also must be represented differently. Table 8.4 lists all
the special character sequences in HTML. The semicolon (;) is necessary to
indicate where the character description ends and normal text resumes.

Table 8.4 Special Character Sequences for HTML Reserved Characters

Sequence	Appearance	Meaning
&lt;	<	Less than
&gt;	>	Greater than
&amp;	&	Ampersand
&quot;	"	Quotation mark

If you're writing HTML code to produce HTML code on a browser screen, you will use the sequences in table 8.4 frequently. For example, to produce a list of the physical style tags, you would need to use the HTML shown in listing 8.8.

Listing 8.8   HTML for Producing a List of Physical Style Tags

```
<H2>HTML Physical Style Tags</H2>
<UL>
<LI>&lt;B&gt ... &lt;/B&gt;</LI>
<LI>&lt;I&gt ... &lt;/I&gt;</LI>
<LI>&lt;U&gt ... &lt;/U&gt;</LI>
<LI>&lt;TT&gt ... &lt;/TT&gt;</LI>
</UL>
```

The resulting screen is shown in figure 8.12.

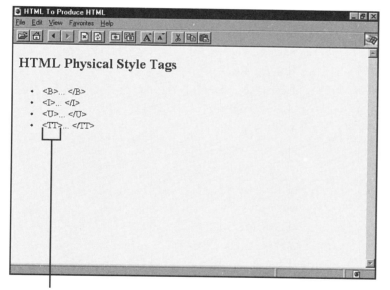

Less than (<) and greater than (>) signs
produced by special character sequences

Fig. 8.12
Writing HTML to produce on-screen HTML requires the use of special character sequences.

Foreign Language Characters

HTML uses the ISO-8859-Latin1 character set, which includes foreign language characters for all Latin-based languages. Since these characters are not on most keyboards, you need to use special character sequences to place them in your documents. Like the other special character sequences in

HTML, these sequences begin with an ampersand (&) followed by a written-out description of the character and a semicolon (;). Table 8.5 lists all the foreign-language sequences available.

Table 8.5	**Foreign Language Characters in HTML**
Character	**Sequence**
Æ,æ	&Aelig;,æ
Á,á	Á,á
Â,â	Â,â
À,à	À,à
Å,å	Å,å
Ã,ã	Ã,ã
Ä,ä	Ä,ä
Ç,ç	Ç,ç
Ð,ð	Ð,ð
É,é	É,é
Ê,ê	Ê,ê
È,è	È,è
Ë,ë	Ë,ë
Í,í	Í,í
Î,î	Î,î
Ì,ì	Ì,ì
Ï,ï	Ï,ï
Ñ,ñ	Ñ,ñ
Ó,ó	Ó,ó
Ô,ô	Ô,ô
Ò,ò	Ò,ò
Ø,ø	Ø,ø
Õ,õ	Õ,õ
Ö,ö	Ö,ö
ß	&szlig;
Þ,þ	Þ,þ
Ú,ú	Ú,ú
Û,û	Û,û
Ù,ù	Ù,ù

Character	Sequence
Ü,ü	Ü,ü
Ý,ý	Ý,ý
ÿ	ÿ

Characters by ASCII Number

You can reference any ASCII character in an HTML document by including the ampersand (&) and pound sign (#) followed by the character number in decimal and a semicolon (;). For example, to include the copyright symbol (©) in an HTML document, you write:

```
Copyright &#169;, 1996
```

However, this is dangerous because you cannot guarantee that the character set mapping will always be US-ASCII or Latin1. For example, a friend of mine was putting chemical information on the Web, and one synthesis involved heating a compound to "270° C." Unfortunately, one particularly incompetent browser decided to render "°" as a "0" instead of a "degree" sign, so his formula ended up asking to heat the compound to 2700 degrees C!

You can find more information on SGML entities, character sets, and more at **http://www.bbsinc.com/iso8859.html**.

Comments

It is possible to include comment lines in HTML that do not show up in browsers. You should consider placing comments in documents that you and others will be working on together. Many stand-alone HTML editors provide templates that include a comment area for information like the author's name and the date the document was last changed. The format for a comment is as follows:

```
<!-- Everything in here is part of the comment. -->
```

This is going to sound extremely bizarre, but for the purposes of compliance with SGML parsing rules, the number of "--" segments in the comment *must* be an even number, while "-" by itself can appear as often as it likes.

> **Note**
>
> Server side include commands embedded in HTML use the same character sequence as comments. This is so that the server-side include commands do not show up even when a server does not support server-side includes. More information about server side includes is available in later chapters.

III

Doing HTML

Nonbreaking Space

You can prevent a browser from breaking a line between two words by inserting a nonbreaking space between the words. Nonbreaking spaces are represented by the special character sequence .

Tip

Nonbreaking space characters can also be used to put in extra white space where you need it. A browser ignores the last two spaces in a sequence of three space characters, but it does print three spaces if you use   .

Horizontal Lines

Horizontal lines are a great way to break up sections of text-intensive documents. Placing a horizontal line is easy: just put an <HR> ("horizontal rule") tag in where you want the line to go. No closing tag is required.

Images

Without the visual appeal of inline images, it is doubtful that the World Wide Web would have become as popular as it has so rapidly. Graphical Web browsers such as Netscape Navigator, Mosaic, and Microsoft Internet Explorer can automatically display images in both the GIF and JPEG formats inside documents.

Graphics Formats: GIF and JPEG

GIF (Graphics Interchange Format) was originally developed for users of CompuServe as a standard for storing image files. Graphics stored in the GIF format are limited to 256 colors.

GIF supports two desirable Web page effects. The first is *interlacing,* in which non-adjacent parts of the image are stored together. As a browser reads in an interlaced GIF, the image appears to "fade in" over several passes. The other effect supported by the GIF format is *transparency*. In a transparent GIF, one of the colors is designated as transparent, allowing the background of the document to show through.

Transparent GIFs

A frequently asked question on the World Wide Web newsgroups is: "How can I create transparent GIFs?" Both UNIX and Windows users can use a program called *giftrans* to create transparent GIFs from existing images. Another useful tool for this purpose is "giftool." Pointers to both are available from **http://melmac.harris-atd.com/transparent_images.html**.

JPEG (Joint Picture Experts Group) refers to a set of formats that supports full color images and stores them in a compressed form. Most popular graphical browsers currently display JPEG images, though previously these images had to be viewed in a separate program. The *progressive JPEG* format, which has recently emerged, gives the effect of an image fading in just as an interlaced GIF would. Transparency is not possible with JPEG images because the compression tends to make small changes to the image data. If a pixel originally colored with the transparent color is given another color, or if a non-transparent pixel is assigned the transparency color, the on-screen results would be dreadful.

Tip

As a general rule, you should use JPEG for color photos so you can harness its full color capabilities. Other graphics and illustrations should be stored in the GIF format.

The <IMG ...> Tag

You must save images as separate files even though they are referenced and displayed inside an HTML document. To place an inline image on a page, you use the <IMG ...> tag.

Syntax: `<IMG SRC="URL">`

Inline images always aligned flush left, although future versions of HTML may allow centering and flush right alignment. For example, to place the World Wide Web Consortium's logo next to its name on its home page (refer to fig. 8.2), the HTML looked like:

```
<H1><IMG ALIGN=MIDDLE ALT="W3C" SRC="Icons/WWW/w3c_96x67.gif">The
World Wide Web Consortium</H1>
```

III

Doing HTML

The SRC attribute, which is mandatory, specifies the URL of the image file. Because URLs can point anywhere, you can reference images on remote servers as well as your local server. Browsers can load images from a server running any protocol supported by the browser, including FTP and Gopher. You can modify the `<IMG...>` tag by several other attributes as well (see table 8.6).

> **Note**
>
> Because browsers can load images from any server on the Internet, browsers establish separate server connections for each image in a document, even if all images are on the same server. For small images, it takes more time to establish the connection than to transfer the image data. Therefore, avoid numerous small images. This is largely fixed using persistent connections in HTTP/1.1.

Table 8.6   IMG Tag Attributes

Attribute	Description
`ALIGN={TOP¦MIDDLE¦BOTTOM}`	Location of text next to image
`ALT="text"`	Text to show instead of image
`ISMAP`	Used to make imagemaps

The ALIGN attribute controls the location of text that follows the image. By default, text appears at the bottom of an inline image. Figure 8.13 shows how you can use the ALIGN attribute to change the text to be aligned with the middle or top of the image. Specifically, ALIGN=MIDDLE aligns the baseline of the text with the middle of the image and ALIGN=TOP aligns the top of the text with the top of the image. Listing 8.9 shows the HTML for this figure.

Listing 8.9   HTML for Figure 8.13

```
<IMG SRC="/images/w3c.gif" ALIGN="MIDDLE">
The World Wide Web (W3) Consortium
<HR>
<IMG SRC="/images/w3c.gif" ALIGN="TOP">
The World Wide Web (W3) Consortium
```

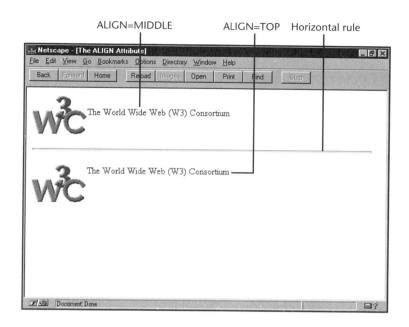

ALIGN=MIDDLE   ALIGN=TOP   Horizontal rule

Fig. 8.13
The ALIGN
attribute lets you
align text with the
middle and top of
an image.

The ALT attribute specifies alternate text to be shown in place of an image in
text-only browsers. Including the ALT attribute tag is a courtesy to dial-up
and dumb terminal users; don't overlook this courtesy. Also, graphical
browsers sometimes fail to load an image, in which case they use the text
specified by ALT instead. For example, to include text-only support in the
previous example, the line would look like this:

```
<IMG SRC="/images/w3c.gif" ALIGN="TOP" ALT="W3C Logo">
The World Wide Web (W3) Consortium
```

In Lynx, this line would appear as:

```
[W3C Logo]The World Wide Web (W3) Consortium
```

ISMAP is a stand-alone attribute that signifies that the image is to be used
as an imagemap. Imagemaps are discussed in Chapter 11, "Graphics and
Imagemaps."

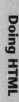

III

Doing HTML

Note

Two Netscape extensions to the <IMG ...> tag that bear an early introduction are WIDTH and HEIGHT. These attributes are set equal to the width and height of the image in pixels. The advantage of doing this is that it allows the browser to leave an appropriately-sized space for the image as it lays out the page. Thus, page layout is finished quickly, without having to wait for the image to load completely so that the browser can determine its size. Use of these tags is strongly recommended.

Hypertext and Hypergraphics

Now to the other half of the HyperText Markup Language—the hypertext part. A hypertext reference is very simple. It consists of only two parts: an anchor and a URL. The *anchor* is the text or graphic that the user clicks to go somewhere. The URL points to the document that the browser will load when the user clicks on the anchor.

In HTML, an anchor can be either text or a graphic. Text anchors usually appear underlined and in a different color than normal text on graphical browsers and in bold on text-only browsers such as Lynx. Graphic anchors (hypergraphics) usually have a colored border around them to distinguish them from plain graphics.

Creating Hypertext Anchors

Any text can be a hypertext anchor in HTML, regardless of size or formatting. An anchor can consist of a few letters, words, or even lines of text. The format for an anchor-address pair is simple:

```
<A HREF="URL">text of the anchor</A>
```

The letter A in the <A HREF> tag stands for "anchor." HREF stands for "hypertext reference." Everything between the <A HREF="*URL*"> and </A> tags is the text of the anchor, which appears underlined or bold, depending on the browser.

Note

Other formatting codes can be used in conjunction with hypertext anchors. For example, to create a text anchor that appears in the level 3 heading style, you write:

```
<A HREF="URL"><H3>text of the anchor</H3></A>
```

The order of nesting formatting codes is not important. It's also possible to write:

```
<H3><A HREF="URL">text of the anchor</A></H3>.
```

Creating Hypergraphics

You can use hypergraphics to create button-like effects and provide a nice alternative to clicking plain text. The format for a graphic anchor is the same as a text anchor. However, instead of putting text between the <A HREF> and </A> tags, you reference an inline image. Figure 8.14 shows a hypergraphic.

```
<A HREF="http://www.w3.org/"><IMG SRC="images/w3c.gif">
</A>Visit the World Wide Web (W3) Consortium's Home Page
```

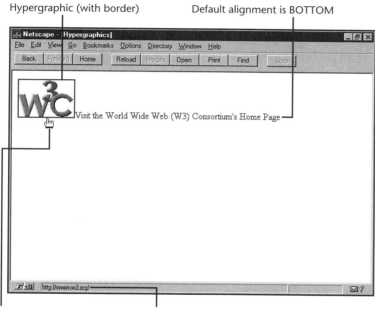

Hypergraphic (with border)   Default alignment is BOTTOM

Mouse pointer changes   URL specified by hyperlink
to a hand on a hyperlink

Fig. 8.14
Hypergraphics
create button-like
objects.

In this example, when the user clicks the W3C logo, the browser jumps to the W3C home page.

Tip

If text or images used in hypertext anchors don't seem to be working right, check to see that the URL in the <A ...> tag is completely enclosed in quotes. Omitting the final quotation mark is a common and easy mistake.

III

Doing HTML

Linking to a Named Anchor

When you link to another document, the browser shows information starting from the top of the linked document. This is fine, unless the document is long and the information you really want displayed isn't near the top. In this case, users have to scroll through the document to find the information you want them to see. An alternative to inflicting this on your users is to set up *named anchors* in longer documents and then have your hyperlink references point directly to the named anchors.

As an example, suppose you have a ten part document stored in a single file longdoc.html and that each section has its own heading. You can set up named anchors on each of the headings using the <A NAME="anchor_name"> and </A> tags as follows:

```
<A NAME="one"><H1>Part One</H1></A>
```

With all of the anchors established, you can instruct a browser to link to a specific anchor by including a pound sign (#) and the anchor's name at the end of the long document's URL:

```
View <A HREF="longdoc.html#seven">Part Seven</A>.
```

When users click on the hypertext "Part Seven," they are taken directly to part seven in the document, rather than to the top of the document from which they would have to scroll all the way down to part seven (see fig. 8.15).

Hypertext pointing to the named anchor   Named anchor text

Fig. 8.15
Linking to named anchors takes users right to the information you want them to see.

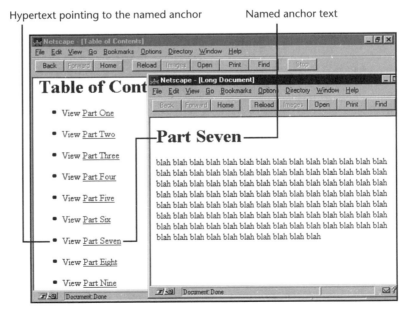

Tip

Named anchors let you set up a miniature "Table of Contents" at the top of long documents with links pointing to the different sections of the manuscript. Users appreciate this courtesy because it spares them from excessive scrolling and searching through the document.

III

Doing HTML

## CHAPTER 9

HTML 2.0, HTML 3.0, and Extensions

In the last chapter, you learned enough HTML tags to start authoring your own pages. Additionally, because these tags are known to almost every Web client program, the documents you write with them should be acceptable to all HTML 2.0-compliant Web browsers.

If you're like most Web authors though, you'll find yourself wanting finer control over your documents before too long. When you reach this point, you're ready to expand your command of HTML to include more advanced tags and tag attributes. But the control comes with a price: many of these advanced HTML entities are not understood by all browsers. Indeed, some of them can only be parsed by one browser! So as you include more advanced features, you increase the chances of "alienating" visitors from your site.

This chapter examines advanced HTML tags from three sources: the HTML 2.0 spec, which attempts to outline the currently accepted HTML standard; the proposed HTML 3.0 spec (which is formally expired, but still the basis for most future HTML work), which promises greater capacity for mathematical expressions and general layout control; and the Netscape extensions to HTML, which can only be properly rendered by the Netscape Navigator browser and other browsers which have chosen to be compatible with Netscape. In particular, you'll learn how to implement:

- The elements of HTML 2.0 beyond those discussed in Chapter 8
- New elements proposed for HTML, including tags for banners, figures, footnotes, admonishments, mathematical characters, and text styles
- Tables as proposed in the HTML 3.0 spec
- Netscape extensions to HTML that control image characteristics, produce rule and list effects, and enhance table spacing

- Frames as proposed by Netscape
- Simple Virtual Reality Modeling Language (VRML) and how to find tools that support VRML creation and viewing

The Evolving Standard

HTML was developed in 1990 at CERN, Europe's major research laboratory for high-energy physics. CERN's intent behind developing the World Wide Web and HTML was to facilitate a global exchange of research information among physicists. This was during a time when the Internet was still used largely for military, research, and academic purposes. The scientists at CERN probably did not anticipate that the Web would evolve into the popular application that it is today.

The evolution of the Web drove the evolution of HTML. The National Center for Supercomputing Applications (NCSA) at the University of Illinois released Mosaic, the first graphical Web client, in 1993, and its greatest claim to fame is a late night hack session which produced the <IMG> tag. Design became a greater issue as more people, desiring better looking pages, started using the Web. This shifted HTML's evolution in the direction of being a design language instead of just a way to mark up documents.

Last year, the HTML 2.0 specification was compiled and released as a Request for Comment (RFC) by the World Wide Web Consortium (W3C). The 2.0 spec sought to summarize the de facto HTML standard and describe how people should be using the HTML that was out there. Since then, the W3C and the Internet Engineering Task Force (IETF) have been considering proposals for future HTML revisions, along with the W3C.

What you are about to read is merely a summary of one instant in HTML's short but dynamic history. HTML will continue to evolve with the Web. The increasing popularity of Java and JavaScript have brought about the need for tags to build applets (Java "mini-applications") and script code right into HTML documents. Browser plug-in programs, like Macromedia's Shockwave, will drive the need for tags to embed other program items into Web pages. No doubt, in another year, the tags you are about to learn will be commonplace and newer tags will have taken their place on these pages.

Note

For the latest information on the HTML specs, visit W3C's Web site at **http://www.w3.org/pub/WWW/MarkUp/**.

HTML 2.0

As noted earlier, the HTML 2.0 spec was written to describe how HTML was being used at the time. The majority of the tags in this spec were covered in Chapter 8. Tags in the spec that were not covered in Chapter 8 are presented in the next three sections. These tags are "new" in the sense that this is the first place in the book that discusses them. They were not necessarily newly introduced as part of the HTML 2.0 spec.

> **Note**
>
> To read the September 22, 1995 release of the HTML 2.0 spec, direct your browser to **http://www.w3.org/pub/WWW/Markup/html-spec/html spec_toc.html**.

Document Type Definitions (DTD)

If you've looked at many HTML files, you've probably seen a tag at the very beginning of the file that looks like:

```
<!DOCTYPE HTML PUBLIC "-//IETF//DTD HTML//EN">
```

Such a tag is a *Formal Public Identifier (FPI)*. FPIs are used to specify the set of rules that apply SGML to the markup tags in the text, and map directly to a Document Type Declaration (DTD) that exists somewhere. Most FPIs you'll see are like the one above, though there are others specific to HTML 2.0, HTML 3.0, and Netscape extensions to HTML.

> **Tip**
>
> You can check your documents' conformance to established DTDs by submitting them to the HTML validation service at **http://www.webtechs.com/html-val-svc/**. The site also provides information on each of the DTDs you can check against.

New Elements in the Document Head

The 2.0 spec includes a number of tags beyond <BASE ...> and <TITLE> for the document head. Probably the most useful of these is the <META ...> tag, which is intended to contain document meta-information. <META ...> requires a name/content pair that can be specified by combinations of three attributes: HTTP-EQUIV, CONTENT, and NAME. HTTP-EQUIV is used to "simulate" an HTTP header right in the HTML document. If you don't

III

Doing HTML

use HTTP-EQUIV, you should use the NAME attribute to give the meta-information a unique name. CONTENT is set equal to the meta-information itself.

An emerging application of the <META ...> tag is for bulletins—messages that Web authors can put on their sites to notify users of changes. Some <META ...> tags that set up a bulletin might look like:

```
<META HTTP-EQUIV="Bulletin-Text" CONTENT="You can now order
from our new online catalog!">
<META HTTP-EQUIV="Bulletin-Date" CONTENT="Tues, 05-Mar-96
00:00:00">
```

The tags above would post a bulletin about the new online catalog at midnight on Tuesday, March 5, 1996. Web users who have bookmark management software that can receive bulletins would be notified of the new catalog by their programs.

The <META ...> tag can also be used to specify document keywords, expiration dates, and reply-to e-mail addresses. You can have as many <META ...> tags in the document head as you need.

Two other document head tags in the 2.0 spec are <NEXTID=n> and <LINK ...>. In the past, <NEXTID=n> was used to assign a unique numerical identifier (n) to a document. Nowadays it is rarely used and the spec discourages authors from including <NEXTID=n> tags in their HTML. The <LINK ...> tag takes the HREF attribute and specifies links to related documents. Related documents might include author information, indexes, glossaries, and earlier versions of the document. Just as with the <META ...> tag, you can put as many <LINK ...> tags in a document head as you like.

New Elements in the Document Body

A handy attribute for ordered, unordered, and description lists is the COMPACT attribute, which compels a browser to render a list in the most space-efficient form that it can. To make a list compact, you simply include the COMPACT attribute in the list's starting tag. Figure 9.1 shows two versions of the same list. The first list is rendered normally and the second is compacted. The HTML to produce the second list is:

```
<UL COMPACT>
<LI>HTML 2.0</LI>
<LI>HTML 3.0</LI>
<LI>VRML</LI>
</UL>
```

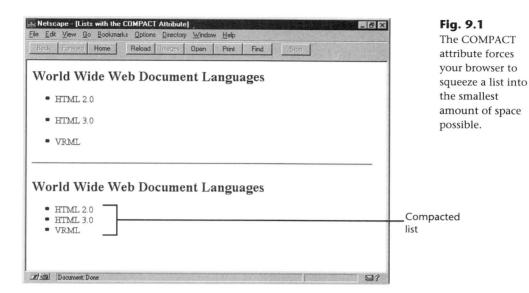

Fig. 9.1
The COMPACT attribute forces your browser to squeeze a list into the smallest amount of space possible.

The <A ...> tag picks up a few interesting, though infrequently used, attributes in the HTML 2.0 spec. The TITLE attribute is meant to suggest a title for the hyperlinked resource. REL and REV are attributes that describe a document's relationship to documents it links to or to documents that link to it, respectively.

The spec also mentions two sets of container tags: <XMP> ... </XMP> for marking up an example and <LISTING> ... </LISTING> for tagging a listing. These tag pairs were originally intended to work like <PRE> and </PRE> in that text between them was taken to contain no markup. However, not all browsers implement this intent consistently, so the spec discourages the use of these tags. You should stick with <PRE> and </PRE> instead.

Forms

The HTML 2.0 spec includes a set of tags used to produce online forms. Forms were an important step in the evolution of Web pages; they were the first means of user interactivity. Today forms are used to set up complicated database queries, conduct market research, take product orders, and collect user feedback. Once entered, form data is packaged and sent to a server for processing by a *script*. Scripts typically compose and return an HTML page as output.

▶ See "Creating Forms," p. 317, to learn how to construct HTML forms.

III

Doing HTML

HTML 3.0

The HTML 3.0 specification is in the final stages of its development and contains some exciting proposals for expanding HTML's ability to well-formatted documents including:

- A <RANGE ...> tag for the document head to facilitate searching
- New tags and attributes to give you finer control over page layout
- Several new physical and logical styles
- A <DIV ...> tag for marking specific divisions of a document (such as the abstract or an appendix)
- Support for footnotes
- A <NOTE ...> tag for including admonishments in your document
- New tags and entities for rendering mathematical characters
- A <FIG ...> tag with several useful attributes to support wrapping of text around figures and placement of captions and overlays
- Tags for creating tables without using preformatted text

The next several sections introduce many of these proposals.

The <RANGE ...> Tag

Placing a <RANGE ...> tag in the document head allows you to set up a range in the document for searching. <RANGE ...> takes the CLASS attribute, which is set equal to SEARCH to set up a search range, and the FROM and UNTIL attributes, which designate the beginning and end of the search range. A sample <RANGE ...> tag might look like:

```
<RANGE CLASS=SEARCH FROM="startspot" UNTIL="endspot">
```

The "startspot" and "endspot" markers are set up in the body of the document using the <SPOT ID="startspot"> and <SPOT ID="endspot"> tags at the points where you want the search range to begin and end, respectively.

Finer Layout Control

A number of HTML 3.0 proposals give authors greater control over page layout. One interesting proposal calls for the addition of <TAB ...> tag, which would allow you to set up your own tab stops in a document. To use a tab stop, you need to first define it using the ID attribute:

```
My first tab stop is <TAB ID="first">here, followed by some other
text.
```

The HTML above sets up the first tab stop in front of the letter "h" in the word "here." To use the tab stop, you use the <TAB ...> tag with the TO attribute:

```
<TAB TO="first">This sentence starts below the word "here."
```

On the browser screen, the "T" in the word "This" will be aligned directly below the "h" in the word "here."

Other enhancements to layout control come in the form of new attributes to existing tags. For example, under HTML 3.0, you can center headings and paragraphs using the ALIGN=CENTER attribute in your <H1>-<H6> and <P> tags. Additionally, the CLEAR attribute will be available on many tags, giving you the ability to clear one or both margins or to leave a specific amount of space between page items.

> **Note**
>
> When specifying a quantity of spacing, the units of the CLEAR attribute can be in pixels, en spaces, or em spaces; for example, CLEAR="5 en" or CLEAR="40 pixels."

Physical and Logical Text Styles

Several new physical and logical styles are proposed in the 3.0 spec. Tables 9.1 and 9.2 summarize these additions. Closing tags are left out of the tables in the interest of space.

Table 9.1   New Physical Styles Proposed in HTML 3.0

Style Name	Tag	Rendering
Strikethrough	<S>	Text is struck through with a slash (/)
Big	<BIG>	Makes text bigger than its current size
Small	<SMALL>	Makes text smaller than its current size
Subscript	<SUB>	Makes text a subscript
Superscript	<SUP>	Makes text a superscript

> **Note**
>
> The HTML 3.0 spec says that <SUB> and <SUP> tags are only appropriate inside the and container tags (discussed below), but the Netscape Navigator browser recognizes these tags outside of a mathematical context.

Table 9.2 New Logical Styles Proposed in HTML 3.0

Style Name	Tag
Abbreviation	<ABBREV>
Acronym	<ACRONYM>
Author name	<AU>
Deleted text	<DEL>
Inserted text	<INS>
Language context	<LANG>
Person's name	<PERSON>
Short quotation	<Q>

Note

Recall that logical styles are often rendered differently on different browsers. You'll need to experiment to see how your HTML 3.0 compatible browser renders these new styles.

Most of the new physical and logical styles are self-explanatory. Text marked with the <Q> style will appear in quotation marks appropriate to the document's language context. The <INS> and <DEL> styles are expected to be useful in the context of legal documents. The <PERSON> style marks a person's name for easier extraction by indexing programs.

The <DIV ...> Tag

The <DIV ...> and </DIV> tags work similarly to the <P> and </P> tags, except that <DIV ...> and </DIV> denote a special division of the document. The <DIV ...> tag takes the CLASS attribute, which describes the type of division being defined. Division types include abstracts, chapters, sections, and appendixes. The <DIV ...> tag can also take the attributes shown in table 9.3, allowing greater control over how that division is formatted. A sample <DIV ...> ... </DIV> container pair might look like:

```
<DIV CLASS=CHAPTER ALIGN=JUSTIFY CLEAR=ALL>
... the text of the chapter goes here ...
</DIV>
```

The above HTML produces a chapter that starts with clear left and right margins and that has justified text throughout.

Table 9.3   Attributes of the <DIV ...> Tag

Attribute	Purpose
CLASS	Specifies the type of document division being marked
ALIGN=LEFT ¦ RIGHT ¦ CENTER ¦ JUSTIFY	Sets the alignment for the entire division
NOWRAP	Turns off auto-wrapping of text. Text lines are broken explicitly with tags.
CLEAR=LEFT ¦ RIGHT ¦ ALL	Starts the division clear of left, right, or both margins

Note

You also can use the CLEAR attribute to specify spacing between the division and any page items around it. For example, CLEAR="2 em" leaves two em spaces between the division and the item it wraps around.

Footnotes

One HTML 3.0 proposal calls for an <FN ...> tag to define footnotes. To set up a footnote, you use the <FN ...> tag together with its ID attribute:

```
<FN ID="footnote1">HTML = HyperText Markup Language</FN>
```

Then, you must tag the footnoted text with an <A ...> ... </A> tag pair that includes an HREF pointing to the footnote. For "footnote1," you could tag every instance of the acronym "HTML" with:

```
<A HREF="#footnote1">HTML</A>
```

When users click on "HTML," they should see the footnote telling them what HTML stands for. The spec calls for footnotes to be displayed in pop-up windows, though it isn't clear that all browsers will be able to support this.

Admonishments

The <NOTE ...> tag lets you set up admonishments like notes, warnings, and cautions on your pages. The text of the admonishment appears between the <NOTE ...> and </NOTE> tags. Additionally, you can include an image with your admonishment using the SRC attribute of the <NOTE ...> tag. SRC and other attributes of <NOTE ...> are summarized in table 9.4.

III

Doing HTML

Table 9.4   Attributes of the <NOTE ...> Tag

Attribute	Purpose
CLASS=NOTE¦CAUTION¦WARNING	Specifies the type of admonishment
SRC="*url*"	Provides the URL of an image to precede the admonishment text
CLEAR=LEFT¦RIGHT¦ALL	Starts the admonishment clear of left, right, or both margins

As with the <DIV ...> tag, you can also use the CLEAR attribute to compel browsers to leave a certain amount of space between the admonishment and surrounding page items. A sample admonishment might look like:

```
<NOTE CLASS=WARNING SRC="images/stopsign.gif" CLEAR=ALL>WARNING!
You are
about to provide your credit card number to a non-secure server!</
NOTE>
```

Mathematical Symbols

If you've ever tried to prepare a document with mathematical content for the Web, you've probably ended up with a substantial headache. Prior to HTML 3.0, mathematical symbols like Greek letters, integral signs, and vector notations had to be read in and placed *as separate images* in the document. Just imagine the number of <IMG ...> tags required, to say nothing about the effort it would take to align them properly! The HTML 3.0 spec calls for tags and entities to make the preparation of mathematical documents much less agonizing.

Under the proposal, all mathematical tags and entities need to be contained inside the and tags. Greek letters are to be drawn from the Symbol font and are incorporated into documents with their entity names. For example, ψ would produce a lowercase psi (ψ) and Ψ would produce an uppercase psi (Ψ). Other variables, notations, and operator symbols are built in through a *large* number of special tags and entities. For a complete run down on the proposals for these new tags and entities, direct your browser to **http://www.hp.co.uk/people/dsr/html3/ maths.html**.

Tip

If you are familiar with the LaTex language for mathematical typesetting, you should have little trouble with HTML math formatting; the two use very similar approaches. If you don't have experience with LaTex and you will be preparing documents with mathematical content for the Web, you can get a jump on things by reading up on LaTex before the HTML math tags and entities become widely supported.

The <FIG ...> Tag

The <FIG ...> tag has been proposed as an alternative to the <IMG ...> tag for larger graphics. As you might expect, <FIG ...> requires the SRC attribute to specify the URL of the image file to be loaded. <FIG ...> can also take the attributes shown in table 9.5. The BLEEDLEFT and BLEEDRIGHT values of the ALIGN attribute align the figure all the way to the left and right edges of the browser window, respectively.

Table 9.5   Attributes of the <FIG ...> Tag

Attribute	Purpose
SRC="*url*"	Gives the URL of the image file to load
NOFLOW	Disables the flow of text around the figure
ALIGN=LEFT ¦ RIGHT ¦ CENTER ¦ JUSTIFY ¦ BLEEDLEFT ¦ BLEEDRIGHT	Specifies an alignment for the figure
UNITS=*unit_of_measure*	Specifies a unit of measure for the WIDTH and HEIGHT attributes (default is pixels)
WIDTH=*width*	Specifies the width of the image in units designated by the UNITS attribute
HEIGHT=*height*	Specifies the height of the image in units designated by the UNITS attribute
IMAGEMAP	Denotes the figure as an imagemap

The <FIG ...> tag is different from the <IMG ...> tag in that it has a companion </FIG> tag. Together, <FIG ...> and </FIG> can contain text, including captions and photo credits, that should be rendered with the figure. Captions are enclosed with the <CAPTION> and </CAPTION> tags and photo credits are enclosed with the <CREDIT> and </CREDIT> tags. Regular text found between the <FIG ...> and </FIG> tags will wrap around the figure unless the NOWRAP attribute is specified.

III

Doing HTML

Figure 9.2 shows an example of a photo with a caption, photo credit, and surrounding text. Listing 9.1 shows the HTML to produce the figure.

Listing 9.1   HTML for Figure 9.2

```
<FIG SRC="drew.jpg" WIDTH=422 HEIGHT=284 ALIGN=LEFT>
    <CAPTION>Drew - 5 months old, Averill Park, NY</CAPTION>
    <P><P><P>The Boxer is a handsome breed, noted for its
    broad, muscular build and unfaltering devotion to its owner.
    Boxers make excellent companions and are especially good with
    children. </P>
    <CREDIT>Photo by Eric Ladd</CREDIT>
</FIG>
```

Fig. 9.2
The <FIG ...> and </FIG> tag pair can be used to contain captions, credits, and text to wrap around the figure.

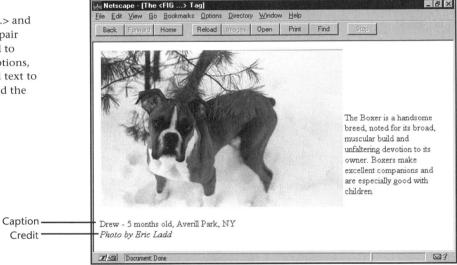

Caption —
Credit —

▶ See "Client-side Imagemaps with the <FIG ...> ... </FIG> Tag Pair," p. 304, to learn how to implement client-side imagemaps with the <FIG ...> tag.

Another feature proposed for the <FIG ...> and </FIG> tag pair is the ability to overlay two images. This is accomplished with the <OVERLAY ...> tag, which specifies a second image to overlay the image given in the <FIG ...> tag. HTML to produce an overlay might look like:

```
<FIG SRC="main_image.gif" WIDTH=250 HEIGHT=186 ALIGN=LEFT>
    <OVERLAY SRC="overlay.gif">
    <P>The image to the left is actually two images,
    one on top of the other.
</FIG>
```

The <FIG ...> tag also plays a critical role in the implementation of client-side imagemaps.

Tables

Until now, the only means for creating tables has been to use preformatted text. HTML 3.0 calls for several table tags that make it possible to build tables on Web pages without having to convert everything to a fixed-width font. Many browsers have already implemented these tags in anticipation of the table tag proposals being accepted into the 3.0 standard.

To understand the table tags better, it helps to take a moment to consider how HTML tables are structured. Tables are made out of one or more *rows*. These rows, in turn, are made up of *cells,* which can contain a data element of the table or a heading for a column of data. If you can keep this breakdown in mind as you read the next few paragraphs, the syntax of the table tags will make much more sense to you.

▶ To learn how to make tables with preformatted text, see "Preformatted Text," p. 176

Table Basics

To start a table, you need to use the <TABLE ...> tag. <TABLE ...> has a companion closing tag </TABLE>. Together these tags contain all of the tags that go into creating a table. The <TABLE ...> tag can take the BORDER attribute, which places a border around the table. By default, a table has no borders.

To put a caption on your table, enclose the caption text in the <CAPTION ...> and </CAPTION> tags. Captions appear centered over the table. The text may be broken to match the table's width. If you prefer your caption below the table, you can include the ALIGN=BOTTOM attribute in the <CAPTION ...> tag.

> **Tip**
>
> Put your caption immediately after the <TABLE ...> tag or immediately before the </TABLE> tag to prevent your caption from unintentionally being made part of a table row or cell.

Because tables are built out of rows, you need to know how to define a row. The <TR ...> and </TR> tags contain the tags that comprise a row of the table. The <TR ...> tag can take the ALIGN and VALIGN attributes. ALIGN controls the horizontal alignment of cell contents in the row and can be set to LEFT, RIGHT, or CENTER. VALIGN controls the vertical alignment and be set to TOP, BOTTOM, or MIDDLE. Values of ALIGN or VALIGN given in a <TR ...> tag apply to each cell in the row and will override all default alignments.

With a row defined, you're ready to put in the cells that make up the row. If a cell contains a table data element, you create the cell with the <TD ...> and </TD> tag pair. The text between <TD ...> and </TD> is what appears in the cell. Similarly, you use <TH ...> and </TH> to create a header. Header cells are exactly like data cells, except that header cell contents are automatically rendered in boldface type and are aligned in the center.

There are default horizontal and vertical alignments associated with each type of cell. Both types of cells have a default vertical alignment of MIDDLE. Data cells have a default horizontal alignment of LEFT, while header cells have the aforementioned CENTER alignment. You can override any of these defaults *and* any alignments specified in a <TR ...> tag by including the desired ALIGN or VALIGN attribute in a <TD ...> or <TH ...> tag. Listing 9.2 shows this in a one row table.

Listing 9.2   Using VALIGN and ALIGN

```
<TABLE>
    <TR ALIGN=RIGHT VALIGN=TOP>
        <TD ALIGN=LEFT VALIGN=BOTTOM>
            Larry
        </TD>
        <TD>
            Curly
        </TD>
        <TD ALIGN=LEFT VALIGN=MIDDLE>
            Moe
        </TD>
    </TR>
</TABLE>
```

Tip

Using indents when writing HTML to produce a table helps you keep better track of what you're doing.

The data element "Larry" is horizontally aligned along the left edge of the cell (ALIGN=LEFT overrides the ALIGN=RIGHT in the <TR ...> tag) and vertically aligned along the bottom of the cell (VALIGN=BOTTOM overrides the VALIGN=TOP in the <TR ...> tag). In the second cell, "Curly" is aligned according to the alignments given in the <TR ...> tag, since there are no alignments specified in the second <TD ...> tag. Finally, "Moe" is horizontally aligned left (again ALIGN=LEFT overrides the ALIGN=RIGHT in the <TR ...> tag) and vertically aligned in the middle (VALIGN=MIDDLE overrides VALIGN=BOTTOM in the <TR ...> tag). Note that Moe's alignment is the same as the default alignment for any data cell, but we had to undo the alignments set forth in the <TR ...> tag to get back to the defaults.

Aligning data elements and headers in your tables may seem a bit confusing, but if you keep the following hierarchy in mind, you can master table alignment quickly:

- Alignments specified in <TD ...> or <TH ...> tags override all other alignments, but apply only to the cell being defined.
- Alignments specified in a <TR ...> tag override default alignments and apply to all cells in a row, unless overridden by an alignment specification in a <TD ...> or <TH ...> tag.
- In the absence of alignment specifications in <TR ...>, <TD ...>, or <TH ...> tags, default alignments are used.

With what you've read so far, you can construct the following table template (Listing 9.3). The template is a good starting point for building any HTML table.

Listing 9.3 Table Template

```
<TABLE>
    <CAPTION>Caption Text</CAPTION>
    <TR>                    <!-- Row 1 -->
        <TD> ... </TD>
        <TD> ... </TD>
        ...
        <TD> ... </TD>
    </TR>
    <TR>                    <!-- Row 2 -->
        <TD> ... </TD>
        <TD> ... </TD>
        ...
        <TD> ... </TD>
    </TR>
    ...
    <TR>                    <!-- Row m -->
        <TD> ... </TD>
        <TD> ... </TD>
        ...
        <TD> ... </TD>
    </TR>
</TABLE>
```

III

Doing HTML

The template above gives you a skeleton for a table with m rows that has a caption over the top and no borders. You can adjust this structure however you like by adding or deleting the appropriate tags and attributes.

Other Table Tag Attributes

For greater control over the appearance of your tables, there are other attributes of the <TD ...> and <TH ...> tags to help you. Either tag can take the NOWRAP attribute, which disables the breaking of data elements and headers onto a new line.

> **Caution**
>
> Use NOWRAP with care! It can produce cells that are inordinately wide if the cell contents aren't kept short.

By default, a cell spans (takes up) one row and one column of a table. You can alter this default by using the ROWSPAN and COLSPAN attributes in a <TD ...> or <TH ...> tag. ROWSPAN and COLSPAN are set equal to the number of rows and columns, respectively, a cell is to span. If you try to extend the contents of a cell into rows that don't exist on the table, the contents of the cell are truncated to fit the number of rows available.

Sample Tables

To illustrate the utility of HTML tables, this section presents some examples of how to use them. The primary intent of the table tags is to give you a means of presenting tabular data without having to resort to preformatted text. Most tables that do this can be constructed from the template given above. For example, the table in figure 9.3 was produced by the HTML shown in listing 9.4.

Listing 9.4   HTML for Figure 9.3

```
<TABLE BORDER>
    <CAPTION ALIGN=BOTTOM>Course Grades - Spring 1996</CAPTION>
    <TR>                    <!-- Row 1 -->
        <TH>Student</TH>
        <TH>Midterm</TH>
        <TH>Final Exam</TH>
        <TH>Course Average</TH>
    </TR>
    <TR>                     <!-- Row 2 -->
        <TD>Sarah Gordon</TD>
        <TD ALIGN=CENTER>89</TD>
        <TD ALIGN=CENTER>95</TD>
        <TD ALIGN=CENTER>92</TD>
```

```
        </TR>
        <TR>                    <!-- Row 3 -->
            <TD>Tim Jackson</TD>
            <TD ALIGN=CENTER>81</TD>
            <TD ALIGN=CENTER>77</TD>
            <TD ALIGN=CENTER>79</TD>
        </TR>

        <TR>                    <!-- Row 4 -->
            <TD>Molly Sanderson</TD>
            <TD ALIGN=CENTER>85</TD>
            <TD ALIGN=CENTER>89</TD>
            <TD ALIGN=CENTER>87</TD>
        </TR>
    </TABLE>
```

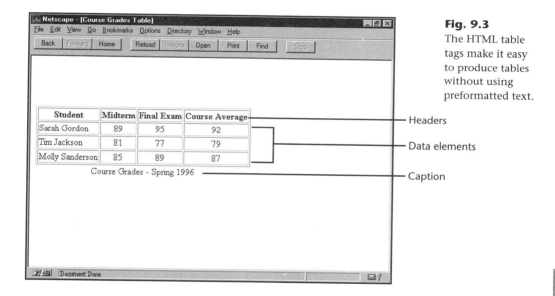

Fig. 9.3
The HTML table tags make it easy to produce tables without using preformatted text.

Note that all grades in the table are centered below their respective column headings. This was accomplished by the ALIGN=CENTER attribute in each of the <TD ...> tags that creates a cell containing a grade. The ALIGN=BOTTOM in the <CAPTION ...> tag placed the caption below the table instead of above it.

Table cells can contain much more than just plain text. Text in data cells can be formatted with any of the formatting tags introduced in Chapter 8. In addition, you can also place images, form input fields, and even other tables inside a table cell. Figure 9.4 shows a one row table with an image in the first and third cells and a heading in the second cell. The table is produced by listing 9.5.

Listing 9.5 HTML for Figure 9.4

```
<TABLE>
    <TR>
        <TD><IMG SRC="images/w3c.gif" ALT="W3C Logo"></TD>
        <TD ALIGN=CENTER><H2>The World Wide Web Consortium and<BR>
        The Internet Engineering Task Force</H2></TD>
        <TD><IMG SRC="images/ietf.gif" ALT="IETF Logo"></TD>
    </TR>
</TABLE>
```

Fig. 9.4
Table cells may contain inline images in addition to text.

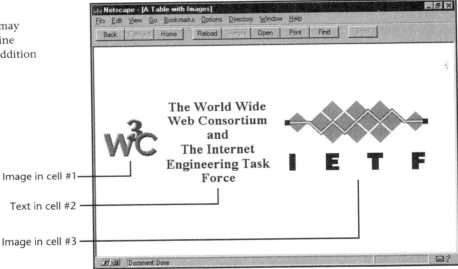

Tables are particularly handy for lining up input fields on an HTML form. Figure 9.5 shows a form that asks for the user's name and address. None of the fields are neatly aligned with each other because the words that precede them are of varying lengths.

By putting the prompting text and the fields in their own table cells, the fields will automatically be aligned. Figure 9.6 shows the same form done with tables. By using COLSPAN in the first two rows, we're even able to get the "City," "State," and "Zip" fields to fit across the same width as the fields above them. The HTML to produce figure 9.6 is shown in listing 9.6.

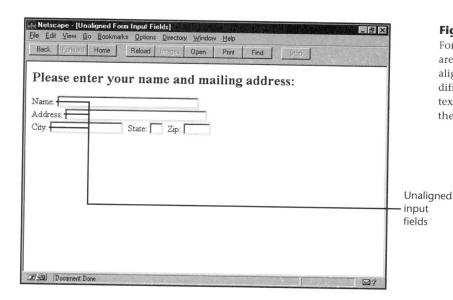

Fig. 9.5
Form input fields
are typically not
aligned because of
differences in the
text that precedes
them.

Unaligned
input
fields

Note

The <INPUT ...> tags shown in the following HTML are used to create the form input
fields. The <INPUT ...> tag is discussed in detail in Chapter 12, "HTML Forms."

Listing 9.6   HTML for Figure 9.6

```
<TABLE>
    <TR>
        <TD>Name:</TD>
        <TD COLSPAN=5><INPUT NAME="name" TYPE="text" SIZE=30></TD>
    </TR>
    <TR>
        <TD>Address:</TD>
        <TD COLSPAN=5><INPUT NAME="address" TYPE="text" SIZE=30></
TD>
    </TR>
    <TR>
        <TD>City:</TD>
        <TD><INPUT NAME="city" TYPE="text" SIZE=11></TD>
        <TD>State:</TD>
        <TD><INPUT NAME="state" TYPE="text" SIZE=2></TD>
        <TD>Zip:</TD>
        <TD><INPUT NAME="zip" TYPE="text" SIZE=5></TD>
    </TR>
</TABLE>
```

III

Doing HTML

Fig. 9.6
Placing form input fields in table cells is an easy way to get them to align properly.

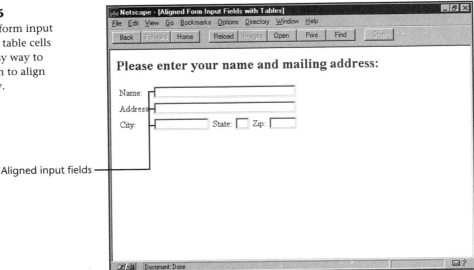

Aligned input fields

Coming Soon!

Even after it is released, the HTML 3.0 spec will continue to evolve. Two items you should look for in the spec in the not-too-distant future are *stylesheets* and *client-side imagemaps*.

HTML Stylesheets

HTML stylesheets contain information on how a document or a portion of a document should be formatted, including text size, font and color, indenting, and other layout instructions. Using stylesheets will help eliminate the need to keep adding new formatting tags to HTML since any new formatting instructions can be placed in the stylesheets and not in the HTML file.

There are different proposals as to how stylesheets should be attached to HTML files. One proposal calls for using the <LINK ...> tag in the document head. By using the many attributes of <LINK ...>, you could attach the stylesheet with the HTML:

```
<LINK TITLE="General Purpose Style Sheet" REL="stylesheet"
HREF="styles/general.style" TYPE="text/css">
```

HREF points to the file containing the stylesheet information and TYPE specifies the MIME type of the stylesheet ("css" stands for "cascading stylesheet").

A second proposal introduces the <STYLE> and </STYLE> container tags. These tags also go in the document head and contain specialized style information that overrides any styles brought in through the <LINK ...> tag. Yet another proposal suggests placing style information into <P> and <DIV> tags. This has the advantage of being able to easily apply different styles to different parts of the same document.

More information on stylesheets can be found at **http://www.w3.org/pub/WWW/Style/**.

Client-Side Imagemaps

Another interesting proposal calls for the support of client-side imagemaps. Imagemaps are multiply-linked images that take users to different URLs depending on where they click on the image. Until recently, imagemap clicks were processed by sending the coordinates of the click to the server. The server then checks a file that defines the linked regions of the map to determine what URL the client (browser) should load. Once this determination is made, the client receives the URL and loads it for presentation to the user.

There is nothing special about the computations that the server does to determine which region of the image the user clicked on. The main reason for having the server do this work is because the file defining the linked regions of the map lives there. Other than that, the client could do the computations just as easily.

The main premise behind client-side imagemaps then, is that the client can do the computations as long as it has the information defining the linked regions of the map. Having the client do the work eliminates the need to open another connection to the server (making image-map processing much faster) and it reduces the load on the server.

The trick to implementing client-side imagemaps is to find a way to store the information that defines the linked regions in your HTML code. This is under consideration for HTML 3.0. Check out the client-side imagemap spec at **http://www.ics.uci.edu/pub/ietf/html/draft-seidman-clientsideimagemap-02.txt**.

Note
Both Netscape Navigator 2.0 and Microsoft Internet Explorer 1.0 support client-side imagemaps.

▶ See "Client-Side Imagemaps," p. 303, to learn more about client-side image-mapping techniques.

Netscape Extensions

As noted at the start of the chapter, some software companies program their browsers to understand tags that are not part of standard HTML. Such tags are called *HTML extensions,* and they are usually associated with the name of the company that devised them.

A leader in developing HTML extensions is Netscape Communications Corporation. The Netscape Navigator browser is widely used, so the extensions that Netscape introduces are usually embraced very quickly by the Web community. Most, if not all, of the Netscape extensions are submitted to W3C and the IETF as candidates for inclusion in upcoming HTML specifications.

The next few sections review the Netscape extensions to HTML, including:

- Extensions to tags in the document head
- Extensions to HTML 2.0 tags
- Entirely new HTML tags
- Extensions to the HTML table tags
- Tags to create frames in the Netscape browser window

Extensions to Tags in the Document Head

Netscape has extended the <META ...> tag in the document head to include a value of "Refresh" for the HTTP-EQUIV attribute. Refresh instructs the browser to reload the same document or a different document after a specified number of seconds. The time delay and the URL of the next document, if applicable, are stored in the CONTENT attribute. The syntax for the <META ...> tag in this situation is:

```
<META HTTP-EQUIV="Refresh" CONTENT="n; url">
```

where *n* is the number of seconds to wait and *url* is the URL of the next document to load. If you want to reload the same document, just use CONTENT="*n*" with no URL specified.

Caution

URLs in the CONTENT attribute should be *fully qualified.*

This dynamic reloading of documents is called *client pull.* The name is appropriate because the client automatically pulls in the next document with no prompting from the user. The client pull technique has already been used on Web pages to produce simple animations and to automatically load and play sounds.

Another extended tag in the document head is the <ISINDEX> tag. The <ISINDEX> tag designates a document as searchable and gives the user an input field into which search criteria is entered. The default prompting text in front of this search field is `This is a searchable index. Enter search keywords:`. The PROMPT attribute is a Netscape extension of the <ISINDEX> tag that lets you change the default prompting text to whatever you like. For example, the following HTML:

▶ See "A One-Field Form: The <ISINDEX> Tag," p. 330 to learn how to use <ISINDEX> to create a searchable document.

Listing 9.7 produces the search field shown in figure 9.7.

Listing 9.7   HTML for Figure 9.7

```
<HEAD>
<TITLE>An Application of the PROMPT Attribute</TITLE>
<ISINDEX PROMPT="Please enter the keyword you wish to search on:">
</HEAD>
```

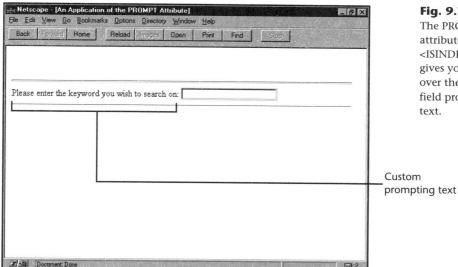

Fig. 9.7
The PROMPT attribute of the <ISINDEX> tag gives you control over the search field prompting text.

Custom prompting text

Extensions to HTML 2.0

Many of the tags you learned back in Chapter 8 have been extended by Netscape, including:

- The list tags (<UL>, <OL>, and <LI>)
- The <HR> tag
- The <IMG ...> tag
- The <BR> tag

The additional attributes to these tags are introduced in the next four sections.

The List Tags

Unordered list items are preceded by bullets. If you nest unordered lists, Netscape automatically changes bullet characters for each new list. The default bullet progression is from solid circle (disc) to open circle (circle) to square (square). The new TYPE attribute of the <UL> tag gives you control over which bullet character to use in nested lists. By setting TYPE equal to DISC, CIRCLE, or SQUARE, you can override the default progression and make Netscape use the bullet you want. This is illustrated in figure 9.8. The nested list in the figure uses solid circles as bullets just as the initial list does. Listing 9.8 shows the corresponding HTML.

Listing 9.8 HTML for Figure 9.8

```
<UL>
    <LI>HTML 2.0</LI>
    <LI>HTML 3.0</LI>
    <UL TYPE=DISC>
        <LI>Mathematical symbols</LI>
        <LI>Tables</LI>
        <LI>Style sheets</LI>
    </UL>
    <LI>Netscape extensions to HTML</LI>
</UL>
```

Fig. 9.8
You can control the bullet character in unordered lists using the TYPE attribute of the <UL> tag.

Nested list with solid bullets

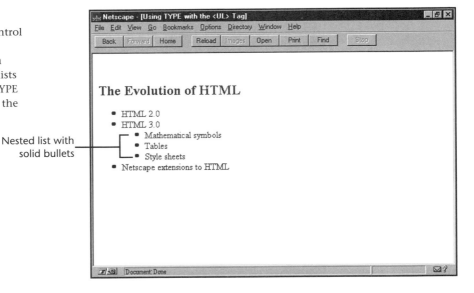

The <OL> tag also picks up the TYPE attribute, but in this case, TYPE changes the numbering scheme used in the ordered list. By default, ordered list items are numbered with consecutive integers starting with "1." By setting TYPE equal to "A," "a," "I," or "i," you can change the scheme to be uppercase letters, lowercase letters, uppercase Roman numerals, or lowercase Roman numerals, respectively. Having these five numbering schemes makes it easy to replicate the standard outline format using ordered lists. Figure 9.9 illustrates this point. The HTML to produce the figure is shown in listing 9.9.

Listing 9.9   HTML for Figure 9.9

```
<OL TYPE="I">
    <LI>Introduction</LI>
    <OL TYPE="A">
        <LI>Problem statement</LI>
        <LI>Results of previous research</LI>
    </OL>
    <LI>Approach</LI>
    <OL TYPE="A">
        <LI>Research objectives</LI>
        <LI>Equipment</LI>
        <OL>
            <LI>Lab equipment</LI>
            <LI>Computing equipment</LI>
        </OL>
        <LI>Techniques</LI>
    </OL>
    ...
</OL>
```

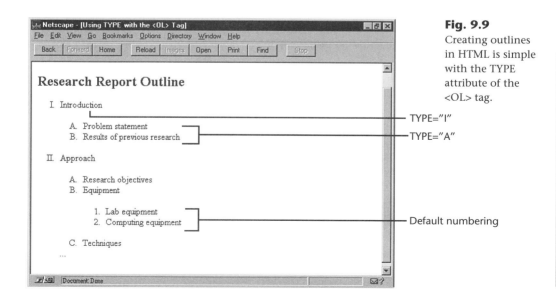

Fig. 9.9
Creating outlines in HTML is simple with the TYPE attribute of the <OL> tag.

III

Doing HTML

Another Netscape extension to the <OL> tag is the START attribute, which lets you change the starting value of the list item numbering. START=1 by default, but you can change it to any number you choose. If you're using a TYPE different from the default numbering scheme, you can still specify a different starting value using numbers. Netscape automatically converts the new starting value to the chosen numbering scheme for you. Thus, listing 9.l0 produces the list seen in figure 9.10.

Listing 9.10   HTML for Figure 9.10

```
<P>Users' favorite Internet applications
after e-mail and the World Wide Web were:
<OL TYPE="i" START=3>
<LI>Usenet newsgroups</LI>
<LI>FTP</LI>
<LI>Telnet</LI>
<LI>Internet Relay Chat (IRC)</LI>
</OL>
```

Fig. 9.10
The START attribute of the <OL> tag lets you begin numbering an ordered list at any value.

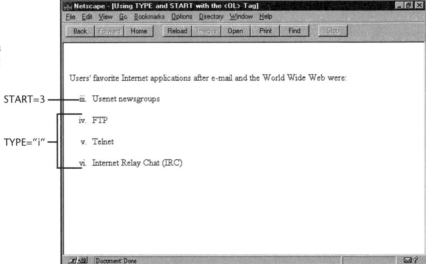

Finally, Netscape extends list type control all the way down to the list item level by adding the TYPE attribute to the <LI> tag. In an unordered list, using TYPE in an <LI> tag lets you change the bullet character for that list item and all subsequent items. For ordered lists, a TYPE attribute in an <LI> tag changes the numbering scheme for that list item and each one after it. The <LI> tag can also take the VALUE attribute in an ordered list. VALUE lets you change the numbering count to any other number you choose.

The <HR> Tag

Netscape has added several attributes to the <HR> tag that give you control over the width, thickness, alignment, and shading characteristics of rule. The new attributes are summarized in table 9.6.

Table 9.6 Attributes of the <HR> Tag (Netscape Extensions)	
Attribute	**Purpose**
WIDTH=pixels ¦ percent	Allows you to change the width of the rule to a set number of pixels or a percentage of the browser screen width
ALIGN=LEFT ¦ RIGHT ¦ CENTER	Sets the alignment of a piece of rule (default is CENTER)
SIZE=n	Controls the thickness of the rule (default is 1)
NOSHADE	Disables the shading Netscape uses when rendering rule, producing a solid bar

Figure 9.11 illustrates some of the new types of rules you can produce with these extensions. Listing 9.11 shows the corresponding HTML.

Listing 9.11   HTML for Figure 9.11

```
<HR>
Normal rule<P>
<HR SIZE=8 WIDTH=40% ALIGN=RIGHT>
Size 8, 40% width, flush right alignment<P>
<HR SIZE=12 NOSHADE>
Size 12, no shading<P>
<HR SIZE=16 NOSHADE WIDTH=80% ALIGN=LEFT>
Size 16, no shading, 80% width, flush left alignment<P>
```

Tip

Since you can't know how many pixels wide every user's browser screen is, you should always specify WIDTH in terms of a percentage rather than a set number of pixels.

The <IMG ...> Tag

The ALIGN attribute of the <IMG ...> tag has been greatly extended by Netscape. The Netscape Navigator understands the values of ALIGN shown in table 9.7.

III

Doing HTML

Fig. 9.11
Netscape extensions to the <HR> tag let you specify width, thickness, alignment, and shading of your horizontal rule.

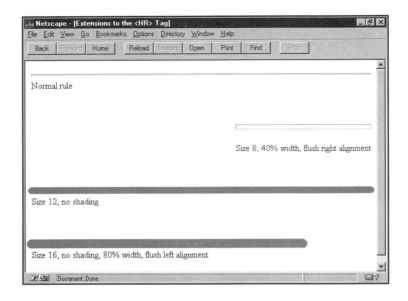

Table 9.7 Values of the ALIGN Attribute of the <IMG ...> Tag (Netscape Extensions)

Value	Effect
TOP	Aligns text following the image with the top of the image
MIDDLE	Aligns the baseline of text following the image with the center of the image
BOTTOM,BASELINE	Aligns the baseline of text following the image with the bottom of the image
TEXTTOP	Aligns the top of the tallest text following the image with the top of the image
ABSMIDDLE	Aligns the middle of the text following the image with the middle of the image
ABSBOTTOM	Aligns the lowest text following the image with the bottom of the image
LEFT	Floats the image in the left margin, allowing text to wrap around the right side of the image
RIGHT	Floats the image in the right margin, allowing text to wrap around the left side of the image

TEXTTOP, ABSMIDDLE, ABSBOTTOM, and BASELINE are small modifications to the TOP, MIDDLE, and BOTTOM values of ALIGN. What's new and interesting are the LEFT and RIGHT values of ALIGN, which produce *floating images* and make it easy to wrap text around an image. Figure 9.12 shows an image floated in the left and right margins with centered text in the open margin next to the image.

Floating image in the left margin —

Text wraps to the left of the image —

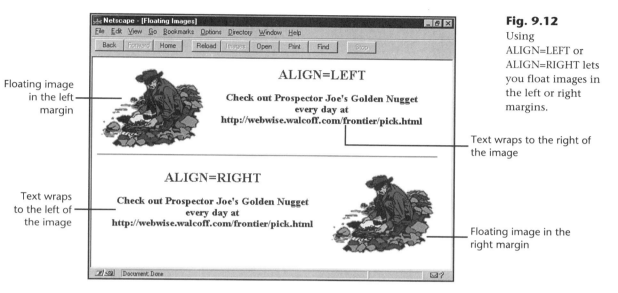

Fig. 9.12
Using ALIGN=LEFT or ALIGN=RIGHT lets you float images in the left or right margins.

Text wraps to the right of the image

Floating image in the right margin

Beyond the new values for the ALIGN attribute, Netscape also adds three other attributes to the <IMG ...> tag. The BORDER=*n* attribute lets you specify the thickness of the border around your images. The default value of *n* is 1, but you can change it to any value you choose, including zero. Setting BORDER to zero is useful with transparent GIFs because it eliminates the rectangular box that would otherwise surround the image.

Caution

Setting BORDER=0 on a hyperlinked image will remove the colored border and users may not be able to tell that the image is linked.

Since it's possible to wrap text around a floating image, it becomes necessary to have a way to put some additional space around the image so that wrapping text doesn't bump right up against it. The HSPACE=*n* attribute lets you insert *n* pixels of white space to the left and right of the floating image. VSPACE=*n* works similarly to put white space above and below the image.

III

Doing HTML

> **Note**
>
> Don't forget the HEIGHT and WIDTH attributes. Technically, these attributes are Netscape extensions to the <IMG ...> tag, but their function is important enough to earn them an early introduction.

The
 Tag

The availability of floating images also makes it necessary to be able to break to the next line that is clear of a floating image. To address this, Netscape added the CLEAR attribute to the <BR> tag. CLEAR can be set to LEFT, to move to the first line whose left margin is clear of floating images; RIGHT, to move to the first line whose right margin is clear of floating images; or ALL, to move to the first line that is completely free of floating images.

Additions to HTML

In addition to new attributes for many existing tags, Netscape has also introduced some entirely new tags to HTML. These new tags apply in the areas of word breaking and text effects.

Word Breaks

Text contained in the <NOBR> and </NOBR> tags will not have any line breaks in it. The tags are meant to prevent breaks at places where it is absolutely necessary to avoid them. You should keep the amount of text between these tags short, as long unbroken strings of text look awful on-screen.

The <WBR> tag can be used two ways. One way is to specify *exactly* where you want a line break inside the <NOBR> and </NOBR> tags. The other way is to indicate a preferred location for text breaks to the browser. <WBR> does not actually create the line break; it just says "It's okay to break the line here."

Text Effects

The <FONT ...> and </FONT> container tags give you control over the size and color of the text they contain. To modify the size of the text, you use the SIZE attribute in the <FONT ...> tag. SIZE can be set to any number between 1 and 7. The default text size is 3. You can also specify SIZE relative to the base font size by indicating how many sizes above (+) or below (-) the base font size you want the text to be. Thus, with a base font size of 3, the following two lines of HTML do the same thing:

```
<FONT SIZE=5>This text is big!</FONT>
<FONT SIZE=+2>This text is big!</FONT>
```

Similarly, to go two sizes below 3, you could use either of the following:

```
<FONT SIZE=1>This text is small!</FONT>
<FONT SIZE=-2>This text is big!</FONT>
```

The base font size is always 3, unless you change it with the <BASEFONT SIZE=*n*> tag. *n* can be any number between 1 and 7.

A popular effect you can create with the SIZE attribute is "small caps." With small caps, each letter in a word is in uppercase, but the first letter of each word is bigger than the others. Figure 9.13 shows some text in small caps as produced by the following HTML:

```
<FONT SIZE=+2>I</FONT> <FONT SIZE=+2>L</FONT>IKE
<FONT SIZE=+2>S</FONT>MALL <FONT SIZE=+2>C</FONT>APS!
```

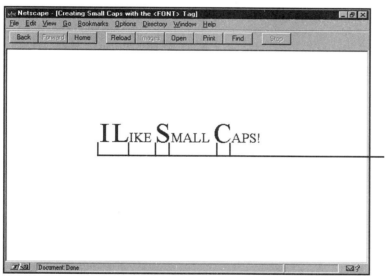

Fig. 9.13
You can create text in small caps using the SIZE attribute of the <FONT ...> tag.

Letters made larger with the <FONT> tag

You can also change the color of text between <FONT ...> and </FONT> by using the COLOR attribute of the <FONT ...> tag. COLOR is set equal to the RGB (Red/Green/Blue) hexadecimal triplet of the color you want. Thus, the HTML:

```
Here is some <FONT COLOR="#FF0000">red text.</FONT>
```

instructs Netscape to render the words "red text." in red.

Tip

To determine the RGB hexadecimal triplet of a desired color, first find that color in Netscape's custom color palette. You can access the palette by choosing the General Preferences option under the Options menu and selecting the Colors tab in the dialog box. Point your mouse to the color you want and click on it. After clicking, the decimal Red, Green, and Blue values should be displayed near the bottom right of the dialog box. Use the Windows calculator in Scientific mode to convert these decimal values to hexadecimal. Then write these three two-digit hex numbers in sequence to produce your color triplet.

Setting Other Colors in Netscape

You can also change the colors of browser window background, body text, unvisited hyperlinks, visited hyperlinks, and active (clicked on) links in Netscape. The BGCOLOR, TEXT, LINK, VLINK, and ALINK attributes of the <BODY> tag can be set equal to an RGB hexadecimal triplet to change their colors from the default values.

Two other Netscape extensions for creating text effects are the <CENTER> ... </CENTER> and <BLINK> ...</BLINK> tag pairs. Text, headings, and images contained between the <CENTER> and </CENTER> tags are centered on the browser screen. Enclosing text in the <BLINK> and </BLINK> tags instructs Netscape to make the text blink.

Extensions to the Table Tags

The Netscape Navigator understands four attributes of the <TABLE ...> tag that are not part of the original HTML 3.0 proposal for tables. These extended attributes are listed in table 9.8

Table 9.8   Attributes of the <TABLE ...> Tag (Netscape Extensions)

Attribute	Purpose
WIDTH=pixels ¦ percent	Sets the width of the table to a specific number of pixels or to a percentage of the browser window width
BORDER=n	Allows the use of borders of varying size
CELLSPACING=n	Controls the amount of space between cells (default value is 2)
CELLPADDING=n	Controls the amount of space between the edges of a cell and its contents (default value is 1)

The WIDTH attribute is useful in creating tables of varying width, but the same advice that applied to the WIDTH attribute of the <HR> tag applies here: always set your WIDTH to be a percentage of the browser screen width. That way, users with browser screens of any size will all see the same, albeit scaled, effect. You may need to see the width of a certain number of pixels if you're placing an image in your table though.

Control over the border size is desirable when nesting tables. You can use the BORDER=*n* attribute to give your main table a wide border and your nested tables smaller borders. If space is at a premium, you can set BORDER=0 to recapture the space that is typically reserved for a border.

Caution

Remember that other browsers treat BORDER as a Boolean attribute: if they see BORDER in the <TABLE ...> tag, they put a border on the table. Otherwise, they don't. This can be a problem when setting BORDER=0. Netscape understands BOR-DER=0 to mean "don't include a border and give me back the space you reserved for a border." Other browsers will look at BORDER=0 and, seeing the word BORDER in the tag, put a border around the table—the complete opposite of what you intended!

CELLSPACING and CELLPADDING are useful in two ways. Setting them to values higher than their default opens a table up and lets the cells "breathe" with more white space. If space is tight, you can set them both to zero to get the most compact table possible.

Note

In a table with CELLPADDING=0, the contents of the cell will be able to touch the edges of the cell. If this is undesirable, change your CELLPADDING to a non-zero value.

Frames

Version 2.0 of the Netscape Navigator supports an exciting new concept called *frames*. Using the frame tags, you can break up the browser window into separate areas that can each load its own HTML document. This is a valuable feature because it lets you put static items, like tables of contents and navigation aids, in small, yet permanent windows while still leaving a considerable amount of space for changing material. Thus, users can look at different documents in the largest frame and always have the useful static items available in smaller frames.

Creating the Frames: The <FRAMESET ...> ... </FRAMESET> Tag Pair

The first step in creating a framed document is to split the Netscape screen up into the frames that you want. You accomplish this with an HTML file that uses the <FRAMESET ...> and </FRAMESET> container tags instead of the <BODY> and </BODY> tags. <FRAMESET ...> and </FRAMESET> are not just container tags though. Attributes of the <FRAMESET ...> tag are instrumental in defining the frame regions.

The <FRAMESET ...> tag can take one of two attributes: ROWS, to split the screen up into multiple rows, or COLS, to split the screen up into multiple columns. Each attribute is set equal to a list of values that tells Netscape how big to make each row. The values can be a number of pixels, a percentage of a browser window dimension, or an asterisk (*), which acts as a wildcard character and tells the browser to use whatever space it has left. For example, the HTML:

```
<FRAMESET COLS="40%,20%,30%,10%">
...
</FRAMESET>
```

breaks the browser window into four columns. The first column has a width equal to 40% of the browser screen width, the second column 20%, the third column 30%, and the fourth column 10%. Similarly, the following HTML:

```
<FRAMESET ROWS="100,150,2*,*">
...
</FRAMESET>
```

splits the window into four rows. The first row is 100 pixels deep and the second is 150 pixels deep. The remaining space is divided between the third and fourth rows with the third row being twice as big (2*) as the fourth (*).

To produce really interesting layouts, you can nest <FRAMESET ...> and </FRAMESET> tags. Suppose you want to split the browser window into eight equal regions. You can first split the screen into four equal rows with the HTML:

```
<FRAMESET ROWS="25%,25%,25%,25%">
...
</FRAMESET>
```

This produces the screen shown in figure 9.14.

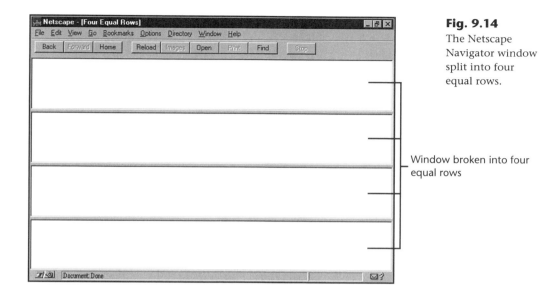

Fig. 9.14
The Netscape
Navigator window
split into four
equal rows.

Window broken into four
equal rows

Next you need to divide each row in half. To do this, you need a <FRAMESET
...> ... </FRAMESET> pair for each row that splits the row into two equal columns. The HTML <FRAMESET COLS="50%,50%"> ... </FRAMESET> will do
the trick. Nesting these tags in the HTML above produces listing 9.12 and figure 9.15. This completes the task of splitting the window into eight equal regions.

Listing 9.12   HTML for Figure 9.15

```
<FRAMESET ROWS="25%,25%,25%,25%">
    <FRAMESET COLS="50%,50%"> <!-- Break Row 1 into 2 columns -->
        ...
    </FRAMESET>
    <FRAMESET COLS="50%,50%"> <!-- Break Row 2 into 2 columns -->
        ...
    </FRAMESET>
    <FRAMESET COLS="50%,50%"> <!-- Break Row 3 into 2 columns -->
        ...
    </FRAMESET>
    <FRAMESET COLS="50%,50%"> <!-- Break Row 4 into 2 columns -->
        ...
    </FRAMESET>
</FRAMESET>
```

III

Doing HTML

Fig. 9.15
Dividing each row
in half yields the
desired eight equal
regions.

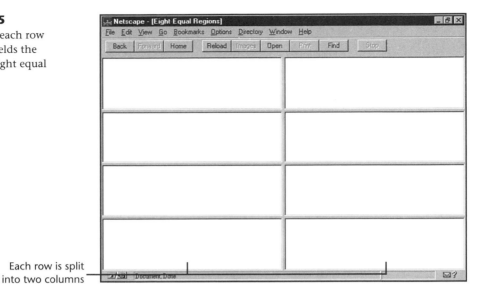

Each row is split
into two columns

Tip

Not sure whether to do a <FRAMESET ...> with ROWS or COLS first? Make a pencil
and paper sketch of what you want the browser window to look like. If you have
unbroken horizontal lines that go from one edge of the window to the other, do your
ROWS first. If you have unbroken vertical lines that go from the top of the window to
the bottom, do your COLS first. If you have both unbroken horizontal and vertical
lines, it doesn't matter which one you do first.

Placing Content in Frames: The <FRAME ...> Tag

With your frames all set up, you're ready to place content in each one with
the <FRAME ...> tag. The most important attribute of the <FRAME ...> tag is
SRC, which tells Netscape the URL of the document you want to load into
the frame. The <FRAME ...> tag can take the attributes summarized in table
9.9 as well. If you use the NAME attribute, the name you give the frame must
begin with an alphanumeric character. The default value of SCROLLING is
AUTO, which means Netscape will automatically put scroll bars in if they are
needed. SCROLLING=YES means Netscape should always put scroll bars in
and SCROLLING=NO means there should be no scroll bars.

Table 9.9   Attributes of the <FRAME ...> Tag

Attribute	Purpose
MARGINHEIGHT=*n*	Specifies the amount of white space to be left at the top and bottom of the frame
MARGINWIDTH=*n*	Specifies the amount of white space to be left along the sides of the frame
NAME="*name*"	Gives the frame a unique name so it can be targeted by other documents
NORESIZE	Disables the user's ability to resize the frame
SCROLLING=YES⎮NO⎮AUTO	Controls the appearance of horizontal and vertical scroll bars in the frame
SRC="*url*"	Specifies the URL of the document to load into the frame

To place content in each of the eight equal regions you created earlier, you can use the HTML shown in listing 9.13. The resulting screen appears in figure 9.16.

Listing 9.13   Placing Content in Frames

```
<FRAMESET ROWS="25%,25%,25%,25%">
    <FRAMESET COLS="50%,50%"> <!-- Break Row 1 into 2 columns -->
        <FRAME SRC="one.html">
        <FRAME SRC="two.html">
    </FRAMESET>
    <FRAMESET COLS="50%,50%"> <!-- Break Row 2 into 2 columns -->
        <FRAME SRC="three.html">
        <FRAME SRC="four.html">
    </FRAMESET>
    <FRAMESET COLS="50%,50%"> <!-- Break Row 3 into 2 columns -->
        <FRAME SRC="five.html">
        <FRAME SRC="six.html">
    </FRAMESET>
    <FRAMESET COLS="50%,50%"> <!-- Break Row 4 into 2 columns -->
        <FRAME SRC="seven.html">
        <FRAME SRC="eight.html">
    </FRAMESET>
</FRAMESET>
```

III

Doing HTML

Fig. 9.16
The <FRAME ...> tag lets you place a different HTML document into each frame.

Content is placed in a frame using the <FRAME...> tag

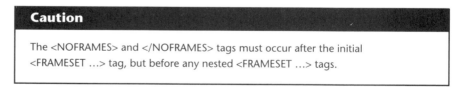

Respecting "Frames Challenged" Browsers

If you create a document with frames, people who are using a browser other than Netscape 2.0 will not be able to see the content you want them to see because their browsers don't understand the <FRAMESET ...>, </FRAMESET>, and <FRAME ...> tags. As a courtesy to users with "frames challenged" browsers, you can place alternative HTML code between the <NOFRAMES> and </NOFRAMES> container tags. Any HTML between these two tags will be understood and rendered by other browsers. Netscape, on the other hand, ignores anything between these tags and just works with the frame-related HTML.

> **Caution**
>
> The <NOFRAMES> and </NOFRAMES> tags must occur after the initial <FRAMESET ...> tag, but before any nested <FRAMESET ...> tags.

Virtual Reality Modeling Language (VRML)

By now, you've probably heard some of the hype surrounding Virtual Reality Modeling Language, or VRML. VRML is a three-dimensional equivalent of HTML that allows you to render interactive 3-D environments in real time over the Web.

The VRML 1.0 spec was written by Mark Pesce, Tony Parisi, and Gavin Bell in late 1994. Since then, VRML has been updated and extended very much as HTML has. VRML 1.1 cleared up a few loose ends from the 1.0 spec. The VRML 2.0 spec, which is nearing completion, has a special focus on action and interaction.

Note

For up-to-date information on the evolving VRML 2.0 standard, consult the VRML FAQ at **http://www.oki.com/vrml/VRML_FAQ.html** or the VRML Architecture Group Web site at **http://vag.vrml.org/**. An excellent text reference on VRML is Que's *Special Edition Using VRML*.

Concepts

VRML is objected-oriented. You create VRML objects and place them in a 3-D environment. VRML browsers let you not only see this environment, but move around in it as well. As you move, the browser must perform many complex calculations to move, scale, rotate, and shade the objects in the environment so that the rendering continues to appear three-dimensional and realistic. This is why early VRML was done on high-powered computing platforms. As algorithms have become more efficient and high-powered computers have become more readily available, VRML has worked its way out of labs and universities and into people's homes and places of work.

Implementation

To view VRML documents, you need a *VRML browser* or a browser with a *VRML plug-in*. As of this writing, there are no VRML Netscape plug-ins for UNIX platforms, though with Netscape's recent acquisition of Paper Software, we should see some plug-ins at least for Irix and Solaris, and hopefully Linux. Other VRML browsers and editors for UNIX can be found at **http://www.sdsc.edu/SDSC/Partners/vrml/software/browsers.html**.

Once you have your objects created, you can place them in a 3-D environment using a *scene assembler*. Scene assemblers let you position and scale objects to create the 3-D effect. Most Web servers can serve VRML documents by using the MIME type x-world/x-vrml, but there are *VRML servers* available that specialize in serving VRML pages. ❖

III

Doing HTML

CHAPTER 10
HTML Editors and Tools

While this book is about running a Web server on a UNIX platform, it is by far the most common case for HTML pages to be created on Macintosh or MS Windows platforms. We will briefly mention UNIX tools for authoring HTML, but most of the discussion will be on Windows tools.

It's easy to write an HTML document. After all, the main document is nothing but ASCII text, most of which is the plain-language text that you're trying to communicate on the page. The tricky part is getting the proper tags in the right place to make your text and images look like you want them to. Browser programs are very literal in the way that they interpret HTML, so errors in your HTML syntax make your page look very unusual. You need to take extra care to ensure that your page comes out looking like you planned.

Because HTML documents are all ASCII code, originally Web documents were written with simple text editors, such as the Windows Notepad. As people began writing longer and more complex documents, many turned to their favorite word processing programs (which can save documents in plain ASCII text) and wrote macros and tools to help them.

As the Web expanded, dedicated HTML editing programs (similar to word processing programs, but designed to produce results for the screen and not the printed page) began to appear. These programs allow Web page creators to more quickly format their text into proper HTML format by allowing authors to have codes placed automatically around text at the click of a toolbar button. Stand-alone HTML editors have since evolved into very advanced HTML authoring systems that provide end-to-end support for the Web page creation process.

In addition to editors and authoring systems, special filters and utilities that convert existing documents to HTML format have cropped up. These applications save authors an immense amount of time; they take information formatted for other programs and mark it up with HTML to produce the same formatting on a Web page.

As you can see, there are many ways you can write your HTML documents; you can use your favorite line editor, a word processor, or a dedicated HTML tool. The choice of which system to use depends on personal preference and your confidence in your use of HTML.

This chapter looks at five types of applications that are useful in developing HTML documents:

- Plain text editors and word processors
- Stand-alone HTML editing tools
- Advanced HTML authoring systems
- Converters and filters for importing other types of documents into HTML
- Analyzers and other tools that check the syntax of your HTML documents

UNIX Editors

Before diving into Windows-based authoring solutions, let's quickly cover the two most popular HTML editors for UNIX, *vi* and *Emacs*.

vi is a very simple text editor that's comparable to the Windows NotePad editor. It has no HTML-specific codes or hotkeys or anything special; it is simply a fast, lightweight, easy-to-use text editor. vi is installed on every UNIX operating system by default.

Emacs, on the other hand, is a much more full-featured, and therefore heavy-weight, beast. It is not standard with all operating systems, so you might have to install it on your machine. You can obtain it from the GNU archives at **ftp://prep.ai.mit.edu/pub/gnu/**.

Emacs has a full LISP interpreter embedded in the application. One particular LISP module, known as *HTML-helper-mode,* has been proven to be very very helpful in creating and managing HTML. It has the following features:

- Automatic entry of common HTML structures when a new .html file is created.
- Special colorization of different sections, such as red for comments, blue for content between header tags, or bold text between <B> tags.

■ Automatic indenting for list items, blockquotes, and many other tags for more readable HTML content.

More information about HTML-helper-mode can be found at **http:// www.santafe.edu/~nelson/tools/**.

Plain Text Editors

You can use any ASCII editor to write HTML pages. The tags necessary to indicate special effects that a Web browser should show are only combinations of ASCII characters (such as <B> at the beginning of text that's supposed to be bold and </B> at the end). In contrast, most word processing programs embed special binary codes in the text to indicate changes in font styles or the location and format of graphics. Because hypertext authors know the HTML codes, they can write in various formatting effects as easily as they can enter sections of text.

This simplicity can be extremely useful. Many veteran HTML authors rely on a simple plain-text editor as they tweak specific points on any given page. Plain-text editors have the advantage of taking up less memory, which allows experienced authors to open multiple Web browser programs simultaneously to see how their page looks in each format. (Although a code for something to be bold is read by Internet Explorer, Mosaic, and Netscape as bold, the way bolded text appears may vary slightly with each browser.)

The major annoyance with plain-text editors is that HTML codes are not treated as complete units. You have to edit each keystroke in the HTML code, whereas many editor programs treat the code as an entire entity. In a plain-text editor, getting rid of the tag pair <B> and </B> around text requires deleting each keystroke. Some of the dedicated editors recognize the combination and eliminate the whole tag (and even delete its companion tag on the other side of the text).

Nevertheless, you will probably need to use a simple editor some time; become familiar with at least one, even if it's not what you usually use to compose your HTML files. You will undoubtedly use one someday to quickly edit your HTML.

MS-DOS Editor

You might not have used it in a very long time, but the MS-DOS Editor is a perfectly good tool for composing or making quick changes to an HTML document. The Editor provides menu options for all of the basic editing operations like cut, copy, and paste. It also has find and replace options to make

III

Doing HTML

it fairly easy to make global changes to your documents. The Editor automatically saves documents in ASCII format, so there's no need to do any special conversions.

The big drawback, of course, is that you have to open an MS-DOS window to get to the Editor. If you're not adverse to this, you can open up a window and type **edit** at the DOS prompt to fire up the Editor.

Windows Notepad

If you can't bring yourself to leave the Windows environment, you can use the Windows Notepad. Notepad is a fine way to edit HTML documents, as long as the documents are not too long. Notepad has a file size limit of 64K; any particularly complex HTML document probably exceeds this file size.

Like the MS-DOS Editor, Notepad saves files in ASCII format. It also provides menu options to cut, copy, paste, and find text, but it does not have a find-and-replace feature.

> **Caution**
>
> Be careful when saving from Notepad that you don't save in the Unicode format. This is an encoded format and you won't be able to see your files with a browser.

Notepad proves most useful if you just need to make a quick tweak on a document that's already mostly edited. You may be able to open the HTML document in Notepad and make the minor adjustment without having to go through the hassle of opening your word processor and activating the proper template.

> **Tip**
>
> If you use Notepad to edit HTML, activate the WordWrap option under the Edit menu. Otherwise, your HTML code can run off the edge of the window and you'll have to scroll to see parts of it.

Windows WordPad

If the document you want to edit is too big for Notepad, Windows will give you the option to open the document in WordPad—a document editor that falls somewhere between a simple editor like Notepad and a full-featured word processor like Microsoft Word.

WordPad offers full editing support through menu options to cut, copy, paste, and find and replace. When saving a document in WordPad, you have a choice of several formats. Be sure to choose the Text Document option.

> **Tip**
>
> You'll need to turn word wrapping on in WordPad as well when you work with plain text documents. You can do this by selecting Options under the View menu. The word wrap radio buttons are on the Text tab of the Options dialog box.

> **Note**
>
> No plain text editor will check the syntax of your HTML for you. If you do most of your HTML authoring in a plain text editor, it's a good idea to check the HTML syntax in your documents before putting them on your server. See the "Analyzers" section at the end of this chapter for programs that will check HTML syntax.

Word Processing Programs

Because many people are already familiar with the editing features of their favorite word processor, a number of HTML authors have turned to creating specialized macros and tools that take advantage of the properties of the word processing programs to make editing HTML easier. Now, even developers are getting into the act, and producing programs designed explicitly as add-ons for commercial word processors.

For whatever reason, be it the strong use of Styles or an easy, powerful macro language, Microsoft's Word seems to be the word processor of choice for those writing HTML editing tools; the vast majority of these types of tools are written expressly for Word for Macintosh or Windows. The first two discussed in this section are simple shareware templates that add helpful toolbars and HTML-specific pull-down menu options to those already available in Word. Quarterdeck's WebAuthor 2.0 is a commercial package that not only provides assistance for HTML authoring, but for syntax checking as well. And, naturally, Microsoft has an offering to enhance Word: Microsoft Internet Assistant turns Word into a fully functional Web browser, in addition to adding support for HTML editing.

III

Doing HTML

CU_HTML

CU_HTML, named after the Chinese University of Hong Kong where it was created by Kenneth Wong and Anton Lam, is a template-based add-on for Word 2 and Word 6.

> **Note**
>
> The information in this section is based on CU_HTML.DOT, version 1.5.3. You can acquire the template and its related files by directing your browser to **http://www.cuhk.hk/csc/cu_html/cu_html.htm**. This document provides information on the current release of CU_HTML and provides a link to the file cu_html.zip, which is the file you want to download.

CU_HTML comes with installation instructions in an HTML format. Use your browser to open the file cu_html.htm. If your browser isn't working, just open the Word document CU_HTML.DOC. After you install CU_HTML's files, you can select the CU_HTML template when you open a new document in Word.

If you choose this template, several new styles equivalent to HTML tags are loaded. From the Style option of the Format menu, you can apply formatting to produce the six heading levels, addresses, preformatted text, ordered and unordered lists, and horizontal rule. You can apply bold, italic, and underline styles using Word's usual formatting toolbar. When you instruct CU_HTML to write your final HTML document, it will convert these formats into the appropriate HTML tags.

There's also an extra pull-down menu, called HTML, and a new toolbar (see fig. 10.1). The HTML menu provides you with some options for tagging text, mostly for linking text in the document to other files (such as graphics or other hypertext links). Buttons on the toolbar replicate the choices found under the HTML menu, giving you quick access to these functions.

> **Tip**
>
> If you don't see the CU_HTML toolbar, place your mouse pointer over any toolbar button, right-click the mouse, and select HTML from the list you see to activate the toolbar.

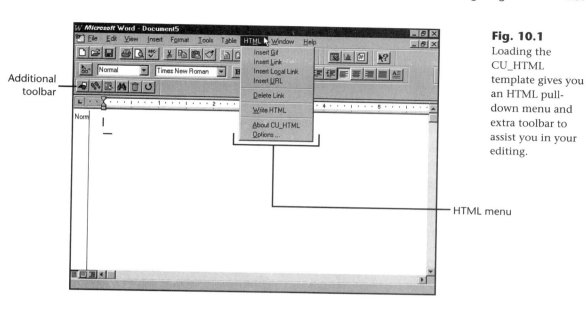

Additional toolbar

HTML menu

Fig. 10.1
Loading the
CU_HTML
template gives you
an HTML pull-
down menu and
extra toolbar to
assist you in your
editing.

After you open a new document, you should save it. CU_HTML requires that you save a copy of the file before formatting text, placing graphics, and writing the final HTML file.

Once you've entered text, you can use the options under the HTML menu to format links to other files. You can link to a graphics file with the Insert Gif option, or another locally stored HTML file with Insert Link. You can create a link to another section of your Web document with Insert Local Link, or link to another document on the Web with Insert URL. The Delete Link option lets you remove any type of link you've inserted.

Like most of the templates for Word, CU_HTML creates files in Word format. You must be sure to save the completed document in HTML format before you try to use it on the Web. To do this using CU_HTML, open the HTML menu and choose Write HTML. This instructs CU_HTML to create an ASCII file in which all Word formatting codes are converted to HTML. The file will have the same name as your Word document, but it will end with the extension .htm.

GT_HTML

GT_HTML is template add-on for Word developed at Georgia Tech. It is as easy to install as CU_HTML, but it supports many more editing features.

WebmasterCD

III

Doing HTML

> **Note**
>
> The following section is based on GT_HTML, version 6.0d. You can download GT_HTML by pointing your browser to **http://www.gatech.edu/word_html/**. Look for the download link to the file gt_html.zip.

Installation of GT_HTML is simple; just copy the template file gt_html.dot into your templates subdirectory for Word. If you activate the template when you open a new document in Word, you have the ability to add the two new toolbars shown in figure 10.2. To activate the toolbars, open the View menu and choose Toolbars. In the Toolbars dialog box, select the Toolbar 1 (Gt_html) and Toolbar 2 (Gt_html) check boxes.

Fig. 10.2
When you install GT_HTML, you have the option of turning on two toolbars to help you edit HTML.

GT_HTML toolbars

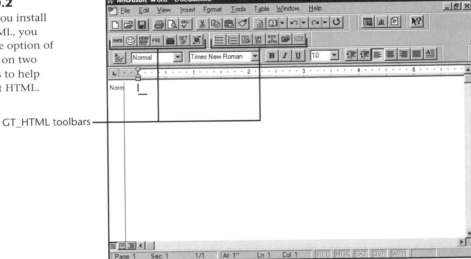

In addition to the two toolbars, GT_HTML adds HTML-related options to most of Word's pull-down menus. The new options appear at the bottom of each pull-down menu and start with the word HTML. Since GT_HTML doesn't load a lot of styles into Word like CU_HTML does, most of your special formatting will be done using the new menu options.

One of the more helpful menu options is the HTML Browser option under the File menu. Selecting this option opens the browser you want to work with GT_HTML. Having quick access to a browser while you edit makes it easier to test your documents as you develop them.

Another helpful menu option is the HTML Toolbox under the Tools menu. You can quickly insert tags for rules, titles, comments, centering and blinking text, and line breaks using selections from the Toolbox. The Toolbox also gives you a way to launch GT_HTML's handy HTML Form Creator and HTML Table Converter. The Forms Creator launches a second dialog box in which you can configure your form input fields, while the Table Converter will convert a simple Word table (no cell in the table spans more than one row or one column) to HTML format. Toolbox items are shown in figure 10.3.

▶ See "Creating Forms," p. 317 to learn about the HTML tags used to create forms.

Fig. 10.3
GT_HTML's Pick a Tag Type dialog box makes it easy to insert many types of HTML tags.

The Format menu includes options for formatting highlighted text as a heading, preformatted text, or a numbered or bulleted list. To apply bold, italics, and underline styles, you can use Word's normal formatting toolbar. GT_HTML converts these formats to HTML tags when it saves the HTML version of your document.

Quarterdeck WebAuthor 2.0

Quarterdeck recently released version 2.0 of its HTML editing plug-in for Word 6.0 called WebAuthor. WebAuthor 2.0 offers a number of enhancements over earlier versions, including new toolbars for text and paragraph formatting, support for HTML 3.0 and Netscape extensions, and faster importing and exporting of documents.

WebmasterCD

III

Doing HTML

> **Note**
>
> The information in this section is based on the trialware version of WebAuthor 2.0. You can download the self-extracting archive containing the trialware files from Quarterdeck's Web site at **http://www.qdeck.com/**. You may evaluate the trialware version of WebAuthor 2.0 for 30 days, after which time the features that convert and save files to HTML will disable. If you choose to purchase the full WebAuthor package after the evaluation period, you will also get WebImage, a useful image editor and converter, and the Quarterdeck Mosaic browser. For current pricing information, consult Quarterdeck's Web site or contact its sales department at (800) 354-3222.

Note

Windows 95 and NT users should note that the current release of WebAuthor only works with Word 6.0 (a 16-bit application). Quarterdeck anticipates releasing a 32-bit version of WebAuthor 2.0 in early 1996. Consult the Quarterdeck Web site at **http://www.qdeck.com/** for the status of this release.

Getting Started

It's easy to install WebAuthor once you've downloaded the archive file. A standard install program will walk you through the installation steps and set up the Windows program group. Once WebAuthor is installed, you'll find an extra option under the Microsoft Word Tools menu, as shown in figure 10.4.

Fig. 10.4
Installing WebAuthor 2.0 adds an HTML Authoring option to the Word Tools menu.

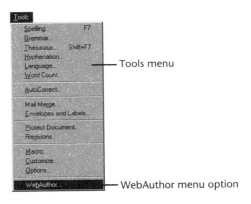

— Tools menu

— WebAuthor menu option

Note

WebAuthor places GIF images in your Windows document by converting the images to the Windows BMP format. When you access WebAuthor through the Tools menu, it checks to see if this converter has been installed. If you get a warning message telling you that your GIF graphics converter has not been installed, you'll need to run your Word Setup program to install it. The filter you want to install is the CompuServe GIF filter.

You activate WebAuthor's capabilities by selecting this new menu option. When you do, you're presented with a dialog box that gives you four options on how to proceed (see fig. 10.5). You can Create a New HTML Document if you have yet to write any or you can Open/Import Existing Documents for Editing. Additionally, you can choose to Convert Existing Documents to HTML or Set/Change Options for Document Conversion to HTML.

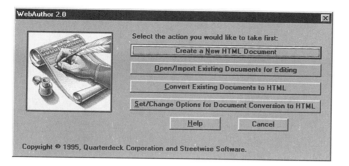

Fig. 10.5
WebAuthor gives
you four different
options when you
activate it from the
Word Tools menu.

Starting a New Document

If you choose to start a new document, WebAuthor immediately presents you
with a dialog box in which you can enter the document's title. If you want to
specify other options in the document head, you can choose the Switch to
Advanced dialog option. The resulting Document Parameters (Advanced)
dialog box is shown in figure 10.6.

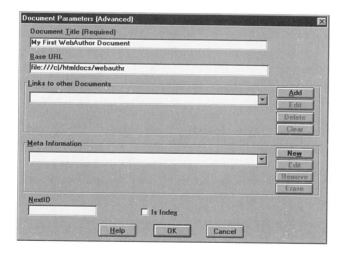

Fig. 10.6
When starting a
new document,
you can set any
document head
option in the
Document
Parameters
(Advanced)
dialog box.

Once you specify a title and other document head information, you'll see a
screen like the one shown in figure 10.7. Note that WebAuthor adds an extra
toolbar to your Word window. Buttons on this toolbar let you create new
documents (Word and HTML), open files (with or without converting), save
files (in Word and HTML formats), toggle to the Edit view where you can
make changes to your document, format characters and lists, or activate one
of WebAuthor's special function managers. The three buttons on the end of
the toolbar, labeled Char, Para, and Form toggle additional toolbars on and
off. Figure 10.7 shows the new toolbar with the additional three turned on.

III

Doing HTML

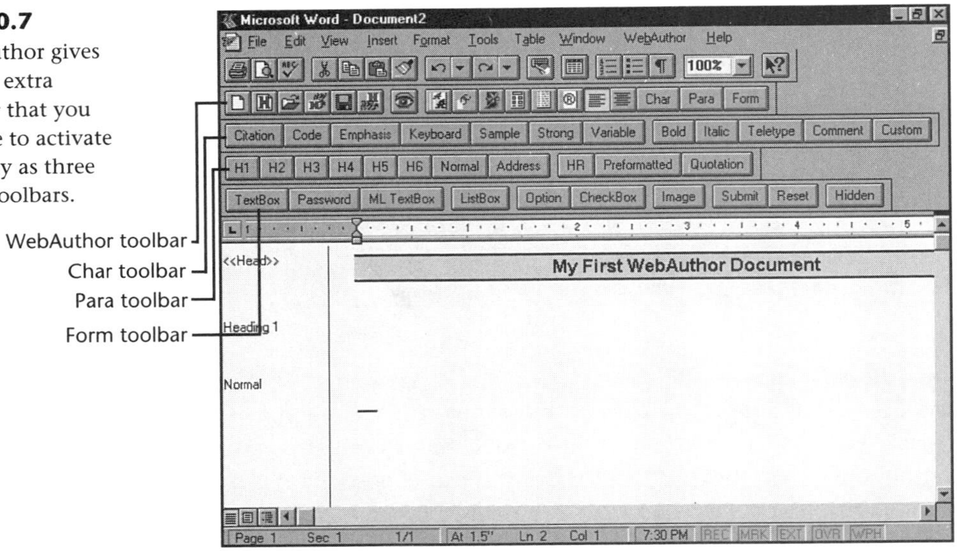

Fig. 10.7
WebAuthor gives
you an extra
toolbar that you
can use to activate
as many as three
other toolbars.

WebAuthor toolbar ⌐
Char toolbar ⌐
Para toolbar ⌐
Form toolbar ⌐

The document view you see in figure 10.7 is called the Edit view. While in this view, you can make additions or changes to your document. The Toggle Document View button in the main WebAuthor toolbar switches you to a near-WYSIWYG view that gives you a sense of how your document might look on a browser screen. You can't make edits while you're in the near-WYSIWYG view, so be sure to toggle back to the Edit view to make changes.

Opening or Converting an Existing Document

If you choose to open or import an existing HTML file, WebAuthor will look for documents that have the DOC, HTM, or RTF (Rich Text Format) extensions. Find the document you want and click OK to load it. Figure 10.8 shows a previously created HTML document loaded into Word by WebAuthor.

> **Tip**
>
> After you load a document, you may find that WebAuthor has placed a blank toolbar in your toolbar area. If so, find the Hide Blank Toolbar button at the left edge of the empty space and click it to recapture the space for your editing window.

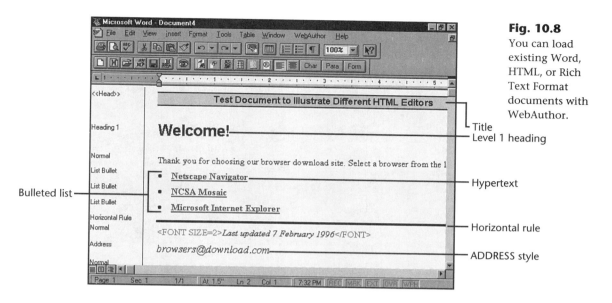

Fig. 10.8
You can load
existing Word,
HTML, or Rich
Text Format
documents with
WebAuthor.

Bulleted list

Title
Level 1 heading

Hypertext

Horizontal rule

ADDRESS style

Converting Existing Documents and Setting Conversion Options

The other two choices you get when activating WebAuthor pertain to converting existing documents to HTML format. If you choose to convert an existing document, WebAuthor lets you select a Word (DOC) or Rich Text Format (RTF). Once you select the file, WebAuthor loads it into Word and then performs the conversion to HTML according to a set of customizable conversion options.

If you choose to set conversion options, you'll activate the Options File Editor. Selections under the Options menu in this program let you specify conversion parameters for logical and heading styles (Styles), physical styles (Direct Formatting), document head information (Document Information), hyperlinks (File Links), and tables (Tables). The Options File Editor with the File Links dialog box active is shown in figure 10.9.

Editing Features of WebAuthor 2.0

Once you have started a new document or have loaded one, it's fairly easy to make edits using WebAuthor's many editing features. The extra Char and Para toolbars make it very easy to apply logical, physical, and heading styles to highlighted text. Buttons on the Form toolbar can be used to drop form elements wherever your cursor is positioned.

III

Doing HTML

Fig. 10.9
The Options File Editor utility program lets you specify how WebAuthor should perform conversions to HTML from Word or RTF formats.

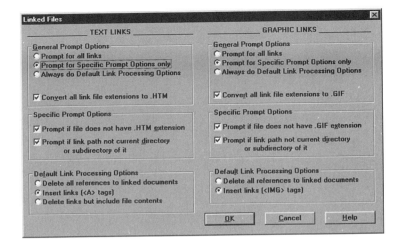

WebAuthor also gives you three different *managers* to assist you with placement of more complicated items. The Anchor Manager lets you specify an internal or external anchor to which a hypertext link can point. The Image Manager dialog box, shown in figure 10.10, prompts you for a GIF or JPEG file, the size of the image, how it should be aligned, and what alternative text should be used if the image is unavailable. The Form Manager walks you through a set of dialog boxes in which you indicate what input fields should be used to build the form, as well as the URL of the processing script and how the form data should be sent to the script. Each of WebAuthor's special managers is accessible by a button on the main WebAuthor toolbar.

Fig. 10.10
WebAuthor's Image Manager prompts you for the basic information needed to place an inline image into your document.

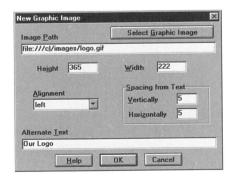

The List button on the main WebAuthor toolbar lets you create any one of the five types of HTML lists. The Insert Symbol buttons gives you a dialog box full of special characters, such as copyright and trademark symbols and characters with diacritical marks.

Saving Documents in HTML Format

To save a document in HTML format, choose Save to HTML under the File menu or click the Save to HTML button on the main WebAuthor toolbar. If you save using an option other than these two, your document will be saved in Word format and will not be suitable for transfer to your server.

Microsoft Internet Assistant for Word

Given the surge of HTML authoring add-ons for Word, it's no surprise that Microsoft itself has produced one. Internet Assistant for Word is a no-cost add-on that turns Word into a Web browser. It includes styles, toolbars, and tools for authoring HTML. Microsoft is also releasing Internet Assistant add ons for each of the Microsoft Office products. Currently only Excel has been released, but by the time this book comes out, others should be available. Look for the Assistants at Microsoft's Office Web site at **http:// www.microsoft.com/msoffice/**.

> **Note**
>
> The information in this section is based on beta release 4 of Internet Assistant version 2.0z. This beta was written to work with Word 7.0 in Windows 95 or with Word 6.0 in Windows NT. For the latest release and links to the downloadable file, direct your browser to **http://www.microsoft.com/msoffice/freestuf/msword/down-load/ia/default.htm**. Microsoft will also ship a copy on floppy disk to registered owners of Word for a shipping and handling charge of $5. Call (800) 426-9400.

After downloading the file, the installation of Internet Assistant is fairly easy. If you have installed a Microsoft program yourself, this process should be familiar. During the installation, you are given the option to make Internet Assistant your default HTML browser. If you choose to do this, the Internet Assistant add-on will be placed in your Word Startup directory. This causes Internet Assistant's functionality to be loaded each time you start Word.

> **Caution**
>
> Be sure to close all open Windows applications, especially Word, before you install Internet Assistant. This minimizes the risk of crashing your computer.

The Internet Assistant Web Browser

When you start Word with Internet Assistant installed, the only difference you'll notice at first is the addition of the Switch to Web Browse View button (see fig. 10.11). Clicking on this button takes you to the browser side of Word

III

Doing HTML

that Internet Assistant creates. As you can see in figure 10.12, the Word browser has most of the usual features found in other popular browsers including forward and backward navigation buttons, reload and stop buttons, and the ability to store the URLs of your favorite sites (Favorites). To return to the Word editing window, you can click on the Switch to Edit View button.

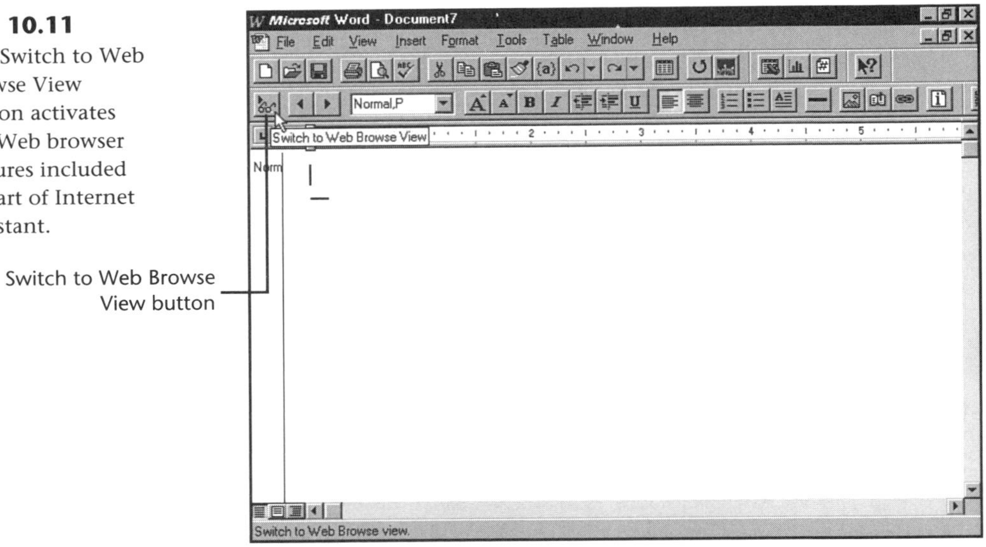

Fig. 10.11
The Switch to Web Browse View button activates the Web browser features included as part of Internet Assistant.

Switch to Web Browse View button

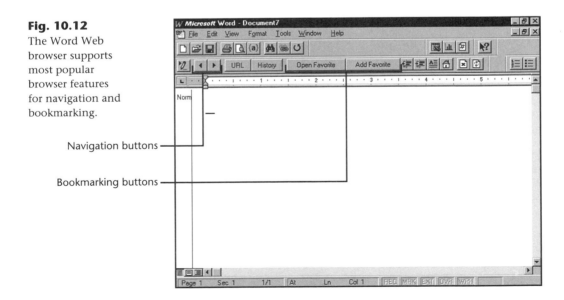

Fig. 10.12
The Word Web browser supports most popular browser features for navigation and bookmarking.

Navigation buttons

Bookmarking buttons

Loading and Editing Documents

When you start a new document, you will find that you have access to a new template called HTML.DOT. This template provides an extensive set of HTML styles and additional menu options and toolbars to support HTML authoring. Figure 10.13 illustrates the modified toolbars. If you want to edit an existing HTML document, Word will automatically open the HTML template when you select a document with an .htm extension.

> **Note**
>
> In the figure, both the Standard and Formatting toolbars are open. Keep in mind that you can customize these toolbars, like all of the toolbars in Word. You can add buttons and rearrange their order; your toolbars may look different, therefore, than those shown in figure 10.13.

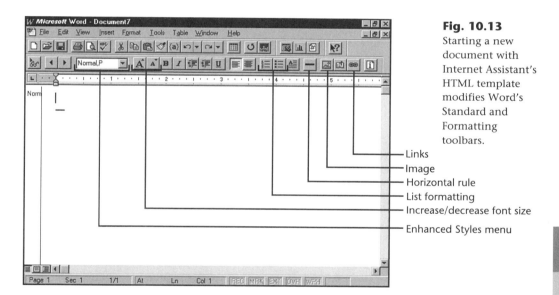

Fig. 10.13
Starting a new document with Internet Assistant's HTML template modifies Word's Standard and Formatting toolbars.

Links
Image
Horizontal rule
List formatting
Increase/decrease font size
Enhanced Styles menu

As you type in the text of your Web page, you can mark it for specific text effects, such as bold or italic, using the standard Word tools. Word automatically translates those effects into HTML tags. You can also format text in HTML modes, such as Strong or Preformatted, by using the styles available under the HTML template. You can select a style using the Styles tool in the formatting toolbar, or you can open the Format menu and choose either Style or Style Gallery.

III

Doing HTML

Internet Assistant also provides a way to place special codes such as diacritical marks, copyright and trademark symbols, or other special punctuation. To access these special characters, open the Insert menu and choose the Symbol option. A dialog box with listings of special characters appears. Double-clicking a specific character places it in the text where the I-beam cursor is located.

Handling HTML Codes Not Supported by Internet Assistant

There are also several HTML tags and effects that Internet Assistant does not accommodate through styles or tools. To enter these additional tags (or any extra HTML code), open the Insert Menu and choose HTML Markup. A dialog box with a large window for entering direct HTML code appears (see fig. 10.14). The entered text is handled and displayed as HTML code without ever being translated into Word format. This feature is nice because it lets you include newly introduced HTML tags in your document, although you do have to type the tags out yourself.

Fig. 10.14
Internet Assistant's Insert HTML Markup dialog box lets you enter unsupported HTML tags.

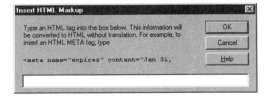

Creating Forms Using Internet Assistant

▶ To learn about the tags used to produce HTML forms, see "Creating Forms," p. 317

Internet Assistant has some fairly extensive features for creating HTML forms. You can begin a form by opening the Insert menu and choosing the Form Field option. This causes Internet Assistant to enter the HTML tags that surround a form. The Form Field dialog box and Forms floating tool palette are shown in figure 10.15.

If you've created forms in Microsoft Access, you may recognize the look of some of these form tools. The Forms tool palette gives you point-and-click access to creating checkboxes, pull-down list boxes, radio buttons, and text boxes. This palette also provides standard Submit and Reset buttons. When you place a field in the form area, additional dialog boxes open to help you create the necessary choices for a pull-down list box or other controls to help make the form work.

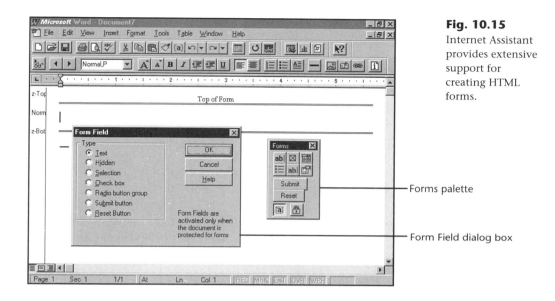

Forms palette

Form Field dialog box

Saving Documents in HTML Format

Internet Assistant for Word saves documents in HTML format by default. The
resulting document is then ready to be used on your Web server. This is a
contrast to many of the third-party templates discussed in this chapter,
which require a special File menu option to save your document in ASCII
format.

HTML Editors

Beyond the templates for word processors, some stand-alone editors are designed completely for the purpose of authoring HTML documents. Many of
the initial versions of these products have been re-released in "professional"
versions that offer souped-up editing capabilities for people who do large
amounts of commercial HTML editing. This section covers some of the more
popular stand-alone HTML editors available.

Netscape Navigator Gold

After setting the standard for browser software, Netscape has taken its
browser a step further by adding document editing features. Packaged under
the name Netscape Navigator Gold, the browser/editor combination provides
a What-You-See-Is-What-You-Get (WYSIWYG) editing environment. What's
more, with Navigator Gold, you can create a Web document *without ever seeing an HTML tag!*

III

Doing HTML

> **Note**
>
> The following information on Netscape Navigator Gold is based on the first public beta release of the software. When the final version of the software is released, a license will cost $79.00. For the most recent information on Navigator Gold, visit Netscape's Web site at **http://home.netscape.com/**.

Getting Started

There are two ways to get started editing a document in Navigator Gold. The first is to load a document into the browser and then switch to the editor. What you see in the editor window will look exactly like what's in the browser window, except that you can make changes to the version in the editor window. Figures 10.16 and 10.17 show the same document in the browser and editor windows, respectively. Notice how little difference there is between them.

Fig. 10.16
A sample document loaded into the Navigator Gold browser.

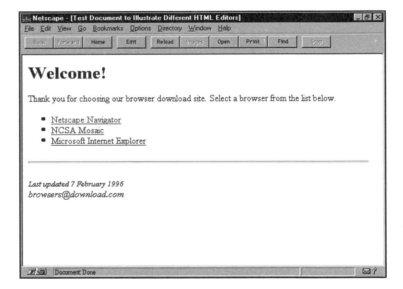

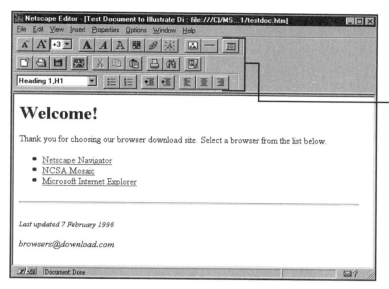

Fig. 10.17
The same sample document loaded into the Navigator Gold editor.

Navigator Gold toolbars

Navigator Gold Toolbars

One thing that is fundamentally different in the editor window is the presence of three toolbars to assist you with your authoring tasks. Most of the buttons in the top toolbar are for formatting text at the font level. You can increase or decrease font size, set the font color, and apply bold, italic, and fixed-width styles. Other buttons let you set up links, place an image, or insert a horizontal rule. The Properties button calls up a dialog box that details the attributes of a selected item and lets you change them if needed.

The middle toolbar handles common file and editing operations. It also provides buttons to open a new browser window, print the edited document, search for a specific text string, and access the Netscape Web Page Starter—a new feature on Netscape's Web site with links to several HTML authoring resources.

Items on the bottom toolbar are for the purpose of formatting text. A pull-down menu lists several styles you can apply to highlighted text. Other buttons let you format ordered and unordered lists, increase or decrease indent levels, and specify left, right, and center alignments.

Note

Depending on your screen width, Navigator Gold's toolbar buttons may be arranged differently from how you see them in figure 10.17.

Opening and Editing a Document

Once you've opened a document by either loading what's in your browser window into the editor or by starting a new one, editing the document becomes almost like using a word processor. Applying a style is just a matter of highlighting the text to be formatted and choosing a style from the pulldown menu or from a toolbar button. You can move images, links, and rules around by simply clicking and holding them, dragging them to where you want them to be, and then releasing your mouse button. This drag-and-drop feature of Navigator Gold makes it easy to place these items exactly where you want them.

Along with the toolbars in the editor window, you also pick up two new menus in your menu bar. The Insert menu lets you place new links, images, rules, line breaks, and non-breaking spaces into your document. Many of these options call up a dialog box in which you can specify the different attributes of the item you're placing. Figure 10.18 shows the dialog box for inserting an image. Note how the information you're asked for in the dialog box directly corresponds to the different attributes of the <IMG ...> tag.

Fig. 10.18

When inserting a new image into a Navigator Gold document, you can specify the attributes of the image in this dialog box.

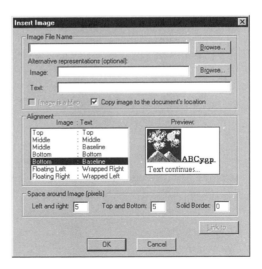

The other new menu is the Properties menu. The different options under Properties let you review and change properties at the font, character, list, paragraph, and document levels.

Perhaps the most curious thing about the Navigator Gold editor is that there is no sign of any HTML tags. You don't see them on-screen and there are no menu options or toolbar buttons that explicitly refer to them. As you read about other HTML editors, you'll see that many of them make explicit mention of tags. Because they do this, the people who use them have to know at least *some* HTML. With Navigator Gold, you could theoretically *not know a single HTML tag* and still be able to author a Web document! The upshot of this is that Navigator Gold will make Web publishing accessible to a much larger group of people. Whether this is beneficial or not remains to be seen.

Publishing Your Documents
In the shipping version of Navigator Gold, you'll be able to publish your finished document right to a Web server with the press of a single button. Navigator Gold will write the HTML file and then transfer it and any necessary image files to the destination server. This saves you from having to save and FTP all of the files by yourself.

HoTMetaL 2.0

If your objective is to write nearly perfect HTML on the first try, you should look into HoTMetaL 2.0 from SoftQuad. There are two versions of HoTMetaL 2.0 available. HoTMetaL FREE 2.0 is intended for use in academe and for internal business purposes. Commercial users are required to purchase HoTMetaL PRO 2.0. When you pay for a license, you also get technical support and some features that are not active in the freeware version, including a spell checker, thesaurus, and user-defined macro capability.

> **Note**
>
> This review of HoTMetaL 2.0 is based on HoTMetaL FREE 2.0, which you can download by visiting **http://www.sq.com/products/hotmetal/hm_ftp.htm**. The features discussed here are also available in the PRO version, along with the added functionality noted above.

Getting Started
When you open a new document in HoTMetaL, you see the window shown in figure 10.19. The figure shows HoTMetaL's standard document template, which is stored in the file tutor.htm. Notice that the tags in the template are

III

Doing HTML

easy to pick out, with starting and ending tags both pointing inward toward the text they contain. Also notice that the template is very complete. All of the tags that are technically required are present, including <HTML>, <HEAD>, <TITLE>, <BODY>, and their corresponding closing tags.

Fig. 10.19
HoTMetaL's standard document template is in proper HTML form and encourages you to title your document immediately.

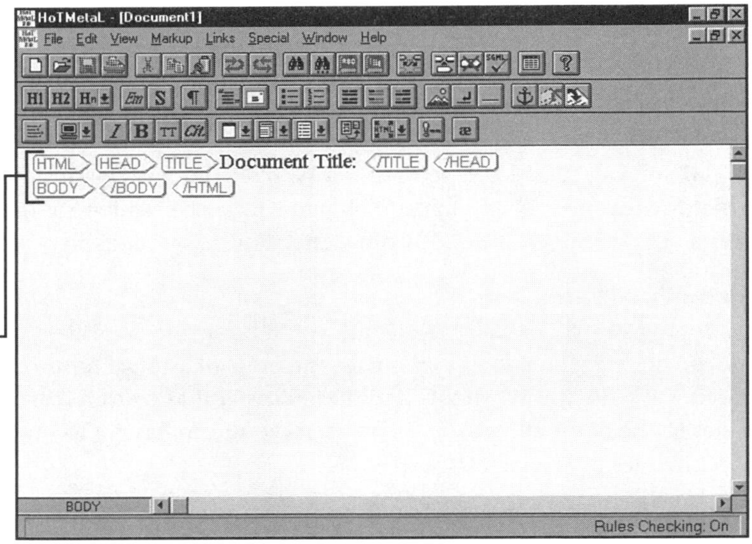

Standard document template

The completeness of HoTMetaL's default template points to one of the program's strengths: it forces you to use good HTML. HoTMetaL's Rules Checking feature makes it almost impossible to insert an inappropriate tag into your document. When Rules Checking is on, the tag insert features of HoTMetaL are context-sensitive and you are limited to inserting only those tags that are legal at the current cursor position. For example, if you were inside the <DL> and </DL> tags, you could only insert <DT> and </DT> tags or <DD> and </DD> tags. HoTMetaL prevents you from inserting other tags by graying them out or by just not presenting them.

Tip

Rules Checking can be annoying if you're a seasoned pro who has developed a particular authoring style. You can turn Rules Checking off or on by pressing Ctrl+K.

In addition to Rules Checking, HoTMetaL also comes with an SGML validator that tests your document for conformance to the rules of proper HTML. These features make HoTMetaL a great choice for the HTML beginner since they encourage good authoring habits right from the start.

The HoTMetaL Toolbars

HoTMetaL provides three toolbars to assist with typical editing tasks. The Standard Toolbar is at the top and provides buttons for frequently used file (New, Open, Save) and editing (Cut, Copy, Paste) operations. Other buttons support searching the document (Find, Find Next), showing, hiding, inserting, and removing HTML tags, and activating the SGML validator. In the freeware version of HoTMetaL, the buttons to activate the Spell Checker and Thesaurus are grayed out.

The Common HTML Toolbar is below the Standard Toolbar and lets you quickly tag markup text with heading styles, frequently used logical styles (Emphasis, Strong, Block Quote, Address), and list tags. Buttons toward the end of the toolbar are not style-related and let you place images, horizontal rules, line breaks, and hyperlinks.

At the bottom, you'll find the Other Toolbar. The Other Toolbar is something of a concession on HoTMetaL's part because it allows for the use of the extensions to standard HTML. This becomes significant when you consider that earlier versions of HoTMetaL refused to recognize these tags and wouldn't even *open* documents that contained them! The HTML extensions are accessible on a pull-down menu that you see when clicking and holding on the HTML Extensions button. Other such pull-down menus give you quick access to tags for the document head, computer-related logical styles (Code, Keyboard, Variable, Sample), compact list tags, and form tags. You can also mark up text with physical styles using buttons in the Other Toolbar. Pressing the Special Characters button produces the floating palette you see in figure 10.20. This palette is handy when coding multilingual pages as it lets you place special characters by pointing to and clicking on them, rather than having to remember the escape sequence of the character. To close the special characters palette, just double-click the button in the upper left-hand corner of the palette.

> ### Note
>
> You can suppress the display of any of the HoTMetaL toolbars by choosing the Toolbars option under the View menu.

III

Doing HTML

Fig. 10.20
The floating
Special Characters
palette makes
placing foreign
language charac-
ters as easy as
pointing and
clicking.

Special Characters
palette

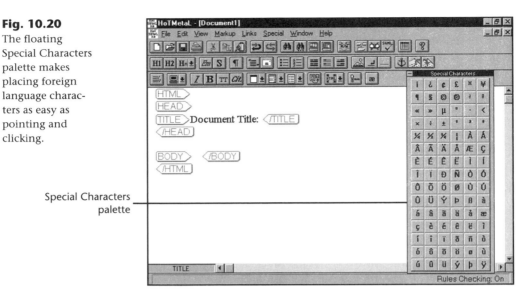

Opening and Editing a Document

Figure 10.21 shows part of an HTML document open in the HoTMetaL window. Note how *all* tags—even tags such as <HR> and <BR>, which ordinarily
occur by themselves—have a closing tag. You can also get a greater sense of
HoTMetaL's tolerance for non-standard HTML tags since it let us load a document that contained <FONT SIZE=–2> and </FONT> tags.

Fig. 10.21
Unlike its
predecessors,
HoTMetaL 2.0 lets
you load docu-
ments with non-
standard HTML
tags.

<FONT> tag

</FONT> tag

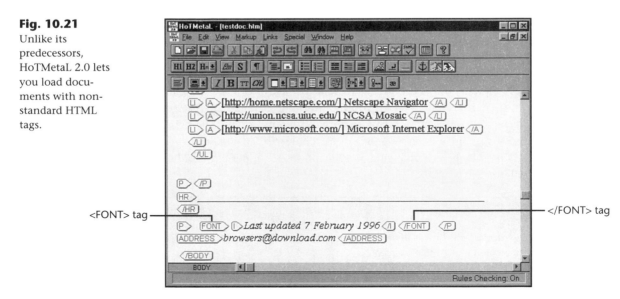

As you edit the document, you'll notice that HoTMetaL treats tag pairs as a single unit. If you delete one tag in the pair, its companion tag and all of the text between them is deleted as well. This is helpful in that it saves you some keystrokes and provides an almost iron-clad guarantee that there will be no stray tags floating around in your document.

> **Caution**
>
> When you delete a tag pair, you also delete all text that appears between the two tags. Make sure you cut and paste this text to another position in your document if you don't want to lose it.

When it's time to insert a tag, choose the Insert Element option under the Markup menu. You can then choose the tag you want to insert from the dialog box that appears. Remember that if Rules Checking is on, you'll be restricted to inserting only those tags that are legal at that point in the document.

Publishing Your Documents

The Publish option under the Links menu is handy if you've developed the pages for a site with all hyperlinks pointing to files on your local hard drive and you need to change those URLs once you place the documents on your server. Once you've validated and saved your documents, you can use the Publish option to prepare your documents for life on the Web server. The Publish dialog box lets you do a search for all URLs that start with the file: protocol and replace them with URLs that start with http:. This dialog box is shown in figure 10.22.

Fig. 10.22
You can quickly convert the local URLs in your documents to URLs appropriate for a Web server.

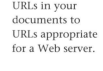

HTMLEd Pro

Hailing from Canada, HTMLEd Pro is the commercial version of the HTMLEd editor that has been around for a few years. Both programs are produced by Internet Software Technologies.

> **Note**
>
> The information about HTMLEd Pro presented here is based on the demo copy of version 1.1. You can download the most recent version from Internet Software Technologies by visiting **http://www.ist.ca/htmledpro/index.html**. If you choose to buy HTMLEd Pro, the license will set you back US$99.95 plus US$10 for shipping and handling.

Getting Started

Just starting up HTMLEd Pro leaves you with an empty editing window. You need to start a new document to activate most of the program's toolbars (which HTMLEd Pro calls *speedbars*) and menu options. When you choose the New option under the File menu, you are presented with a dialog box that lets you set up a basic template for your new document. Checkboxes in the dialog box let you include <HTML>, <HEAD>, <BODY>, and corresponding closing tags. You can also specify your document's title and include comments to indicate that you wrote the document and the date you started it. Once you've filled in the dialog box and clicked OK, you'll see a screen much like the one in figure 10.23. Notice that once the new document is open, HTMLEd Pro's speedbars are no longer grayed out and many new items appear in the menu bar.

> **Note**
>
> You can also choose to create a new document with a custom template of your own design. Just select the New with Document Template option under the File menu.

HTMLEd Pro Speedbars

One of the first things you notice about HTMLEd Pro is all of its speedbars. There are five across the width of the screen and you can even put one down the right-hand side! You can toggle the display of each speedbar on or off under the Options menu.

When all speedbars are displayed, the topmost one is the Standard Speedbar. Buttons on this speedbar handle the most frequently used options like file and editing operations, paragraph and line breaks, horizontal rules, placing images, setting up hyperlinks, formatting unordered and definition lists, centering text, and applying bold and italics styles.

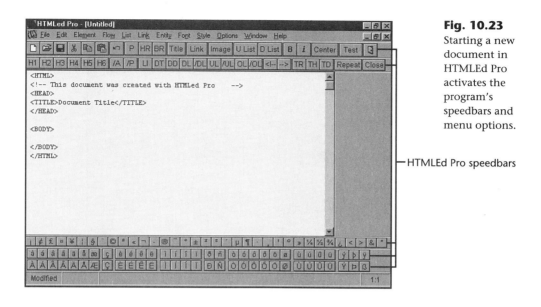

Fig. 10.23
Starting a new document in HTMLEd Pro activates the program's speedbars and menu options.

HTMLEd Pro speedbars

Just below the Standards Speedbar is the Common Tags Speedbar. Here you'll find many of the tags you use most, like heading styles, list and table tags, and tags for creating comments. The closing tags of many popular tag pairs are also available.

The first of the three speedbars at the bottom of the window is the Extended Characters speedbar. Placing any of the characters in this speedbar is as easy as clicking its button. This relieves you from having to remember or look up the escape sequences to produce these characters.

The other two speedbars along the bottom are the Special Characters speedbars. The two are essentially identical with the upper bar supporting the lowercase versions of characters in the lower bar. If you're editing other-than-English language HTML, you'll want to have these two speedbars active.

The speedbar on the right-hand side of the screen is the Custom Speedbar. Each button in this bar is custom designed by you. To place a button on the bar, right-click your mouse while it is pointing to an empty spot on the bar and choose New Button. Once you've placed the button, you can right-click again and choose Modify to get the Edit Custom dialog box, highlight the button you wish to edit, and then select the Edit button as shown in figure 10.24. Custom buttons are great for tag combinations, such as bold and italics, that would otherwise require the application of two or more separate styles.

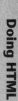

III

Doing HTML

Fig. 10.24
You can customize
buttons on
HTMLEd Pro's
Custom speedbar.

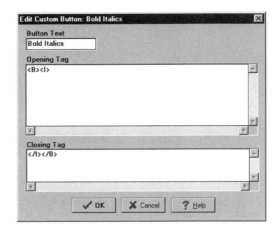

Opening and Editing Documents

Once you have a document open, HTMLEd Pro provides extensive support
for inserting tags and marking up text through a large number of pull-down
menus. HTMLEd Pro supports all of the tags proposed in HTML 3.0 and many
of the Netscape extensions to HTML.

Most of the text formatting styles are found under the Font or Style menus.
Specifically, the Font menu lets you apply any of the physical text styles and
gives you access to the <FONT …> and <BASEFONT …> tags. The Style menu
is home to the heading styles and the logical text styles.

Under the Element menu, you'll find options to activate HTMLEd Pro's Table
Designer and Form Designer. The Table Designer makes it easy to set up a
simple table of any number of rows or columns and to place headers and data
in each of the table's cells. The Form Designer, shown in figure 10.25, is particularly nice because it lets you drag-and-drop form elements around on a
blank worksheet. Click OK when you're done to place the appropriate HTML
in your document.

If you or a friend needs to get a home page up quickly, the HTML Page
Builder under the Options menu is probably the way to go. The Page Builder
"interviews" you over a series of several dialog boxes and composes a home
page based on your responses. One of the Page Builder's dialog boxes appears
in figure 10.26.

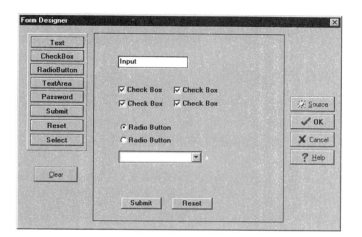

Fig. 10.25
HTMLEd Pro's
Form Designer lets
you drag-and-drop
form elements on
a blank page.

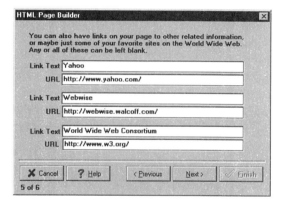

Fig. 10.26
The HTMLEd Pro
HTML Page Builder
"interviews" you
and creates a
personal home
page based on your
responses.

You can further customize the editing environment by defining your own
Quick Keys under the Quick Keys tab of the Preferences dialog box located
under the Options menu. Rather than typing the same text in over and over,
you can store frequently repeated text under one of the Quick Keys and save
your fingers the extra effort.

Publishing Your Documents
When you save your documents, you can choose a DOS or UNIX (no carriage
returns) file format. If your documents need to end up on a remote server,
you can choose the Save Remote option under the File menu to save directly
to that server using the FTP protocol.

III

Doing HTML

You can also save a document without HTML tags. This option is useful when you've downloaded an HTML file and just want the plain-text content of the document. By saving the document without the HTML tags, you automatically strip out the HTML, leaving just a text file.

HotDog Pro

HotDog Pro is a popular new HTML editor from Sausage Software in Australia. You have to pay to license the commercial version, but there is a freeware version (just called HotDog) available as well.

> **Note**
>
> You can download HotDog Pro from Sausage Software's Web site at **http://www.sausage.com/**. You have 30 days to review the demo. After that, you can pay US$99.95 to license HotDog Pro or let the demo expire. If you choose to pay for a license, Sausage Software will send you a registration number by e-mail, saving you shipping and handling charges.

Getting Started

When you first start HotDog Pro, you see the screen shown in figure 10.27. Note that HotDog Pro gives you a standard document template, complete with <HTML>, <HEAD>, <TITLE>, and <BODY> tags, without having to start a new document. You can create and save your own custom templates in HotDog Pro, but you'll need to choose the New option under the File menu to load them.

HotDog Pro Toolbars

HotDog Pro has two toolbars at the top of the editing window and two informational bars at the bottom of the window. The topmost toolbar, shown in figure 10.27 with buttons containing both text and icons, is called the Button Bar. The buttons on the Button Bar are preconfigured to perform the tasks you will probably do most often when editing HTML. However, it is very easy to customize the Button Bar to your own editing habits. Choose the Customize Button Bar option under the Tools menu to open the dialog box shown in figure 10.28. In the dialog box, you can remove buttons from the bar by dragging them to the trash or add a new button to the bar by specifying the text label, icon, tool tip, and function of the new button.

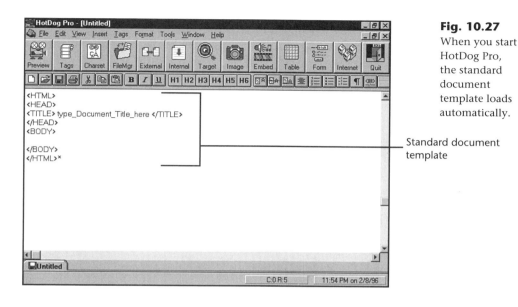

Fig. 10.27
When you start HotDog Pro, the standard document template loads automatically.

Standard document template

Tip

You can reduce the amount of space the Button Bar takes up by changing them to "text only" buttons. This is done on the Display tab of the Options dialog box. You can shut off the Button Bar, as well as any other toolbar or informational bar, under the View menu.

Fig. 10.28
You can remove buttons from the Button Bar or add your own custom buttons.

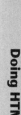

Immediately below the Button Bar is the Elements Bar. This toolbar has significantly smaller buttons than the Button Bar, but it provides you with single-click access to a large number of program options. Buttons on the

III

Doing HTML

Elements bar let you do common file and editing operations, apply physical or heading styles, align text after an image, create a list, insert a paragraph or line break, or place a horizontal rule very quickly.

The first informational bar is immediately below the horizontal scrollbar in figure 10.27. This bar is called the Documents Bar. A different tab, much like the tabs you see at the bottom of an Excel workspace to denote the different spreadsheets in the space, shows up on the bar for each document you have open. HotDog Pro lets you save multiple files together in what's called a *project*. Opening or saving a project opens or saves each file contained in the project. This is a handy feature because the sites you develop are not likely to be comprised of just one page. You'll author many pages in creating a site and HotDog Pro's project capability is a great way to keep track of them all. The Project Manager, accessible under the File menu, lets you perform different tests on documents in a project and prints a report for you when the tests are complete.

Directly below the Documents Bar is the Status Bar. The Status Bar lets you know what the program is doing at any point and provides time and date information as well.

Opening and Editing Documents

You open documents in HotDog Pro with the Open option of the File menu. A new twist is that you can open multiple files at once from the Open File dialog box.

Once you're editing, HotDog Pro supplies you with lots of helpful editing tools. The Tags and Entity palettes are shown in figure 10.29. You can select and insert just about any piece of HTML markup you'll ever need from these two palettes. If a palette with the complete list of HTML tags is too much to scroll through, you can use options under the Tags menu to call up smaller versions of the palette that have similar tags grouped together. For example, the Graphics palette contains the <IMG ...> and <FIG ...> tags, along with standard and extended attributes for each. The Entity palette is useful when you have a lot of special characters in your document.

Tip

You can activate the Tags or Entity palettes quickly by pressing the F6 or F7 keys, respectively.

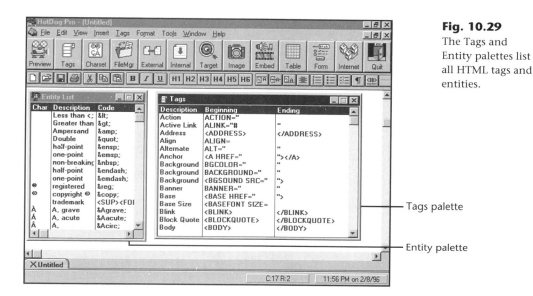

Fig. 10.29
The Tags and
Entity palettes list
all HTML tags and
entities.

Tags palette

Entity palette

Options under the Insert menu use easy-to-follow dialog boxes to guide you
through the insertion of complicated tags and tag sequences. The Insert List
dialog box is shown in figure 10.30. Notice the options to create unordered,
ordered, definition, and plain lists, as well as fields for entering a heading,
specifying the bullet character, and making the list compact. Other options
under the Insert menu let you insert embedded program items and marquees
(a Microsoft Internet Explorer extension to HTML).

If you find you're performing a certain operation frequently and there is no
shortcut key for that operation, you can define your own shortcut key in the
Shortcut Keys dialog box (choose Tools, Shortcut Keys).

Caution

If you define a shortcut key that HotDog Pro assigns to another operation at startup,
your definition will override the startup definition. However, the shortcut key will
continue to appear next to the operation to which it was originally assigned.

Publishing Your Documents

Once you're done editing, you should spell check your document and validate the HTML. HotDog Pro can do both with options under the Tools menu.

III

Doing HTML

Fig. 10.30
Dialog boxes
accessible from the
Insert menu guide
you through the
placement of
complex HTML
tags.

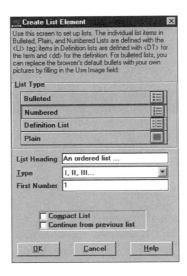

After you make these checks on your document, you'll want to look at them
in a browser to see how they appear on-screen. If you don't want to open a
separate browser program to do this, you can try HotDog Pro's Real-time Output ViewER (ROVER) to test your document. Figure 10.31 shows the HotDog
Pro editing window with a ROVER window open below it. The ROVER window provides a near-WYSIWYG display of how your document will look.

Fig. 10.31
HotDog Pro's Real-
time Output
ViewER (ROVER)
supports a near-
WYSIWYG display
of your
document's online
appearance.

ROVER window —

Kenn Nesbitt's WebEdit

WebEdit is another Windows-based text editor designed to ease the editing of HTML documents. Specifically, WebEdit includes support for every feature of every version of the HTML specification, from HTML 1.0 through the current draft specification for HTML 3.0, including optional features and special non-standard extensions supported by browsers such as Netscape. The latest version also includes the new HTML extensions defined by Netscape 2.0 and Microsoft's Internet Explorer 2.0. Moreover, WebEdit makes all of these features available in a consistent, well-organized fashion, with a minimum number of keystrokes, allowing you to create HTML documents rapidly.

Note

This section on WebEdit is based on the shareware version of WebEdit 1.4b, which is included on the CD-ROM or which can be downloaded from Nesbitt Software's Web site. The URL is **http://www.nesbitt.com/**. You have 30 days to use the software. After that, the commercial license is US$79.95 and the educational license is US$39.95. When you pay for the license, Nesbitt Software will send you a registration number by e-mail, saving you shipping and handling charges. Some of the advanced features are disabled in the demo version and are only available in the "unlocked" version.

Caution

The 16-bit version of WebEdit can only handle file sizes of 64K or less. Windows 95 and Windows NT users will be pleased to know that a 32-bit version of WebEdit is scheduled for release on April 1, 1996. The 32-bit version will be able to handle files of any size.

Getting Started

When WebEdit starts, it creates a new HTML file without any HTML tags. To add all the basic structural HTML tags, simply click on the plus sign (+) and they are added to the blank file. The resulting screen is shown in figure 10.32.

Fig. 10.32
The Plus (+)
button on the
WebEdit toolbar
automatically
places document
structure tags into
a blank file.

Plus (+) button ——

Template created
by clicking the ——
Plus (+) button

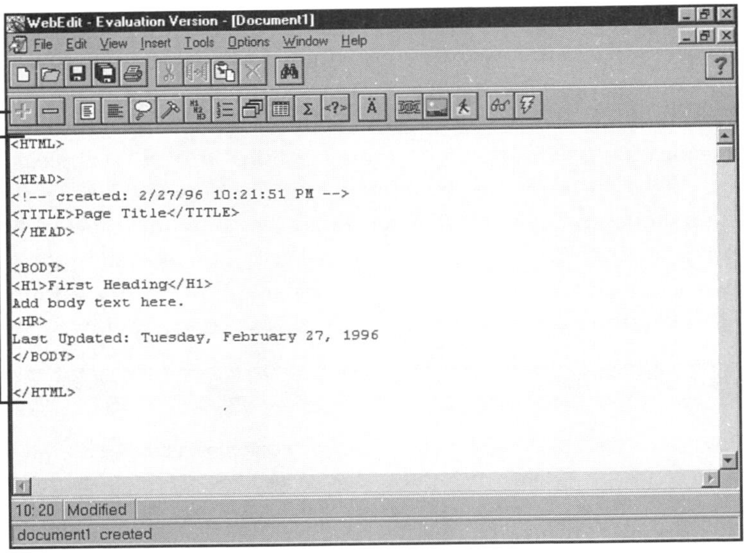

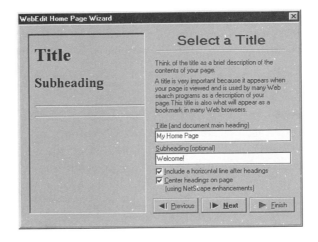

If this is your first time creating a page, WebEdit includes a Home Page Wizard. The Home Page Wizard allows you to create a simple home page with colored or textured backgrounds, inline images, a paragraph of text, links to other sites and pages, and contact information. Figure 10.33 shows one of the Home Page Wizard's dialog boxes.

Fig. 10.33
WebEdit's Home
Page Wizard
authors a custom
home page for you
based on informa-
tion it collects
through a series of
dialog boxes.

WebEdit Toolbars

Figure 10.34 shows the two toolbars WebEdit provides for quick access to frequently used program functions. Buttons on the top toolbar are primarily for common file (New, Open, Save, Save All, Print) and editing (Cut, Copy, Paste, Delete, Find) operations.

Buttons on the lower toolbar are for more HTML specific functions. You've already seen how the Plus button works to place document structure tags into a document. The corresponding Minus (–) button removes all HTML tags from a highlighted portion of the file. Following the Plus and Minus buttons are ten buttons that give you access to practically any HTML tag you might need. Clicking any of the first nine of these buttons produces a drop-down list with the tags available under that button. Figure 10.34 shows the tags available under the List and Misc Tags button. Other buttons play host to document structure, block style, logical style, physical style, heading style, form, table, and math tags.

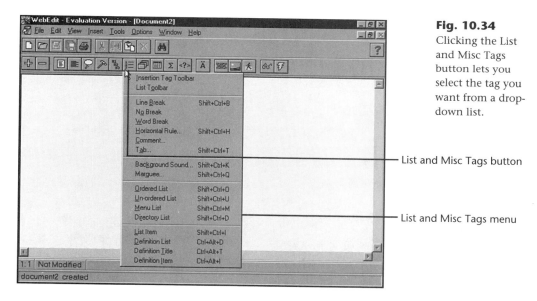

Fig. 10.34
Clicking the List and Misc Tags button lets you select the tag you want from a drop-down list.

— List and Misc Tags button

— List and Misc Tags menu

III

Doing HTML

Caution

WebEdit has floating toolbars corresponding to each of the drop-down boxes. However, these toolbars are locked until you enter your registration code, so don't try to activate them until after you have entered your code.

The remaining buttons on the lower toolbar allow you to define custom tags, gain access to special characters sets, and place hyperlinks, images, and figures into your documents. The two buttons on the end each provide a different way to look at the documents you have under development. The View Document with Browser button fires up whatever browser you've selected to work with WebEdit and the Quick Preview button activates WebEdit's Quick Preview feature (see fig. 10.35). Quick Preview splits the screen in half and allows you to see the HTML source code on the left-hand side and what the document might look like on a browser on the right-hand side.

> **Note**
>
> WebEdit's Quick Preview feature can only handle HTML tags up through those in the HTML 2.0 specification, even though the program provides full support for HTML tags from the HTML 3.0 and Netscape and Microsoft extensions to HTML.

Fig. 10.35
WebEdit's Quick Preview gives you a quasi-WYSIWYG display of your documents.

Editing window

Quick Preview toggle button

Quick Preview window

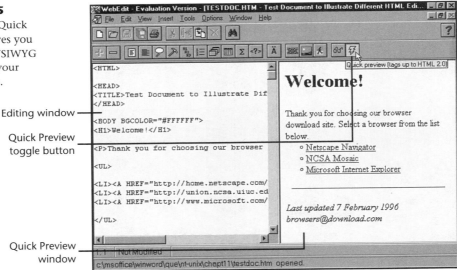

WebEdit Editing Features

Apart from its very thorough support of most HTML tags, WebEdit offers other features that make HTML authoring easier. WebEdit uses extensive dialog boxes to walk you through the placement of links, images, figures, forms, and tables in your documents. Input fields in these dialog boxes let you specify any or all of the attributes you might put into the HTML tags that place these items. WebEdit also features a near-WYSIWYG Table Builder that lets you compose a table right on-screen. The Table Builder dialog box is shown in figure 10.36.

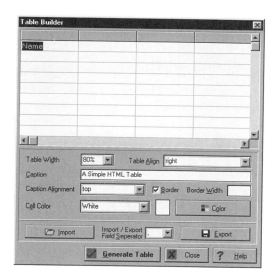

Fig. 10.36
The WebEdit Table Builder allows you to create a table right in the dialog box.

If you're putting imagemaps on your pages, you can use WebEdit's Map Builder to define the hot regions and their associated URLs. To activate the Map Builder, click the Use Mapping check box you see in the Image dialog box and then click the Map Builder button. The Map Builder supports both server-side and client-side imagemaps.

If you like to use color in your Web pages, you probably know the frustration of having to find out the Red/Green/Blue (RGB) codes for the color and then having to convert those numbers to hexadecimal (base 16) so you can specify the color in your HTML code. Using the Hexadecimal Color Value option under the Insert menu, you can choose the color you want from either a pre-configured or custom color palette. Once you choose the color and click on OK, WebEdit converts the decimal RGB values to hexadecimal and places the hexadecimal triplet for the color right into your document.

Publishing Your Documents
Once you have created your document, you should proofread it. WebEdit helps with this process, by including spellcheckers for multiple languages.

III

Doing HTML

Note

The spellcheck feature is locked until you purchase your license and enter your registration code.

Once your documents are spellchecked, you can save them individually (Save) or all at once (Save All). The Export option under the File menu lets you export the files in either UNIX or Macintosh formats, making cross-platform development much easier.

Advanced Editing Systems

The job of maintaining a Web site goes well beyond the creation of HTML pages. Just by looking at the Table of Contents of this book, you can see that there are other tasks involved. You need to plan your site and configure your server according to the plan. You may need to write scripts to process data collected by online forms. Or you may need to develop a database interface or provide support for real-time interactivity. Whatever the purpose of your site, you will most certainly find yourself doing more than just HTML.

The programs you've read about so far can only assist you with the HTML authoring component of your job as a site administrator. However, some forward-thinking companies are releasing software to assist you with all aspects of site administration, including document authoring and management, script authoring, and controlling access to the server. The next two sections point out the highlights of two such software packages: Netscape's LiveWire Pro and Microsoft's FrontPage.

Netscape LiveWire Pro

Netscape unveiled LiveWire Pro at the March 1996 Netscape Developer's Conference in San Fransisco. The LiveWire Pro package comes with:

- Netscape Navigator Gold 2.0
- LiveWire Site Manager
- LiveWire Server Extensions
- A Java-compatible scripting language
- LiveWire Server Front Panel
- Native support for several databases
- A developer's version of Informix

You have already read about Navigator Gold 2.0 and how it can support you in creating Web pages. The LiveWire Site Manager gives you a graphical depiction of your site and lets you restructure the site using drag-and-drop operations. A page that is dragged and dropped to a new location will automatically have all links pointing to it reassigned to its new URL. The Site Manager also checks the validity of external links, supplies several Web page templates and page creation wizards, converts documents prepared in other programs (like Microsoft Word or Novell WordPerfect) to HTML form, and converts many types of images to a Web-compatible format.

The LiveWire Server Extensions are meant to plug in to the Netscape Application Programming Interface (NSAPI) and become an integral part of the server's operations. Server Extensions let you interpret and run scripts, install, remove and update applications created in LiveWire, and make local or remote additions and updates to pages.

Using Java is sometimes overkill in the case of small programs that perform relatively simple tasks. Netscape's Java-based scripting language gives programmers an easy-to-learn way of creating scripts to take care of these tasks. Scripts written in the Netscape scripting language can run on both the Netscape Navigator and Netscape server software. You can even compile the code to produce executable versions of your scripts.

The LiveWire Server Front Panel gives you a Web-like interface to operations of your server. The Front Panel lets you install, remove, and update applications running on your Netscape server. It also monitors these applications and provides you with an almost-real-time display of performance information.

If you're building a database into your site, you'll want to make use of LiveWire's easy connectivity to many popular Structured Query Language (SQL) databases, including those from Oracle, Informix, Sybase, and Microsoft. You can also use LiveWire to create the applications that allow users to query, browse, or update these databases.

Note

The beta release of LiveWire Pro is due out during the second quarter of 1996—right around the time this book is being published. For the most up-to-date information on LiveWire's specifications and pricing, consult Netscape's Web site at **http:// home.netscape.com/**.

III

Doing HTML

Microsoft FrontPage

When it bought out Vermeer Technologies, Inc., Microsoft acquired the rights to Vermeer's FrontPage software package for Web site content creation and management. Now released under the name Microsoft FrontPage, the software has been made compatible with the Microsoft Office suite so that corporate users can easily create Intranet or Internet documents right on their desktops. The client portion of Microsoft FrontPage includes:

- FrontPage Explorer
- FrontPage Editor
- Templates for entire Web sites and individual Web pages
- Wizards for creating different sites and pages
- WebBots that support common Web server functions
- Personal Web Server software

The server side of FrontPage is called Server Extensions. Server Extensions are CGI-based applications that are compatible with Netscape and Microsoft Web server software.

The FrontPage Explorer gives you several ways to look at your entire site. The Outline View presents documents in a hierarchical format, much like the way files are presented in File Manager (Windows 3.1 or 3.11) or in Windows Explorer (Windows 95). You can expand an element of the hierarchy to see the documents below it or collapse an element to see a more compressed view. The Link View shows how the pages of your site link to one another and the Summary View gives you a sortable list of the pages on the site and their properties. Additionally, FrontPage Explorer lets you restructure the site by dragging and dropping documents. Any link changes required after dragging and dropping are done automatically. FrontPage Explorer also validates internal and external links, gives you access to FrontPage's many templates and wizards, lets you control access to pages on your site, and makes it simple to port your site to another server.

The FrontPage Editor supports you in HTML authoring tasks. The Editor lets you easily create basic HTML constructs like headings and lists, as well as more complicated constructs like forms. You can convert images that aren't in GIF or JPEG format using the Editor's image conversion facility. The Editor also converts RTF and text files to HTML format. You can even create imagemaps (clickable images) right in the Editor.

FrontPage's templates and wizards guide you in creating individual Web pages or your entire Web site. Web templates include a Normal Web, Personal Web, Project Web, and Customer Support Web. The Corporate

Presence Web and Discussion Web Wizards walk you through the creation of a site according to your specifications in wizard dialog boxes. FrontPage has ready-made templates for many types of pages commonly found on a site including Frequently Asked Questions (FAQ), Feedback, Guest Book, Press Release, Table of Contents, and What's New pages. The Personal Home Page and Forms Page Wizards let you custom-design a personal page and online forms.

FrontPage WebBots handle common Web site functions without you having to program them. You can use WebBots to implement searches, feedback forms, threaded discussion groups, user registration, and tables of contents.

So that you can get a server up and running right away, FrontPage also includes an NCSA-based Personal Web Server that fully supports HTTP and CGI standards.

Note

For the latest price information on Microsoft FrontPage, consult Microsoft's Web site at **http://www.microsoft.com/**.

Note

Web site administrators with higher-end site management needs should keep their eyes open for Microsoft's Internet Studio. Internet Studio was originally designed only for use with the Microsoft Network, but Microsoft decided in February 1996 to forego the MSN-only version and develop its first release based on Internet standards. Keep watching Microsoft's Web site for information on Internet Studio pricing and release date.

Document Conversion Tools

HTML filters are useful tools that let you convert a document produced with any kind of editor (including ASCII text editors) to HTML. Filters are useful when you work in an editor that has its own proprietary format, such as Word, WordPerfect, or Rich Text Format (RTF).

HTML filters are attractive if you want a utility to convert your document with tags to HTML as you continue to work in your favorite editor. Filters tend to be fast and easy to work with, because they take a file name as input and generate an HTML output file.

III

Doing HTML

> **Note**
>
> The World Wide Web Consortium maintains a good list of HTML filters and converters. Check it out at **http://www.w3.org/hypertext/WWW/Tools/Filters.html**.

Converting Word Documents

Word for Windows and Word for DOS documents can be converted to HTML using the CU_HTML and GT_HTML add-ons mentioned earlier. A few stand-alone conversion utilities have also begun to appear. Because Word can read other word processor formats (including WordPerfect and RTF), you can use these filters when error checking is required or when a dedicated filter for your word processor is not available.

> **Note**
>
> You can find many other Word filters by visiting **http://www.w3.org/hypertext/WWW/Tools/Word_proc_filters.html**.

Converting WordPerfect

The utility WPTOHTML converts WordPerfect documents to HTML. WPTOHTML is a set of macros for WordPerfect versions 5.1 and 6.0. You can also use the WordPerfect filter with other word processor formats that WordPerfect can import.

> **Note**
>
> A link to download WPTOHTML can be found at **http://www.w3.org/hypertext/WWW/Tools/Word_proc_filters.html**.

If the documents you need to convert were created in WordPerfect 6.1, you can use Novell's Internet Publisher to do the conversion.

> **Note**
>
> Internet Publisher is available free-of-charge from Novell at **http://wp.novell.com/elecpub/intpub.htm**.

Converting FrameMaker

FrameMaker release 5 includes a filter to translate FrameMaker documents to HTML. This release also lets you export your document in RTF format, in which case you can use the RTF converter RTFTOHTM discussed next.

> **Note**
>
> To learn more about FrameMaker 5, consult the Adobe site **http:// www.frame.com/PRODUCTS/fm5.html**.

Converting Rich Text Format (RTF)

RTFTOHTML is a common utility that converts RTF documents to HTML. While most versions are available for UNIX and Macintosh systems, there is a version for DOS as well.

> **Note**
>
> The DOS binary file for RTFTOHTML can be downloaded from **http:// www.georgetown.edu/acc/software/rtftohtm.zip**. Note the name is abbreviated because of DOS's eight-character limit on file names.

Because many word processors handle RTF formats, you can import an RTF document into your favorite word processor, and then run one of the word processor specific filters. However, RTFTOHTML seems to be faster at performing this conversion.

Converting PageMaker

EDCO produces the PM2HTML converter in both freeware and production versions. The production version costs $49.00 and can handle a greater number of conversions.

> **Note**
>
> The freeware version of PM2HTML is available by anonymous FTP at **ftp:// ftp.gate.net/pub/users/edco/**. This is a busy site, so it may take you a while to access it.

III

Doing HTML

The World Wide Web Consortium's list of filters reports that Adobe has released an HTML authoring plug-in for PageMaker 6.0, but a search of Adobe's Web and FTP sites yielded no information about this add-on.

Converting Excel Spreadsheets

There are a couple of good options for converting Excel spreadsheets into HTML table format. Microsoft has created a simple Internet Assistant that is available from the Microsoft Web site. Also, XL2HTML.XLS contains a Visual Basic macro for Excel 5.0 that allows you to specify a range of cells and then generate the HTML that converts data in the cells to table form. XTML is an add-on for Excel 5.0 that can do this conversion as well.

> **Note**
>
> You can learn more about XL2HTML.XLS at **http://www710.gsfc.nasa.gov/ 704/dgd/xl2html.html**. XTML lives under Ken Sayward's directory at **http:// users.aol.com/ksayward/xtml/**.

Converting Lotus Notes

Lotus Notes users can now convert their documents to HTML format with Lotus InterNotes Web Publisher. Lotus Notes databases can be converted to HTML by using the program TILE from Walter Shelby Group, Ltd.

> **Note**
>
> Lotus has online information about Lotus InterNotes Web Publisher at **http:// www.lotus.com/inotes/**. You can get information on how to order TILE at **http://tile.net/info/about.html**.

Converting Interleaf

Interleaf users can use Cyberleaf 2.0 to not only convert Interleaf documents to HTML, but Framemaker, RTF, WordPerfect, and ASCII documents as well. Additionally, Cyberleaf converts graphics to either GIF or PostScript formats and it converts tables to GIF images, PostScript files, or HTML 3.0 markup.

> **Note**
>
> Cyberleaf 2.0 for Windows NT is due for release in early 1996. For the latest information, consult Interleaf's Web site at **http://www.ileaf.com/ip.html**.

HTML Analyzers

If the editing tool you use doesn't have a syntax checker, you might encounter problems once your documents are up on the Web. Mismatched or incorrect tags can produce on-screen results that detract from the content you're presenting. Another problem is that as HTML documents age, links may point to files or servers that no longer exist (either because the locations or documents have changed). It is, therefore, good practice to validate the hyperlinks in a document on a regular basis.

Several HTML analyzers exist to help you avoid these problems. These handy utility programs are often Web-based and using them is a matter of pointing your browser to the appropriate page and letting the utility know the URL of the document to analyze. Others live on your hard drive and process the HTML files right on your machine.

> **Caution**
>
> Make sure Access Control is not enabled or Web-based HTML checkers will not have access to your files.

Doctor HTML

Doctor HTML is a Web-based HTML analyzer that lets you perform several different tests on your documents, including:

- Spell checking
- An analysis of the document structure that looks for unclosed or extraneous tags
- An image analysis that loads each image and measures how much bandwidth each consumes
- An image syntax check that makes sure you've used WIDTH, HEIGHT, and ALT attributes in your <IMG ...> tags
- Proper table and form structure tests
- A check on hyperlinks that reports all links that timeout after 10 seconds
- A command hierarchy analysis that displays all HTML commands in the document

The command hierarchy analysis also indents nested tags, making them easier to read. The hierarchy test is best used in combination with one or more of the other tests.

III

Doing HTML

> **Note**
>
> To check your documents with Doctor HTML, direct your browser to **http://imageware.com/RxHTML.cgi**. The form-based interface lets you specify which tests you want done and the URL of the document to test.

HTML Check Toolkit

The HTML Check Toolkit measures how well your documents conform to the rules of standard HTML. You can choose Strict, HTML 2.0, HTML 3.0, Mozilla (recognizes Netscape extensions to HTML), and HotJava (recognizes HTML used to embed Java applets) conformance tests. The report you get back can include a display of the input, the parser output, and the formatted output. In addition to being able to supply a URL to test, you can also submit a smaller chunk of HTML code for testing.

> **Note**
>
> You can open the HTML Check Toolkit at **http://www.webtechs.com/html-val-svc/**.

WWWeblint

WWWeblint "picks the lint" off your HTML documents by performing an extensive number of tests. Some highlights of WWWeblint's analysis include checking for:

- Proper document structure
- Unknown tags or attributes
- Overlapping tags
- The presence of a title in the document head
- The use of ALT in <IMG ...> tags
- Inappropriate nesting of tags
- Unmatched quotation marks
- Existence of local anchors

WWWeblint supports elements proposed in HTML 3.0, including table and math tags. You can ask WWWeblint to check a URL or you can supply a chunk of code for it to test.

> **Note**
>
> You can clean the lint off your documents by checking out **http:// www.unipress.com/weblint/**.

HTML_ANALYZER

A popular hyperlink analyzer is HTML_ANALYZER. It examines each hyperlink and the contents of the hyperlink to ensure that they are consistent. HTML_ANALYZER functions by examining all of a document's links, and then creating a text file that has a list of the links in it. HTML_ANALYZER uses the text files to compare the actual link content to what it should be.

HTML_ANALYZER actually does three tests. It validates the availability of the documents pointed to by hyperlinks (called *validation*). It looks for hyperlink contents that occur in the database but are not, themselves, hyperlinks (called *completeness*). And it looks for a one-to-one relation between hyperlinks and the contents of the hyperlink (called *consistency*). Any deviations are listed for the user.

> **Note**
>
> You can download the compressed archive that contains the HTML_ANALYZER files from **http://www.gatech.edu/pitkow/html_analyzer/README.html**.

> **Note**
>
> Because new HTML authoring tools become available all the time, you should check one of the following Web sites for the most up-to-date information. The World Wide Web Consortium maintains a list of HTML editing tools at **http://www.w3.org/ hypertext/WWW/Tools/**. You can read Mag's Big List of HTML Editors by pointing your browser to **http://union.ncsa.uiuc.edu/HyperNews/get/www/ html/editors.html**. And of course, Yahoo provides an extensive list of editing tools at **http://www.yahoo.com/Computers_and_Internet/Internet/ World_Wide_Web/HTML_Editors**.

III

Doing HTML

## CHAPTER 11

Graphics and Imagemaps

As with the earlier chapter on HTML authoring tools, this chapter will briefly mention the UNIX graphics tools available, but will mostly talk about the Windows tools, since we anticipate that's what the majority of you folks will be using, even if the site is hosted on a UNIX platform.

One of the strongest draws to the World Wide Web is graphics. In 1993 with the 2.0 release of NCSA Mosaic, inline graphics became part of Web pages and made them much more interesting than plain-text documents. Now, just a handful of years later, it's possible to animate the graphics on a Web page by using server push techniques (for the Netscape Navigator) or by using Java, the newest trend in Web programming languages. While these applications are compelling, they are, unfortunately, outside the scope of an introductory chapter on graphics.

Web graphics basically come in two flavors: GIF (for Graphics Interchange Format), a format developed by CompuServe, and JPEG (for Joint Picture Experts Group). Each format has its merits and drawbacks. You'll want to choose one or the other based on how you're using images on your pages. If you have designers at your disposal to produce your graphics, all you need to do is take the hand-off from them and put the files where they belong on your server. Otherwise, you'll need to develop some expertise in a graphics program so you can create your own.

In Chapter 9, you learned how to use the <IMG ...> tag to place an inline image in your documents. You later saw that sandwiching an <IMG ...> tag between the <A ...> and </A> tags set up a linked graphic, or hypergraphic, that users can click on to jump to another document. An extension of this idea is the *imagemap*. Imagemaps are graphics that have been divided into special sections called *hot regions*. Clicking on different hot regions instructs the browser to load different URLs. You've probably seen imagemaps on the main pages of many Web sites, where they provide a popular point-and-click interface to the rest of the site. The first implementation of imagemaps placed the burden of figuring out which URL to load squarely on the server (*server-side imagemaps*), but the current trend is to shift this burden to the client (*client-side imagemaps*).

In this chapter, you learn about:

- The basics of the GIF and JPEG graphics formats
- Several different graphics programs and what features they have to assist with the development of Web page graphics
- Server-side and client-side imagemaps
- Tools to help you create and test imagemaps

Graphics Standards

There are a large number of graphics storage formats in the world, but only two are used in the Web graphics realm: GIF and JPEG. GIF is the format originally put forward in HTML standards, but more and more browsers are able to display JPEG images as well.

> **Note**
>
> It is often possible to configure a browser to use a helper application to display images stored in formats other than GIF or JPEG. For example, you can instruct the browser to run a TIFF format viewer if it encounters an image file that has a .tif extension.

The next few sections look at some of the specifics of the GIF and JPEG formats.

GIF

The GIF format was originally developed by CompuServe as a standard for storing and transmitting images. GIF is an 8-bit format, meaning that GIF images are limited to 256 colors. The current GIF specification, released by CompuServe in 1990, is GIF89a.

How GIF Works

Image data in GIF format is organized into related blocks and sub-blocks that can be used to reproduce the graphic. When transmitting a GIF, a program called an *encoder* is used to produce a GIF data stream of control and data blocks that are sent along to the destination machine. There, a program called a *decoder* parses the data stream and assembles the image.

GIF employs a compression scheme called *LZW compression* to reduce the amount of data it needs to send to completely describe the image. LZW compression works best on simple images like line drawings or graphics with a only a few distinct colors. For more color-rich images, LZW is less efficient, producing compression ratios around 2:1 or less.

Interlaced GIFs

When you place an inline GIF on a Web page, the browser reads it in over the course of one pass over the area the image is to occupy. During the pass, each pixel is set to exactly what it has to be to produce the image. The problem with this approach is that it can take a while for the entire image to be read in. One way to reduce this time and still give the user an idea of what the whole image looks like is to use *interlaced* GIFs.

An interlaced GIF file contains the same image data as a regular GIF file, but it is organized differently. As a browser decodes an interlaced GIF, it receives *incomplete* information about the *entire* image. As it presents this information on-screen, an incomplete version of the whole image shows up. Because it is incomplete, the quality of the image will not be very good, but it is usually good enough to impart a sense of what the final image will look like. As it continues to read more data, the approximation to the actual image is improved, producing a "fade in" effect. When the browser reaches the end of the file, it has all of the image data and it makes the last few changes to the approximate image to reproduce the original. The advantage to this approach is that the user can quickly get a sense of the what the entire image looks like without having to wait for the whole thing to load.

Transparent GIFs

Another attractive feature of the GIF format is *transparency*. In a transparent GIF, one color is designated as transparent. When the image is displayed, all pixels colored with the transparent color are instead set to the color of the background. This gives the effect of the background color "showing through" the image in certain places. Figure 11.1 shows images with and without a transparent background. Note how the oval in the image with the transparent background appears to just be sitting on the background, whereas the oval on the non-transparent background appears to be sitting on a rectangular box that is sitting on the background.

III

Doing HTML

Fig. 11.1
Transparent GIFs
have one color
that is always
changed to the
background color,
allowing the
background to
show through.

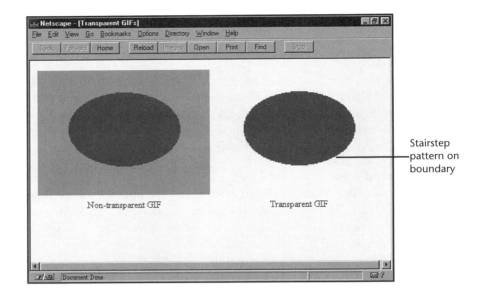

When you knock out the background behind an object in an image, you tend
to get a "stairstep" pattern along the boundary, rather than a smooth curve.
You can see this with the oval on the right in figure 11.1. To alleviate the
stairstep pattern, you can use *anti-aliasing*. By anti-aliasing the image, you
change the color of pixels on the boundary to a color halfway between the
color inside the boundary and the color outside the boundary. By being colored with this middle-ground color, the boundary appears less jagged.

> **Note**
>
> A number of the programs discussed in the "Graphics Programs" section of this
> chapter can create interlaced and transparent GIFs.

Animation

You can create simple animations using GIF files. The GIF89a standard allows
you to store the images that make up the animation in the same file. When a
decoder detects a file with multiple images, it decodes and presents them in
sequence to produce the animation.

Not all browsers have decoders that are sophisticated enough to properly
present an animation. Version 2.0 of the Netscape Navigator does,
though. If you're using Netscape 2.0, you can check out the URL **http://
members.aol.com/royalef/gifanim.htm** to see some sample GIF
animations and learn how to create them.

JPEG

The JPEG format refers to a set of standards for compressing full-color or gray-scale still images. JPEG's ability to work with full-color (16.7 million colors, 24 bits per pixel) images make it preferable to the GIF format (256 colors, 8 bits per pixel) for working with photographs and nature-related art where the entire color spectrum is in play.

How JPEG Works

JPEG can handle so many colors in a relatively small file because it *compresses* the image data. You can control how big or small the image file ultimately is by adjusting the parameters of the compression. A highly compressed file can be very small, but the quality of the image on-screen will suffer for it.

When you decompress a JPEG image, there is always some amount of *loss,* meaning the image will not look exactly the way it did originally. Fortunately, JPEG's compression/decompression scheme is such that the lost image data is in the higher color frequencies where it is harder for the human eye to detect the differences. In spite of this loss, you can still use JPEG to achieve compression levels of about 10:1 or 20:1 without appreciable change in the image. This means you've changed from storing 24 bits per pixel to 1 or 2 bits per pixel—a very impressive savings! As noted above, you can take the compression ratios even higher, but as you do, the loss becomes more and more detectable.

Progressive JPEGs

One attractive feature of the GIF format was the ability to interlace images. Interlacing reorganizes the image data so that as the file is read in, the image "fades in" over several passes, rather than just being read in from top to bottom. The analogous effect on the JPEG side is produced with *progressive JPEG* or *p-JPEG.* A machine displaying a p-JPEG presents a lower-quality approximation to the entire image after the first pass, followed by improvements in quality during subsequent passes. Thus, the user gets to see a rough version of the image right away and doesn't have to wait for the whole thing to display from top to bottom. The drawback of p-JPEG is that each pass over the image requires as much computational effort as the first, so the later passes are not necessarily faster.

In a Windows environment, you have a few options for converting to p-JPEG. The Independent JPEG Group (IJG) offers a series of command line programs for working with JPEG and p-JPEG files. You can download the source code from **ftp://ftp.coast.net/SimTel/msdos/graphics/jpegsrc6.zip**. Version 1.C of LView Pro (described later in this chapter) can also handle p-JPEGs.

> **Note**
>
> There is no analogy for transparency in the JPEG format. The approach to transparency requires the selection of one color to be transparent. Because there can be data loss in JPEG compression/decompression, it's possible that a pixel colored with the transparent color may change to a slightly different color during the compression/decompression computations. Similarly, a pixel colored with a non-transparent color could become transparent and disappear. Either situation would undo the transparency effect you want to achieve.

Growing Acceptance

More and more browsers are warming up to the JEPG format and are able to display JPEG images without launching a helper application. Browsers that can fully support JPEGs and p-JPEGs include:

- Netscape Navigator 2.0
- Microsoft Internet Explorer 2.0 (under Windows 95)
- Spyglass Enhanced Mosaic 2.1
- UdiWWW 1.0.010
- Java 1.0

> **Note**
>
> An extensive list of frequently asked questions about the JPEG format can be found at **http://www.cis.ohio-state.edu/hypertext/faq/usenet/jpeg-faq/top.html**.

When Should I Use JPEG over GIF?

There are a number of situations in which you might choose the JPEG format over the GIF format. If preservation of more than 256 colors is important, you want to use JPEG. If you try to store a full-color image as a GIF, the first thing that happens is that it gets knocked down to 256 colors. You can imagine how much different this might look when you consider that full, 24-bit color supports over 16 million colors!

Another factor is speed. A well-compressed JPEG version of an image is likely to be much smaller than a GIF of the same image. Smaller file size means faster transmission time over the Internet. In some cases, once the file arrives at the browser or image decoder, you can further speed things up by configuring the decompression process to use reduced accuracy in doing the necessary calculations. However, this will increase data loss and reduce image quality.

A third reason is portability. With GIFs, you're locked into 256 colors. JPEGs make no predetermination of how many colors to use, so it is more useful for transferring images among systems with different display hardware.

On the flip side, you'll want to use GIFs for images with a few distinct colors, for black-and-white art like line drawings, and for images with sharp color changes. Most logos and icons found on Web pages fall into this category. Also, if you need an image with a transparent background, you have to use the GIF format because there is no way to achieve transparency with JPEGs.

Graphics Tools

Some Web authors work in conjunction with graphics people who design and develop all of the images that go into a Web site. Other authors have to create the graphics themselves. If you ever find yourself in the latter situation, you'll need to know how to use one of the many graphics programs on the market. This section gives an overview of five such programs with emphasis on how they can help you create graphics for the Web.

UNIX Tools

The most common UNIX graphics tools are xpaint and xv. Xpaint is included with the X11R6 distribution, and is a simple paint program (see **http:// www.x.org**). The descriptions below for Microsoft Paint work very well for xpaint too. Xpaint is "donateware" says the author, so if you like it, send him money or cookies or something.

Xv is a full image manipulation program. If xpaint is the poor man's Adobe Illustrator, xv is a poor man's Adobe Photoshop. Not only can it be used to view images, it has a very extensive array of color and palette manipulation tools, can convert into and from a large number of content types, and cut and paste regions of the image. Xv is available from **ftp:// ftp.cis.upenn.edu/pub/xv/**.

Finally, Adobe PhotoShop is available on a couple UNIX platforms, and is the UNIX graphics creation tool of choice for most high-end graphics sites.

Microsoft Paint

Windows users have a basic graphics program right at their disposal in Microsoft Paint. Paint's main window is shown in figure 11.2.

Paint's tool palette lets you select one of many tools you can use to create and color graphical items and text. The lower four tools let you create rectangles with square or rounded corners, polygons, and ellipses. You can color the regions you create with the Pencil, Brush, Airbrush, or Fill tools.

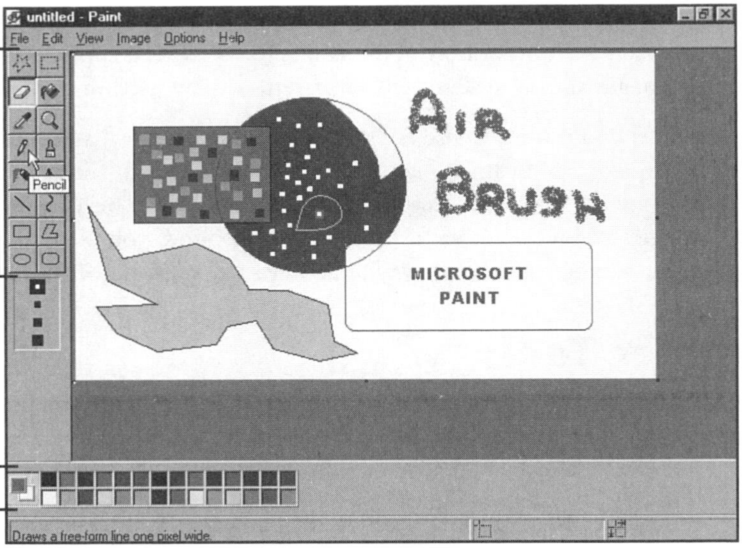

Fig. 11.2
Microsoft Paint is
a basic graphics
program that
comes bundled
with Windows.

Tool palette—

Color palette—

Tip

To create circles in Paint, use the Ellipse tool while holding down the Shift key.

The Text tool enables you create pieces of text in various sizes and fonts. Be sure to turn on the Text Toolbar under the View menu when placing text as this will make changing text attributes easy.

The rest of Paint's tools are equally handy. If you just need a simple line or curve, the Line and Curve tools (found just above the Rectangle and Polygon tools, respectively) provide an easy way to produce one. The Magnify tool increases the magnification of the image so you can do detailed work on small parts of it. The Erase tool can erase anything you've drawn by moving the tool over the image and holding down the left mouse button.

At the bottom left of the Paint window, you'll find the color palette. Left-clicking on a color sets the foreground color to that color. Right-clicking a color does the same thing for the background. The default foreground/background combination is black on white.

Most of Paint's menu options are fairly standard or self-explanatory. The Image menu gives you options to flip, rotate, stretch, or skew your image and to modify its size and colors.

One useful feature that you find in Paint and most other graphics programs is a readout of the x and y coordinates of the pointer or cursor as you move it over the graphic. When you learn about imagemaps later in the chapter, you'll see that knowing certain coordinates on the image is critical to defining the hot regions on an imagemap.

For all of its features, Paint has one major drawback in the context of creating Web graphics: it can't save images in the GIF or JPEG formats. If you want to use a Paint graphic on the Web, you need to convert it from a Windows bitmap to a GIF or a JPEG using a format converter or a different graphics program.

LView Pro

LView Pro is a great little shareware program you can use to edit existing graphics or convert them to GIF or JPEG format. It offers most of the same image manipulation features—such as flip and rotate—that Paint does, plus several other options that give you very fine control over image appearance.

WebmasterCD

> **Note**
>
> The information on LView Pro presented here is based on the evaluation copy of version 1.C/32. You can download the latest version of LView Pro by pointing your browser to **http://www.std.com/~mmedia/lviewp.html**. A license costs US$30.00 plus US$5.00 for shipping and handling.

Figure 11.3 shows the LView Pro window along with its extensive tool palette. Almost every tool in the palette corresponds directly to one of LView Pro's menu options.

Tool palette ——

Fig. 11.3
LView Pro's tool palette enables you to make modifications to most aspects of an image.

III

Doing HTML

One nice feature is that LView Pro will let you open multiple images. This makes it easy to cut, copy, and paste objects from one image file to another. When you save an image, you can use LView Pro as a format converter and choose a format different from the original.

Notice that LView Pro doesn't have tools to create rectangles, polygons, and ellipses like Paint does. Indeed, the only LView Pro tool for creating anything is the Add Text tool. It stands to reason then that you'll probably have to use a different program to create your graphics. But what LView Pro lacks in ability to create, it makes up for with its ability to make very particular changes to an image.

LView Pro lets you change just about any facet of the image you could ever want. Tools on the palette call up dialog boxes to modify quantities like:

- Image brightness and contrast
- Red, Green, and Blue (RGB) color components
- Hue, Saturation, and Value (HSV) values
- Luminance and Chrominance (YCbCr) values
- Transformation maps and filters for RGB color components

Other tools let you convert the entire image from color to grayscale or to its photographic negative.

Used in conjunction with a program that has more graphics creation capabilities, LView Pro is a powerful editing tool that you can use to fine-tune the images you make for your Web pages.

Paint Shop Pro

Another good shareware program for graphics work is Paint Shop Pro from JASC, Inc. Paint Shop Pro handles many types of image storage formats, lets you do the most common image manipulations, and even comes with a screen capture facility.

Note

The following information on Paint Shop Pro is based on the Shareware 3.11 version of the program. You can download this version from **ftp://ftp.the.net/mirrors/ ftp.winsite.com/pc/win95/desktop/psp311.zip**. A license costs US$69.00 plus US$5.00 for shipping and handling.

Figure 11.4 shows an image loaded into Paint Shop Pro along with the many available tool panels that give you single-click access to Paint Shop Pro's functions. The Zoom panel lets you zoom in to magnifications as high as 16:1 and out to magnifications as low as 1:16. Tools on the Select panel sample colors, move the image around in the window, define a custom area of the image to clone or resize, and change the foreground and background colors. The Paint panel is a welcome addition to Paint Shop Pro that was not available in earlier versions. It supports 22 different tools that you can use to make your own graphics. These tools let you create brush, pen, pencil, marker and chalk effects; draw lines, rectangles and circles; fill a closed region with color; add text; and sharpen or soften part of an image. The Histogram window gives you a graphic representation of the luminance of all colors in the image, measured with respect to the brightest color.

Tip

You can toggle any of the tool panels on or off by using options found under the View menu.

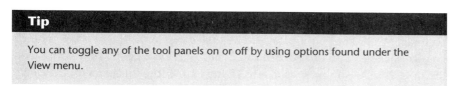

Zoom panel   Select panel

Toolbar

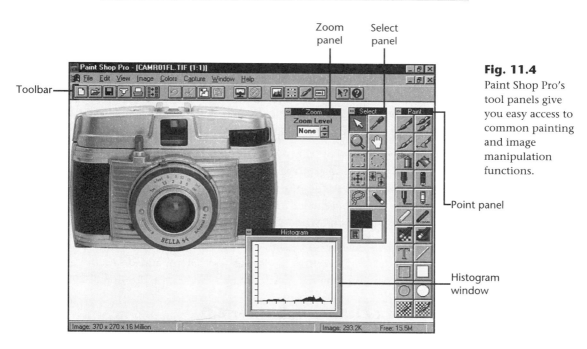

Fig. 11.4
Paint Shop Pro's tool panels give you easy access to common painting and image manipulation functions.

Point panel

Histogram window

III

Doing HTML

Paint Shop Pro is a versatile program that can open images stored in 25 raster (pixel-based) formats, including GIF and JPEG, and 9 meta/vector (image components stored as geometric shapes that combine to produce the entire image) formats, including CorelDRAW!, Micrografx, and Ventura. However, it can only save in one of the raster formats. Nevertheless, Paint Shop Pro is still handy for converting to pixel-based formats. The Batch Conversion option under the File menu lets you select any number of files to convert to a new storage format.

TWAIN refers to a set of industry standards that allow graphics programs to work with image acquisition hardware like scanners. If you have a TWAIN-compliant scanner attached to your computer, you can use the File|Acquire option to scan in a new image. The Select Source option, also under the File menu, lets you choose what device you want to use for the acquisition.

Under the Image menu, you'll find options to do many of the standard manipulations like flipping the image upside down, creating a mirror image of an image, and rotating the images. The Image|Resample option allows you to change the size of an image with the jagged edges you get by standard resizing. You'll also find several effect filters under the Image menu that let you add or remove noise, enhance darker or lighter colors, and blur, sharpen or soften the image. You can even define effect filters of your own.

The Colors menu is host to many standard functions such as adjustment of brightness, gamma correction and RGB values, and conversion to grayscale or photographic negative versions of an image. You can also load, modify and save color palettes from the Colors menu. The Increase and Decrease Color Depth options allow you to change the number of colors being used to render the image.

One very useful feature of Paint Shop Pro is its screen and window capture facility. Options under the Capture menu let you capture the whole screen, a single window on the screen, the client area inside a window, or a user-define area. You can also choose whether or not the mouse pointer should be included in the capture and which hotkey will activate the capture.

Paint Shop Pro alone is a very capable image editing program, but you can also purchase it bundled with Kai's Power Tools SE for added functionality. To order this combination package, contact JASC sales at 1-800-622-2793.

Micrografx Picture Publisher 6.0

Micrografx Picture Publisher 6.0 is an image creation and editing program that comes as part of Micrografx's ABC Graphics Suite. The Picture Publisher main window is shown in figure 11.5.

Fig. 11.5
Micrografx Picture
Publisher 6.0 is a
feature-rich image
creation and
editing program.

To completely describe all of Picture Publisher's many features would fill
several chapters, so the discussion here is limited to those features related to
creating Web graphics. In addition to image painting capabilities that exceed
those of Microsoft Paint and editing capabilities that at least match those of
LView Pro, Picture Publisher supports the creation of Web graphics with features like:

- Transparent and interlaced GIF creation

- Effect filters to sharpen or smooth image edges or to lighten or darken
  an image

- Layers that act like sheets of acetate; you can place image objects on
  separate layers and then overlay them to produce the entire image

- Anti-aliasing of object edges

- Easy-to-create 3-D effects like drop shadows

- Support for creating custom textures like wood grain or brushed steel

- Filters that let you export your image in one of over 30 formats, including GIF and JPEG

- A highly customizable editing environment that lets you create your
  own "toolboxes" of tools, commands, and macros.

The other programs that come bundled with Picture Publisher 6.0 add value
to the entire ABC Graphics package. ABC FlowCharter makes it easy to create

III

Doing HTML

diagrams and charts. Micrografx Designer is a useful graphics illustrator program and the ABC Media Manager puts over 30,000 clipart images, photos, and diagramming symbols at your fingertips.

For all you get, you'd probably expect that the Micrografx ABC Graphics Suite isn't shareware—and you'd be correct. However, a license for the entire package costs substantially less than what other stand-alone graphics programs might run you. Since software prices can change rapidly, you should consult your software dealer or Micrografx (1-800-671-0144) for the most up-to-date price information.

> **Note**
>
> To learn more about the complete Micrografx product line, check out their newly redesigned Web site at **http://www.micrografx.com/**.

Adobe Photoshop

Adobe Photoshop sets the industry standards for both high-end imaging and importing other graphics. Additionally, there are versions of Photoshop that run on Macintosh, Windows, Silicon Graphics, and Sun platforms, making it the most powerful, cross-platform graphics application discussed in this chapter.

Just as with Micrografx Picture Painter, a full description of all of Photoshop's features would fill volumes. Photoshop supports many of the useful features noted for Picture Publisher like transparent and interlaced GIFs, layers, anti-aliasing, drop shadows, and broad graphics file support, plus several others including:

- Numerous plug-in programs that support custom effect filters and emerging image formats like progressive JPEG
- Many options for dithering to lower color depths and different color palettes
- Highly efficient memory management
- A flawless interface with other Adobe products like Illustrator and PageMaker

Because it is so powerful, Photoshop doesn't come cheap. Depending on what platform you want to run Photoshop on, a single license can set you back almost $1000. Check with your software retailer or Adobe for current pricing.

Note

For more information about Photoshop and other Adobe products, visit their Web site at **http://www.adobe.com/**.

Implementing Imagemaps

As noted at the start of the chapter, there are two kinds of imagemaps. The original kind is the server-side imagemap, in which the server does the work to determine what hot region the user clicked on. The newer variety is the client-side imagemap, in which the client makes this determination.

The major difference between the two approaches is where you find the information that defines the map hot regions and the URLs associated with those regions. For a server-side imagemap, the information is found in a *map file* that resides on the server. With client-side imagemaps, the information is embedded in the HTML code that produces the page the imagemap is on.

Server-Side Imagemaps

When a reader clicks on an image that is part of a server-side imagemap, the mouse coordinates relative to the upper-left corner of the image are sent to the server for processing by an *imagemap script.* The script looks at a map file to decide which hyperlink to follow based on the mouse coordinates.

In order for a server-side imagemap to work, several configuration steps are necessary. First, depending on what server software you use, certain imagemap support files must be present on your server. Second, you must create the graphic and determine the coordinates that define the various hot regions. These coordinates, along with the URLs associated with each hot region, are used to make up the map file. Finally, you need to set up the <IMG ...> tag that places the image so that the client knows it's dealing with an imagemap and what the name of the map file is.

Configuring Your Server for Server-Side Imagemaps

The NCSA, CERN, Netscape, and Windows httpds feature imagemap support, although there are differences among them. Important differences are noted as the section progresses. NCSA httpd requires two files for imagemap support. The first is a script called *imagemap,* which must be compiled for your machine and placed in the cgi-bin directory. CERN httpd requires a similar file. With Netscape and Windows httpds, the imagemap script is pre-installed and ready to go.

III

Doing HTML

Second, for NCSA and CERN httpds, you need write permission to the imagemap.conf file in the server's conf directory. This file maps image names, which you create, to their associated map files. You have to add a line to this file for each new imagemap you create. The format of the imagemap.conf file is simple:

```
image_name : physical_path
```

The path to the map file is not an URL. It's the physical path on your system. A sample imagemap.conf is included below.

```
homepage : /maps/homepage.map
buttonbar : /maps/buttons.map
usmap : /maps/countries/us.map
```

The Netscape and Windows httpds do not require an imagemap.conf file.

Creating a Graphic and Defining Hot Regions

Standard HTML requires that the image you use for an imagemap be in the GIF format. You can use any of the image editing programs discussed earlier in the chapter, possibly with a GIF conversion tool, to make the GIF file itself. The most difficult part of making an imagemap is mapping image coordinates to corresponding actions.

Imagemap scripts can process hot regions that are rectangles, circles, and polygons. Lines in a map file define these regions using the minimum number of (x,y) coordinates required to completely describe the region. Rectangles are defined by the coordinates of the upper-left and lower-right corners, circles by the coordinates of its center and a point along the circle itself, and polygons by the coordinates of its vertices. Coordinates are measured with respect to the upper-left corner of the image, which is taken to have the coordinates (0,0). The x-coordinate increases as you move to the right along the image and the y-coordinate increases as you move down the image.

Each line in a map file defines one hot region and specifies the URL associated with the hot region. For example:

```
rect URL upper_left(x,y) lower_right(x,y)
circle URL center(x,y) edge_point(x,y)
poly URL vertex1(x,y) vertex2(x,y) vertex3(x,y) …
```

Caution

All URLs in the map file should be *fully qualified*.

Note

The CERN imagemap facility uses the keywords rectangle, circle, and polygon instead of NCSA's and Netscape's rect, circle, and poly. In addition, the format of the map file is slightly different.

Netscape's imagemap script recognizes the keyword point in a map file as well. It is followed by the URL and the coordinates of the point.

You can also include a line in the map file beginning with the keyword default, which specifies what action to take if the coordinates of the mouse click are outside any hot region.

Caution

If you're doing imagemaps on a Netscape server, avoid using point and default lines in the same map file. If one or more point lines is specified, a click outside of a hot region is taken to be a click at the nearest hot point. This means that any default URL is disregarded.

Figure 11.6 shows a GIF file to be set up with links to several government sites. The image contains a rectangle, a circle, and a pentagon (5-sided polygon) whose defining coordinates and associated URLs are shown in table 11.1.

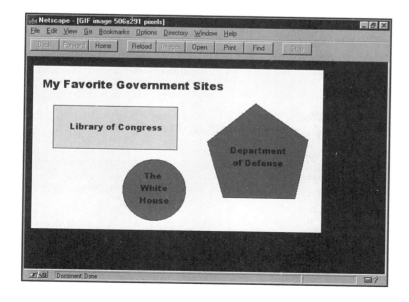

Fig. 11.6
A GIF file to be linked to three different government sites.

III

Doing HTML

Table 11.1 Defining Coordinates and URLs for Sample Imagemap		
Shape	**Coordinates**	**URL**
Rectangle	(36,70),(252,146)	http://www.loc.gov/
Circle	(214,219),(269,221)	http://www.whitehouse.gov/
Polygon	(389,61),(480,125), (459,231),(334,230), (305,131)	http://www.dtic.dla.mil/ defenselink/

> **Note**
>
> At this stage, your only option for finding the necessary coordinates is to use the pointer in your graphics program and read the coordinates from the program window. Later in the chapter, you'll learn about imagemap tools that let you create a map file without knowing the coordinates. These tools let you trace over shapes on your graphic and it figures out the coordinates for you.

Using the coordinates and URLs in table 11.1, you can write the map for the imagemap. In this case, the file would be:

```
rect http://www.loc.gov/ 36,70 252,146
circle http://www.whitehouse.gov/ 214,219 269,221
poly http://www.dtic.dla.mil/defenselink/ 389,61 480,125 459,231
334,230
```

Apache Internal Imagemap Handling

Apache, like the Netscape server and several others, is able to handle imagemaps internally. This means that no CGI process is required to service the imagemap request - one simply references the map file directly, and Apache itself translates the selected point coordinates into a new URL to redirect the browser.

This is done by setting the MIME type of your map files (which end with, say, .map) to a "special" MIME type using the "AddType" directive. In particular:

```
AddType application/x-httpd-imap map
```

The server, when asked to get this file, "knows" that file type is special and treats it with some internal machinery. This machinery is defined in the "mod_imap" module.

One would call this from HTML as any other imagemap file, but now one can do so locally, without a call to the imagemap CGI program. For example:

```
<A HREF="main-menu.map">
<IMG SRC="menu.gif"  ALT="Menu" ISMAP>
</A>
```

The URL's in "main-menu.map" can be relative URL's as well, making life easier for those who move directories around a lot. Because CGI is avoided, internal imagemaps are more efficient as well.

Optional: Linking to the Imagemap

If you'd prefer to use the CGI method for implementing imagemap functionality, use these instructions instead of the ones above, though the above method is strongly recommended over this one.

After you create a map file for an image, you must make it an anchor to include it in an HTML file, like this:

```
<A HREF="/cgi-bin/imagemap/govtsites">
<IMG SRC="images/govtsites.gif" ISMAP></A>
```

The hypertext reference must contain the URL to the imagemap script followed by a slash (/) and the name of the map defined in the imagemap.conf file. The actual picture is then included with the <IMG ...> tag. The <IMG ...> tag also includes the ISMAP attribute, indicating that the image placed by the tag is to be an imagemap.

For this example to work, there must also be a line in the imagemap.conf file pointing to a map file for the imagemap "govtsites." That line might look like this:

```
govtsites :/maps/govtsites.map
```

Client-Side Imagemaps

Having the server do the work to find out where the user clicked and where to send the user based on the click involves a lot of wasted resources. The client has to open another http connection to the server to pass the coordinates and get the response back regarding what URL to load next. The computations the server has to do to find out what hot region the user clicked on are straightforward and there's no reason they couldn't be done by the client. And slow transmission times between client and server means that users may have to wait quite a while from the time they click the mouse to the time the new URL is loaded.

Until recently, the compelling reason for having the server do the imagemap computations was because the map file data resided on the server. If there were a way to get this information to the client, then the client could do the computations and the imagemap process would become much more efficient. This is the spirit behind client-side imagemaps.

Currently, there are two proposals for implementing client-side imagemaps. Both provide a way to get the map file data to the client, but specifics of each

III

Doing HTML

approach are different. One proposal suggests the use of the <FIG ...> ... </ FIG> tag pair with map file data contained in <A ...> tags between them. The other proposes a new tag pair—<MAP ...> and </MAP>—with <AREA ...> tags between them to contain the map file data.

Client-Side Imagemaps with the <FIG ...> ... </FIG> Tag Pair

The key to using the <FIG ...> and </FIG> tags for a client-side imagemap is that these tags can contain text that acts as an alternative to the image being placed by them. Thus, any text between the <FIG ...> and </FIG> tags is much like text assigned to the ALT attribute of the <IMG ...> tag. For example, the HTML:

```
<IMG SRC="logo.gif" ALT="Company Logo" WIDTH=120 HEIGHT=80>
```

and

```
<FIG SRC="logo.gif" WIDTH=120 HEIGHT=80>
Company Logo
</FIG>
```

essentially do the same thing.

To implement the government sites map as a client-side imagemap with the <FIG ...> and </FIG> tags, you need to place the information previously found in the map file between these tags. This is done with the <A ...> tag as shown in listing 11.1.

Listing 11.1   Implementing the Government Sites Map

```
<FIG SRC="images/govtsites.gif" WIDTH=530 HEIGHT=300>
<B>Select a government site to visit:</B>
<UL>
<LI><A HREF="http://www.loc.gov/" SHAPE="rect 36,70,252,146">Library
of Congress</A></LI>
<LI><A HREF="http://www.whitehouse.gov/" SHAPE="circle
214,219,269,221">
The White House</A></LI>
<LI><A HREF="http://www.dtic.dla.mil/defenselink" SHAPE="polygon
389,61,480,125,459,231,334,230,305,131"></A></LI>
</UL>
</FIG>
```

The HREF attribute in each <A ...> tag contains the URL to load when the user clicks on a hot region and the SHAPE attribute contains the information needed to define each hot region. SHAPE is assigned to the shape of the hot region, followed by a space, and then followed by the coordinates that specify the region. Each number in the coordinate list is separated by a comma.

SHAPE also has a secondary function in this setting. If the image file specified in the SRC attribute of the <FIG ...> tag is placed on the page, the browser ignores any HTML between the <FIG ...> and </FIG> tags, unless it is an <A ...> tag with a SHAPE attribute specified.

On the other hand, if the image is not placed, the browser renders the HTML between the two tags. The result for the HTML above is a bulleted list of links that can act as a text alternative for your imagemap. This is an important feature of client-side imagemaps done with the <FIG ...> and </FIG> tags: they degrade into a text alternative for non-graphical browsers, browsers with image loading turned off, browsers that don't support the <FIG ...> and </FIG> tags, or when the desired image file cannot be loaded.

Tip

Make sure that the alternative text between the <FIG ...> and </FIG> tags is formatted nicely into something like a list or a table. Users will appreciate this extra effort.

Note

For the full scoop on the <FIG ...> ... </FIG> tag pair proposed for HTML 3.0, visit **http://www.w3.org/pub/WWW/MarkUp/html3/figures.html**.

Client-Side Imagemaps with the <MAP ...> ... </MAP> Tag Pair

While working on a version of Mosaic that could read from CD-ROM, people at Spyglass had an immediate need for client-side imagemaps. Their solution was to introduce a <MAP ...> and </MAP> tag pair to contain the hot region information previously found in map files. Each map defined by these tags is given a unique name so that it can be referenced from the <IMG ...> tag used to place the graphic for the imagemap.

To define a map for the government sites map above, you would use the HTML shown in listing 11.2.

Listing 11.2   Defining a Map for the Government Sites Map

```
<MAP NAME="govtsites">
<AREA SHAPE="RECT" COORDS="36,70,252,146" HREF="http://www.loc.gov/">
<AREA SHAPE="CIRCLE" COORDS="214,219,269,221"
HREF="http://www.whitehouse.gov/">
<AREA SHAPE="POLYGON" COORDS="389,61,480,125,459,231,334,230,305,131"
HREF="http://www.dtic.dla.mil/defenselink/">
</MAP>
```

III

Doing HTML

The NAME attribute of the <MAP ...> tag gives the map information a unique identifier. The <AREA ...> tags between the <MAP ...> and </MAP> tags are used to define the hot regions and the URLs to which they link. You can have as many <AREA ...> tags as you like. If the hot regions defined by two <AREA ...> tags overlap, the <AREA ...> tag that is listed first gets precedence.

The <AREA ...> tag can also take a NOHREF tag, which tells the browser to do nothing if the user clicks on the hot region. Any part of the image that is not defined as a hot region is a NOHREF region, so if users click outside of a hot region, they won't go anywhere by default. This saves you from setting up an <AREA SHAPE="DEFAULT" ... NOHREF> tag for all of your maps.

The HTML used to define a map region can reside in the same file in which the <IMG ...> tag for the graphic lives or in an entirely different file. If the map definition is in the same file, you reference the map with the HTML:

```
<IMG SRC="images/govtsites.gif" WIDTH=530 HEIGHT=300
USEMAP="#govtsites">
```

The USEMAP attribute in the <IMG ...> tag tells the browser it's dealing with a client-side imagemap and what the name of the map is. If you store all of your map information in a separate HTML file, the tag to link to the map would be:

```
<IMG SRC="images/govtsites.gif" WIDTH=530 HEIGHT=300
USEMAP="maps.html#govtsites">
```

Storing all of your maps in a single file is a good idea if you're placing the same imagemap on several pages. This is frequently the case with navigational button bars.

Note

To read the Spyglass proposal for client-side imagemaps, visit the URL **http:// www.ics.uci.edu/pub/ietf/html/draft-seidman-clientsideimagemap-01.txt**.

Using Client-Side and Server-Side Imagemaps Together

Client-side imagemaps are a great idea since they permit faster imagemap processing and enhance the portability of your HTML documents. Unfortunately, not all browsers support even one of the client-side imagemap approaches just described. Since you want to write HTML that is friendly to as many browsers as possible, you should consider combining server-side and client-side imagemaps whenever possible.

To combine a Netscape- or Windows-style server-side imagemap with the <FIG ...> and </FIG> tag approach to client-side imagemaps, you can modify the earlier example to be:

> **Listing 11.3   Using <FIG...> and </FIG>**

```
<FIG SRC="images/govtsites.gif" WIDTH=530 HEIGHT=300>
<A HREF="maps/govtsites.map"><IMG SRC="images/govtsites.gif"
WIDTH=530 HEIGHT=300 ISMAP></A>
<B>Select a government site to visit:</B>
<UL>
<LI><A HREF="http://www.loc.gov/" SHAPE="rect 36,70,252,146">Library
of Congress</A></LI>
<LI><A HREF="http://www.whitehouse.gov/" SHAPE="circle
214,219,269,221">The White House</A></LI>
<LI><A HREF="http://www.dtic.dla.mil/defenselink" SHAPE="polygon
389,61,480,125,459,231,334,230,305,131"></A></LI>
</UL>
</FIG>
```

The second line in the HTML above is new. It places the same map graphic on the page and links it to the map file govtsites.map on the server. If the browser recognizes the <FIG ...> tag and places the image it specifies, the additional line of HTML is ignored.

To combine a Netscape- or Windows-style server-side imagemap with the <MAP ...> and </MAP> tag approach, you can modify the earlier HTML to be:

```
<A HREF="maps/govtsites.map">
<IMG SRC="images/govtsites.gif" WIDTH=530 HEIGHT=300
USEMAP="#govtsites" ISMAP>
</A>
```

Flanking the <IMG ...> tag with <A ...> and </A> tags makes it point to the govtsites.map map file on the server. You need to include the ISMAP attribute in the <IMG ...> tag to let the browser know that the image is linked as a servers-side imagemap as well.

> **Note**
>
> You can also link NCSA- and CERN-style server-side imagemaps to client-side imagemaps. Instead of the HREF in the <A ...> tag pointing directly to the map file, you need to make it point to the imagemap script.

Doing HTML

Imagemap Tools

Whether you're creating a server-side or client-side imagemap, it can be cumbersome to determine and type in all of the coordinates of the points you need to define hot regions. Luckily, there are programs to help you through this process that will let you load your imagemap image, trace out the hot regions right on the screen, and then write the appropriate map file or HTML file to implement the imagemap. These next few sections describe some of these programs and tell you how to get them.

MapEdit

MapEdit 2.1 is a shareware imagemap tool produced by Boutell.Com, Inc. This version of MapEdit supports client-side images and images in the JPEG format, and cleans up a number of small bugs in the 2.0 release.

Using MapEdit is easy. To begin, select the Open/Create option under the File menu. The dialog box you see prompts you for several things. First, you need to specify if you are doing a server-side or client-side imagemap. If you choose server-side, you then need to select either NCSA or CERN formats and specify a name for the map file. If you choose client-side, you need to tell MapEdit the name of the file to which it should write the HTML code. Finally, you tell MapEdit the file containing the image for the imagemap. When you click OK, the image file is loaded into the MapEdit window and you're ready to start defining hot regions.

You can choose Rectangle, Circle, or Polygon tools under the MapEdit Tools menu. Each tool lets you trace out a hot region shaped like the name of the tool. To use the Rectangle tool, point your mouse to the upper-left corner of the rectangular hot region and click the left mouse button. Then move your mouse pointer to the lower-right corner of the region. As you do, a black rectangular outline is dragged along with the pointer, eventually opening up to enclose your hot region (see fig. 11.7).

With the mouse pointer pointing at the lower-right corner, left-click the mouse again. When you do, you see a dialog box like the one shown in figure 11.8. Type the URL that is associated with the hot region you're defining into the dialog box, along with any comments you want to include, and click OK. MapEdit puts this information into the file it's building and is then ready to define another hot region or to save the file and exit.

> **Note**
>
> Comments in a server-side imagemap map file are offset with a pound sign (#).

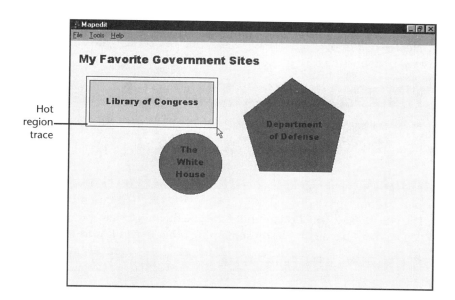

Hot
region
trace

Fig. 11.7
MapEdit lets you
trace out a hot
region using your
mouse.

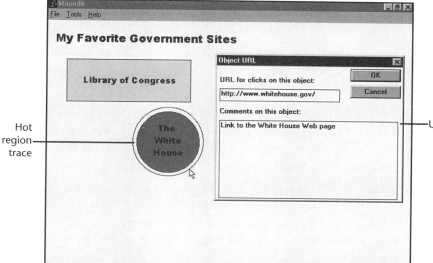

Hot
region
trace

Fig. 11.8
Once a hot region
is defined, MapEdit
prompts you
for the associated
URL and any
comments.

URL dialog box

III

Doing HTML

MapEdit's Circle and Polygon tools work similarly. With the Circle tool, you place your mouse pointer at the center of the circular region (this is sometimes difficult to estimate!) and left-click. Then move the pointer to a point on the edge of the circular region and left click again to define the region and call up the dialog box. To use the Polygon tool, simply left-click on the vertices of the polygon in sequence. When you hit the last unique vertex (i.e., the next vertex in the sequence is the first one you clicked), do a right-click instead to define the region and reveal the dialog box.

> **Tip**
>
> If you're ever unhappy with how your trace is coming out, just press the Esc key to erase your trace and start over.

Other MapEdit Tool menu options let you move an entire hot region, add or remove points from a polygon, and test the imagemap file as it currently stands. The Edit Default URL option under the File menu lets you specify a default URL to go to if a user clicks on something other than a hot region.

> **Note**
>
> You can download MapEdit 2.1 by directing your browser to **http://www.boutell. com/mapedit**. After a 30 day evaluation period, you must license your copy of MapEdit at a cost of US$25.00. Site licenses are also available. Educational and non-profit users do not have to pay for a license, but they should register their copies of MapEdit.

Web Hotspots

Web Hotspots 2.0 is a shareware imagemap tool developed by Keith Doty at 1Automata. Web Hotspots supports both server-side and client-side imagemaps and can load graphics in both GIF and JPEG formats. Figure 11.9 shows the government sites graphic loaded into the Web Hotspots window. You can see in the figure that Web Hotspots provides you with buttons that let you change between tracing tools quickly.

In addition to the usual rectangle, circle and polygon tools, you also get a freeform region tool that lets you define unsually-shaped hot regions. As you define a region, Web Hotspots shades it for you, making it easy to see in relation to objects in the graphic. The shading feature is illustrated in figure 11.10.

> **Note**
>
> Web Hotspots converts a freeform region into a many-sided polygon, so the line for the freeform region in the map file or <AREA ...> tag in the HTML file will start with the keyword polygon. You can see all of the vertices in the many-sided polygon that describes the freeform region in figure 11.10.

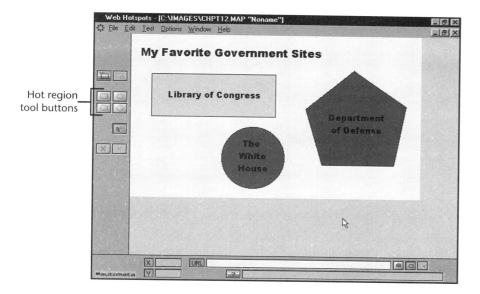

Fig. 11.9
You can access
Web Hotspots
tools quickly using
buttons in the
main window.

Hot region
tool buttons

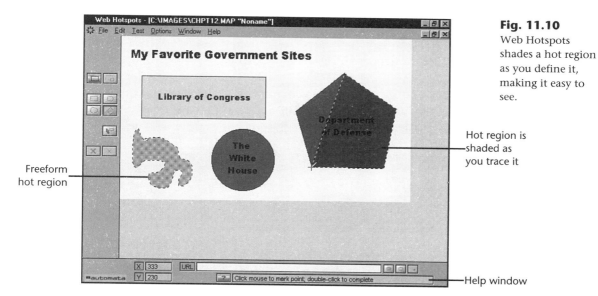

Fig. 11.10
Web Hotspots
shades a hot region
as you define it,
making it easy to
see.

Hot region is
shaded as
you trace it

Freeform
hot region

Help window

Once a hot region is defined, you can type in the associated URL into the
URL edit box near the bottom of the window.

Web Hotspots offers a number of other useful features beyond its basic functionality including:

- A context-sensitive help box
- A zoom feature that lets you increase or decrease the size of the image
- A testing mode that supports live testing over the Internet (you need to have WinSock installed to do this)
- Image rescale and rotate options
- The ability to move a hot region to the front of the map file or HTML file, giving it precedence over the other regions

> **Note**
>
> You can download an evaluation of Web Hotspots 2.0 from **http://www.cris.com/~automata/hotspots.shtml**. After 30 days, you can remit US$49.00 plus US$5.00 shipping and handling to purchase a license. The US$49.00 price is valid through May 1, 1996.

Map THIS!

Map THIS! is a freeware imagemap tool written by Todd C. Wilson. It only runs on 32-bit Windows platforms, but that's about the extent of its limitations. Map THIS! can help you with server-side and client-side imagemaps and can load images in both the GIF and JPEG formats. Figure 11.11 shows the Map THIS! main window with the government sites graphic loaded.

Fig. 11.11
Map THIS!
is a freeware
imagemap tool
that supports
server-side and
client-side
imagemaps on
graphics in both
GIF and JPEG
format.

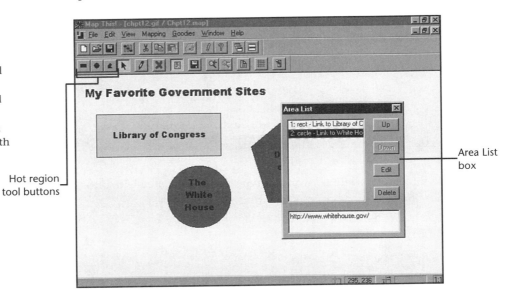

Most of Map THIS!'s features are accessible through buttons in the main window. The rectangle, circle, and polygon tools occupy the first three buttons in
the second row. The circle tool is particularly nice because you drag out the
circle from one point on the circle to the point that is diametrically opposite
it, rather than trying to start on the exact center of the circle. As you use one
of the tools, you get instructions on what to do next in a box at the lower left
of the window. You can enable the shading feature to make the hot regions
you define easier to see.

The Area List, shown in figure 11.11, is a floating box that you can activate to
show the regions you've defined and what URLs they're linked to. You can
also turn on a grid pattern to help you measure out hot regions with greater
accuracy.

Map THIS! lets you work on multiple images. You have the choice of cascading or tiling the windows that contain the images. When it's time to save
your work, you can save in CERN or NCSA format for server-side imagemap
map files or in HTML format for client-side imagemaps. Other useful features
of Map THIS! include:

- Adding points to or deleting points from polygons
- Color support all the way up to 24-bit color
- Zoom in and out
- A Preferences window in which you can set the map type and color
  choices for outlining and shading hot regions
- A Mapfile Information window in which you can specify a default URL,
  the map title, your name, and other descriptive comments
- Context-sensitive menus accessible by right-clicking the mouse

---

Note

To download the latest version of Map THIS!, point your browser to **http://
www.ecaetc.ohio-state.edu/tc/**.

Testing

A great feature of the imagemap tool programs is that you can use them to
test your imagemaps. MapEdit's test mode presents the imagemap graphic to
you and lets you click on it. If you click on a hot region, the URL dialog box
opens and displays the URL associated with the region on which you clicked.

Web Hotspots' test mode allows you to test your imagemap right on the Internet. As long as you have an active WinSock layer, Web Hotspots will fetch the URL that goes with the hot region on which you clicked. The Map THIS! testing mode opens up a completely separate window (see fig. 11.12). As you move your mouse pointer over a hot region, its corresponding URL shows up in the box at the bottom of the screen.

Fig. 11.12
As you move your mouse over a hot region in the Map THIS! test window, the URL you'd jump to shows up at the lower left.

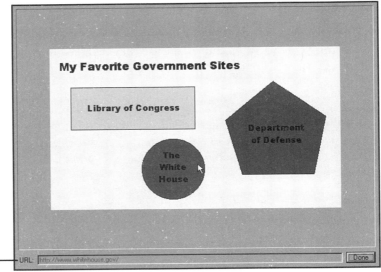

URL of selected hot region

If none of these programs are available to you, you'll have to put your map or HTML files on your server and test them with a browser. You can make small changes to these files using a simple text editor, if needed.

Tip

If you're testing a client-side imagemap with a browser, make sure the browser can implement the approach (<FIG ...> or <MAP ...>) that you used.

## CHAPTER 12

HTML Forms

Static Web pages are fine for presenting information, but they don't harness the full capabilities of Web technology. The Web community's craving for interactivity has led to the incorporation of animation, audio, and video clips, and other multimedia items into Web pages. One of the earliest types of interactivity on Web pages were HTML *forms*—sets of clickable buttons and boxes, text fields, and menus into which the user enters data. The browser then passes the data to a *script* on a server that processes the data and sends a response back to the browser.

This powerful form of interactivity initially allowed for querying of databases and for soliciting feedback from Web users. As encryption technology improved, forms became a common part of electronic commerce sites where they gave Internet shoppers a secure interface for entering their orders, shipping addresses and credit card numbers. Recent innovative applications of HTML forms include real-time chat and conducting online research.

On the client side of HTML forms are a few basic yet versatile tags that make it easy to create familiar graphical elements for data input and to specify where and how to send the form data.

In this chapter, you learn:

- ■ The basics of form data flow
- ■ How to create HTML forms
- ■ The two methods clients use to pass form data to a server
- ■ How to query a script without filling out a form

Overview of Form Data Flow

Before learning about the HTML tags used to create forms, it is helpful to have a perspective on the "path" that form data takes as it moves from the browser to the processing script. Once a user enters the data, the browser *encodes* it and makes a call to the server where the processing script resides. One part of this call indicates which script the server should run and the other part passes the form data.

Once the server has the data and knows which script to run, it starts the script and passes the form data to the script by the *Common Gateway Interface (CGI)*—a set of specifications that allows clients to make calls to server scripts, regardless of platform. The script processes the data and creates a response to be sent back to the client. Typically this response is an HTML file, but it can also take the form of things like a plain text file or a URL. The response is (in most cases) handed back to the server which then passes it on to the browser for display to the user.

> **Note**
>
> When a script produces an HTML document, it is sometimes referred to as generating HTML "on-the-fly."

Form Support in HTML

Like other elements of HTML, forms have a similar appearance in different browsers, but the appearance is not identical. The appearance of a form always matches the graphical environment in which the form is displayed. For example, Windows pull-down menus and check boxes look significantly different than they do in X Windows. This platform portability is part of the power of forms. Authors of HTML forms don't need to worry about the details of interacting with the user's graphical operating system—the browser handles all the details. This is what allows you to use the same HTML form under Windows, Mac, OS/2, X Windows, and even in text-mode with Lynx.

HTML's form support is very simple, and yet surprisingly complete. A handful of HTML tags can create the most popular elements of modern graphical interfaces, including text windows, check boxes and radio buttons, pull-down menus, and push buttons. In fact, using HTML forms in conjunction with server scripts is arguably the fastest and simplest way to create cross-platform graphical applications! The only programming required is the script itself, and the programmer can choose the language.

Creating Forms

Composing HTML forms might sound like a complex task, but there are remarkably few tags that you need to master to do it. All form-related tags occur between the <FORM ...> and </FORM> container tags. If you have more than one form in an HTML document, the closing </FORM> tag is essential for distinguishing between the multiple forms.

Each HTML form has three main components: the *form header,* one or more *named input fields,* and one or more *action buttons.*

The Form Header

The form header is really just the <FORM ...> tag and the attributes it contains. The first of these is the ACTION attribute. You set ACTION equal to the URL of the processing script so that the client knows where to send the form data once it is entered. ACTION is a mandatory attribute of the <FORM ...> tag. Without it, the browser has no idea where the form data should go.

The ACTION URL can also contain extra path information at the end of it. The extra path information is passed on to the script so that it can correctly process the data. It's not found anywhere on the form and is therefore transparent to the user. Allowing for the possibility of extra path information, an ACTION URL has the form:

```
protocol://server/path/script_file/extra_path_info
```

You can use the extra path information to pass an additional file name or directory information to a script. For example, on some servers the imagemap facility uses extra path information to specify the name of the map file. The name of the map file follows the path to the imagemap script. A sample URL might be:

```
http://cgi-bin/imagemap/homepage
```

The name of the script is `imagemap`, and `home page` is the name of the map file used by imagemap.

> **Note**
>
> On many CGI capable servers, you will find the script executable files in the cgi-bin directory. Having a special directory for the executable files helps the server administrator keep ill-intentioned users from getting to portions of the server where they might do serious harm.

III

Doing HTML

The second attribute found in the <FORM ...> tag is the METHOD attribute. METHOD specifies the HTTP method to use when passing the data to the script and can be set to values of GET or POST. When using the GET method, the browser will append the form data to the end of the URL of the processing script. The POST method sends the form data to the server in a separate HTTP transaction. More specific information about the differences between these two methods can be found in the "HTTP Methods" section later in this chapter.

METHOD is not a mandatory attribute of the <FORM ...> tag. In the absence of a specified method, the browser will use the GET method.

Caution

Some servers may have operating environment limitations that prevent them from processing a URL that exceeds 1 kilobyte of information. This can be a problem when using the GET method to pass a large amount of form data. Since the GET method appends the data to the end of the processing script URL, you run a greater risk of passing a URL that's too big for the server to handle. If this is a concern on your server, you should use the POST method to pass form data.

Actually, the absolute safe limit, and one we should definitely mention, is 256 characters for the whole URL—meaning, if the URL including the script name is 40 characters, the part after the ? mark or / can only be 215 characters. There is no fundamental limit, but the specs (will) only require applications to support 256-character URL's to be considered compliant. If you've got more than that, use POST.

In summary, a form header follows the syntax:

```
<FORM ACTION="URL" METHOD={GET¦POST}>
```

Following the form header are the tags to create named input fields and action buttons. We discuss these tags next.

Named Input Fields

The named input fields typically comprise the bulk of a form. The fields appear as standard GUI controls such as text boxes, check boxes, radio buttons, and menus. You assign each field a unique name that eventually becomes the variable name used in the processing script.

Tip

If you aren't coding your own processing scripts, be sure to sit down with your programmer to agree on variable names. The names used in the form must exactly match those used in coding the script.

You can use several different GUI controls to enter information into forms. The controls for named input fields appear in table 12.1. The TYPE="FILE" control allows you to create forms that ask for files as input. This control is a Netscape extension to standard HTML and is only supported by the Netscape Navigator browser.

Table 12.1   Types of Named Input Fields

Field Type	HTML Tag
Text Box	<INPUT TYPE="TEXT" ...>
Password Box	<INPUT TYPE="PASSWORD" ...>
Check box	<INPUT TYPE="CHECKBOX" ...>
Radio Button	<INPUT TYPE="RADIO" ...>
Hidden Field	<INPUT TYPE="HIDDEN" ...>
File	<INPUT TYPE="FILE" ...>
Text Window	<TEXTAREA ...> ... </TEXTAREA>
Menu	<SELECT ...> ... <OPTION> ... </SELECT>

Note

Even though it is a text-only browser, Lynx emulates GUI elements to achieve complete support for forms.

III

Doing HTML

The <INPUT ...> Tag

You may have noticed in table 12.1 that the versatile <INPUT ...> tag, together with the appropriate TYPE attribute, is used to produce most of the named input fields available to form designers. The following sections discuss each of the different possible TYPE attributes in greater detail.

Text and Password Fields

Text and password fields are simple data entry fields. The only difference between them is that text typed into a password field appears on-screen as asterisks (*).

◀ To learn more
about encryp-
tion and other
security issues,
see Chapter 6,
"Managing an
Internet Web
Server,"
p. 103

Caution

Using a password field may protect users' passwords from the people looking over their shoulders, but *it does not protect the password as it travels over the Internet.* To protect password data as it moves from browser to server, you need to use some type of encryption or similar security measure.

The most general text or password field is produced by the HTML (attributes in square brackets are optional):

```
<INPUT TYPE="{TEXT¦PASSWORD}" NAME="Name" [VALUE="default_text"]
[SIZE="width"] [MAXLENGTH="width"]>
```

The NAME attribute is mandatory as it provides a unique identifier for the data entered into the field.

The optional VALUE attribute allows you to place some default text in the field, rather than having it initially appear blank. This is useful if there is a certain text string that the majority of users will enter into the field. In such cases, you can use VALUE to put the text into the field, thereby saving most users the effort of typing it.

The optional SIZE attribute gives you control over how many characters wide the field should be. The default SIZE is 20 characters. MAXLENGTH is also optional and allows you specify the maximum number of characters that can be entered into the field.

Note

Previously the SIZE attribute used to take the form SIZE="width,height" where setting a height other than 1 produced a multiline field. With the advent of the <TEXTAREA ...> ... </TEXTAREA> tag pair for creating multiline text windows, height has become something of a vestige and is ignored by most browsers.

A simple application of text and password fields would be to provide a user login interface. For example, listing 12.1 produces the screen in figure 12.1.

Listing 12.1 HTML for Figure 12.1

```
<HTML>
<HEAD>
<TITLE>XYZ Corporation Login Screen</TITLE>
</HEAD>
<BODY>
<H1>Welcome to XYZ's Computer System!</H1>
<HR><P>
Please enter your ID and password.<P>
<FORM ACTION="http://www.xyz.com/cgi-bin/login.cgi" METHOD="POST">
ID:   <INPUT TYPE="TEXT" NAME="Username" SIZE="10" MAXLENGTH="10"><P>
Password:  <INPUT TYPE="PASSWORD" NAME="Password" SIZE="10"
MAXLENGTH="10"><P>
<INPUT TYPE="SUBMIT" VALUE="Log On">
</FORM>
</BODY>
</HTML>
```

The Log On button you see is an action button. Action buttons are described more fully later in the chapter.

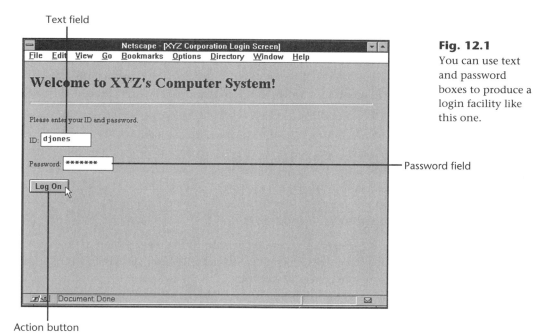

Text field

Fig. 12.1
You can use text and password boxes to produce a login facility like this one.

Password field

Action button

Note

The <INPUT ...> tag and other tags that produce named input fields just create the fields themselves. It's up to you as the form designer to include some descriptive text next to each field so that users know what to information to enter.

Tip

Because browsers ignore white space, it's difficult to line up the left edges of text input boxes on multiple lines because the text to the left of the boxes are of different lengths. One solution is to put label text to the right of input boxes. Another solution is to set up the text labels and input fields as cells in the same row of an HTML table.

Check Boxes

You can use check boxes to provide users with several choices, from which they may select as many of them as they want. An <INPUT ...> tag to produce a check box option has the syntax:

```
<INPUT TYPE="CHECKBOX" NAME="Name" VALUE="Value" [CHECKED]>
```

Each checkbox option is created by its own <INPUT ...> tag and must have its own unique NAME. If you give multiple check box options the same NAME, there will be no way for the script to determine which choices the user actually made.

Check boxes only show up in the form data sent to the server if they are selected. Check boxes that are not selected do not appear. For check boxes that are selected, the VALUE attribute specifies what data is sent to the server. This information is transparent to the user. The optional CHECKED attribute will preselect a commonly selected check box when the form is rendered on the browser screen.

Figure 12.2 shows an expanded version of the login screen in figure 12.1. The expanded screen has several options that the user can specify at login time. Because people generally want to check their electronic mail, the Check for New Messages option is preselected. The HTML to produce the check box options in figure 12.2 is:

```
<B>Login Options -</B> Select any, all or none of the following:<P>
<INPUT TYPE="CHECKBOX" NAME="Suppress" VALUE="Yes">Suppress
greeting screen<P>
<INPUT TYPE="CHECKBOX" NAME="Email" VALUE="Yes" CHECKED>Check for
new messages<P>
<INPUT TYPE="CHECKBOX" NAME="Schedule" VALUE="Yes">Display today's
schedule<P>
```

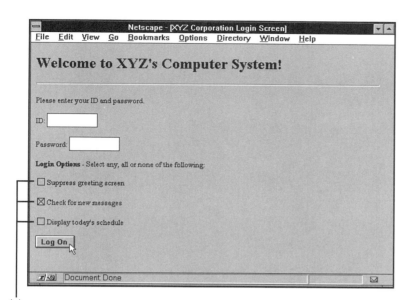

Fig. 12.2
Check boxes like
this one give users
many options
from which they
can choose as
many as they like.

Check boxes

Radio Buttons

Radio buttons are used to present users with several options from which they
may select one and only one option. When you set up options in a radio button format, make sure that the options are mutually exclusive so that a user
won't try to select more than one.

The HTML to produce a set of three radio button options is:

```
<INPUT TYPE="RADIO" NAME="Name" VALUE="VALUE1" [CHECKED]>Option 1<P>
<INPUT TYPE="RADIO" NAME="Name" VALUE="VALUE2">Option 2<P>
<INPUT TYPE="RADIO" NAME="Name" VALUE="VALUE3">Option 3<P>
```

The VALUE and CHECKED attributes work exactly the same as they do for
check boxes, though you should only have one preselected radio button option. A fundamental difference with a set of radio button options is that *they
all have the same NAME.* This is permissible because the user can only select
one of the options.

Figure 12.3 shows one more extension to our login screen, giving the user the
choice of a UNIX shell or to load X Windows at login. The HTML to produce
the radio buttons is:

```
<INPUT TYPE="RADIO" NAME="X_WIN" VALUE="NO" CHECKED>UNIX
Shell  
<INPUT TYPE="RADIO" NAME="X_WIN" VALUE="YES">Start X-Windows<P>
```

III

Doing HTML

Fig. 12.3
Radio buttons
present users with
multiple options
from which they
may select one
and only one
option.

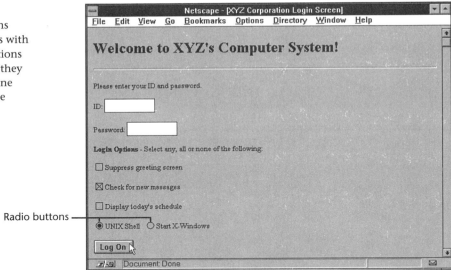

Radio buttons ——

Note that the two radio button options are side-by-side in figure 12.3, separated by nonbreaking space. This is fine for radio button or check box options described with a small amount of text.

Hidden Fields

Technically, hidden fields are not meant for data input. However, you can send information to the server about a form without displaying that information anywhere on the form itself. The general format for including hidden fields is:

```
<INPUT TYPE="HIDDEN" NAME="name" VALUE="value">
```

One possible use of hidden fields is to allow a single general script to process data from several different forms. The script needs to know which form is sending the data, and a hidden field can provide this information without requiring anything on the part of the user. For example, all forms processed by the script can have a hidden name of FormID and hidden values of Sales, Order, Followup, NewUser, and so on.

A closely related use of hidden fields is to use a generic script to process several forms that vary only in one or two fields. For example, a generic script to send comments via e-mail might use a hidden field to specify the e-mail address. This way, the user doesn't have to type an address or even know where the mail is going, but because the form contains the address information in a hidden field, a single script can still be used to send automated feedback to several different e-mail addresses.

> **Note**
>
> In general, anything you can do with hidden fields, you can do by specifying extra path information in the form's ACTION attribute. However, hidden fields appear as regular data items in a form and may therefore be easier to process, especially if there are multiple hidden items.

A third possible use of hidden fields is to embed state information into forms generated on-the-fly. For example, a form that is generated in response to a previous form can contain the original contents of the first form in a hidden field. This way, when the data from the second form is sent, the data from the first form is sent, too, and the processing script has a complete history of the necessary information. This can be useful in a search for returning preliminary results to the user while still maintaining a record of the original query.

Files

The Netscape Navigator supports an extension to the <INPUT ...> tag that allows a file to be specified as input. To accomplish this, you need to do two things. The first is to add the ENCTYPE attribute to the form header to let the browser know that it will be sending a file. The modified form header looks like:

```
<FORM ACTION="URL" METHOD="POST" ENCTYPE="multipart/form-data">
```

The second change is to set the TYPE attribute in the <INPUT ...> tag to FILE:

```
Enter file name:<INPUT TYPE="FILE" NAME="filename">
```

III

Doing HTML

> **Note**
>
> Because the browser will be transferring an entire file as part of the form data, use the POST method for this type of form so that you don't run the risk of creating too large a URL for the server to process.

The <TEXTAREA ...> ... </TEXTAREA> Tag Pair

Text and password boxes are used for simple, one-line input fields. You can create multiline text windows that function in much the same way by using the <TEXTAREA ...> and </TEXTAREA> container tags. The HTML syntax for a text window is:

```
<TEXTAREA NAME="Name" [ROWS="rows"] [COLS="columns"]>
Default_window_text
</TEXTAREA>
```

The NAME attribute gives the text window a unique identifier just as it did with the variations on the <INPUT ...> tag. The optional ROWS and COLS attributes allow you to specify the dimensions of the text window as it appears on the browser screen. The default number of rows and columns varies by browser. In Netscape Navigator the defaults are 1 row and 20 columns, while in Microsoft Internet Explorer they are 3 rows and 30 columns.

Multiline text windows are ideal for entry of long pieces of text such as feedback comments or e-mail messages. Figure 12.4 shows a text window being used as an online suggestion box. The corresponding HTML is shown in listing 12.2.

Listing 12.2   HTML for Figure 12.2

```
<HTML>
<HEAD>
<TITLE>XYZ Corporation Suggestion Box</TITLE>
</HEAD>
<BODY>
<H1>XYZ Corporation Suggestion Box</H1>
<HR><P>
<FORM ACTION="http://www.xyz.com/cgi-bin/suggest.cgi" METHOD="POST">
<TEXTAREA NAME="Suggest" ROWS="10" COLS="60">
Enter your suggestions here.
</TEXTAREA>
<P>
<INPUT TYPE="SUBMIT" VALUE="Submit Suggestion">
</FORM>
</BODY>
</HTML>
```

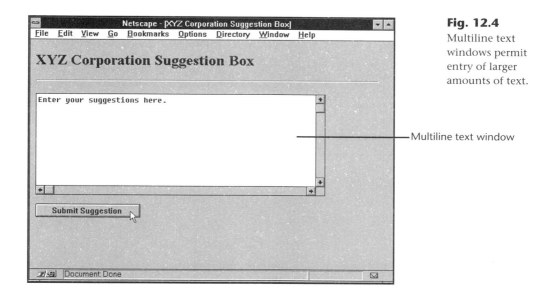

Fig. 12.4
Multiline text
windows permit
entry of larger
amounts of text.

Multiline text window

The <SELECT ...> ... </SELECT> Tag Pair

The final technique for creating a named input field is to use the
<SELECT ...> and </SELECT> container tags to produce a pull-down or
scrollable menus of options. Listing 12.3 shows the HTML used to create
a general menu.

Listing 12.3   HTML That Produces a General Menu

```
<SELECT NAME="Name" [SIZE="size"] [MULTIPLE]>
<OPTION [SELECTED]>Option 1
<OPTION [SELECTED]>Option 2
<OPTION [SELECTED]>Option 3
...
<OPTION [SELECTED]>Option n
</SELECT>
```

In the <SELECT ...> tag, the NAME attribute again gives the input field a
unique identifier. The optional SIZE attribute lets you specify how many options should be displayed when the menu is rendered on the browser screen.
If there are more options than there is space for displaying them, they will be
available either by a pull-down window or by scrolling through the window
with scroll bars. The default SIZE is 1. If you want to let users choose more
than one menu option, you can include the MULTIPLE attribute. When

III

Doing HTML

MULTIPLE is specified, users can choose multiple options by holding down the Control key and by using the mouse to click on the options they want.

Note

If you specify the MULTIPLE attribute and SIZE=1, a one-line scrollable list box is displayed instead of a drop-down list box. This is because you can only select one item (not multiple items) in a drop-down list box.

Each option in the menu is specified with its own <OPTION ...> tag. If you want an option to be pre-selected, you can include the SELECTED attribute in the appropriate <OPTION ...> tag.

Figure 12.5 shows the menu produced by listing 12.4.

Listing 12.4   HTML for the Menu in Figure 12.5

```
<HTML>
<HEAD>
<TITLE>XYZ Corporation Report Generator</TITLE>
</HEAD>
<BODY>
<H1>XYZ Corporation Report Generator</H1>
<HR><P>
Select the reports you want to generate.<P>
To select multiple options, hold down the Control key while clicking
the mouse.<P>
<FORM ACTION="http://www.xyz.com/cgi-bin/reports.cgi" METHOD="POST">
<SELECT NAME="Reports" SIZE="4" MULTIPLE>
<OPTION SELECTED>Bi-weekly Payroll
<OPTION>Accounts Payable
<OPTION>Accounts Receivable
<OPTION>YTD Revenue
<OPTION>YTD Expense
<OPTION>YTD Profit and Loss
<OPTION>Balance Sheet
</SELECT>
<P><INPUT TYPE="SUBMIT" VALUE="Submit Report Request">
</FORM>
</BODY>
</HTML>
```

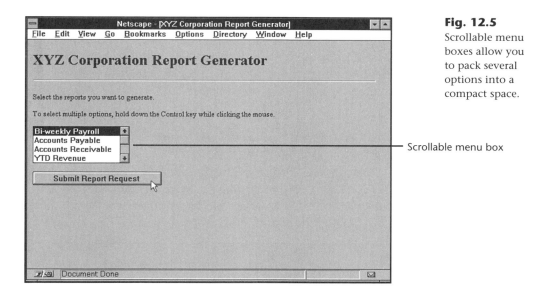

Fig. 12.5
Scrollable menu boxes allow you to pack several options into a compact space.

Scrollable menu box

You may have noticed that there are no VALUE attributes for the <SELECT ...> or <OPTION ...> tags. This is because the values passed to the server are the text items that appear after each <OPTION ...> tag.

Tip

You can replace radio buttons with pull-down menus to save space on-screen. Including the MULTIPLE option in a <SELECT ...> tag allows menus to replace check boxes, as well.

Action Buttons

The handy <INPUT ...> tag returns to provide any easy way of creating the form action buttons you have seen in the preceding figures. Buttons may be of two types: submit and reset. Pressing a submit button instructs the browser to package the form data and send it to the server. Pressing a reset button clears out any data entered into the form and sets all the named input fields back to their default values.

III

Doing HTML

Any form you compose should have a submit button so that users can submit the data they enter. The one exception to this rule is a form containing only one input field. For such a form, pressing Enter automatically submits the data. Reset buttons are technically not necessary, but are usually provided as a user courtesy.

To create submit or reset buttons, you use the <INPUT ...> tags:

```
<INPUT TYPE="SUBMIT" VALUE="Submit Data">
<INPUT TYPE="RESET" VALUE="Clear Data">
```

The VALUE attribute is used to specify the text that appears on the button. You should set VALUE to a text string that concisely describes the function of the button. If VALUE is not specified, the button text will read "Submit Query" for submit buttons and "Reset" for reset buttons.

> **Note**
>
> Normally, forms include only one submit button. In some cases, however, you may want to include multiple buttons that take different actions. You can achieve this by naming submit buttons with a NAME attribute so that the NAME and VALUE of the button pressed show up in the query string. However, this capability is not yet part of standard HTML and is not supported by many browsers.

A One-Field Form: The <ISINDEX> Tag

There is an exception to the rule about forms having headers, input fields and action buttons. You can use the <ISINDEX> tag to create a single field form. No other tags are required. <ISINDEX> fields are used to allow a user to enter search criteria for queries against Gopher servers or database scripts. For example, you may be maintaining a directory of employees where you work that is searchable by a person's last name. You can use an <ISINDEX> field as a front-end to search the directory. Figure 12.6 shows such a field. The user would enter the last name to search on and press Enter to initiate the search.

Fig. 12.6
The <ISINDEX> tag creates a single field form that can be used for entry of search criteria

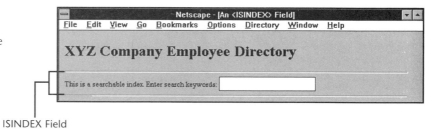

ISINDEX Field

You may be wondering where the data entered into an <ISINDEX> field goes. After all, there's no <FORM …> tag with an ACTION specified. How does the client know which URL to send the data to? The answer is that it sends the data to the URL of the page containing the <ISINDEX> field. This requires one of two things: (1) that the page be created by some sort of a script, since a static HTML page could not receive and process the data, or (2) that the <ISINDEX> field be part of a Gopher document, since Gopher servers are configured to process such queries.

▶ Chapter 13, "CGI Scripts and Server APIs," contains more details on how to create scripts that return HTML documents. See p. 339

Note in figure 12.6 that the <ISINDEX> field is preceded by the default text `This is a searchable index. Enter search keywords:`. The Netscape Navigator supports a PROMPT attribute of the <ISINDEX> tag that allows you to alter this default and make the text in front of the field more descriptive. For example, the following HTML produces the page shown in figure 12.7.

```
<BODY>
<H1> XYZ Company Employee Directory</H1>
<ISINDEX PROMPT="Enter the last name to search by:">
</BODY>
```

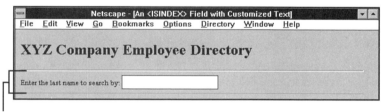

Fig. 12.7
Netscape lets you customize the text in front of an <ISINDEX> field.

ISINDEX field with customized prompt

Passing Form Data

Once the user clicks the submit button after filling out a form or presses Enter after specifying an <ISINDEX> query value, the form data or query is packaged by the browser for transmission to the server. There are two key aspects to this transmission: the *HTTP method* used to transmit the data and the *URL encoding* used to format the data. All form data or query information gets encoded, regardless of which HTTP method is used. Once you understand how the encoding works, it becomes easy to make calls to the same script with the same data later on.

HTTP Methods

In the earlier discussion of form headers, you learned that there are two HTTP methods by which form data can be passed to the server. The GET method attaches form or query data onto the end of the URL of the processing script. The POST method sends form data to the server in a separate transaction. If you don't specify the METHOD attribute in the <FORM ...> tag, the client will use the GET method by default.

> **Note**
>
> Query data entered into an <ISINDEX> field is always sent by the GET method.

The GET Method

The default GET method appends data onto the end of the URL specified in the ACTION attribute in the case of forms and onto the end of the URL of the page containing the <ISINDEX> field in the case of an <ISINDEX> query. A URL created by the GET method has the form:

```
protocol://server/path/filename/extra_path_info?query_string
```

where the query string is the form data or <ISINDEX> query data formatted as described in the "URL Encoding" section below.

> **Caution**
>
> If your form contains several input fields, it's possible that your query string will grow too large for the server to process (more than 1 kilobyte of data). If this is a concern, use the POST method.
>
> Since <ISINDEX> query information is generally short, use of the GET method is not a problem.

The POST Method

The POST method sends the form data to the server in a separate HTTP transaction, passing it to the standard input device on the server's operating system. By sending the data separately, you no longer need to be concerned about a URL becoming too long for the server to process. Even though it is sent separately, the data is still encoded in the same way as data sent by the GET method.

> **Note**
>
> The HTTP protocol supports the ability to POST data files of any type from browser to server, even outside of a script context. However, this capability is not yet widely supported by browsers or servers. Form data is of MIME type x-www/url-encoded.

URL Encoding

The browser must somehow convert all data represented graphically in a form to a string of text it can send to the server. This involves both packaging the form data and then formatting it for proper transmission to the server.

Packaging Form Data

The form designer assigns each field, or graphical control, a unique name using the NAME attribute, except for submit and reset buttons. This naming provides a way for the server to associate data with where it came from.

The browser translates the entire contents of a form into a single text string using the following format:

```
name1=value1&name2=value2&name3=value3...
```

where name1 is the name of the first form variable and value1 is the value of that variable as entered by the user. For example, the URL from a form that adds names and phone numbers to the employee directory described earlier might look like this:

```
http://www.xyz.com/cgi-bin/add.cgi?name=Beth+Roberts&number=2025551234
```

Because you give each field in a form a unique name, the processing script can figure out what each form entry represents. The type of graphical control in which a user enters a value is not specified directly in the information sent to the server. This lack of specification is okay, though, because the processing script can use each field's unique name to figure out the control type if necessary.

Note

Query data entered into an <ISINDEX> field is simply added on to the end of the URL. For example, a query to the employee phone directory might take the form:

```
http://www.xyz.com./cgi-bin/lookup.cgi?Adams
```

Since there is only one input field, it is impossible to confuse the meaning of the query data and there is no need to use a name=value packaging approach.

Formatting Rules

Most operating environments interpret spaces in character strings as some type of delimiter indicating the start of a new field, a new parameter, and so on. Consequently, you must remove spaces from all form data and queries in order to ensure that the data is successfully received by the processing script. By convention, all spaces become plus signs (+).

III

Doing HTML

This replacement presents a minor problem. What if a query itself contains a plus sign? Or what if form data contains an equals sign or ampersand, both of which are used to package the form data? There must be some way to distinguish between those characters inside form data versus those characters used to package the data. Consequently, when these characters appear in the form data itself, they are *escaped* by converting them into their hexadecimal ASCII representations, beginning with a percent sign (%). For example, the string "#$%" is converted to "%23%24%25". In hexadecimal ASCII, 23 represents the pound sign (#), 24 represents the dollar sign ($), and 25 represents the percent sign. For programming convenience, most nonalphanumeric characters are represented in hexadecimal ASCII notation.

> **Note**
>
> The exact range of characters represented in hexadecimal ASCII is not important because the decoding operation converts all character sequences beginning with a percent sign to their hexadecimal ASCII equivalent. Even if letters and numbers in a query string were encoded this way, they would still be decoded properly.

In summary, for both form data and <ISINDEX> queries, any data inside the form or query itself is converted according to the following rules:

- All spaces in the data are converted to plus signs (+).
- Nonalphanumeric characters are represented by their hexadecimal ASCII equivalents.

Storing Encoded URLs

As you have seen in the previous discussion of URL encoding, packaging form or query data into a single text string follows a few simple formatting rules. Consequently, it is possible to "fake" a script into believing that it is receiving form or query data without using a form. To do this, you simply send the URL that would be constructed if a form were used. This may be useful if you frequently run a script with the same data set.

For example, suppose you frequently search the Web index Yahoo for new documents related to the scripting language JavaScript. If you are interested in checking for new documents several times a day, you could fill out the Yahoo search query each time. A more efficient way, however, is to store the query URL in your browser's hotlist or bookmark list. Each time you select that item on the hotlist, a new query is generated as if you had filled out the form. The query URL stored in the hotlist would look like:

```
http://search.yahoo.com/bin/search?p=JavaScript
```

Innovative Uses of Forms

Forms have come a long way from just being front-ends for search facilities and directory updates. Currently forms are used to conduct electronic commerce, to conduct research on who is using the Web, and to have fun! The following are some examples.

Electronic Commerce: The Nashville Country Store

The Nashville Country Store at **http://www.countrystore.com/** is an example of doing business over the Web or electronic commerce. As technology to keep Internet transactions secure has emerged, Web users have developed more confidence in buying merchandise online. Figure 12.8 shows a screen from the Country Store that uses check boxes, text fields and pull-down menus to create an shopping interface for visitors. Hidden fields are used to keep track of a shoppers' purchases as they browse through the store.

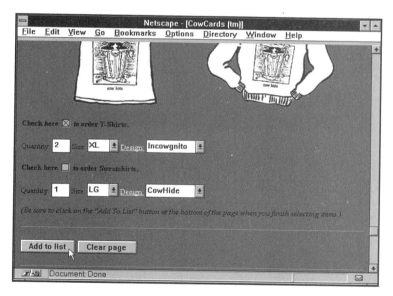

Fig. 12.8
HTML forms support electronic commerce by providing users with an interface to facilitate their shopping.

Research: Georgia Tech GVU Web Surveys

The Graphics, Visualization, and Usability Center at Georgia Tech has conducted four World Wide Web user surveys since January 1994. Online forms collect data on user demographics and the results are made publicly available on the Web. The last survey occurred in October 1995, with the next one planned for April 1996. You can visit the GVU Center's Web site at **http://www.cc.gatech.edu/gvu/user_surveys/**.

III

Doing HTML

Fun: The Dreaded Matching Question '95

In a play on the popular testing format, a faculty member at Tulane University has put a 26-item matching question online. The question tests knowledge of popular culture and is taken from actual exams given in the course Management of Promotion. Figure 12.9 shows the first few items in the question. The boxes next to the numbered items in the first column are text boxes into which you type the letters of the matching item from the second column. You can take the test at **http://129.81.234.19/courses/ dmq95.htm**.

Fig. 12.9
HTML forms allowed one faculty member to replicate a matching question online.

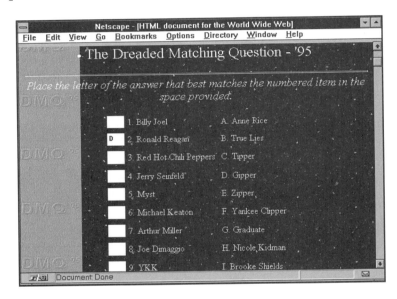

Part IV

Applications

CHAPTER 13

CGI Scripts and Server APIs

By now, you know enough to get your server up and running. You can create and publish HTML documents and display images. You can sit and watch people from around the world log onto your server but you still seem to have this nagging feeling that there's something missing. Maybe your server should be doing…something. You know, something like searching documents or even displaying one of those cute little access counters that tell how many people have linked to your page. Your server just seems a little reactive and not interactive.

It's time to talk about creating dynamic documents on your server. One of the earliest means of creating documents on-the-fly is through the use of the *Common Gateway Interface* (CGI). Using CGI scripts, your server can interact with third-party applications that can execute document searches, query databases, or return a dynamically-created HTML page. You can give users that customized and professional feel to your server.

There are other means of creating interactive services on your Web servers. *Server Side Includes* are customized capabilities offered by Web server applications that allow you to produce dynamic documents but without the resource overhead of CGI script processing. In addition, some servers offer the ability to directly extend the capability of the server program itself using a technology known as *Application Programming Interfaces* (APIs).

This chapter covers the following topics:

- An introduction to the CGI standard and CGI scripting
- Use of Server Side Includes
- Use of Web server APIs

Introduction to CGI

Normally, Web servers respond to requests from Web browsers in the form of HTML documents and images. The browser sends a URL to the server and the server sends the file, whether it's an HTML document, GIF or JPEG graphic, sound file, or movie, to the browser via an HTTP connection. Sometimes, the browser sends a URL that does not point to a document but instead points to an application. The server activates this application which then responds to the browser with the requisite information. This application is a CGI script. This section covers how this script interacts with the Web server and browser.

One important feature of HTML 2.0 is the capability for Web designers to use the language to create interactive forms. These forms collect data entered by the user; the Web browser processes this data and sends it via an HTTP request to a Web server. Usually, the Web server will receive requests for HTML documents or graphic images. However, the HTML form implies that a specific action is requested of the server. With this type of request, the server knows to ignore the content of the form data and redirect the information to a CGI script specified in the HTML form page.

The CGI script is actually a third-party application developed in a language such as C, C++, PERL, Visual Basic, or really any language supported by the operating system in which the server is running. However, some languages lend themselves to CGI scripting more than others and we'll discuss those later in this chapter.

How the CGI Works

The process through which the Common Gateway Interface works is quite simple.

1. The browser accumulates data from an HTML form and prepares it for transmission to the server.

2. The server reads the URL enclosed in the browser request and activates the application.

3. The server relays the information from the HTML form to the CGI application.

4. The CGI script processes the form data and prepares a response. This processing can include a database query, a numerical calculation, or an imagemap request. The response is usually in the form of an HTML document. However, the response is cleverly phrased by the CGI application to convince the Web browser that it originated from the server.

5. The CGI application passes the response to the server which immediately redirects it to the Web client. The server does not usually affect the output of the CGI application.

This process is outlined in figure 13.1. Note that the server merely passes information to the script. The script receives the data from the Web server through some mechanism unique to the language in which the script was developed. As long as this mechanism is in place, any programming language can be used to implement a CGI script.

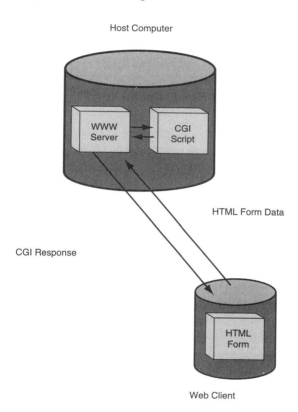

Host Computer

WWW Server

CGI Script

HTML Form Data

CGI Response

HTML Form

Web Client

Fig. 13.1
The CGI script works with the Web server to respond to certain Web browser requests.

IV

Applications

Client-Server HTTP Header Formats

Web browsers communicate with Web servers via the HTTP protocol. Not only does this protocol specify the physical packet structure of the protocol, but it also defines the manner in which the server and browser exchange information. For example, a Netscape Navigator client might send the following text to a Web server for a simple file request:

```
GET /article1.html HTTP/1.0
Accept: text/html
Accept: image/gif
Accept: image/jpeg
User-Agent: Mozilla/2.0b5 (Windows; I; 32bit)
 ...a blank line...
```

This message header informs the server that the browser is looking for the file article1.html and intends to use version 1.0 of the HTTP specification. The browser then informs the server as to which file formats it can interpret. In the above message, this list is truncated from what browsers usually express, but the server is informed that the client can interpret several text and graphics MIME types. The browser then informs the server as to its brand of client; in this example, the browser is defined as Netscape Navigator. Finally, the browser passes a blank line to complete the request.

The server will respond with a message generally like the following:

```
HTTP/1.0 200 OK
Date: Thursday, 01-Feb-96 19:15:32 GMT
Server: Apache 1.0.3
MIME-version: 1.0
Last-modified: Friday, 15-Dec-95 17:54:01 GMT
Content-type: text/html
Content-length: 7562
 ...a blank line...
<HTML><HEAD><TITLE>Article....
```

In this response, the server provides enough information to allow the browser to process the requested data. The server denotes that it too is providing data using the HTTP v.1.0 protocol. Furthermore, it returns an HTTP code of 200 OK which tells the browser to relax and the requested file was not only found but is being returned in this message. The date and server type are described in the header. The server type is included as the browser may interpret certain features not described in other servers. The server tells the Web client which version of MIME encoding is being used so that the browser can reprocess the data. The browser is also informed as to the MIME type of the data and the size of the file; this last datum is important as it allows the browser to inform the user as to the progress of the data transfer. Finally, a blank line (actually, two carriage return/line feed pairs, i.e. CRLFCRLF) separate the HTTP headers from the body of text.

The server needs to be flexible enough to provide the file in a format that is accessible to the client. For example, the server would need to provide a GIF file if a browser, which could only process GIF files, requests a file that is offered in JPEG.

IV

Applications

For information about HTTP specifications see **http://www.ics.uci.edu/pub/ietf/http/**.

As mentioned previously, the HTTP server doesn't usually process output from a CGI application; the response is merely funneled through the server back at the browser. The message, however, must be configured so as to conform to the HTTP message header specifications. We will discuss later in this chapter ways that you can program your CGI script to insert an HTTP header at the beginning of your response to ensure correct processing by a Web browser.

HTML Forms and CGI

By using an HTML form page, you can allow users to enter data that is processed by a CGI script. As discussed earlier in this book, users can enter text and specify options using forms developed with HTML. The types of data input options are as follows:

- Multiline text entry fields
- Pop-up selection menus
- Radio buttons
- Check boxes

Figure 13.2 shows an example of an HTML form that can be used to transfer data to a CGI application. Note that this sample page contains text, check boxes, radio buttons. The HTML code for this page is shown in listing 13.1.

Listing 13.1   Transfer Data to a CGI Application with This Form

```
<HTML>
<HEAD>
<TITLE>
Forms Test
</TITLE>
</HEAD>
<BODY>
<FORM ACTION="http://hoohoo.ncsa.uiuc.edu/cgi-bin/post-query"
METHOD=POST>
A normal text field:
<TEXTAREA NAME="comments1"></TEXTAREA><p>
<HR>
<DL>Please indicate your favorite holiday:
<DD>
```

(continues)

Listing 13.1 Continued

```
<INPUT TYPE="radio" NAME="holiday" VALUE="Christmas">Christmas
<DD>
<INPUT TYPE="radio" NAME="holiday" VALUE="Thanksgiving">Thanksgiving
<DD>
<INPUT TYPE="radio" NAME="holiday" VALUE="Easter">Easter
<DD>
<INPUT TYPE="radio" NAME="holiday" VALUE="NYDay">New Year's Day
</DL>
<DL>Please put a check next to the applications you own:
<DD>
<INPUT TYPE="checkbox" NAME="msword" VALUE="No" CHECKED>Microsoft
Word
<DD>
<INPUT TYPE="checkbox" NAME="photoshop" VALUE="No">Adobe Photoshop
<DD>
<INPUT TYPE="checkbox" NAME="netscape" VALUE="No">Netscape
<DD>
<INPUT TYPE="checkbox" NAME="excel" VALUE="No">Microsoft Excel
</DL>
<INPUT TYPE="submit" VALUE="Submit This Form">
</FORM>
</BODY>
</HTML>
```

Fig. 13.2
You can use several types of HTML forms to retrieve information from Web users.

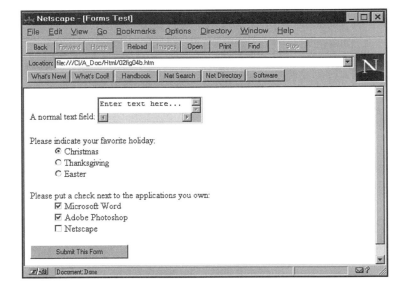

Note that all of the form elements in the above code use the NAME attribute. The idea is that the user enters text in a field or checks a radio button; this data is assigned a variable corresponding to the value of the NAME attribute. The CGI script uses these data by referencing the corresponding variable name. For example, the response from a post-query script to the above example is shown in figure 13.3.

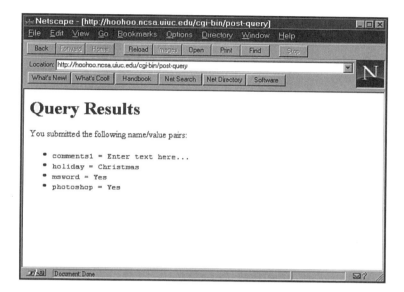

Fig. 13.3
A post-query script
is useful for
displaying the
values of an HTML
form.

Note

A *post-query script* is a generic term for any script that merely echoes back the results of an HTML form submission. In the nominal NCSA httpd software distribution, a simple CGI script entitled post-query reflects the values of the entered text data. Post-query scripts are one of the simplest implementations of CGI scripting and are useful for debugging HTML form pages.

Two alternative methods of transferring form data to a CGI script are POST and GET. These are the possible values of the METHOD attribute in the opening <FORM> tag. You're limited to passing no more than 24KB of data back to the server using GET. POST, however, allows transfer of much more data. This results from the fact that a request made through the GET method concatenates all the HTML form variables into a single string; this string is appended to the URL in the HTTP message that identifies the CGI script. Requests made through the POST method combine all the form parameters into an internal variable that is passed to the script.

The CGI Environment

In order to get the CGI application to run on any operating system, there needs to be some mechanism to convey the form data from the HTTP server to the CGI application. With UNIX, this is done through the use of environment variables, standard input and output. With Web servers running under the MacOS, AppleEvents are used to convey data to and from the CGI script and Web server. With Windows 3.1, Windows 95, and Windows NT, CGI variables are exchanged using a Windows private profile file in key-value format.

CGI Variables

The variables described in this section are passed from the browser to the server; they pertain to information about the browser. Your CGI application can use these variables to display information about the server, the user, the user's browser, or the user's connection to the server. The CGI environment variable is included in parentheses where applicable.

- Server Software (SERVER_SOFTWARE)

  The name and software version of the Web server answering the request and launching the CGI application.

  Example: Apache 1.0.3

- Server Name (SERVER_NAME)

  The server's host name or IP address.

  Example: www.mcp.com

- Server Port (SERVER_PORT)

  The port number that received the request.

  Example: 80

- Server Admin (SERVER_ADMIN)

  The administrative contact for the web server, as obtained from the web server config files. Useful for giving a feedback email address in case of unrecoverable problems.

- CGI Version (GATEWAY_INTERFACE)

  The version of the CGI standard to which the server replies.

  Example: CGI/1.1

- Request Protocol (SERVER_PROTOCOL)

  The name and version of the protocol used by the client for this request.

  Example: HTTP/1.0

■ Request Method (REQUEST_METHOD)

The HTTP method specified in the request.

Examples: GET, HEAD, POST

> **Note**
>
> Most of the headers in an HTTP request are made available to the CGI environment by taking the name of the header, turning it into all-capitals, and prepending HTTP_ to the front of it (i.e., if the browser sends Foo: Bar, the CGI script will see HTTP_FOO as a variable, and Bar as the value of that variable). This is the case with some of the variables below.

■ Referrer (HTTP_REFERRER)

The URL of the document from which the CGI script was referred, if the browser sends it.

Example: http://www.anywhere.com/cgi-test.html

■ From (HTTP_FROM)

The e-mail address of the Web browser user.

> **Note**
>
> The From variable is not used by every browser because of privacy concerns although it is included in the HTTP specification.

■ User Agent (HTTP_USER_AGENT)

This variable contains the description of the browser software. This is useful, although not used by all browsers, for using CGI specific to various browsers.

Example: Mozilla/2.0b6 (Windows; I; 32bit)

■ Logical Path (PATH_INFO)

This is the part of the URL after the / right after the name of the CGI script, but before any ?— for example http://host/script.cgi/path?foo would set the PATH_INFO to be path, if the script was really script.cgi.

■ Physical Path (PATH_TRANSLATED)

If a logical path is specified in the client message, the server can try and map that as a path onto the document tree of the running Web server. In the above example, the server would see if a request to /path would have mapped to an actual resource on the server, and returned the full pathname to that (i.e., /web/htdocs/path/).

- Script URI (SCRIPT_NAME)

  The name of the CGI script specified by the request.

  Example: `http://host/cgi-bin/foo?argument` would result in a SCRIPT_NAME of `/cgi-bin/foo`.

- Script Filename (SCRIPT_FILENAME)

  The actual filename of the CGI program on the file system.

  Example: `http://host/cgi-bin/foo?argument` could result in a SCRIPT_NAME of `/usr/local/etc/httpd/cgi-bin/foo`.

- Query String (QUERY_STRING)

  The encoded version of the query data. This data follows the ? in the URL and is usually the result of a query from an HTML form.

  Example: `http://host/phonebook.cgi?Joe%20Smith+5551321` would result in `Joe%20Smith+5551321`.

- Remote Host (REMOTE_HOST)

  The IP host name of the Web browser making the request, if available.

  Example: s115.slipper.net

- Remote Address (REMOTE_ADDRESS)

  The IP address of the Web browser making the request.

  Example: 167.142.100.115

- Authentication Method (AUTH_TYPE)

  The protocol-specific method of authentication used to validate the user if the document is protected and the server supports authentication. This corresponds with the AuthType directive in Apache.

- Authenticated User Name (REMOTE_USER)

  The name of the authenticated user if the document is protected and the server supports authentication.

- Content Type (CONTENT_TYPE)

  The MIME type/subtype of the HTML form data contained in a PUT or POST request.

  Example: text/plain

- Content Length (CONTENT_LENGTH)

  The number of bytes of data contained in a PUT or POST request. This allows the browser to display the progress of a lengthy transmission to the user.

  Example: 42

- Accept (HTTP_ACCEPT)

  The list of MIME types accepted by the client. You can pass parameters for some of the MIME type/subtype combinations.

  Example: text/plain, text/html, image/gif

Apache Extensions to the CGI Environment

There are a few environment variables beyond those specified in the CGI 1.1 specification which Apache supports.

DOCUMENT_ROOT

As one would guess, this is the document root for the server, as specified in the server configuration files. This is useful for, for example, allowing PERL scripts to find a common definitions file without having to hardcode the path location in each PERL script. You might have a lib or data directory off of your document_root where you store extra PERL libraries or dynamic data, so to reference it in a PERL script you'd say, for example,

```
require "$ENV{'DOCUMENT_ROOT'}/lib/common.pl";
```

This way you can move your document tree around without having to worry about having hardcoded paths—everything would be based around the DocumentRoot as specified in the server configuration files.

REDIRECT_...

Apache supports custom error responses. It is usually useful, if that custom error response is a CGI script, to be able to get some information about the original request which caused the error. So, Apache takes each CGI variable from the old request and prefixes it with REDIRECT_ into the new environment. So for example:

```
QUERY_STRING -> REDIRECT_QUERY_STRING
PATH_INFO -> REDIRECT_PATH_INFO
```

Then, whatever appropriate new values for the old variables are defined.

There are two more special environment variables defined in this instance: REDIRECT_URL and REDIRECT_STATUS. REDIRECT_URL is simply the URL of the custom error response, while REDIRECT_STATUS is the error code which triggered this response. So for example, you might have

```
ErrorDocument 500 /error-handler.cgi
```

In this case, the REDIRECT_URL become /error-handler.cgi and the REDIRECT_STATUS is 500.

HTTP_COOKIE

If you are running with the `mod_cookie` module, you will see another environment variable you wouldn't normally see, `HTTP_COOKIE`. This is the legendary Netscape cookie functionality, where the server gives the web browser a token (cookie) when they first talk to each other, and then the browser sends it with every request. This token is unique and random, but usually guaranteed to be persistent for at least a user's "session", so it is possible to map this token to a "user". Usually it'll look something like this:

```
HTTP_COOKIE = s=myhost20434482411973732
```

What the key actually is isn't important—it's basically just a random number that mod_cookie makes up when it needs one. The important thing is that it can be used as a key in a database, or logged for tracking purposes. For example, if you see a CGI script hit 10 times, 3 times with one cookie, 3 with another, and 4 with another, you can be pretty sure you only had 3 people using that script, instead of 10 people once or 1 person ten times.

Notes on Certain CGI Variables

There are three variables that may or may not be set depending on other factors in the server configuration.

REMOTE_HOST

This is the DNS-resolved hostname matching the IP number of the client making the request from the server. If the server was compiled with DMINIMAL_DNS, or if the directive `LookupHostname` is set to `Off`, that variable will be set to the same value as REMOTE_ADDR, which is just the IP number. If your CGI program requires the hostname, and you have DNS resolution turned off for performance reasons, you can get the hostname by performing a `gethostbyaddr` call in C, or PERL, or whatever its equivalent is in other languages. Also, not every IP address is set to respond to reverse-DNS lookups, so even if the server is normally resolving every IP number, you might not be able to get a hostname for that number.

REMOTE_USER

This variable is only set if the script was placed under password-based authentication—this is the username that was used to get access. A very common bug report is "my CGI scripts aren't getting REMOTE_USER set!"—when in actuality what happened was that the CGI script was in a different directory (say, /cgi-bin/) from the other password-protected pages, and cgi-bin wasn't protected in the same way as those other pages. Since browsers cache passwords, and also since there's very rarely any user-interface level distinction between viewing a protected page and viewing an unprotected page, it's easy to understand why this may seem confusing. But don't worry, that's why you own this book.

REMOTE_IDENT

This is the string returned by a lookup to the client's machine using the ident protocol, as defined in RFC831. This will only return something if the IdentityCheck directive is set to On in the server config files, and of course if the remote site is actually running an ident daemon.

Setting Extra Variables

If you compiled in support for the module mod_env, there are two directives available to you for adding further information into the CGI environment.

PassEnv

PassEnv will let you pass through any environment variable from the shell environment from which the server is launched. For example

```
PassEnv USER
```

will pass along the contents of the USER variable from the shell of the user to the CGI environment.

SetEnv

This will let you explicitly set a particular variable in the environment. For example

```
SetEnv LIBDIR /www/lib
```

might be the best way to pass on to your CGI scripts where their libraries are, just as

```
SetEnv DEBUG 3
```

might be the best way to set the debugging level for your scripts.

Server APIs

Besides the CGI and SSI specifications, there is one other major means by which you can add functionality your server. Both Apache and Netscape support the notion of an API to the server—this is so code can be written to a published interface, compiled, and linked into the server such that the server and extra code become one actual program. This can give a tremendous boost to performance, and it can also allow the content creator to control certain deep aspects of the server that CGI does not allow.

Both the Apache API and the Netscape API are written in C, so modules to those servers must be written in C as well.

The Apache API provides a very generalized interface to the functionality of the server. Almost all the functionality beyond the core of the server is implemented through this API— all user authentication functions, the CGI interface, all access control functions, all "URL-munging" functions like Alias and Redirect. Apache modules can be written to implement "handlers" for certain data types—this is how functionality such as internal imagemap handling and Server Side Includes are implemented. Even logfile functionality is implemented as a module. This modular approach makes it very easy to "drop in" new functionality on top of or in place of older functionality. It allows server owners to tune their servers for optimum performance—for example, if you don't want to use the internal imagemap functionality, you can compile Apache without that module, and save yourself a couple dozen kilobytes per running child process, which may be significant at higher levels.

Examples of functionality that people have done using an API which normal CGI could not provide, either at all or in an efficient manner:

- Totally configurable logging into any syntax (mod_log_config)
- Authentication to an MSQL database (mod_auth_msql). This can be used as a prototype for other database interfaces as well.
- Automatic cookie maintenance for session tracking (mod_cookie)
- Radical new Server-Side Include functionality, beyond existing NCSA-style SSI syntax.

Note

The specifications for the Apache API can be found at **http://www.apache.org/docs/API.html**, or on the CD-ROM included with this book.

The NSAPI specification is available at **http://www.netscape.com/newsref/std/server_api.html**

Using HTTP Cookies

Cookies (as briefly mentioned above, under the "HTTP_COOKIE" CGI environment variable description) are a new HTTP mechanism proposed by Netscape Communications, but as of this writing, cookies are also supported by the Microsoft Internet Explorer and a couple other browsers as well. Cookies are designed to communicate state information to the browser from the server. This is in contrast to standard the HTTP process where server information outside of the HTTP response is not communicated to the browser.

When a browser first visits a "cookie-enabled" Web site, the site can send back a `Set-Cookie:` header in the HTTP response. On subsequent visits to that site, or to particular other sites within that domain, the browser sends one or more `Cookie:` headers in the request, and the server can change the cookies sent by sending yet more `Set-Cookie` headers back to the client. Possible applications include client preferences, such as user accounts and personal information, for online shopping services.

The syntax for a cookie header is as follows:

```
Set-Cookie: name=Value; expires=Date;
path=Path; domain=Domain_Name; secure
```

The cookie `name` is the only required attribute and identifies the cookie. You can set an expiration date with the `expires` tag; after that date, the cookie becomes invalid. The `domain` keyword is used by the server to validate the cookie; while searching the cookie list for valid entries, the `domain` keyword is matched against the domain of the requesting host. This enables the server to match the cookie from many other browsers making similar requests. Similarly, the `path` keyword is used to validate the cookie request. The cookie is transferred if the path defined by the requesting browser matches the cookie `path` attribute. The `secure` keyword alerts the server to transfer the cookie only if the connection is made using the Secure Sockets Layer protocol.

> **Note**
>
> The Cookie specifications are available at **http://www.netscape.com/newsref/std/cookie_spec.html**. As of this writing, the implementation of the cookie mechanism has not been finalized; consult the specifications before attempting to utilize cookies. It looks like cookies will make it into the HTTP specifications, but with guidelines on the user interface issues.

IV

Applications

## CHAPTER 14

More Scripting Options

As the World Wide Web has expanded and included more and more information, users have clamored for more interactivity beyond "point-and-surf." Especially with the advent of online information requests and product ordering, a need has developed for efficient data gathering and validation without the time-consuming and cumbersome process of developing CGI scripts and the inherent slow transmission of information across phone lines.

Enter the new world of scripting, with JavaScript and Visual Basic Script. With a compatible browser or add-on software components, much of the necessary interactive work is accomplished on the client machine without the need for exchanging information back and forth with the server.

In this chapter, you learn about:

- What functionality scripts add to HTML documents
- The basics of Netscape's JavaScript
- What is possible with Microsoft's Visual Basic Script
- New options for linking outside applications with ActiveX and Network Loadable Objects

Concepts

Scripts are small sections of code embedded in HTML tags or stand-alone sections of commands that are triggered by specific events in the document.

Normal HTML tags define static page appearances (headings and graphics), user interfaces (forms and links), and other features in addition to the text that appears on-screen. Scripts add interactivity to normal HTML tags by looking for events such as mouse clicks, mouse movements, and entering and leaving form fields.

For example, the tag `<input type="button" value="Click Me, Please" onClick="sayHowdy()">` is the normal definition of a button up to the `onClick` statement. This addition to the tag calls a function called `sayHowdy` when the button is pushed.

Functions are defined using HTML script tags. If the browser does not recognize the script tag, the actual tag is ignored and any subsequent text is handled like any other text on the page.

Note

Using script tags with HTML documents requires the following format:

```
<SCRIPT>
Statements...
</SCRIPT>
```

The optional, but recommended, attribute "language" specifies which scripting commands are being used:

```
<SCRIPT LANGUAGE="JavaScript">
JavaScript statements...
</SCRIPT>
```

The language specification for Visual Basic Script is "VBS." There is no limit to the number of statements enclosed by script tags, or the number of occurrences of scripts in an HTML document.

JavaScript and Visual Basic Script, while similar in purpose and function, are implemented in different ways. JavaScript capability is included as part of the browser, notably Netscape 2.0. No additional files or programs are needed to add JavaScript capability, just an HTML document embedded with a valid script.

At the moment, Visual Basic Script is an add-on application that requires a set of VBS files on the client machine in order to function; Internet Explorer 3.0 includes VB Script. When the browser finds the <script> command denoting VB Script, it will invoke the VB compiler add-on to handle the text denoted by the tags.

Because VB Script is a subset of Microsoft's Visual Basic programming language, it is likely that it will remain a separate application from the browser, although the two will be closely linked.

Both script languages discussed in this chapter allow Web authors and administrators to add interactivity to Web pages, including functions to respond to queries, ask questions, validate data, calculate expressions, and link to external controls and applications.

Checking for Helper Applications

How do I know if a user has the proper "helper application" or right browser to view my page? In two words, you don't. Unless you have control over the types of browsers end-users have on their computers, it's a good idea to identify pages that require compatibility with a script language.

Tip

To prevent your script from appearing on-screen with an incompatible browser, it's also a good idea to encompass the material between the "<script>" and "</script>" tags with comment HTML tags "<!--" and "-->". This will prevent your script from cluttering an otherwise attractive page.

When planning which scripting language to use, keep in mind that not all browsers support all scripts, if any. At publication, Microsoft announced support for JavaScript in its Internet Explorer, while Netscape has not yet reciprocated for VB Script. Other scripting possibilities are also on the horizon based on other popular Web languages, including Tcl, Python, and Caml.

JavaScript

JavaScript is a set of commands that are included in HTML documents to add additional interactivity and functionality to Web pages. It began its life as LiveScript until collaboration with Sun Microsystems and its object-oriented language called Java caused a name change. Although JavaScript is not directly derived from Java, it is very similar in its form and construction. The primary difference between the two is that JavaScript is interpreted while Java is compiled.

Interpreted versus Compiled

Interpreted languages are evaluated line by line at run-time. Compiled languages are passed through a compiler, where it is converted into a form readily usable by the computer. Interpreted languages are easier to work with in areas like HTML page design, but they sacrifice a lot in speed. A compiled program runs very fast since the interpretation of commands was done "ahead of time."

For example, a JavaScript function can verify that users enter valid information into a form requesting a ZIP code. Without any network transmission, an HTML page with embedded JavaScript interprets the text and alerts the user with a message for invalid input. Or, you can use JavaScript to perform an action (such as play an audio file, execute an applet, or communicate with a plug-in) in response to the user opening or exiting a page.

With an effective script, it is possible to respond without any network transmission to user-initiated events, such as mouse clicks and form entries.

JavaScript Isn't Java

An important distinction to make is the difference between JavaScript and Java, which has caused confusion for a great number of folks. Java is a full-fledged object-oriented programming language. It makes use of a compiler to create stand-alone applications and browser applets. Applets are separate files downloaded to the client computer that can add special effects to HTML pages (scrolling banners are the current rage), but the code still resides in a separate file from the browser.

JavaScript, although related to Java, was developed by Netscape and does not require compiling. JavaScript exists as a set of commands supporting interactive levels above and beyond HTML without the need for server-based CGI programs.

JavaScript's vocabulary is much smaller than Java's, and is easily understandable by authors currently working with HTML. Java is a full-blown programming language, and benefits from knowledge of C and C++. Programming in Java requires a set of development tools, including a compiler and class library. All that is needed to take advantage of JavaScript is a text editor or HTML authoring application and a compatible browser, such as Netscape Navigator 2.0.

Note

For the most up-to-date information, check out Netscape's home page at **http://home.netscape.com**. It includes access to online documentation for JavaScript and links to pages exploiting JavaScript.

JavaScript Basics

In order to understand what is happening inside a section of JavaScript code and how to use it on your pages, it is necessary to understand a few key ideas of how JavaScript is constructed.

Objects and Properties

An object is similar to a noun. Cars, people, buildings, dogs, pencils, and coffee cups can all be considered objects. They're tangible things we can touch and feel. Properties help define the object. They can be variables or other objects.

Let's create an object called `libraryBook` with the properties of title, author, and dueDate. In JavaScript, we can define the object like this:

```
libraryBook = new checkOutBook("Return of the Native",
➥"Thomas Hardy", "04/15/96")
```

This line calls a function which results in a creation of a new object with the following values:

```
libraryBook.title = "Return of the Native"
libraryBook.author = "Thomas Hardy"
libraryBook.dueDate = "04/15/96"
```

Writing a function to create an object is covered later in this section.

> **Tip**
>
> JavaScript is case-sensitive, which can lead to confusion when creating objects and errors at run-time. For example, `libraryBook` and `LibraryBook` would be two different objects in JavaScript. It is important to strictly adhere to one style for naming items in JavaScript — your sanity depends on it.

Now, include another object called `libraryInfo` with the properties of branch, address, phone, which contains the following values:

```
libraryInfo.branch = "Downtown"
libraryInfo.address = "111 Higgins St."
libraryInfo.phone = 4065551212
```

To add more information to our `libraryBook` example, add the `libraryInfo`:

```
libraryBook.publicLibrary = libraryInfo
```

Here's what just happened. A new property named `publicLibrary` was added to `libraryBook`. This new property was assigned the value from the `libraryInfo` object. The properties for `libraryBook` are listed in table 14.1.

Table 14.1 Values of *libraryBook* Object

Object/Property Name	Value
libraryBook.title	"Thomas Hardy"
libraryBook.author	"Return of the Native"
libraryBook.dueDate	"04/15/96"
libraryBook.publicLibrary.branch	"Downtown"
libraryBook.publicLibrary.address	"111 Higgins St."
libraryBook.publicLibrary.phone	4065551212

JavaScript assigns values by adding properties to objects. If an object is added as a property, then the parent object (`libraryBook`) inherits the properties of the child (`publicLibrary`).

Methods and Functions

Methods and functions are the verbs of JavaScript. These are the items that "do" something. JavaScript includes a set of predefined methods and functions, in addition to allowing users to create their own special-purpose items.

Functions and methods begin with the `function` declaration:

```
function printTextAndLine (string) {
document.write(string + "<HR>")
}
```

First, `function` lets the browser know that this is the definition of a process. Until the end of the function declaration is reached, no statements are executed. The function must be called somewhere else in the document before anything happens.

The name of the function follows. The name is used to invoke the function later on. The last item is an argument list surrounded by parentheses. In our example, there is only one argument called `string`.

The body of the function is enclosed in curly brackets ({ }). When the closing bracket is reached, the function definition is completed.

> **Tip**
>
> JavaScript text is treated like any other HTML text. Extra spaces and carriage returns are ignored, but should be used to make the code more readable. Normally in coding, a carriage return is used to delineate the start of a new command or line. In JavaScript, command lines are separated with a semicolon.

When a function is added to an object, it is called a method.

Continuing with the `libraryBook` example, let's define a new function called `printCheckout`:

```
function printCheckout() {
document.write("Your book: " + this.title + "<BR>");
document.write("  Due on: " + this.dueDate + "<P>");
}
```

This function is added to the object the same as another object:

```
libraryBook.printInfo = printCheckout
```

To invoke the method requires a single statement:

```
libraryBook.printInfo().
```

> **Tip**
>
> There are two ways of formatting text inside JavaScript. The first uses standard HTML tags generated by the document.write function. In order for these to work, they must be sent to the screen encapsulated in quotation marks like any other text.
>
> The second is with JavaScript codes, which are included in the string expression NOT enclosed in quotation marks. JavaScript formatting codes are listed in table 14.2.
>
> The following two statements would yield the same results, a break at the end of the line:
>
> ```
> document.write("Something<BR>another line")
> document.write("Something  \n another line")
> ```

Table 14.2   JavaScript Text Formatting Codes

Code	Purpose
\b	backspace
\f	form feed
\n	new line
\r	carriage return
\t	tab character

JavaScript can use an additional set of codes to format text displayed with document.write. These codes are included in the string with a plus sign (+) and no quotation marks.

Creating Objects

Creating objects is a two-step process.

1. Create a function which defines the object.
2. Assign a variable to the function using new.

Going back once again to the libraryBook, a function to create a book object could look something like this:

```
function book(title, author, dueDate) {
this.title = title;
this.author = author;
this.dueDate = dueDate;
}
```

Our library book is defined with the following statement:

```
libraryBook = new book("Return of the Native","Thomas Hardy","04/15/96")
```

> **Tip**
>
> JavaScript supports a special object called `this`. In general, this refers to the calling object. It is especially useful for validating form information.
>
> For example, the tag `<input type="text" name= "ssn" width="9" onChange="validId(this)>` will call the function `validId` with the information entered by the user in the ssn text box.

In turn, we can create other objects using the same definition:

```
libraryBook2 = new book("Life Among the Savages","Shirley
➥Jackson","03/18/96")
collegeLibraryBook = new book("Red Shirt, Green Shirt","Sandra
➥Boynton","05/01/96")
```

Variables

Unlike Java, JavaScript does not enforce explicit data types.

> **Note**
>
> An explicit data type can only handle a specific type of data, such as integers, floating point decimals, or strings. Implicit data types are defined on-the-fly as a value is assigned to the variable. For example, a variable called `weekDay` is assigned a number representing the day of the week, 3 for Wednesday. When it's time to print the text, the variable can change type by a simple expression such as, "if weekDay = 3 : weekDay = "Wednesday".

JavaScript supports four basic kinds of variables: `object`, `numeric`, `string`, and `date`. As discussed earlier, JavaScript is based on objects. While similar to other variables, it is different in a key behavior. The "value" of objects are changed by adding properties, methods, and other objects. So, while a variable can be a property of an object, an object is never a property of a variable.

The next two variables, `numeric` and `string`, are straightforward. Numeric is any number, integer or floating-point decimal. A string is any collection of characters, including letters, numbers, and special characters.

> **Note**
>
> JavaScript has a feature called *automatic type conversion*. This feature will convert a string variable to numeric and vice versa, depending on its use.

For example, the variable x is assigned to 10, and the variable increment is assigned to "3." The statement "x = x + increment" evaluates to 13. The first type encountered by JavaScript is numeric, so the second variable is also converted to a numeric value. If increment was assigned to "Bob," the statement would return an error, since numeric conversion is impossible for "Bob."

Using implicit typing, JavaScript has eliminated the need for commands found in other languages, such as val and str, used to convert strings to numeric values and vice versa. It also places more responsibility on the person writing the code to manage variables to ensure that inconsistent data types are not brought together in a 3 + "Bob" situation.

Dates

The date data type does not contain a "date" the way we normally think of a date. JavaScript calculates the date and time based on the number of milliseconds since midnight on January 1, 1970. It sounds a little complicated, but it is a fairly standard form of calculating dates and times with computers.

Where it starts to get complicated is assigning a new date variable. The date is entered "yy,mm-1,dd,hh,mm,ss". Translated, this means entering the year, the month minus one, the day, hours, minutes, and seconds. For example:

```
docFirstDay = new Date(96,0,13,6,15,00)
```

This creates a variable called docFirstDay with a value of January 11, 1996 at 6:15 am.

Accessing the current date requires creating a new variable, usually called today, the same way docFirstDay was created. Then, each component is accessed through separate methods:

```
today.getMonth()
today.getDate()
today.getYear()
today.getHours()
today.getMinutes()
today.getSeconds()
```

Tip

Don't forget to add 1 to the month. JavaScript begins its year with January equal to 0.

You can add and subtract the values from date methods. For example, using the onLoad event handler, you could check the current date against the date the document was modified and inform the user if the information they're going to read is out of date.

Note

The date on the client's computer is used for all date calculations. So, if your date is based on the correct date and time, and the client computer is set to 1/1/85, any calculation based on the current time will be inaccurate.

Adding JavaScript to HTML

As seen in some of the previous examples, adding JavaScript to HTML is a fairly simple matter. There are a couple of points to keep in mind when deciding where to place the scripts.

- When an HTML document is called by a browser, the page is loaded into memory before its tags are evaluated and displayed. For this reason, it's best to place all function definitions inside the <head> tags at the beginning of the document, where they are loaded into memory before the user has a chance to initiate any events. The exception is JavaScript code that is executed with the rest of the page. It should be included inside the <body> tags so it is processed at the proper time.

- Browsers incompatible with script languages will display any text inside the <script> tags as text, so it's best to use comment tags to hide it. Hiding the script will not interfere with a compatible browser's ability to load and run it.

With this ability in mind, JavaScript can reside in two places inside an HTML document.

- As statements and functions using <script> tags.
- As event handlers using HTML tags.

Scripts

Now that some of the basic building blocks are in place for creating JavaScript procedures, it's time to try some examples.

Listing 14.1 illustrates a simple script to display text on a page.

Listing 14.1   A Simple HTML Document with JavaScript

```
<html>
<head>
This is an HTML page.
</head>
<body>
```

```
This begins the body of an HTML page.
<script language="JavaScript">
<!-- Hide text from old browsers
document.write("<hr>Hello from JavaScript.<hr>")
alert("You have entered a JavaScript-powered page")
//finish hiding script -->
</script>
That's all, folks.
</body>
</html>
```

Examining the code line by line reveals what is happening. First, under HTML commands, a simple text line is displayed on the screen. Then, the script flag is encountered, letting the browser know that the following lines will need to be interpreted as JavaScript commands.

The two JavaScript lines, *alert* and *document.write*, are both methods for displaying information on the screen. The alert function beeps and displays a dialog box with a message, which can then be cleared by the user. The next line displays text on the screen like normal HTML text. Since JavaScript commands are interpreted separate from the browser, any formatting needs to be inserted into the string before it is sent to the page. In this example, the <hr> tag inserts a horizontal line above and below the JavaScript text to separate it from the HTML text on the screen.

HTML text ——
JavaScript
text
JavaScript Alert box

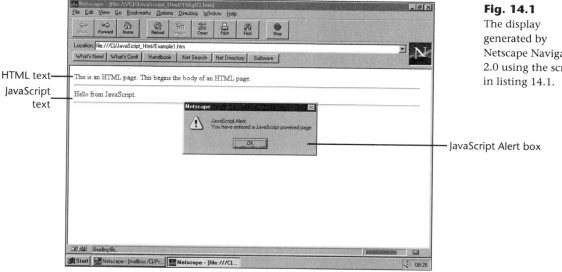

Fig. 14.1
The display generated by Netscape Navigator 2.0 using the script in listing 14.1.

Fig. 14.2
The display
generated by a
noncompatible
browser only
shows HTML text.
The script
commands are
ignored and
hidden by
comment tags.

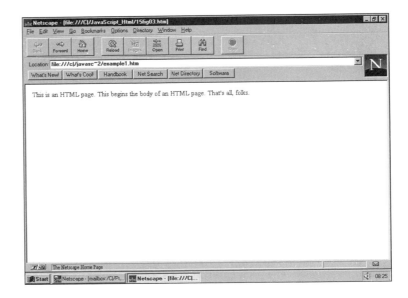

Listing 14.2 illustrates the placement of functions and events that
trigger them. The code produces figure 14.3.

Listing 14.2   A Simple JavaScript Event-Handling Function

```
<html>
<head>
This is an HTML page.
<script language="JavaScript">
<!-- Hide text from old browsers
function outTheWindow() {
newWin =open("","DisplayWindow","toolbar=no,directories=no,menubar=no");
newWin.document.write("<HEAD><TITLE>HTML On The Fly!</TITLE><HEAD>");
newWin.document.write("<H1>Now is the time to make HTML work.</H1>");
}
//finish hiding script -->
</script>
</head>
<body>
This begins the body of your average HTML page.
<form>
<input type="button" name="button" value="Press Here For Results"
➥onClick="outTheWindow()">
</form>
</body>
</html>
```

When the document is loaded, the outTheWindow function is defined for future use. A button is drawn on the screen inside a form. Clicking the button is detected by the onClick event handler (table 14.3), which triggers the function.

The function itself is the basis for some intriguing possibilities with script languages. JavaScript opens a new window in the browser and begins to generate HTML code. The initial value that is left blank can also contain a URL to another file on your server, or any other address on the Web.

Event Handlers

Event handlers, coupled with the basic programming functions, allow Web developers to implement client-based interactivity. JavaScript includes a basic set of event handlers that provide the capability to deal with most things a user will do with a form or the mouse pointer (see table 14.3).

Table 14.3   JavaScript Event Handlers

Name	User Event	Example
click	Click on form element or link	onClick
mouseover	Mouse pointer moved over a link or anchor	onMouseOver
blur	Remove input focus from form element	onBlur
focus	Form element selected for input	onFocus
select	Form element's input field selected	onSelect
change	Changed value of text, textarea, or select element	onChange
load	Navigator loads page	onLoad
unload	User exits the page	onUnload
submit	Form is submitted	onSubmit

The following script shows how additional information can be provided for links to other items by using the onMouseOver event to place a custom message in the status bar.

```
<html>
<body>
If you need more information about JavaScript, check out
<a href="http://home.netscape.com/" onMouseOver="window.status=
➡'The Netscape Home Page'; return true"> Netscape.</a>
</body>
</html>
```

Fig. 14.3

The display generated by listing 14.2. Note the status bar at the bottom of the screen, where the link's URL is replaced by text from the event handler tag.

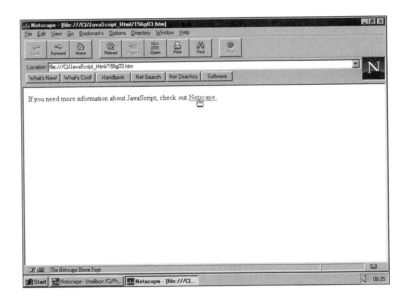

The real power of event handlers is evident in validating user information (see listing 14.3).

Listing 14.3   A Script To Validate User-Entered Information

```
<html>
<head>
<script language="JavaScript">
<!-- Hide script from old browsers
function checkPassword(string) {
if (string="password") {
newWin = open("download/safezone/index.html","DisplayWindow",
➥"toolbar=no,directories=no,menubar=no");
}
else {alert("Invalid password.")
}
// end script hiding -->
</script>
<body>
Please type your name in the box:
<form>
<input type="password" name="name" size=8
➥onBlur="checkPassword(this.value)" value="">
</form>
</body>
</html>
```

After entering a password in the form box, it is checked against the generic password. If "password" is entered, then a new window is opened with a different HTML document.

Obviously, this is not a secure way to deal with passwords, but you get the idea of the kind of validation and entry-checking possible without accessing the server.

The Future of JavaScript

As of publication, JavaScript is implemented as part of Netscape 2.0 and 2.01. This is not the end of its development, however, as Netscape has reserved words for future properties and methods. Proposed HTML specifications will limit script actions to events generated within form tags, but currently, JavaScript capabilities extend beyond the defined limits. Two examples are the OnLoad and OnUnLoad events, triggered when a page is entered and exited, which are possible to include within body tags.

Netscape also has plans to support JavaScript from the server through a compiled form of the language. When a Web page containing server-side JavaScript is encountered, it will only perform the code locally. This type of application can be used to track the current browser connection and other information from the user. In this form, JavaScript could be pressed into CGI service without dealing with PERL or C. Future plans call for JavaScript-related applications to provide access to standard database products.

JavaScript can also interact with the exposed properties and methods of Java applets and plug-ins. Once the object is declared on the page, JavaScript can get and set properties and call methods within scripts by using its standard object hierarchy, beginning with the class or plug-in name as the object name.

Visual Basic Script

Visual Basic Script, also known as VB Script, is a new scripting language packaged with Microsoft's Internet Explorer 3.0. VB Scripts are connected to events, defined by attaching "On" handlers to HTML tags. The event triggers the script, which interacts with its environment through a set of objects representing HTML page element, history list, plug-in applications, object files, and applets.

The syntax of VB Script is based on Visual Basic, although VB Script offers a much smaller and simpler set of commands to work with. It is used to validate form data, create new Web pages on-the-fly, and perform other operations with user input.

While VB Script resembles the object-oriented JavaScript, it is not necessary to understand object-oriented programming.

Visual Basic Script Isn't Visual Basic

VB Script is described by Microsoft as a "fast, lightweight" subset of Visual Basic designed for use inside HTML pages. While requiring a compiler on the host machine, VB Script has no ability to create user interfaces. Every item manipulated by VB Script must first exist in the HTML page. The files required to integrate VB Script with a browser take approximately 200K of disk space.

Microsoft Visual Basic is a programming language geared towards developing applications for Windows. It includes editors, debuggers, and compilers for the creation of independent applications. It consumes approximately 1 MB of disk space for the basic set of tools.

Note

Updates on Microsoft's development and support of Visual Basic Script can be found through Microsoft's Web site at **http://www.microsoft.com/intdev/vbs/**.

Visual Basic Tools

Since VB Script is a subset of Visual Basic, it is upwardly compatible to Visual Basic for Applications which is upwardly compatible with Visual Basic. For Web managers and developers already familiar with Visual Basic, the trip to productivity and interactivity will be a short one.

Note

Browsers often employ "helper applications" to extend the capabilities of HTML documents. Some of these applications are built-in or generally included as part of the software package (some sound and graphics), while others are added later by the user (animation and compressed files).

If a browser sees an item tag it doesn't recognize, it checks its list of helper applications and calls the matching program to handle the information between the tags.

Data and Variable Types

VB Script's only data type is called a *variant*. A variant can contain different types of information depending on how it's assigned or used. Since it's the only data type in VB Script, all functions return it.

Since different types of information may be passed to the variant, the command **VarType** is used to return information about what kind of data is stored within. At a simple level, variants contain string or numeric data. If it is used in a mathematical equation, it is treated as a number; if used in a string, it behaves like a string.

Since the basic types of data come in many varieties, the variant is equipped with subtypes to help further define its use. Subtypes include boolean, integer, single, and double (floating point numbers), date and string. Information can be translated from one subtype to another using the conversion functions included with VB Script.

Variables are declared using the `Dim` statement. For example:

```
Dim TotalBill
```

creates a variable called `TotalBill`, which is a variant. Its subtype is empty, since no value has been assigned yet. Variables can also be declared implicitly by using a valid name somewhere within your script. For example:

```
ItemCharge = 10.50
```

creates a variable named `ItemCharge`, which is a variant of subtype single, since it has been assigned a floating point value.

Standard Naming Rules

Variable names follow a simple set of standard rules that also apply to all other user-defined items.

- Must begin with an alphabetic character.
- Can't contain an embedded period.
- Are restricted to 255 characters in length.
- Must be a unique name within the scope it's used.

When a variable is declared within a procedure, only commands and statements within that procedure can access or change the value of the variable. This is called local scope. If a variable needs to have a scope that extends to all procedures within a script, it should be declared outside of a procedure definition. It has script-level scope.

Local scope variables retain their value only while the procedure is running. Once the procedure returns control to the script, the variable is lost until created again by calling the procedure again. A script-level variable will maintain its value until the script is completed.

VB Script also supports arrays. The only difference in declaration is the addition of parentheses with the number of elements.

```
Dim ExecutiveBoard(12)
```

Since all arrays include a 0 element, the previous example contains 13 elements. Arrays can contain up to 60 dimensions.

Tip

To create a dynamic array, whose size can change during run-time, use the `ReDim` statement.

```
ReDim ItemsOrdered()
```

Note the difference with the parentheses. A dynamic array does not use a size value.

To increase or decrease the size of the array, use `ReDim` with a value. Changing the number of elements will clear existing values in the array unless the `Preserve` statement is used.

```
ReDim ItemsOrdered(6)
...
ReDim Preserve ItemsOrdered(7)
```

Procedures

Procedures come in two varieties with VB Script, `Sub` and `Function`.

A `Sub` procedure can accept parameters and perform actions, but does not return a value when it is completed. If it doesn't accept parameters, it is declared with a set of empty parentheses.

```
Sub AddNumbers(First,Second)
     NumSum = First + Second
     MsgBox "The sum of " & First & " and " & " Second " is " &
     ➥NumSum & "."
End Sub
```

A Function is similar to a Sub, but it can return a value. This is accomplished by assigning a value to the function name.

```
Function AddNumbers(First,Second)
     AddNumbers = First + Second
End Function
```

Tip

Like functions in JavaScript, Subs and Functions should be declared in the <head> portion of an HTML page. This ensures the procedures are loaded and ready by the time the user sees the page and has a chance to act.

Working with Forms

One of VB Script's most powerful uses is for data validation without server interaction. This makes it possible to ensure users submit information that your server is expecting, preventing unexpected error messages.

Values from forms are referenced using their names. For example, a text box named "SSN" is accessed using SSN.value in a calling function.

Using Objects

In order for VB Script to get and set object properties from OLE controls or Java classes, it is first necessary to define the object using the <object> declaration with the "ID" parameter to identify it.

Once it is inserted, its properties and methods are invoked by using the appropriate syntax.

For properties and values, use the name and a dot:

```
PictureButton.Caption = "Display Image"
```

For event handlers, use an underscore:

```
Sub PictureButton_Click ()
...
End Sub
```

Embedded Objects

One key item that is included with Microsoft's entry into scripting is control of Object Linking and Embedding (OLE) controls, expanded and renamed as ActiveX.

Getting ActiveX

An ActiveX software development kit (sdk) is available for download from Microsoft's Internet Developer Web site at **http://www.microsoft.com/intdev/sdk/ sdkdownl.htm**. It includes ActiveX development tools and a copy of Internet Explorer 3.0. This is a very large download (12 MB), which is also available in 2 MB or 1 MB chunks if your modem is slower or your Internet connection is less-than-reliable.

OLE controls, also called OCXs, are graphical objects with well-defined external interfaces which may be manipulated by Visual Basic and other Microsoft-related tools.

These controls are embedded in HTML documents in formats similar to Netscape's plug-ins, although the formal standard is still under development.

ActiveX expands the capabilities of OCX controls by adding additional tools for embedding a wide variety of software components directly into a Web page, including graphics viewers, animation sequences, credit card transaction objects, or spread sheet applets. For example, the ActiveMovie API released by Microsoft is an ActiveX control that plays video sequences within the browser.

ActiveX controls can be included as part of VB Script or JavaScript applications to extend interactivity and functionality of Web pages. It will also extend beyond Microsoft's browser to Netscape with a plug-in module co-developed by Microsoft and nCompass Labs. By implementing multiple-browser support, ActiveX could become a very popular way of including live objects in HTML documents.

The new object controls also allow authors and developers easier access to client-server communications, including WinSock TCP, FTP Client, HTTP, HTML, POP, SMTP, and NNTP.

Note

For the most recent W3 Consortium proposal regarding HTML embedded objects, check out the W3 Web site at **http://www.w3.org/pub/WWW/TR/ WD-insert9512221.html**. This site also includes other HTML and Web standards information useful for Web administrators and authors.

Two important properties planned for Internet-aware OCXs are known as `ReadyState` and `OnReadyStateChange`. This will allow specific OCXs to declare their current state and trigger actions based on changes to that state. This could lead to interesting developments in OCX planning, as it allows an OCX to progressively load itself while supporting greater levels of functionality and responsibility for actions.

For example, a button could be active as soon as the button state code is loaded, even though graphics display is not fully rendered or active.

But, Microsoft is not alone in its pursuit of easy-to-use embedded objects. Oracle has developed Network Loadable Objects (NLOs) for its PowerBrowser software. NLOS are programs and program modules that load and run on the client machine, and are similar in function to a CGI application on the server. NLOs offer the developer access to the user interface and client network access facilities, which are especially useful for long-term operations which must maintain states across network access.

One of the first ready-made NLO programs being offered by Oracle supports integrating a Netscape plug-in interface, so HTML pages with this type of content can be loaded and displayed correctly by PowerBrowser.

NLOs are similar to Visual Basic controls in the sense that they are third-party applications that can be plugged into the browser to implement new functions. However, this also means they share a common drawback. NLO programs are binary objects, which makes it easier to insert viruses or Trojan horses into the code. One recommendation is to distribute NLOs in combination with their source code so they can be inspected and compiled by the user. However, because NLOs are similar to other plug-in modules, they can also be downloaded and scanned for corruption before you run them on your system.

CScript

CScript is an extension of the Server Sides Includes specification. It is implemented as a part of SSI+. CScript is an enhanced subset of the C programming language. With CScript you are able to include complete C-like programs within an HTML page without needing to compile the program. CScript is the natural complement to JavaScript; while JavaScript is client-based, CScript is server-based. Like JavaScript, CScript follows the C syntax conventions. Anyone familiar with C will be able to use CScript. CScript is native to WebQuest NT 2.0, and currently is only available with WebQuest NT 2.0.

Note

More information about CScript is provided with WebQuest NT 2.0 files, including SSIPLUS.HTM. Also, information is available at Questar's Web site, **http:// www.questar.com/**.

Features

CScript is a complete programming language. Most of the features of C are available within CScript. Like C, CScript includes variables, flow control, operators, string manipulation, type casting, assignment, and outputting. Also, CScript has some unique features relevant to the World Wide Web like ODBC, Cookies, and SMTP mail. The following is a quick overview of some of the elements of CScript.

CScript Basics

The CScript tag allows you to embed C-like code directly into a HTML file. All the semantics and features of a high-level object-oriented language like C are available without a compiler or the limitations of CGI. CScript is added to a HTML file using the opening `<!--#cscript` tag and the closing `-->` tag.

Listing 14.4 shows a simple CScript that calls a DLL called WQODBC.DLL. This DLL connects to the `nwind` datasource, queries the datasource and returns data in the specified format.

Listing 14.4   ODBC Manipulation Using CScript

```
<!--#cscript
WQODBC,Connect("nwind",NULL,NULL,FALSE,LOCAL_SOCKET);
WQODBC,Query("nwind","SELECT Freight,Freight,Freight,Freight
➥FROM Orders","String: %s<BR>Currency(10.2f): $%10.2f<BR>
➥Currency Left Aligned(-10.2f): $%-10.2f<BR>Percent:
%%%.2f<P>",TRUE,LOCAL_SOCKET);
WQODBC,Disconnect("nwind",FALSE,LOCAL_SOCKET);
-->
```

In listing 14.5, flow control and logical operators are used to find out if the variable USER_NAME matches the name on a hard coded list. If the name matches, the second message is displayed. If the name does not match the first message, You are not on the list is displayed.

Listing 14.5   Flow Control and Comparison Using CScript

```
<!--#CScript
if( !strstr( "Kevin Alan Sue", USER_NAME )
{
print( "<p>You are not on the list" );
exit(0);
}
else
print( "<p>Yes,  you are on the list" );
-->
```

Variables

All variables are represented as self-allocating objects, and are available in the following formats:

- Form objects, like standard SSI environment variables
- Ordinals, standard C data types: int, float and char
- Nonstandard data types: text, logic, and dword

- Strings, text objects
- Structures, user defined data types
- Arrays, sequential list of CScript data types and structures.

Flow Control

A complete implementation of flow control is available with CScript using standard operands.

- if, else, switch
- for, while, goto
- break, exit

Operators

Mathematical, logical, and comparison operators are implemented as in C.

- Math: +, −, *, /, ^
- Logic: &, |, !
- Comparison: ==, >, <, >=, <=, !=, !>, !<

## CHAPTER 15

Search Engines and Annotation Systems

The previous chapters covered the basics of setting up a Web server, writing HTML, and creating forms and scripts. The last chapters in this book use the tools acquired in the first part of the book to build or explain several useful applications that can be built with Web servers.

This chapter starts off with an introduction to search engines, a mechanism to search through simple databases, and more sophisticated indexing and retrieving software that search through an entire Web server and present the resulting list in a hypertext document in accordance with the tradition of the Web. Specifically, you look at two popular freeware Web search engines, namely, *ICE* and *Glimpse*.

This is the age of information sharing. Data is of little use if it cannot be shared and shared alike. The second part of this chapter presents techniques for using Web technology as a workgroup tool for information sharing. Several vehicles for conducting workgroup discussion are presented, including list servers, newsgroups, and Web conferencing systems. This chapter also discusses methods for creating annotation capability.

In this chapter, you learn the following:

- How to build simple search and retrieval scripts for simple databases
- How to set up and use an advanced search engine to search an entire Web server
- How to use Web technology as a workgroup tool, including document annotation capabilities and Web conferencing systems

Searching Simple Databases

In the last chapter, you saw how to write a simple script to search an on-line phone book for names and numbers. Although this can be considered a simple database application, it differs from what is normally thought of as a database because users can view but not enter information. Creating Web database applications that can modify, add, and delete information from databases is covered in Chapter 17, "Database Access and Applications Integration." This chapter is more concerned with search and retrieve applications that are used as guide maps around the vast Web.

Even though an organization centrally maintains many types of data, that data often still needs to be made available to hundreds or even thousands of users, either internally or externally. Examples of this type of data include a company phone and address book, a product catalog that maps product numbers to titles, or a list of regional sales offices and contacts. All of these types of information can be stored in a relational database, but there's really no need for anything more than a simple text file if the goal is to quickly and easily make information available. A simple Web search routine can achieve the desired result without all the headaches of maintenance that is associated with a relational database. However, there are performance limitations related to the size of such a simple database, so if your applications will be used for data sets with more than a couple hundred records at most, you may want to consider a more industrial-strength solution.

Grepping for Data

In the previous chapter, the phone book example demonstrated how to search a text file containing names and phone numbers. At the heart of the search is the grep command, which simply looks for pattern matches in a file. One of the benefits of this approach is that the text file need not be in any certain format. The grep command just reads each line of the file for a match; it doesn't care how many columns there are or what characters are used to separate fields. Consequently, the phone book script from the previous chapter can be used to search any text file database. That script has been generalized from the phone book example and is reprinted here for convenience. Figure 15.1 shows the resulting search form.

> **Tip**
>
> You can make searches case-sensitive by removing the -i option from the grep command.

Listing 15.1   Simple PERL Search Script

```
# search.pl
# Invoke the perl compiler
#!/bin/perl

# Define the location of the database
$DATABASE="/usr/local/etc/httpd/cgi-bin/phone.txt";

# Define the path to cgiparse
$CGIPATH="/usr/local/etc/httpd/cgi-bin";
# Convert form data to variables
eval '$CGIPATH/test/cgiparse -form -prefix $';

# Determine the age of the database
$mod_date=int(-M $DATABASE);

#Display the age of the database and generate the search form
print <<EOM;
Content-type: text/html

<TITLE>Database Search</TITLE>
<BODY>
<H1>Database Search</H1>
The database was updated $mod_date days ago.<p>
<FORM ACTION="/cgi-bin/search.pl" METHOD="POST">
Search for: <INPUT TYPE="TEXT" NAME="QUERY">
<INPUT TYPE="SUBMIT" VALUE="SEARCH">
</FORM>
<p><hr><p>
EOM

# Do the search only if a query was entered
if (length($query)>0) {
  print <<EOM;
Search for <B>$query</B> yields these entries:
<PRE>
EOM

#Inform user if search is unsuccessful
$answer = 'grep -i $query $DATABASE';
if (!$answer) { print "Search was unsuccessful\n" ;}
else { print $answer\n" ; }

print <<EOM;
</PRE>
</BODY>
EOM
}
```

Fig. 15.1
This generalized database search form is used with the preceding search script to search any text file database.

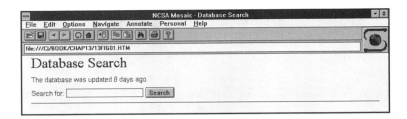

To use the script for data other than the phone book, simply change the name and location of the text file containing the desired information. Because the script uses the generic grep command, it can be used with almost any text file for any purpose.

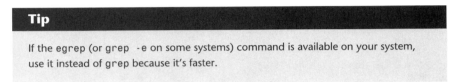

Tip

If the egrep (or grep -e on some systems) command is available on your system, use it instead of grep because it's faster.

Generating Text Files from Databases

To take advantage of the simple search routine above, you must have some text file data to start with. If your data is currently in another format, such as a proprietary database, you must first convert it to an ASCII text file. You can easily create the necessary text file by exporting the data from the native format to ASCII text. Almost all databases include the capability to export to text files.

Tip

For easiest use of the search script, export data so that there is exactly one record per line. This produces the neatest output from the script.

After the text file has been created, you simply need to specify its path in the search script.

Choosing Between Several Databases

With a few simple modifications, you can generically use the script to search one of many databases that all have different paths. This can be done most efficiently in one of two ways. You can allow the database to be chosen by selecting one of several hyperlinks, in which case extra path information in the URL can be used to specify the database. On the other hand, you can allow the user to choose which database to search in a fill-in form.

Choosing via Hyperlinks

Suppose you want users to be able to choose between several different divisional phone books. One way to do this is to include a pre-search page on which the user selects the database by clicking the appropriate hyperlink. Each link calls the same database search script, but each link includes extra path information containing the path to the database. The following HTML code demonstrates how the hyperlinks are constructed:

```
<H2>Company Phonebooks</H2>
<A HREF="/cgi-bin/search.pl/db/IAphone.txt">Iowa Locations</A>
<A HREF="/cgi-bin/search.pl/db/CAphone.txt">California Locations</A>
<A HREF="/cgi-bin/search.pl/db/KSphone.txt">Kansas Locations</A>
```

The name of the search script in this example is `/cgi-bin/search.pl` and the databases are named `/db/IAphone.txt`, and so on. The search script itself needs to be modified to use the extra path information.

First, the name of the database to search is now specified in the extra path information rather than hard-coded into the script. Therefore, the line at the top of the script that specifies the path to the data needs to read the extra path information. This is done by reading the PATH_INFO environment variable. In PERL, the syntax for this is

```
$DATABASE=$ENV{"PATH_INFO"};
```

Second, the ACTION attribute of the form, which is generated inside the script, needs to specify the path to the database, as well. This way, after the user performs the initial query, the correct database is still in use. This is done by changing the <FORM ACTION...> line to the following:

```
<FORM ACTION="/cgi-bin/search.pl$DATABASE">
```

> **Note**
>
> No slash (/) is necessary to separate the script name (`/cgi-bin/search`) from the extra path information because $DATABASE already begins with a slash.

These are the two modifications necessary to implement choosing a database via hyperlinks. The hyperlinks to other databases are now included in the search form also. The resulting form is shown in figure 15.2. The complete modified script code is included below. Only new or changed lines have been commented.

Listing 15.2 Modified PERL Search Script

```
# search2.pl
#!/bin/perl

# Get database name from extra path info.
$DATABASE=$ENV{"PATH_INFO"};

$CGIPATH="/usr/local/etc/httpd/cgi-bin";
eval '$CGIPATH/test/cgiparse -form -prefix $';

$mod_date=int(-M $DATABASE);

# Show the current database and list other available databases.
# The <FORM ACTION ...> line now includes the database name
#   as extra path info.
print <<EOM;
Content-type: text/html

<TITLE>Database Search</TITLE>
<BODY>
<H1>Database Search</H1>
Current database is $DATABASE.
It was updated $mod_date days ago.<P>
You can change to one of the following databases at any time:<P>
<A HREF="/cgi-bin/search/db/IAphone.txt">Iowa Location</A><BR>
<A HREF="/cgi-bin/search/db/CAphone.txt">California Locations</A><BR>
<A HREF="/cgi-bin/search/db/KSphone.txt">Kansas Locations</A><P>
<FORM ACTION="/cgi-bin/search2.pl$DATABASE" METHOD="POST">
Search for: <INPUT TYPE="TEXT" NAME="QUERY">
<INPUT TYPE="SUBMIT" VALUE=" Search ">
</FORM>
<p><hr><p>
EOM

if (length($query)>0) {
  print <<EOM;
Search for <B>$query</B> yields these entries:
<PRE>
EOM

$answer = 'grep -i $query $DATABASE';
if (!$answer) { print "Search was unsuccessful\n" ;}
else { print $answer\n" ; }

print <<EOM;
</PRE>
</BODY>
EOM
}
```

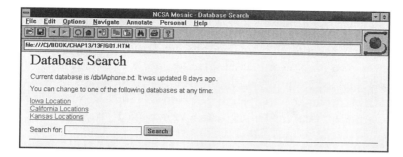

IV

Applications

Fig. 15.2
Now the interface allows the user to use hyperlinks to select a new search database.

Choosing via a Form

Depending on the application, it may be more convenient for users to choose their database via a form rather than via hyperlinks. The initial form uses option buttons to choose the desired database, and after that the chosen database is active for all searches. Figure 15.3 shows the initial form used to select the database.

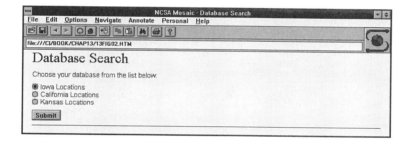

Fig. 15.3
In this form, you select the search database and then proceed to the search form.

Listing 15.3 shows the form's code.

Listing 15.3   Using Pull-Down Menus Instead of Hyperlinks

```
<TITLE>Database Search</TITLE>
<BODY>
<H1>Database Search</H1>
Choose your database from the list below:<P>
<FORM ACTION="/cgi-bin/search3.pl" METHOD="POST">
<INPUT TYPE="RADIO" NAME="DATABASE" VALUE="/db/IAphone.txt" CHECKED>
 Iowa Locations<BR>
<INPUT TYPE="RADIO" NAME="DATABASE" VALUE="/db/CAphone.txt">
 California Locations<BR>
<INPUT TYPE="RADIO" NAME="DATABASE" VALUE="/db/KSphone.txt">
 Kansas Locations<P>
<INPUT TYPE="SUBMIT" VALUE=" Submit ">
</FORM>
<p><hr><p>
```

The initial selection form passes the path of the chosen database in the input field named "DATABASE", so only two modifications are necessary to the original search script that receives this information. First, the path to the database is now read from the initial selection form, so a separate line defining $DATABASE is no longer necessary. Second, the search form must have a way to keep track of the current database. This is conveniently accomplished by including a hidden input field in the search form named "DATABASE". This way, whether the search form is called from itself or from the initial selection form, it always knows the path to the correct database. The code for the search script is in listing 15.4. Only the new or changed lines are commented. The resulting search form appears in figure 15.4.

Listing 15.4   Search Script Code

```perl
# search3.pl
#!/bin/perl

$CGIPATH="/usr/local/etc/httpd/cgi-bin";
eval '$CGIPATH/test/cgiparse -form -prefix $';
# $DATABASE is now defined as a form variable

$mod_date=int(-M $DATABASE);

# A hidden field <INPUT TYPE="HIDDEN" NAME="DATABASE" ...> stores the
database path.
print <<EOM;
Content-type: text/html

<TITLE>Database Search</TITLE>
<BODY>
<H1>Database Search</H1>
The current database is $DATABASE.
The database was updated $mod_date days ago.<p>
<FORM ACTION="/cgi-bin/search3.pl" METHOD="POST">
<INPUT TYPE="HIDDEN" NAME="DATABASE" VALUE="$DATABASE">
Search for: <INPUT TYPE="TEXT" NAME="QUERY">
<INPUT TYPE="SUBMIT" VALUE=" Search ">
</FORM>
<p><hr><p>
EOM

if (length($query)>0) {
  print <<EOM;
Search for <B>$query</B> yields these entries:
<PRE>
EOM

$answer = 'grep -i $query $DATABASE';
if (!$answer) { print "Search was unsuccessful\n" ;}
else { print $answer\n" ; }
```

```
print <<EOM;
</PRE>
</BODY>
EOM
}
```

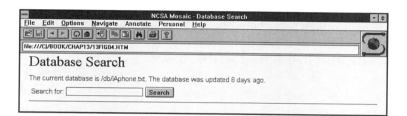

Fig. 15.4
Once the search
database is selected
in a separate form,
this form is used to
perform the
search.

Searching Multiple Files and Directories

The previous examples searched only one file at a time. However, grep is flexible enough to search multiple files and directories simultaneously.

Searching Multiple Files

In the previous example, the user was allowed to choose between several different phone directories. However, it's also possible to search several files at
the same time. The script is easily modified to do this because the grep command can search multiple files simultaneously. Instead of specifying one file
in the $DATABASE environment variable, specify a path to the directory con-
taining the phone text files (/db). So the line beginning $DATABASE= in the
original script (search.pl) changes to the following:

```
$DATABASE="/db/*.txt";
```

The grep command now searches all files in the /db directory that correspond
to the specified wildcard pattern for the desired information.

Searching Multiple Directories

Taking it a step further, the grep command can also accept multiple files in
different directories. For example, you can specify the following database
files:

```
$DATABASE="/db/phone*.txt /db2/address*.txt"
```

Now, the grep command searches all TXT files in the /db directory beginning
with phone and all TXT files in the /db2 directory beginning with address.

Searching Directories Recursively

By combining the `grep` command with a directory command, it's even possible to recursively search subdirectories. To do this, change the $DATABASE line to the following:

```
$DATABASE='find /db -name '*.txt''
```

Because the `find` command operates recursively on directories, $DATABASE contains the names of all TXT files under the /db directory and its subdirectories.

Accommodating Formless Browsers

Although most Web browsers today have forms capability, not all do. To allow these browsers to search for information, it's common to offer an alphabetical or numerical index of data as an alternative to entering a form-based query. Typically, you create a hyperlink for each letter of the alphabet and specify a URL for each hyperlink that performs the appropriate search. For example, in a phone book listing where last names are listed first, you could search for capital Cs at the beginning of a line to get a listing of all last names beginning with C. To create a hypertext index that can submit this type of search automatically, use the following code:

```
<H1>Phone Book Index</H1>
Click on a letter to see last names beginning with that letter.<P>
<A HREF="/cgi-bin/search?%26A">A</A>
<A HREF="/cgi-bin/search?%26B">b</C>
...
<A HREF="/cgi-bin/search?%26Z">Z</Z>
```

> **Note**
>
> The queries in this example begin with the caret (%26 = ^) to force grep to look for the specified character at the beginning of a line.

Searching an Entire Web Server

So far, you have only looked at searching collections of simple text files. However, one of the most useful utilities on any Web server is the capability to search for words anywhere on the server, including plain text and HTML files. It's theoretically possible to simply `grep` all HTML and TXT files under the document root (and other aliased directories), but this can be very time-consuming if more than a handful of documents are present.

The solution to the problem of searching a large Web server is similar to that used by other types of databases. We maintain a compact index that summarizes the information present in the Web server's content area. As data is added to the database, you just keep updating the index file. The usual method of maintaining the integrity of the index file is to run a nightly (or more frequent) indexing program that generates a full-text index of the entire server in a more compact format than the data itself.

Indexing with ICE

A popular indexing and searching solution on the Web is ICE, written in PERL by Christian Neuss in Germany. It's freely available on the Internet at **http://www.igd.fhg.de/~neuss/me.html** and is included on the WebmasterCD. In the discussion that follows, you learn how ICE works and how it can be modified to include even more features. By default, ICE includes the following features:

- Whole-word searching using Boolean operators (AND and OR)
- Case-sensitive or case-insensitive searching
- Hypertext presentation of scored results
- The ability to look for similarly-spelled words in a dictionary
- The ability to find related words and topics in a thesaurus
- The ability to limit searches to a specified directory tree

> **Note**
>
> Because it's written in PERL, ICE can run on any platform for which PERL is available, including UNIX, Windows NT, Mac, DOS, and OS/2. However, some modifications are necessary because of the differences in file systems employed by these operating systems.

ICE presents results in a convenient hypertext format. Results are displayed using both document titles (as specified by HTML <TITLE> tags) and physical file names. Search results are scored, or weighted, based on the number of occurrences of the search word or words inside documents.

The ICE Index Builder

The heart of ICE is a PERL program that reads every file on the Web server and constructs a full-text index. The index builder, ice-idx.pl in the default distribution, has a simple method of operation. The server administrator specifies the locations and extensions (TXT, HTML, and so on) of files to be indexed. When you run ice-idx.pl, it reads every file in the specified directories and stores the index information in one large index file (by default, index.idx). The words in each file are alphabetized and counted for use in scoring the search results when a search is made. The format of the index file is simple:

```
@ffilename
@ttitle
word1 count1
word2 count2
word3 count3
...
@ffilename
@ttitle
word1 count1
...
```

Running the Index Builder

The index builder is typically run nightly or at some other regular interval so that search results are always based on updated information. Normally, ICE indexes the entire contents of directories specified by the administrator, but it can be modified to index only new or modified files, as determined by the last modification dates on files. This saves a little time, although ICE zips right along as it is. On a fast UNIX workstation, ICE indexes 2–5 MB of files in under 15 seconds, depending on the nature of the files. Assuming an average HTML file size of 10 KB, that's 200–500 separate documents.

UNIX users can run the index builder nightly using the UNIX cron facility for scheduling regular events. To use the crontab command, a system administrator must add your name to the cron.allow file. The following is a typical cron entry for ICE that runs the index-builder nightly at 9:34 PM (21:34):

```
34 21 * * * /usr/local/etc/index/ice-idx.pl
```

Windows NT users can use the native at command to schedule the indexing utility.

Tip

It's often a good idea to schedule cron jobs at odd times because many other jobs run on the hour by necessity or convention. Running jobs on the hour that don't have to run at this time increases the load on the machine unnecessarily.

Space Considerations

Searching an index file is much faster than searching an entire Web server using grep or a similar utility; however, there is a definite space/performance tradeoff. Because ICE stores the contents of every document in the index file, the index file can theoretically grow as large as the sum of all the files indexed! The actual compression ratio is closer to 2:1 for HTML because ICE ignores HTML formatting tags, numbers, and special characters. In addition, typical documents use many words multiple times, but ICE stores them only once, along with a word count.

> **Note**
>
> When planning your Web server, be sure to include enough space for index files if you plan to offer full-featured searching.

The Search Engine

The HTML code that produces the ICE search form is actually generated from within a script (ice-form.pl) but calls the main search engine (ice.pl) to do most of the search work. The search simply reads the index file previously generated by the index builder. As the search engine reads consecutively through the file, it simply outputs the names and titles of all documents containing the search word or words. The search form itself and the search engine can be modified to produce output in any format desired by editing the PERL code.

Tips and Tricks

The ICE search engine is powerful and useful by itself. However, there's always room for improvement. This section discusses several modifications you can make to ICE to implement various additional useful features.

Directory Context

A very useful feature of ICE is the ability to specify an optional directory context in the search form. This way, you can use the same ICE code to conduct both local and global searches. For example, suppose you're running an internal server that contains several policy manuals and you want each of them to be searchable individually, as well as together. You can simply require that users of the system enter the optional directory context themselves; however, a more convenient way is to replace the optional directory context box with option buttons that users can use to select the desired manual.

A more programming-intensive method is to provide a link to the search page on the index page of each manual. The URL in the link can already include the optional directory context so that users don't have to enter this themselves. This way, when a user clicks the link to the search page from within a given manual section, the search form automatically includes the correct directory context. For example, you can tell the ICE search to look only in the /benefits directory by including the following hyperlink on the Benefits page:

```
<A HREF="/cgi-bin/ice-form.pl?context=%2Fbenefits>Search this
manual</A>
```

> **Note**
>
> The slash of /benefits must be encoded in its ASCII representation (%2F) for the link to work properly.

For this to work, you need to make the following necessary modifications to ice-form.pl:

- Set the variable $CONTEXT at the beginning of the script (using cgiparse or your favorite parsing utility) based on what was passed from the search URL.

- Automatically display the value of $CONTEXT in the optional directory context box:

```
<INPUT TYPE="TEXT" NAME="CONTEXT" VALUE="$CONTEXT">)
```

Speed Enhancements

If the size of your index file grows larger than two or three megabytes, searches will take several seconds to complete due to the time required to read through the entire index file during each search. A simple way to improve this situation is to build several smaller index files, say, one for each major directory on your server, rather than one large one. However, this means you can no longer conduct a single, global search of your server.

A more attractive way to break up the large index file is to split it up into several smaller ones, where each small index file still contains an index for every file searched, but only those words beginning with certain letters. For example, ice-a.idx contains all words beginning with "a," ice-b.idx contains all words beginning with "b," and so on. This way, when a query is entered, the search engine is able to narrow down the search immediately based on the first letter of the query.

> **Note**
>
> In the event that your server outgrows the first-letter indexing scheme, the same technique can be used to further break up files by using unique combinations of the first two letters of a query, and so on.

To break up the large index file alphabetically, you need to modify the ICE index builder (ice-idx.pl) to write to multiple index files while building the code. The search engine (ice.pl) also needs to be modified to auto-select the index file based on the first letter of the query.

Searching for Words Near Each Other

Although ICE allows the use of AND and OR operators to modify searches, it only looks for words meeting these requirements anywhere in the same document. It would be nice to be able to specify how close to each other the words must appear as well. The difficulty with this kind of a search is that the ICE index doesn't specify how close to each other words are in a document. There are two ways to overcome this.

First, you can modify the index builder to store word position information, as well as word count. For example, if the words "bad" and "dog" each occur three times in a file, their index entries might look like the following:

```
bad 3 26 42 66
dog 3 4 9 27
```

In this case, 3 is the number of occurrences, and the remaining numbers indicate that dog is the 4th, 9th, and 27th word in the file. When a search for bad dog begins, the search engine first checks if both bad and dog are in any documents and then whether any of the word positions for bad are exactly one less than any of those for dog. In this case, that is true, as bad occurs in position 26 and dog occurs in position 27.

There's another way to search for words near each other. After a search begins and files containing both words are found, those files can simply be read by the search program word-by-word, looking for the target words near each other. Using this method, the index builder itself doesn't have to be modified. However, the first method usually results in faster searches because the extra work is done primarily by the index builder rather than by the search engine in real-time.

Glimpse

For larger databases of text (say, more than a couple dozen megabytes of text) a more scalable and robust solution than ICE can be found in a publicly available package from the University of Arizona called *Glimpse*.

> **Note**
>
> Glimpse is available from **http://glimpse.cs.arizona.edu/**.

The program is written in C and is thus not as instantly portable as the PERL-coded ICE, but the developers have ported it to a large number of different UNIX platforms. Glimpse is comprised of two main tools: the indexer, called glimpseindex and the search command called glimpse. You first build the index by pointing glimpseindex at a particular directory with a couple of command-line calls describing where to store the index files. A typical command line to the indexer looks something like the following:

```
glimpseindex -H "searchdir" "documentroot"
```

The *documentroot* is the root tree of your Web files. The indexer builds a number of files that begin with the prefix .glimpse_—these files are stored in the *searchdir* directory, which you might not want to store in the main Web directory.

To run a query against the index, you use glimpse with some command-line options, as the following shows:

```
glimpse -H "searchdir" "query"
```

For example,

```
glimpse -H /www/searchdir radio
```

finds all files that contain the word "radio." Glimpse supports some amazing options, such as the ability to search for words with a given number of spelling errors (that is, one spelling error allows "ratio," two allows "ration"), you can combine logical AND and OR clauses, and you can even limit the scope of the results to file names that match particular patterns.

One of the most significant advantages of glimpse, though, is that its algorithms allow a variable size for the index, with the caveat that smaller indexes result in slower searches. So if you have a fast machine but relatively little spare disk space, you can set the index so that it is smaller. The allowed ranges are tiny (index is 2–3% the size of the indexed data), small (7–9%), or medium (20–30%). This is configured using different command-line options with glimpseindex.

Integrating this functionality into your server is done using another package available from the Glimpse folks called GlimpseHTTP. The most significant part of this package is a CGI script called aglimpse. Put the aglimpse file in the right place (perhaps your cgi-bin directory?) and edit the configuration options at the top of the script. These options set things such as the home of your .glimpse_ files, the document root for your Web server, and so on. With this you should now have an efficient, full-featured search engine for your Web server.

Harvest

At some point, you may find that ICE, Glimpse, and other search engines that build indexes of file-system contents break down, either because you start heavily using server-side includes or because you start having a large amount of content that only CGI scripts access. At this point, instead of gathering data from the file system for the index, you really want to gather data from the Web server itself. This robot-based searching is the basis for several commercial Internet search engines out there, such as AltaVista, Infoseek, Lycos, and WebCrawler. You can also get this functionality for your own server using Harvest.

Note

Harvest project's home page is **http://harvest.cs.colorado.edu/**.

Harvest is a reasonably complex system, and while indexing content over the network is one of its primary goals, it is far from a drop-in replacement for Glimpse. One of the bigger goals for the Harvest project is to create an infrastructure for "distributing" indexes, using a network of *Gatherers* and *Brokers*. The Gatherers slurp content from Web sites, create indexes of the content they find, and hand those off to the Brokers, who then publicize the existence of those indexes and handle queries. It is worthwhile to note that as of this writing, Netscape's new Catalog Server interfaces with this infrastructure, providing information about the content it indexes in the Summary Object Interchange Format (SOIF) format, just as used by Harvest.

Harvest is mentioned here as the "future" of server indexing, and if you desire functionality beyond that provided by ICE or Glimpse, you should really invest the time and effort to explore the Harvest project.

Other Web Search Solutions

While the Net seems vastly endless in its repertoire of solutions to choose from, it becomes more and more incumbent upon you to thoroughly study the feature sets of the various search systems while deciding on one that best suits your Web site with respect to operating system, Web server, volume and value of content, security, and so on. The following list should serve as a basic checklist of things to consider before deciding on any one of the solutions:

- Compatibility with operating system
- Compatibility with Web server
- Boolean searches (AND, OR, and NOT operators)
- Synonym searches
- Plural searches (a search for "woman" also returns all documents with reference to "women")

- Weighted results

- Ease of installation and integration

- Amount of programming involved

The following table shows a list of available commercial, shareware, and freeware search systems that may be used on a Web site. It is important to note that this list is, by no means, exhaustive.

Product	Company	URL
Excite	Architext Software	www.excite.com
Livelink Search	OpenText Corp.	www.opentext.com
Verity	Verity, Inc.	www.verity.com
CompasSearch	CompasWare Development, Inc.	www.compasware.com
NetAnswer	Dataware Technologies, Inc.	www.dataware.com
Fulcrum Search Server	Fulcrum Technologies, Inc.	www.fultech.com

Including Content

A very desirable enhancement to a search system is to include some sort of summary of each document presented in the search results. Infoseek, Lycos, and AltaVista do exactly this by displaying the first couple of sentences of each document on its search results page. This helps users quickly find the documents most relevant to their topic of interest.

To include summary content, store the first 50–100 words in every document in the index file created by the index builder. Doing this, however, requires yet more storage space for the index file, and therefore may not be desirable. You could also have the script that displays results itself open the files returned in the search and grab the first 50–100 words from the file, but that imposes something of a burden on the file system if the script is heavily used. Once again, you have a tradeoff between efficiency and disk space, which is in many ways a good thing.

Web Conferencing—Discussion and Annotation Systems

The World Wide Web was originally developed as a medium for scientific and technical exchange. One of the important elements of that exchange is the sharing of ideas about other people's work. This has been common on UseNet news for many years now, but articles are limited largely to plain ASCII text. The Web, with its superior hypertext presentation, presents opportunities for richer exchange but has developed as a remarkably one-sided communications medium thus far. This is unfortunate for those who want to take advantage of the Web's superior document capabilities along with the flexibility and interactivity of UseNet.

Why Is the Web One-Way?

The Web has developed primarily as a one-way medium simply because the great majority of Web servers and clients have not supported any kind of interactive behavior; Web servers can only serve documents, and Web clients can only browse documents. However, these limitations are not fundamental to either the HTTP protocol or HTML. The ingredients necessary for worldwide annotation of Web documents and posting new documents to servers are already in place, but these have not yet been implemented. There are, however, a few exceptions, that are discussed in the following sections.

Group Annotations

The most notable exception is NCSA Mosaic, which supported a feature called *group annotations* in the first few versions. This feature allows users to post text-only annotations to documents by sending annotations to a group annotation server, which NCSA provided with earlier versions of their Web server. Group annotations, however, have been abandoned in later versions of Mosaic in favor of the HTTP 1.0 protocol, which supports group annotations in a different manner.

CGI and HTTP POST

The second exception is CGI scripting, which allows data to be received rather than sent by a server. The data is usually simple text, such as a query or form information, but it can also be an entire document, such as an HTML file, spreadsheet, or even an executable program. The new file upload capabilities for forms as supported by Netscape 2.0 and other browsers is a great step in the right direction.

Because HTTP and HTML already support most (if not all) of the ingredients necessary for a more interactive Web, it's probably only a matter of time before these features are incorporated into browsers and servers alike. In the meantime, however, prototypes of what the future holds have been constructed using news, e-mail, and CGI scripts.

News and the Web

UseNet news makes available today in plain ASCII text some of what the Web will do tomorrow in HTML. In fact, the NNTP protocol is in many ways superior to the HTTP protocol for the purpose of disseminating small messages very widely, for it pushes messages to other news servers instead of waiting for them to be pulled on demand like HTTP.

News can effectively be used as both a private or public tool for information exchange. Public newsgroups are the most familiar, with worldwide distribution and the ability for anyone to post articles to these groups. By running your own news server, you can also create entirely private newsgroups or semi-private groups, which the public can read but not post to. The ability to control who can read news and who can post to a local server makes news a useful tool for workgroup discussion.

> **Tip**
>
> Many Web browsers can both read and post news. This simplifies the use of both news and hypertext in an organizational context by providing a common interface for viewing both kinds of documents.

While news is an excellent medium for conducting entirely private (inside a corporate network) or entirely public conversations (UseNet), it's not as well suited for allowing discussions between a select group of individuals located all over the world. It's possible to create a special news server for this purpose and use password security to ensure that only the intended group of people can read or post news to the server. However, users of the system are inconvenienced because most newsreaders expect to connect to one news server only. If users were already connecting to another news server to receive public news, they have to change the configuration information in their newsreader to connect to the special server. Fortunately, there are other answers to this problem.

Hypermail

E-mail is a more flexible method of having semi-private discussions among people all around the world. Using a mailing list server (list server), it is possible to create a single Internet e-mail address for a whole group of people. When an item is sent to the mailing list address, it's forwarded to all members of the list. This approach has several advantages over running a news server, in addition to the previously mentioned convenience issue.

> **Note**
>
> A popular UNIX-based list server is majordomo, available from **http://www.greatcircle.com/majordomo/**.

First, e-mail is the most widely accessible of all Internet services. Individuals are more likely to have e-mail access than any other Internet service. Secondly, e-mail is something that users typically check regularly for new messages. Consequently, there is less effort involved in receiving "news" or discussion items from a mailing list than in checking for news in a separate newsreader. The same applies to posting news, which tends to encourage use of the system.

> **Tip**
>
> Through various e-mail gateways, it's possible to do almost anything by e-mail that can be done on FTP, Gopher, news, or the Web, only slower.

A very nice complement to a mailing list is a *mailing list archive*, which stores past items on the mailing list. Public mailing list archives are frequently found on FTP sites, but they can also be stored on the Web. A really powerful tool called *Hypermail* converts a mailing list archive into a hypertext list of messages, neatly organized to show message threads. Mail archives converted with Hypermail can be sorted by author, subject, or date.

> **Note**
>
> Because Hypermail uses the standard UNIX mailbox format, it can even be used to convert your personal mail on a UNIX workstation to hypertext. This allows you to read mail in hypertext, a capability not yet supported by most e-mail readers. The ability to read and write HTML in an e-mail reader is a useful and interesting addition to e-mail and the Web.

More information on Hypermail can be obtained from **http://www.eit.com/software/hypermail/hypermail.html**. It is reasonably easy to compile and install on any UNIX workstation.

Annotation Systems

While e-mail and news are both valuable tools for workgroup discussion, they still lack an important feature: the ability to make comments on a document in the document itself. In the paper world, this is accomplished with the infamous red pen. However, the equivalent of the editor's pen in the world of hypertext markup is just beginning to appear. The ultimate in annotation is the ability to attach comments, or even files of any type, anywhere inside an HTML document. For now, however, it's at least possible to add comments to the end of an HTML page. Several people are working on annotation systems using existing Web technology. The following sections take a brief look at a few of them.

HyperNews

Not to be confused with Hypermail, HyperNews does not actually use the NNTP protocol, but it allows a similar discussion format and is patterned after UseNet. You can see examples of HyperNews and find out more about it at **http://union.ncsa.uiuc.edu/HyperNews/get/hypernews.html**.

W3 Interactive Talk (WIT)

A similar system originating at CERN allows new "proposals," or comments, to be submitted in response to a given document. This is a practical way for a group of engineers, for example, to discuss a document. Some degree of security is possible by requiring users to have a valid user name and password before they can post comments. This can be combined with user authorization procedures to control who can see documents as well. More information is available from **http://www.w3.org/pub/WWW/WIT/**.

Web Conferencing Systems

The glaring deficiency of the Web, namely, that it has been a one-way drive, has not gone unnoticed, however. There are quite a few systems available that employ the traditional client-server architecture to implement Web conferencing systems.

One commercially available Web conferencing product is WebNotes for Windows NT, a product of OS TECHnologies Corporation. WebNotes is a client-server solution where the "client" is any HTML capable Web browser (Mosaic, Netscape, and so on). The WebNotes server software maintains discussion threads of topics of discussion, remembers "already-seen" messages by users, and allows users to post discussion material either as text or as HTML documents with inline graphics. It also employs a text search engine that facilitates retrieving discussions based on the result of a search query.

> **Note**
>
> More information and a live demonstration of WebNotes can be found on OS TECHnologies' home page at **http://www.ostech.com**.

Other Web conferencing systems that can be found on the Net include, but are not limited to:

- Agora Web Conferencing System—**http://www.ontrac.yorku.ca/agora**
- WebBoard from O'Reilly and Associates—**http://webboard.ora.com/**
- Futplex System—**http://gewis.win.tue.nl/applications/futplex/index.html**
- Cold Fusion Forums from Allaire—**http://www.allaire.com/**
- InterNotes from Lotus—**http://www.lotus.com/inotes**

Some of these systems also let users upload files to the server, thereby allowing them to upload picture binaries to inline their message content with graphics.

Academic Annotation Systems

Many of the annotation-like systems on the Web today are academic in nature. At Cornell, a test case involving a computer science class allows students to share thoughts and questions about the class via the Web. Documentation on the Cornell system is available at the following Web site:

http://dri.cornell.edu/pub/davis/annotation.html

The Cornell site also has useful links to related work on the Web. Some of the related systems that have been developed use custom clients to talk to an annotation database separate from the Web server itself, much like the early versions of Mosaic. This architecture may well be the future of annotations and the Web.

On the lighter side, take a peek at MIT's Discuss->WWW Gateway to get a behind-the-scenes look into an American hall of higher education. For a particularly novel and entertaining use of the Web, take a peek at the Professor's Quote Board at the following site:

http://www.mit.edu:8008/bloom-picayune.mit.edu/pqb/

Summary

In this chapter, you learned how to write a simple query system to search a textual database and to publish the result on the Web. You also took a look at how to use existing search engines to implement search functionality on a Web server and search through the entire Web server's HTML content. The later section of the chapter gave you an overview of the future applications of the World Wide Web and to look at the Web not as a one-way street but as a totally interactive solution over the Internet. In the future, the Web browser will take on the role of the universal client and act as a front-end to access all kinds of servers like Web, news, e-mail, FTP, bulletin board, database, and other client-server applications—even operating systems. ❖

## CHAPTER 16

Usage Statistics and Maintaining HTML

Setting up your server is literally just the start of your work. Administering, maintaining, and monitoring usage are important tasks that will keep you busy after your server is operational. The rapid growth of Internet usage and the growing interest in analyzing that usage means that there is a lot of work you have to do. Among your major tasks will be setting up the mechanism for monitoring usage statistics, monitoring and presenting those statistics, and checking that the HTML code is correct.

Once your Web server is up and running, there's still a lot of work to do to keep it running smoothly and to maintain a responsive and professional looking site. Ongoing maintenance activities are associated both with the server itself and with the data files on the server.

Your customers—those people who put up the content of the WWW site and expect it to provide some return on investment—need to know if other people are coming to the site and what they do when they are there. Fortunately, with some effort, you can tell them. A tremendous amount of information about the client systems and activities of the WWW site is captured and available for analysis.

You are able to find out information such as how often your server is being accessed, what files are being accessed most, what client is accessing your server and how often—almost everything but how much money the user has to spend. You can convert the data into graphical summaries of any or all this information quite easily using programs designed to gather server usage statistics.

When the volume of information on your server becomes large, checking all the information to ensure that all hyperlinks operate correctly and that all intended files have been linked to your server becomes more and more difficult.

As the number of related documents grows, the only practical way to do this is to use automated programs that check your documents for you.

In this chapter, you learn:

- How to extract and interpret information from the server access and error logs
- What tools are available for analyzing and graphing usage statistics
- What tools are available for ensuring the integrity of your HTML files
- How to automatically find new and changed files on your server

Understanding Usage Logs

When your Web server is running, every document or file request is logged as a separate entry in the server's log file. By default, this file is named logs/access.log under the server root directory, as defined in the HTTPD configuration file. Errors are logged separately in logs/error.log. The access and error logs are very similar, but are discussed separately for clarity.

The Log Formats

All major Web servers produce logs in a format known as *CLF*, for Common Logfile Format. Quite a few utilities are available, both freeware and commercial, to analyze these logs on most major platforms. The format includes just the basic information about the request (see below). Notably missing from this format are the type of browser used, the "referring" URL and any cookies used. Diagnostic information about errors is also not included, that's recorded in a separate error log.

The Access Log

Most server programs either have a default directory for storing log files or allow you to configure the server program to set where the log files should be kept. Usually, the files "access_log" and "error_log" are kept in a subdirectory under the main server directory called "logs". You may have configured the server to log elsewhere, however.

Information in the access log includes (in this order):

- The reverse-DNS hostname of the machine making the request. If the machine has no reverse-DNS hostname mapped to the IP number, or if the reverse-DNS lookup is disabled, this will just be the IP number.
- The user name used in any authentication information supplied with the request.

- If "identd" checking is turned on, the user name as returned by the remote host.
- The precise date and time that the transfer took place, including offset from Greenwich Mean Time.
- The complete first line of the HTTP request, in quotes.
- The HTTP response code.
- Total number of bytes transferred

Note that if the value for any of this data is not available, a "-" will be put in its place. For example, if the requests are to a space not protected by a password, the field for the login name is replaced with the dash.

The extra information can be recorded to a log file using one of the specialized logging modules for Apache, as described in Chapter 5. Since there aren't standard tools for analyzing that extra information, it probably doesn't need to be mentioned here, but we can point to it.

Note

Extra information can be captured by using particular extra Apache modules and configuration options—these are covered in Chapter 5.

The following is an excerpt from an access log generated Apache, on the Apache Web site.

Listing 16.1   Sample Logfile from the www.apache.org Web Site

```
sf-110.sfo.com - - [01/Mar/1996:01:42:47 -0800] "GET / HTTP/
1.0" 200 3920
dyn79.ppp.pacific.net.sg - - [01/Mar/1996:01:42:49 -0800] "GET /
docs/ HTTP/1.0" 200 1770
as1s12.erols.com - - [01/Mar/1996:01:42:52 -0800] "GET /images/
apache_pb.gif HTTP/1.0" 200 2326
dyn79.ppp.pacific.net.sg - - [01/Mar/1996:01:42:57 -0800] "GET /
images/apache_sub.gif HTTP/1.0" 200 6083
port46.fishnet.net - - [01/Mar/1996:01:42:59 -0800] "GET /images/
apache_pb.gif HTTP/1.0" 200 2326
narfi.ifi.uio.no - - [01/Mar/1996:01:43:01 -0800] "GET /docs/
directives.html HTTP/1.0" 200 3907
sf-110.sfo.com - - [01/Mar/1996:01:43:02 -0800] "GET /dist/ HTTP/
1.0" 200 1833
sf-110.sfo.com - - [01/Mar/1996:01:43:03 -0800] "GET /icons/
blank.gif HTTP/1.0" 304 -
sf-110.sfo.com - - [01/Mar/1996:01:43:03 -0800] "GET /icons/
back.gif HTTP/1.0" 304 -
```

(continues)

```
Listing 16.1  Continued
sf-110.sfo.com - - [01/Mar/1996:01:43:03 -0800] "GET /icons/
➥text.gif HTTP/1.0" 304 -
sf-110.sfo.com - - [01/Mar/1996:01:43:03 -0800] "GET /icons/
➥dir.gif HTTP/1.0" 304 -
sf-110.sfo.com - - [01/Mar/1996:01:43:03 -0800] "GET /icons/
➥tar.gif HTTP/1.0" 304 -
ts20-04.tor.inforamp.net - - [01/Mar/1996:01:43:04 -0800] "GET /
➥images/apache_pb.gif HTTP/1.0" 200 2326
dyn79.ppp.pacific.net.sg - - [01/Mar/1996:01:43:07 -0800] "GET /
➥images/apache_home.gif HTTP/1.0" 200 1465
sf-110.sfo.com - - [01/Mar/1996:01:43:17 -0800] "GET /docs/ HTTP/
➥1.0" 200 1770
sf-110.sfo.com - - [01/Mar/1996:01:43:24 -0800] "GET /docs/
➥compat_notes.html HTTP/1.0" 200 3593
narfi.ifi.uio.no - - [01/Mar/1996:01:43:30 -0800] "GET /
➥docs/ HTTP/1.0" 200 1770
sf-110.sfo.com - - [01/Mar/1996:01:43:32 -0800] "GET /
➥docs/install.html HTTP/1.0" 304 -
194.158.228.97 - - [01/Mar/1996:01:43:43 -0800] "GET /
➥images/apache_pb.gif HTTP/1.0" 200 2326
narfi.ifi.uio.no - - [01/Mar/1996:01:44:03 -0800] "GET /
➥ HTTP/1.0" 200 3920 -
```

From these pieces, it is possible to put together a wide variety of statistics on your server usage, including:

- Which documents are accessed most frequently
- Which hours of the day, days of the month, and so on are the busiest
- Which domains or countries access your server most (e.g. gov, .edu, .com, .uk [United Kingdom], .se [Sweden], and so on.)
- The total volume of byte traffic.

Because every document access is recorded, log files can grow very quickly. This is compounded by the fact that inline image files are processed as separate requests; for example, a request for a document with three inline GIFs actually shows up as four separate requests—one for the document and three for the GIFs. Even on a lightly loaded server, the access log can grow to several megabytes each month. More heavily loaded Web servers can generate several megabytes per day. (Here's a clue: the average logfile entry is probably around 80 bytes—multiply that by your hit rate and you'll see how much space is being consumed). If you want to save historical log data, it is a good idea to move the current logfile to an archive and compress it. Compression can typically cut a logfile down to 10 percent of its original size, at least. You might want to do this automatically at the beginning of each month, week, or even at midnight every night.

> **Note**
>
> If you want to see document requests as they happen rather than after the fact, you can use the UNIX `tail` command to display each new line added to the log file. Simply enter **tail** -**f** *access_log*.

The Error Log

The error log is the place where the Web server will record any problems it encounters. Some of these problems are rather noteworthy—such as access that failed because the object requested was missing, or there was a system error. Others are merely warning messages that may or may not be indications of serious problems. In any event, it is worth consulting on a regular basis to make sure things are working right and your customers see a professionally maintained Web site.

The format of the logfiles is pretty simple: a timestamp and the warning message. For example:

```
[Sat Apr  6 00:58:54 1996] send lost connection to client
➡202.229.54.36
```

This is an example of a simple warning—for some reason the server lost the connection. It's impossible to tell whether it was the server or client that is at fault; oftentimes this will appear on older browsers when they stop loading the page, for example. However, it is useful debugging information if you are having problems. If you see a very large number of these, comparable in number to your access log itself, there might be problems with your Internet access provider. Other log entries that describe this condition are:

```
[Sat Apr  6 01:00:41 1996] read timed out for async02.acm.org
[Sat Apr  6 10:54:44 1996] request lost connection to client
➡ remote209.compusmart.ab.ca
```

These will typically be the majority of the entries, if your site is well-maintained. There are other, more ominous warning messages, however. For example,

```
[Sat Apr  6 09:19:49 1996] access to /export/pub/apache/robots.txt
➡ failed for homer-bbn.infoseek.com, reason: File does not exist
```

In this case, someone was trying to access a file which did not exist. This may indicate that your pages have a broken link somewhere; if you are using the configurable logging module and are recording the "Referrer" field from the request, you can find it immediately; if you aren't, you can try and see where this user went before trying to get the broken link.

However, a warning like this does not *always* indicate a problem with your site. For one thing, some browsers out there have bugs which occasionally force them to request the wrong object, usually because their rules for resolving relative URL links into full URLs for the request can be broken. Furthermore, you may have rearranged the content on your site into a new hierarchy without providing redirection, so browsers or proxy caches with older copies of your pages ask for the old objects. With Web crawling search engines like Infoseek or WebCrawler, these old references may be requested several months after the change.

The request above in particular, however, is for a file named robots.txt. This file is the commonly accepted way of informing "robots" of policies for your site regarding what content on your site may be indexed, if any.

> **Note**
>
> More information may be found at **http://info.webcrawler.com/mak/ projects/robots/norobots.html**

If you have user authentication turned on anywhere, you'll also see occasional warnings about "user not found" or "password mismatch" if they enter the wrong user/password combination. For example:

```
[Sat Apr  6 10:22:08 1996] access to /www/private/ failed for
➥ ppp66.isp.net, reason: DBM user george not found
```

If your CGI script has problems, any messages sent to the "STDERR" pipe will be recorded in the logfile. For example:

```
[Fri Apr  5 10:01:24 1996] foo.cgi: Insecure dependency in eval
➥ while running with -T switch at lib/CGI/Imagemap.pm line 317.
```

This is a warning from the PERL 5 interpreter invoked by this CGI script. Another major CGI-related error message is "malformed header from script", i.e.:

```
[Fri Apr  5 10:01:24 1996] access to /www/htdocs/foo.cgi failed
➥for test09.host.com, reason: malformed header from script
```

This will occur if the script is not following the rules for CGI output. Other warning messages are largely self-descriptive.

Sifting Usage Data

The access file is a great record of your server's activity, but it's pretty tough to get anything meaningful out of the raw data. You need to sift through and sort the log files and turn them into valuable demographics that illustrate the usage of the Web site. This will justify the investment in the successful pages and assist in understanding how to improve the less successful pages. This information can be used to support the quality of the server or justify the need to upgrade.

There are a wealth of tools and products available for sifting and analyzing the access log file. They range from simple operating system commands to sophisticated relational databases.

Quick and Dirty Analysis with UNIX and DOS

Although there are a number of programs available to analyze access logs, the following are simple steps for finding answers quickly. Using some simple searches, however, you can find many items you need without having to write a line of code. For starters, look at the basic search tools available under UNIX and DOS.

Searching in UNIX

On a UNIX workstation, the simplest way to search a text file is to use the time-honored `grep` utility. For example, to find all access log entries containing `fred`, enter:

```
grep 'fred' access_log
```

> **Tip**
>
> Search strings containing characters that are special to your UNIX shell must be *escaped* by enclosing them in single quotes (for example, `'fred;george'`); you might as well get in the habit of doing this all the time.

`grep` has many powerful capabilities in addition to basic searching. For example, you could search for all lines except those containing `becky` using the `-v` option:

```
grep -v 'becky' access.log
```

Other useful `grep` options include:

- `-i`   Turns off case-sensitive searching
- `-c`   Returns only a count of all matching lines
- `-n`   Displays the line number of each matching line

You can also use multiple options to help limit your search by putting multiple option flags behind the dash. For example, if you want to search for all lines not containing the word "becky" and you want to shut off case-sensitive searching while looking for the term "becky," type:

```
grep -vi 'becky' access.log
```

Searching in DOS

The DOS `FIND` command performs nearly the same function as UNIX's `grep` command. To search for all instances of `nasa.gov` in the access log, enter:

```
FIND "NASA.GOV" ACCESS.LOG
```

> **Note**
>
> With `FIND`, all search strings must be enclosed in quotes, regardless of whether they contain special characters.

Although the DOS `FIND` command does not have as many options as `grep`, it has enough for simple log-file searching, including:

`/v`   Displays all lines not containing the search string

`/c`   Returns only a count of all matching lines

`/n`   Displays the line number with each matching line

`/i`   Does a case-insensitive search

Because the log files are just ASCII text, you can also open your logs in a word processor and use the search features that are part of that particular program. You can also write macros to search for particular strings of text, such as certain error codes, to help you scan through your logs faster.

Useful Search Patterns

Now it's time to put `grep` to work looking for useful data in the access log. Without writing a line of programming code, you can see:

- A history or count of all accesses from an address or class of addresses
- A history or count of all accesses to any file or directory
- The number of total accesses to your server, excluding inline GIFs
- A history or count of all accesses during a given time period

Sifting by Address

Suppose you get a couple of calls one day from users wanting to know why they can't get to the weather map anymore. You ask for their addresses and discover that they never should have had access in the first place. What do you do now? To verify their claims and assess the damage, you can start by simply searching for their addresses in the log file. Suppose the unauthorized users are from **iam.illegal.com** and **ur.illegal.com**. To see what they've looked at besides the weather map, you can simply search for **illegal.com** by entering:

```
FIND "illegal.com" access.log
```

The result is a fascinating chronicle of unauthorized activity. If there are too many lines to count, use `FIND /C` or `grep -c` to do the dirty work for you, and e-mail the results to your boss on a good day.

This scenario is not all that unlikely, by the way. Basic Web server security is good, but only as good as the rules that are made for it. More often than not, problems arise when people make assumptions or generalizations that turn out to be false. You may think, for example, that all addresses in a certain subnet (beginning with 127.34.26, for example) are located on your network, only to find out later that the first 20 addresses belonged to another company. The trick here is just to be aware of what you're doing when you're doing it. Taking the "easy way out" can sometimes open up more of a hole in your security than you really intended.

If you're running a restricted-access Web server, you might want to check now and then to make sure that no one has gotten in from the outside. You can do this easily by looking for all accesses not from your site:

```
FIND /V "widgets.com" ACCESS.LOG
```

In this case, anything returned by the search indicates a possible security breach. If you're running on a UNIX machine, run a `grep -v` command analogous to the previous DOS `FIND` command as a `cron` job every week and mail yourself the results so that you don't forget to check now and then.

Sifting by File or Directory

Perhaps you've recently added a new feature to your Web site and want to see how much attention it's getting. Just search your logs for the directory or file name and you're in business. To see how many times your What's New page has been read in the current logging period, simply enter:

```
FIND "whatsnew.htm" ACCESS.LOG
```

Or if you've added a whole new directory of stuff (called "/stuff"), try:

```
FIND "/stuff" ACCESS.LOG
```

> **Note**
>
> The correct URL to get an automatic directory index is the directory name followed by a slash (/). Some servers, like NCSA's HTTPD for Windows, return an error if the trailing slash is omitted. Most others, however, generate a Redirect URL (status code 302) and then a second request containing the proper URL, causing the document request to show up twice, which distorts true usage figures.

> **Tip**
>
> The ease with which simple searches can find all accesses to a given directory is a strong argument for maintaining a close relationship between the hyperlink structure of documents and the physical directory structure.

Computing Total Accesses

One measure of your Web server's utilization or exposure is the number of total document requests. This is not necessarily a measure of effectiveness because many people who visit your site may spend only a few seconds there and travel on. This is especially true now because of the Web's notoriety. In fact, the ratio of tourists to seriously interested patrons of the Web may even be lower than the percentage of sales resulting from direct-mail campaigns. Fortunately, Web space is a lot cheaper. Nonetheless, the number of documents requested or "hits" is of major interest.

If nothing else, measuring your server's growth in utilization can give you a good indication of when you'll have to buy more powerful hardware. Without running a more advanced usage statistics program, you can get a good feel for your server's growth simply by counting the number of total document accesses. In general, you want to exclude GIF files, however, because inline GIFs show up as separate document requests, which distorts the true number of HTML pages accessed. Of course, if providing images is a major part of your site, you may not want to exclude them in the count. But, for example, to find out many HTML pages have been accessed on your server minus the GIF files, enter:

```
FIND /C /V ".gif" ACCESS.LOG
```

To see how many accesses occur during some specified time period, simply run this command every six hours and compute the difference between each run. For more regular time periods, however, such as days and hours, you can use the next technique.

Computing Accesses During a Given Period

The access log turns out to be in a very convenient format for finding out how many document requests have been processed in most common time periods. For example, if you want to find out how many documents were transferred between 3:00 and 4:00 p.m. on October 25, 1994, use:

```
FIND /C "25/Oct/1994:15" ACCESS.LOG
```

Using this technique, you can look at total accesses in a given hour, day, month, or year. By piping the output of one FIND or grep command into another, you can obtain even more detailed information. For example, to find all accesses from red.widgets.com in the month of October, use:

```
FIND "red.widgets.com" ACCESS.LOG | FIND "/Oct/"
```

The first `FIND` command finds all occurrences of `red.widgets.com`, while the second `FIND` looks only in that data for occurrences of `/Oct/`. (Of course, if you haven't cleaned up your log files for a while, you end up with data from this and all previous Octobers since you last purged or archived your file.) In UNIX, the same thing can be accomplished using regular expressions in a single `grep` command. For example:

```
grep 'red.widgets.com.*/Oct/' access.log
```

> **Note**
>
> In UNIX, the dot is part of regular-expression syntax, which means "any character." When followed by an asterisk, it means "a sequence of any characters." Consequently, the expression above actually finds redAwidgetsBcom as well as red.widgets.com.

Usage Utilities

Now for the really neat stuff. What has been described above gives you a lot of answers about your site and its usage. But they require separate actions and still give you raw output. There are numerous products—some free, some commercial—that take all the grunt work out of collecting and totaling usage statistics. These programs range from freeware that still requires some programming effort on your part to commercial packages that provide easy-to-use graphical user interfaces to set up and customize. They all take the raw data in your log files and create reports and graphs customized to your specifications.

Amongst the freeware offering, one of the best is *wwwstat* (available from **http://www.ics.uci.edu/WebSoft/wwwstat/**). Wwwstat is good because it produces thorough and nicely-formatted output and can be used with *gwstat,* which turns the output of wwwstat into attractive usage graphs (in GIF format, of course). Gwstat is available from **ftp:// dis.cs.umass.edu/pub/gwstat.tar.gz**, and both wwwstat and gwstat are available on the WebmasterCD.

wwwstat

Wwwstat is a PERL script that reads the standard access-log file format and produces usage summaries in several categories. Wwwstat produces summary information for each calendar month and can be run for past months as well as the current month. Summary categories include:

- Monthly Summary Statistics
- Daily Transmission Statistics
- Hourly Transmission Statistics
- Total Transfers by Client Domain (.edu, .gov, and so on and country codes)
- Total Transfers by Reversed Subdomain (the address of every computer that accessed the server)
- Total Transfers from each Archive Section (the number of accesses to each file on the server)

Figure 16.1 shows an example of Daily Transmission Statistics generated by wwwstat.

Fig. 16.1
Wwwstat generated these Daily Transmission Statistics.

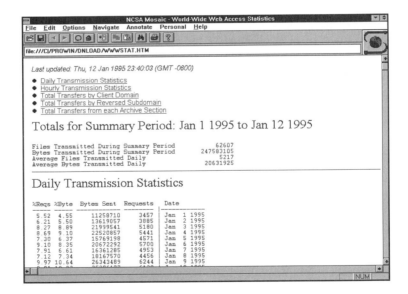

Figure 16.2 shows wwwstat's summary of statistics by client domain, which brings home the truly global nature of the Internet. Part of the wwwstat distribution is a file containing all the country codes in use on the Internet.

Because wwwstat is a PERL program, and a simple one at that, it can run on most other implementations of the PERL interpreter on other platforms.

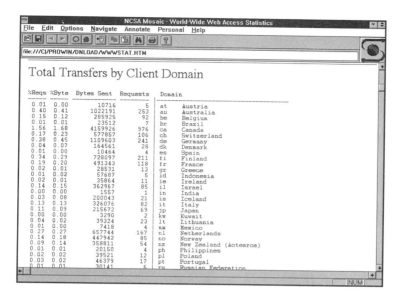

Fig. 16.2
Wwwstat's output of country codes and names.

gwstat

Gwstat takes the output of wwwstat and turns it into illustrative graphs. gwstat produces two sizes of GIF files—thumbnail sketches and full-size graphs like the hourly-usage graph (see figs. 16.3 and 16.4). You can specify the sizes of both the thumbnail and full-size graphs.

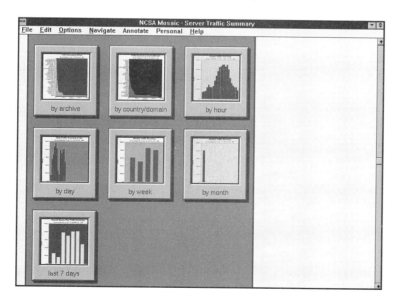

Fig. 16.3
Gwstat's thumbnail sketches.

> **Note**
>
> The graphical window-boxes in figure 16.3 are not created by gwstat, but can be created with the utilities needed to run gwstat. Instructions for doing this are available from **http://dis.cs.umass.edu/stats/statsimage.html**.

Fig. 16.4
Hourly-usage
graph produced by
gwstat.

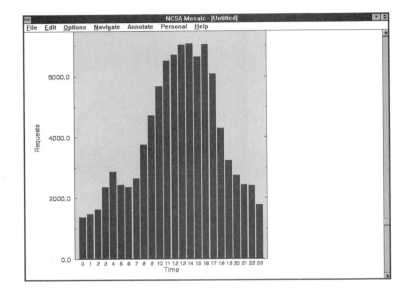

Gwstat requires three other programs to run, so installation can be time-consuming if you don't already have the other programs. However, the results are well worth it. Gwstat is designed to work exclusively under the X Windows system on UNIX workstations, so unfortunately, there is no way to port it to other platforms. Besides wwwstat and PERL, gwstat needs Xmgr, ImageMagick, and GhostScript. Information on these programs and hyperlinks to them is available at **http://dis.cs.umass.edu/stats/gwstat.html**. At that location, there are also instructions for creating a composite imagemap (refer to fig. 16.3).

statbot

Another popular WWW log analyzer is statbot. It works by "snooping" on the log files generated by most WWW servers and creating a database that contains information about the server. This database is then used to create a statistics page and GIF charts that can be "linked to" by other WWW resources.

Because statbot "snoops" on the server log files, it does not require the use of the server's cgi capability. It simply runs from the user's own directory, automatically updating statistics. Statbot uses a text-based configuration file for setup, so it is very easy to install and operate, even for people who have no programming experience.

You can find statbot at **http://www.xmission.com/~dtubbs/club/ cs.html**.

AccessWatch

A third freeware product is AccessWatch, a PERL script from Bucknell University. It converts the analyzed data into an HTML file. Here is an example of AccessWatch output. It was generated for a subdirectory of HTML files about creating an online newspaper, called CReAte.

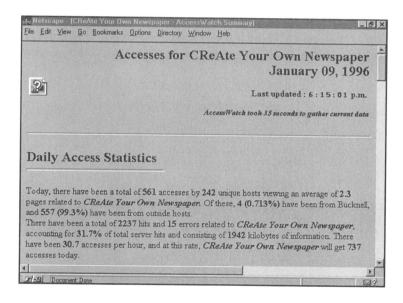

Fig. 16.5
An example of AccessWatch output.

It then adds detailed data in HTML tabular form. You can view the full page at:

> **http://www.eg.bucknell.edu/~dmaher/accesswatch/crayon/**

AccessWatch is available from **http://www.eg.bucknell.edu/~dmaher/ accesswatch/getAccessWatch.html**.

You can find a long list of other analysis tools in the Yahoo directory **http:// /www.yahoo.com/Computers_and_Internet/Internet/ World_Wide_Web/HTTP/Servers/Log_Analysis_Tools/**.

Commercial Products

Commercial products will be proliferating soon. Two early offerings are WebTrends and net.Analysis. WebTrends is a mid-range product that functions more in a batch processing mode. Net.Analysis is a high-end product complete with an Informix database and real-time capability. Both offer great flexibility in customizing reports.

Reports generated by WebTrends include statistical information as well as colorful graphs that show trends, usage, market share, and much more. Reports are generated as HTML files that can be viewed by a browser on your local system or remotely from anywhere on the Internet. WebTrends claims it can read the log files of all available servers. You can download an evaluation copy from **http://www.webtrends.com/** and try it out with your server. It is highly recommended that you try out any software for an evaluation period before you purchase it.

Figures 16.6 through 16.13 are some examples of WebTrends output available from its Web site. These are representative of the kinds of output possible from all of the packages.

Fig. 16.6
This graph illustrates what Internet domains connected and the number of user sessions over a sample day.

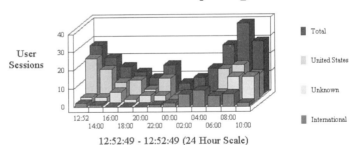

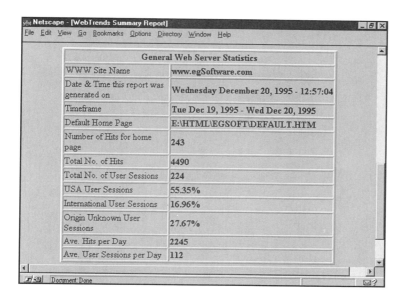

Fig. 16.7
This table includes additional information such as total and average hits per day.

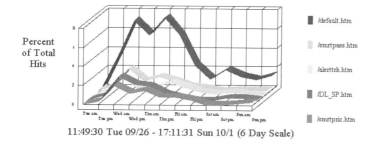

11:49:30 Tue 09/26 - 17:11:31 Sun 10/1 (6 Day Scale)

Fig. 16.8
This graph illustrates the hits to the pages over a set period of days.

IV

Applications

Fig. 16.9
This table includes additional information such as total number of hits and user sessions.

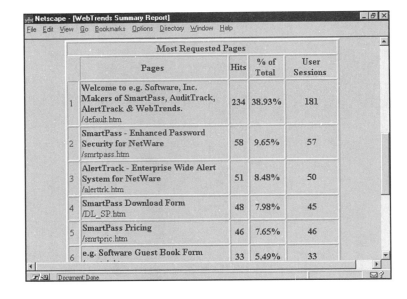

Fig. 16.10
This graph illustrates the activity as percentage of total visits.

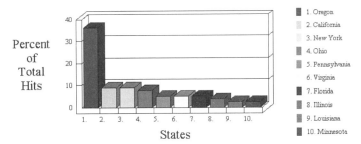

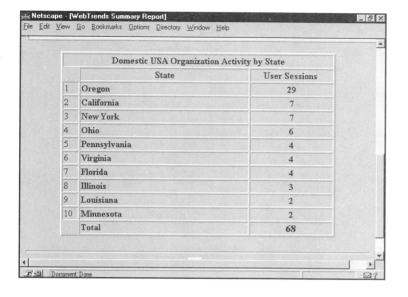

Fig. 16.11
This table includes additional information such as the number of user sessions per state.

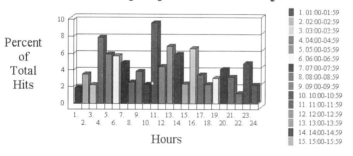

Fig. 16.12
This graph illustrates the activity over a 24-hour period as percentage of total visits.

IV

Applications

Fig. 16.13
This table includes additional information that contrasts the weekdays and weekends as well as indicates the busiest and slowest times.

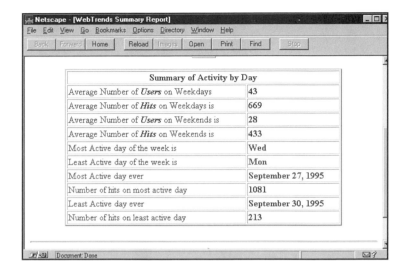

net.Analysis

Net.Analysis is a product designed for complex real-time log analysis. It places the log into an Informix database and runs a host of customizable queries to present as complete an analysis as possible. Here are two examples of the results generated by net.Analysis.

Fig. 16.14
You can present data in a pie chart.

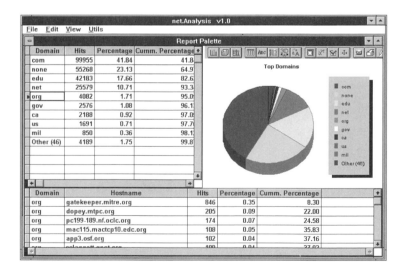

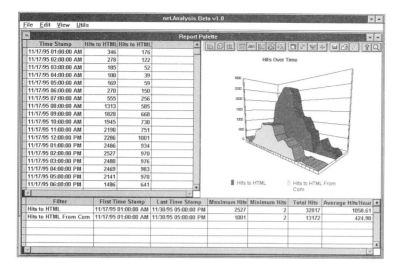

Fig. 16.15
net.Analysis is available from: http://www. netgen.com/

Note

These examples are not meant as an endorsement of any particular product. There are literally new products and updates daily. You should check what is currently available, download evaluation copies, and decide for yourself what you want.

A list of other programs to analyze log files is available from **http:// union.ncsa.uiuc.edu/HyperNews/get/www/log-analyzers.html**.

Also there is a list at the Yahoo directory at:

http://www.yahoo.com/Computers_and_Internet/Internet/ World_Wide_Web/HTTP/Servers/Log_Analysis_Tools/index.html

Checking HTML

As your server grows, it becomes more and more difficult to find broken hyperlinks, both to documents on your own server as well as documents on other servers. This is especially true if many people are responsible for creating and editing documents on your server. Fortunately, there are tools to help you analyze the structure of your HTML database and find problems. Some of these tools are freely available on the Internet.

HTML Analyzer

HTML Analyzer is a C program that both finds broken links and attempts to ensure that the HTML database is well-organized and makes sense to users. It is available in various forms from:

http://wsk.eit.com/wsk/dist/doc/admin/webtest/ verify_links.html

ftp://ftp.cc.gatech.edu/pub/gvu/www/pitkow/ html_analyzer

ftp://ftp.ncsa.uiuc.edu/Web/Mosaic/Contrib/

The file name will be something like html_analyzer-0.30.tar.gz. The documentation for HTML Analyzer is contained in the program's distribution.

The basic philosophy of HTML Analyzer is that the text of any given hyperlink should always point to the same place and that no other text should point to that same place. This is necessary in order for users to get a clear picture of the organization of the HTML database. HTML Analyzer performs three checks on a database of HTML files—validity, completeness, and consistency.

Checking for Validity

The first check performed by HTML Analyzer is for link validity. This ensures that all hyperlinks point to valid locations (that is, no server errors are returned). Empty hyperlinks (such as HREF=""), local links (such as HREF="#intro"), and links to interactive services (Telnet and rlogin) are not checked. Even without running the other two checks, validity checking helps to ensure that users of your site won't be frustrated by broken links.

Checking for Completeness

The completeness check ensures that each anchor's contents always occur as a hyperlink. If a hyperlink contained the text Beginner's Guide, for example, and the same text occurred as regular text (not a hyperlink) elsewhere, this is reported. The intent of the completeness check is to improve user-convenience by expecting a hyperlink everywhere there can be, and also to prevent user confusion because the same text sometimes occurs in a hyperlink but not in others.

Checking for Consistency

The final check ensures that every occurrence of a hyperlink anchor points to the same address and that every occurrence of that address is pointed to by the same hyperlink anchor. In other words, HTML Analyzer checks to see that there is a one-to-one correspondence between hyperlink anchors and their respective addresses.

Here is an example of the results of HTML_Analyzer.

In this example, there is no file /u/CIMS/Demo_Description.html located on the server named nsidc1.colorado.edu, an httpd server listening on port 1729. The first series of tests discovered this and notified the user. It also discovered an incomplete link and an inconsistent link.

Listing 16.2   Sample Results of HTML_Analyzer

```
+++++++++++++++++++++++++++++++++++++++++++++++++++
VERIFYING LINKS…
WWW Alert:  HTTP server at nsidc1.colorado.edu:1729 replies:
HTTP/1.0 500 Unable to access document.
WWW Alert:  Unable to access document.
WARNING:  Failed in checking:
 http://nsidc1.colorado.edu:1729/u/CIMS/Demo_Description.html
   With content of:  Description of this demo
   In local file: ./temp/example.html

VERIFYING COMPLETENESS...
WARNING: These filenames contain the content:
   Description of this demo
 Without a link to:
  http://nsidc1.colorado.edu:1729/u/CIMS/Demo_Description.html
example.html

 VERIFYING CONSISTENCY OF LINKS…
WARNING: Link used inconsistently.
  HREF: http://nsidc1.colorado.edu:1729/u/CIMS/More_info.html
  occurs 1 time with content:
Free Text Frame
  as in file: ./temp/example.html, but also
  occurs 1 time with content:
More Info Frame
  as in file: ./temp/example.html

VERIFYING CONSISTENCY OF CONTENTS…
WARNING: Content used inconsistently.
  CONTENT:
Free Text Frame
  occurs 1 time with href: http://nsidc1.colorado.edu:1729/u/CIMS/
  ➥Even_more_info .html
  as in file: ./temp/example.html, but also
  occurs 1 time with href: http://nsidc1.colorado.edu:1729/u/CIMS/
  ➥More_info.html
  as in file: ./temp/example.html

 +++++++++++++++++++++++++++++++++++++++++++++++++++++
```

MOMspider

MOMspider is a PERL program originally written as a class project in distributed information systems at the University of California. MOMspider stands for Multi-Owner Maintenance Spider and is similar to other spiders and robots that traverse the World Wide Web looking for information. MOMspider is available from **http://www.ics.uci.edu/WebSoft/MOMspider/** and requires *libwww-perl*, a library of PERL code for the World Wide Web available from the same site.

Because MOMspider is designed to follow hyperlinks anywhere on the Web, it has many features for controlling the depth of searches and is respectful of other sites' wishes not to be visited by automated robots like MOMspider. MOMspider also has an interesting feature that can build a diagram of the structure of the documents it finds. In addition, MOMspider can avoid sites that are known to cause problems for Web-roaming robots. Examples of these kinds of sites are those that use scripts to generate all output rather than static HTML documents.

Finding What's New

When your Web site is being maintained by many people independently, such as an internal server in a large organization, it becomes impractical, if not impossible, to require that HTML authors tell you every time they create or modify a page on your server. However, it is highly desirable that server administrators be able to quickly and easily find out what new items have been added each day in order to spot potential problems before they spread too far.

In addition to administrative concerns, information about new or modified documents on the server is helpful for users who can look on the What's New page and see that the server is continually being updated with valuable information.

In UNIX, it's possible to find all new or modified files in an entire directory tree with a single command:

```
find directory_name -mtime 1
```

The `find` command looks recursively down the directory tree specified by *directory_name* to find all files that meet the specified requirements. The `-mtime` option looks for all files that have been modified in the previous number of days—in this case, 1. You can narrow the search to include only new files (not directories) using the `-type f` option. You can also look for files of a certain extension using the -name `'search_pattern'`. For example, to find only `.html` files modified in the last week, enter:

```
find directory_name -mtime 7 -type f -name '*.html'
```

By including a find command like these examples in a shell or PERL script, you can easily generate a list of What's New pages, as in the following PERL example. The script is available as "whatsnew.pl" on WebmasterCD.

WebmasterCD

Listing 16.3   PERL Script That Generates a What's New Page

```perl
#!/usr/bin/perl

# whatsnew.pl--David M. Chandler--January 13, 1995
# This program finds all files underneath the search directory which
# have been created or modified within the last day. The output is an
# HTML What's New page with hyperlinks to the new pages.

# Invoke the script and redirect the output to your What's New page
# whatsnew.pl >whatsnew.html

#Put your server's document root here
$SEARCHDIR="/httpd/htdocs";

#Create header for What's New document
print "<TITLE>What's New<TITLE>\n";
print "<H1>What's New!</H1>\n";
print "The following documents were created or modified
➥yesterday:<P>\n";
print "<DL>\n";

#Find all new/modified HTML files in the past day
for each $file (`find $SEARCHDIR -type f -mtime 1 -name '*.html'`)
{
  #Construct the URL from the filename by removing the
# directory path
  if ($file =~ m%$SEARCHDIR/(.*)%) {
  $url = $1; }

  #Find the document title
  chop($title = `grep '<TITLE>' $file`);
  if ($title =~ m%<TITLE>(.*)</TITLE>%i) {
    $anchor = $1; }

  #Create the What's New listing
  print "<DD><A HREF=\"$url\">$anchor</A>\n";
}
print "</DL>\n";
```

Windows for Workgroups users can accomplish this task easily in File Manager by using the Date Sort tool, which lists all files in chronological order. Likewise, many Windows-based shells, such as Norton Desktop or PC Tools for Windows, have similar features in their file management utilities. DOS users aren't fortunate enough to have the `-mtime` option available to list only those files modified recently; however, it is possible to see a directory listing sorted by date so that a quick scan reveals any new or modified files. To list a directory with the most recently created or modified files last, use:

```
DIR /OD directory_name
```

To list a directory with the most recently created or modified files listed first, use:

```
DIR /O-D directory_name
```

Summary

This chapter will set you well on the way to managing the usage of your Web site. You will be able to furnish the content managers with detailed and organized data on the accesses to the site and its pages. You will also be able to check the HTML pages that get placed on the server to see if they are linked properly. This will help to make your site more professional and productive. ❖

## CHAPTER 17

Database Access and Applications Integration

The previous two chapters really lay the groundwork for one of the most exciting and interesting uses of the Web: using a World Wide Web client as an interface to the wealth of data contained within a structured database. It's in this capacity that the flexibility and usability of the Web really shines through, making the difference between a static, unchanging site and a site that responds dynamically to the user's preferences and environment.

This is also the fastest-growing area of the Web. At first, as people were just getting accustomed to HTML and the Web, most sites featured fairly static HTML pages. Even if well-designed, the ultimate effect was a very easy to use and splashy catalog with the ability to reference other sites. Database integration changes all of that. Databases allow the user to search through reams of data far too large to browse through manually, even in summary form. They allow for different views of the same data, creating and utilizing data relationships on-the-fly. And most importantly, by using live data on the Web, the site is always kept up-to-date, accurate, and interesting.

In this chapter, you learn about:

- The online needs that a database interface can help you meet and the software and programming needed to make a database link work

- How typical database applications on the Web look to the database programmer

- A few widely used tricks that database programmers use to make implementing online databases easier

- Advantages and disadvantages of using browsers as database clients

- Emerging technologies that will make integrating structured data into the Web much easier and provide Web authors with much more flexibility and control

Getting Started

The different uses for database interfaces on the Web is as complex and interesting as the Web itself. Customers visiting a well-wired retail site can easily check the status of their orders, browse through a customized list of inventory items, or request to be notified via e-mail when a product becomes available. A tourist planning a trip to a city may search for available suites at a resort, register online for activities that interest them, or download the menu—and the pages which later show the scenic points of the city are customized to the user's interests. The site is now much more useful than its equivalent paper counterpart, since it reflects the data on the site in a manner that is customized to each particular user.

All of the data just described can be easily stored within a traditional database. Full-text indexing methods do not really apply to these cases, since the queries and updates use structured data. Customers wanting to purchase a product do not want to retrieve documents that describe the marketing techniques for the product, which a full-text index may return.

> **Tip**
>
> As a general rule of thumb, if your data is structured and well-ordered, such as a mailing list or a parts list, then you should consider using a database. If your data has little or no structure and includes a significant amount of free-flow text, you might be better off using a text indexing method. If your data has both free-form text and structured fields, such as a collection of documents with author/content headers, then you might want to consider a hybrid approach. Some databases have support for free-form text or binary data built in.

The integration of the database to your Web site is done through the CGI interface. You write programs that take user input, do some extra processing, and return a Web page back to the user that shows the effects of the user's work. However, the difference is the extra processing; rather than just execute a program or perform a fairly simple task, you will usually access a database *engine*. The database engine, or *server*, takes your input, performs a search or other operation on the data within the database, and returns the results of that operation. The exact details of how this is done vary widely based on the type of database to which you connect.

If your data is not already in an accessible database, then the first step toward making your data available on the Web is to load it into a database of some sort. There are a large number of databases on the market, including commercial, shareware, and freeware solutions. The databases range from simple structured tables with indexes on various fields—such as the cbase library from Citadel—up to fully scaleable, high-performance SQL databases from companies such as Informix, Oracle, Sybase, and so on. Database software for UNIX machines may be as cheap as $100, or may cost hundreds of thousands of dollars. Most of the reliable, good-performance database engines for small UNIX machines cost thousands of dollars, but are usually easier to program and will handle higher user loads more reliably than their freeware or shareware cousins. In general, the more complex your data and the more users it needs to be able to handle at once, the more expensive the commercial product will need to be.

> **Tip**
>
> If your application only needs to look up the value of a single field that matches the user's input exactly, you might not need a database. Why not use PERL's associative arrays to rapidly access a record if you know the record's name?

Once the data is stored within an accessible database, the next step is to choose an interface language that can accept input in CGI format, query or modify the database, and then return results in the HTML language. Because PERL seems to be the de facto language for use with Web servers, many database solutions involve custom PERL libraries that can interface with several popular database languages. These PERL dialects are available at **ftp:// ftp.demon.co.uk** (and mirrored at **ftp://ftp.cis.ufl.edu/pub/perl/ scripts/db/**), and can assist with the interface to Informix, InterBase, Oracle, Postgres, SyBase, Unify, Ingres, X.500 directories, and common C-Tree and NDBM formats.

Most commercial database packages may also be accessed through the development tools that are sold to access the database. For example, Informix's embedded SQL-within-C language (ESQL/C) can be used directly to program database interfaces, or can be used in cooperation with a PERL wrapper to handle post-processing. In many instances, using existing database tools is the easiest route for database programmers who are already familiar with the database tools from that vendor.

Control Flow and a Sample Application

Because of the design of the Web, designing a database interface for the Web is different than traditional procedural or event-driven database applications.

The program must be designed to work with *pages*; your database program is called when a form is submitted or a link is chosen, and must generate a new HTML page to be returned to the user.

Caution

Turn off Crawler Access!

One of the great features of a database-driven Web environment is the great flexibility and custom appearance that can be generated for a user. However, this sometimes drives Web indexing programs, such as Alta Vista and WebCrawler or even internal harvesting applications, crazy as they try to index every single page on your server since they cannot detect that each page is actually the output of a program. For the benefit of both the search engines on the Net and your own performance and throughput, use the */robots.txt* server control file to limit the scope of the crawlers to your static data and away from your database applications. If you have non-form links that can modify the database, this step is critical to maintaining database integrity.

As an example of a database interface on the Web, we'll walk through a fairly simple "query-add-delete-edit" database application. This typical application can be used as a basis to build up more complex database systems, involving more advanced topics such as relational table joining and data integrity concerns.

This Web database application has several database activities, which are fairly typical of database programs on the Web:

- *Gathering Query Information*   The query is usually given to the user in a normal, static HTML form, with a database CGI program as the "Submit" destination URL (see fig. 17.1). In this example, the user may use the data entered in the screen either as a Query-By-Example, or he or she can insert the record directly into the database using the Add submission button.

- *Execution of User's Query*   The Query is submitted to a CGI program, which examines the data entered by the user, translates it into an appropriate format for the database language involved (such as SQL), and submits it to the database engine. The program then gathers the results and displays the list of found items in an HTML format (see fig. 17.2). Each found item is then a link to the "Update" database program, which will display a "detailed" view of that particular record and allow the user to modify the record. If the search found only one record, it might go directly to the found record's update screen. If no results are found, it might lead the user to an Add screen, with the data entered by the user already filled out in the form.

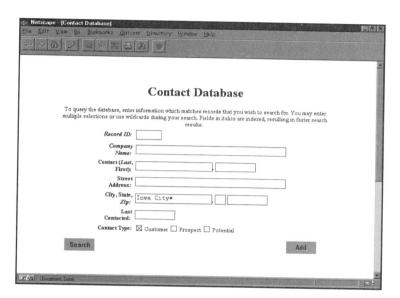

Fig. 17.1
The user may enter a query-by-example from this screen, or may add a new record directly into the database.

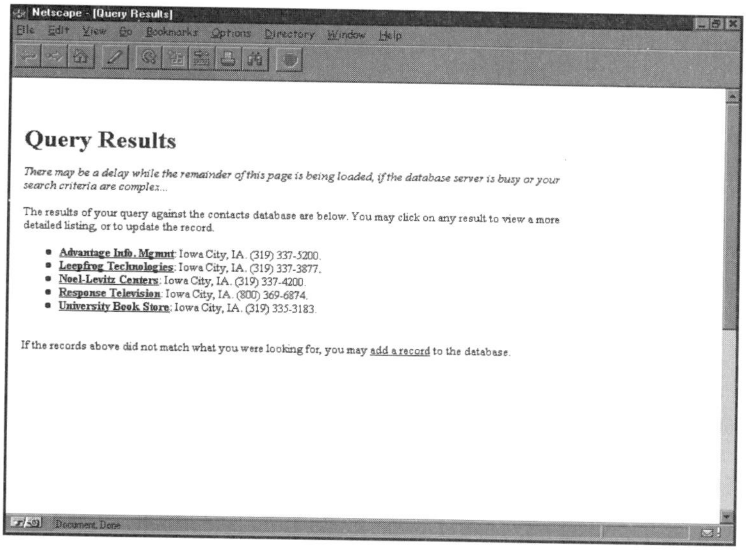

Fig. 17.2
The result of a query is an HTML document containing a link to each of the different records found. The link URL tells the CGI program which record to retrieve.

■ *Adding a Record* An empty or default record is shown to the user in an HTML Form, either from a static HTML file or from the query program after an unsuccessful query. After the user completes the form, the form is submitted to a database CGI program that will validate the data entered within the form and, if the data is valid, add it to the database. If the data is not valid for whatever reason, the form should be redisplayed to the user with the work-in-progress intact and the problem emphasized in the form for the user to correct. Alternatively, a page may be returned to the user that informs him that the data was incorrect and instructs him to hit "Back," correct the error, and then try again by resubmitting the form.

■ *Modifying a Record* When the user clicks on a field to view or update a record, the program returns back a form with the existing data already appearing on the form. The user makes the modifications and submits the new data back to the database CGI programs (see fig. 17.3). Again, after form submission, the update program must check to make sure that the new data meets data constraints and is valid. The form uses a hidden input field to keep track of which record is being modified.

Fig. 17.3
The user can modify the data directly on the screen, updating the record within the database.

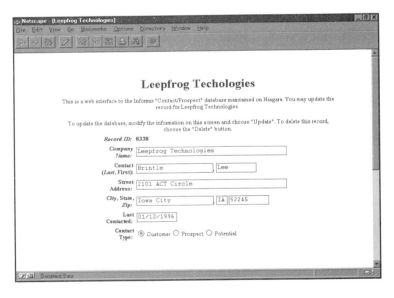

■ *Deleting a Record* After going through a confirmation step, the record is deleted from the database. Note that this causes the "Update" screen to reflect incorrect information: the record may no longer be modified, but it may be added back into the database. Handling this type of problem is one of the difficulties of using the Web as an interface to a typical database application.

This sample application is an integration between several static HTML pages and the following six database programs:

dbquery	Given the user's CGI input, return a list of found records or a message of "nothing found." Each record is a link to the *dbfetch* program to retrieve the detailed view of a record.
dbinsert	Called from the static "blank record" template, this program will validate and insert the user's new record into the database.
dbfetch	Given the primary key of a record, this program will generate a detailed view using an HTML form. The form includes a link to the *dbconfirm* program to confirm the deletion of a record, and a submission destination to the *dbupdate* program to update the record.
dbupdate	Updates the database to reflect changes made by the user.
dbconfirm	Asks the user if he is sure he wants to delete; links "Yes" response to the *dbdelete* program.
dbdelete	Deletes a record from the database.

With a handful of fairly simple CGI programs, this database now has a client-server interface that can run on a variety of platforms, ranging from high-end workstations to very inexpensive ASCII terminals.

Programming Hints

Following are a few programming hints that will make your Web applications easier to use and more effective.

Use Hidden Input Fields

Hidden fields can be a great benefit to the database designer. Hidden fields are fields that are included in HTML forms and are submitted with the rest of the user's data entry, but the user never sees them and cannot normally change the values. A programmer may use hidden fields to pass along to later database programs information that is not of interest to the user, such as the record IDs of the row being updated, user format preferences, generation numbers, temporary file names, and so on.

In the above example, the database programmer may have chosen to implement all six programs in a single CGI script, and rely on hidden fields to indicate which of the six functions should be executed on the current input information.

Caution

Although the HTML specification requires the user's browser to submit all data in the order that it was received, not all Web browsers do that. However, all browsers that I could find either send the fields correctly (that is, in order) or in reverse order. Therefore, a hidden field that needs to be known before any of the rest of the data can be processed (such as a "which function to perform" tag) should be included at the very top *and* very bottom of an input form.

Whistle While You Work

Because the CGI program is doing more complex tasks than retrieving a file from a disk, there may be a much longer delay when loading Web pages, particularly if the user enters complex search criteria or the database machine is heavily loaded. If the delay is too long, the user might cancel the download, hit back, and try again, which may frustrate both the user and the rest of the system as query after query is started and then canceled. To avoid this situation and to let the user know that the system is indeed processing his input, output a header immediately that indicates that the database is working and will return results shortly. Even a simple "Working…" message as the first line of the document will help avoid this problem.

However, you must also check to make sure that your Web server will not save up the output of your program until it is finished. Some Web servers do this under some circumstances so that they can inform the user's browser how long the resulting document will be. With such servers, use the "pass through" or "http direct" option for your queries; the "Content-Length:" field of the HTTP header is optional and your program may choose to skip it if the length of the data is not known.

The default type of service for the Apache server is to buffer 8 kilobytes of CGI script output before passing it off to the network layer for transmission. To avoid this buffering, you must make your script an *nph script*. *nph* stands for nonparsed headers, and it literally means that the server removes itself as the middleman and the CGI script talks directly to the client. Currently the only way to designate a script to be an nph script is to name the first four letters of the script's `nph-` (i.e., `/www/htdocs/nph-foo.cgi`.

Use POST and GET Submission Types Correctly

When implementing an HTML Form, the form designer may choose whether the user's data will be submitted using the GET or POST methods. According to the HTML 2.0 specification, the GET method should be used when submitting the form has no side effects on the database (such as queries, or the start of an update), and the POST method should be used when submission will change the state of the database (such as add, update, or delete operations). This is not just a trivial distinction: most browsers will confirm from the user before submitting a form twice using POST, and will silently submit a form twice with GET. Obviously, you don't want the user to accidentally add the same record twice to the database.

> **Note**
>
> One HTML guideline that is commonly available on the Web *incorrectly* states that the difference between the two should be the length of the data being submitted, and to use POST when dealing with possible long sets of data. This is not how the HTML 2.0 designers intended the two methods to be used nor how browsers are implemented, but it does reflect an important practical consideration: many Web servers cannot handle GET methods when dealing with longer data sets. Check your Web documentation or experiment if unsure, but try to use GET and POST in the spirit that they were intended.

At the time of this writing, the America Online browser cannot handle POST forms at all. Therefore, database programmers who wish to provide functionality to AOL users cannot use POST in their applications. Hopefully, this will be fixed on AOL's end before too much longer, and Webmasters may always use the appropriate method.

Always Maintain Security

Implementing secure CGI programs is important since the programs can possibly alter data on the machine itself. However, with database programming, the problem is magnified greatly since the programs work directly with data that can be fairly easily corrupted if the programmer is not careful. An important thing to remember is that the user can alter *any* of the data on a form, even in ways not usually possible using a normal Web browser. For example, a radio button may be returned to the CGI script as a value that is not legal and never appeared in any of the choices to the user. The values of hidden fields may be changed by a malicious user at any time. Fields that have a length limitation that the browser normally enforces may be submitted with longer strings (this one is particularly painful if using a language like C and directly writing user values into arrays of fixed length). As a database programmer who is concerned about the integrity of the data, you cannot assume that any of the data that comes from the user's browser will fit the constraints of the calling page.

As an example of such a potential pitfall, consider a Web interface where a user may update his or her address information online. The application starts off requesting the user's name and address password, verifies it, and returns a form with the user's ID number in a hidden recordid field and the data entry fields populated with the user's existing address information. The user modifies the information, submits the form, and the database program updates the record number in the recordid field to reflect the changes that the user made.

The problem here is that the user may change the ID number manually to any other ID number in the system, and the update program will then update the wrong user's record. A better solution would be to store the ID number in a special format and then encrypt the ID number using a key known only to the server. If the ID number is modified by a potential data vandal, the format will not match up after decryption and the database server may reject the request.

User Authentication

The Web is rapidly advancing in its ability to have servers automatically recognize and verify which user is accessing a CGI program, but such automatic solutions to this problem are still too sparsely implemented to be able to be used in a generic environment. However, database programmers may still make use of password fields or HTML's almost-official browser authentication to verify users at the beginning of the application, and have the browser keep track of authentication credentials as the user moves through the application.

User Preferences

If your site already has users who are logging in or registering themselves, then one of the best things that your site can do is track their interests and preferences to customize the site for that user. This makes your site come "alive" and become more interesting and useful to all of the users, since they get information that is customized and appropriate for their interests. It also makes your site more memorable and more likely to be revisited and passed around through word-of-mouth, which is an important consideration for sites that are seeking popularity.

For example, a real-estate server might remember that a user is interested in a certain price range, location, and style, as well as the last date that they visited the site. When the user returns to the site, the home page might include a listing of new properties added since his last visit, each one in the style and price range that interests the user. When touring a new property online, the descriptions might change slightly to emphasize the features that interest the user.

Browsers as Database Front Ends

Creating a Web interface to a database may do more than just give users outside your company access to your information—it may also provide an easy, cross-platform solution for in-house use. Once a good, robust gateway is written between the Web and your existing database server, your users can immediately have cross-platform access and update ability to that database by using their Web browser as a database client. Almost every hardware platform and operating system has a World Wide Web browser available, which eliminates the need for your MIS staff to worry about creating a client for Macintosh, Windows, and UNIX. In addition, if you use large numbers of ASCII terminals, then your database is still accessible through plain-text Web clients, such as Lynx and Panda.

The largest shortcoming of this approach is that you are restricted to the level of functionality that all of your Web browsers support. All data and forms are displayed inside the browser rather than as a separate application. If your application needs its own menu bar rather than links within the page, or floating palettes, spreadsheets, graphical editing, or any of a number of custom controls, it will be difficult to implement using the Web and standard HTML.

Since the formal HTML 2.0 specification does not offer database programmers enough flexibility and control to be able to implement "real" clients for databases, many people decide to go with extensions or extra features that are offered on particular Web browsers. These features either completely or partially close the gap between what the database programmer wants the database interface to do, and what the browser can actually handle.

One good example of such an extension is Java and JavaScript. Created by Sun Microsystems, Java allows you to program in one language that works across many platforms, allowing you to "break" the HTML rules when a needed functionality is not supported by HTML. For example, you might use a Java applet to allow the user to draw a line on a graphical image of a map, connecting two cities in the U.S. that he wants to visit. This provides an easier method of collecting this data than asking the user to type in the two cities' names. Other browser extensions include the ability to handle validation callbacks after filling in an entry field for data validation, ability to search graphical images, use multiple editing windows, and so on. However, users who are not using a browser that supports such extensions either will not be able to use the database interface, or will need to use some sort of a work-around.

There are new products on the market that create a hybrid between a platform-specific client interface and a Web interface. One such product is InterAp from Stac Electronics (**http://www.stac.com/Homepages/ Software/intcont.html**), which allows you to create advanced applications that can interoperate with the Web and other Microsoft Windows applications. Similar applications are available from other vendors, and Microsoft has announced increased Internet functionality to many of its products and services.

Advanced Topics and a Look Ahead

There are many issues dealing with the peculiar workings of the Web that cause some sticky situations for database programmers. Most of these issues apply only when using the Web to update databases, rather than merely searching them online, and most of the issues are traditional database issues cast into a different light because of the Web interface.

Use of the Back Button

Because the user may click on the Back button at any time, implementing user flow paths becomes a rather complex issue. The database programmer must keep in mind that at any screen, the user can choose the Back icon and go back to a prior page, abandoning the current flow path without the server's knowledge. Unless steps are taken, this may lead to the double-updating of records, or the re-writing of older data on top of newer data. The user might also be able to go back after deleting a record and attempt illegal operations, such as attempting to update that record. The database programs should be able to handle such odd situations gracefully.

The database designer should also be able to handle the user submitting the same request multiple times, and intelligently ignore subsequent requests if appropriate. For example, if the user adds a record to a database, clicks on "Back," and then re-submits the same form to add a record, the system should tell the user that the item has already been added into the system and his current request has been ignored.

Concurrency Control

When designing an interface to a database that includes the ability to update or change the data within the system, the database programmer needs to keep in mind Web peculiarities. In general, most of the issues revolve around how Web browsers retrieve information: when the user clicks on a link or submits a Form, the browser opens up a connection, downloads the new page from the Web server, and then closes the connection. From the server's point of view, the server does not know what the client does after the page is downloaded; if the user clicks on Back, or even quits his browser application, the server is not informed of this fact.

This behavior makes implementing concurrency control difficult, since the server cannot afford to lock a record while the user is editing it, for fear that the user is not really editing the record at all, but has gone off to browse someplace else or has quit the application. Also, dealing with cursors of things to do can be problematic because the items in the current working set are added and deleted by other users. Coordinating multiple users working on a common working set requires a lot of programming acrobatics and usually results in some training issues to the end users.

One partial solution to this problem is to use the client pull features available on some Web browsers. The browser presents the page to the user for his actions, and allows the user to modify that page for a reasonable period of time. During that period, the database considers that data "checked out" by the user doing the modifications, and will not permit others to modify it or put it on their To-Do lists. After a certain period of time, the server will automatically "check in" the object, and the version that the user has checked out is now stale. However, the browser will also load, automatically, a new version of the page, which should indicate to the user that his update period has expired and he needs to re-load this page in order to check the object back out. There is still a period during which the user can check out the page and then quit the application, but the user is at least notified when their lock becomes stale. Browsers which do not support client pull will behave normally, except that they will not receive notification of their outdated lock status.

Heavy Server State Management

Some database applications require the database process to build up a rather complex state within the server, such as a cursor of currently active rows from a query. This state can be expensive to rebuild on every page fetched from the server, which slows down the responsiveness of the site and adds greatly to the server load. Even the basic overhead of re-establishing a connection with the database server every single time a page is fetched may cause a noticeable impact on performance.

One fairly straightforward solution is to have the page teach the browser the information the server will need to re-use by using hidden buttons within a Form. Remember that the user does not see the value or contents of hidden buttons, but they are returned by the browser at the time the form is submitted. For example, a list of "customers to visit today" may be submitted on every page submission, allowing the user to walk down the list without re-querying the database to rebuild the list after every update. However, some browsers are limited in the number of items that can be on a form or do not work correctly for very long lists, so this technique might not be usable when the lists can get long. Also remember that not all browsers return items on a form in the same order, in spite of the HTML 2.0 specification.

Another solution is to use temporary files located on the server to store the server's state. This has the advantage of being able to store lists of almost any size, and allows the user to keep the list updated regardless of moving back and forth using the "Back" button. The server would send a hidden field (or a parameter to the CGI script) that indicates which temporary file on the server to use. However, since there is no way for the server to know when the user is finished with the list, the server must delete the list on its own after some period of time. And because the user may bookmark a page and re-visit it later, the server should be able to handle a page submission after it has already deleted the user's temporary list, usually by rebuilding the state within the list.

One fairly complicated solution is to use a fairly complex server to reconnect the database server process with the client's browser across multiple page retrievals. That is, the database process continues running even after it has completed the request for an "expensive" page. If the user finishes that page within a given period of time, that process can continue onward with the state it has already built up, without the overhead of rebuilding it. There are commercial applications that will perform the reconnect, and are usually phased-in after a database site becomes so heavily used that performance issues are starting to effect user satisfaction with the interface.

Custom HTTP Servers

If your application is expected to get very heavy usage (millions of hits a week, or a large amount of processing on a smaller number of hits), one way to improve performance is to bypass the standard Web server. Rather than using programs that are called from the standard Web server (such as CGI programs called from the Apache server), a custom program handles all HTTP requests and transactions directly, speaking and understanding the raw HTTP protocol. The custom server must handle many of the nit-picky details of content negotiation itself that are usually handled by the HTTP server, but the overall effect of going this route might be better performance and easier handling of machine resources. However, it requires a significant understanding of Internet programming and the HTTP 1.0 specification.

For example, the standard Apache server can be run on the normal HTTP port on a machine to handle most of the general requests and for pages that require some of the Apache server's features. Once the user accesses pages that are the performance-critical sections of the application or accesses sections that need additional functionality not easily added to a standard server, the browser connects to a second server on the same machine, on port 8080. The second server is a simple, single-minded process dedicated to maintaining the database interface. Because it does not have all of the features of the full-blown Apache server, it is significantly smaller (in one common case, only 67K) and executes significantly faster than running the same processes off Apache using CGI scripts.

Because writing your own HTTP server is a fairly complicated and difficult task, an interesting option recently made available is to use the extensibility of the Apache server, as of release 1.0.0. This release of the server permits programmers to add their own modules at link time to provide additional or alternate functionality to the standard Apache server. Rather than writing an entirely new custom server to handle your database applications, modules may be added to the Apache server to permit it to communicate directly with the database and to maintain connections while awaiting new requests. At the same time, modules that are not directly needed in the performance-critical points of your overall Web application may be left out of the custom server, resulting in a smaller, quicker custom executable, without having to re-write all of HTTP.

Licensing Issues

Most commercial UNIX databases are sold with a certain number of user licenses, which, by copyright law, must still be obeyed by the Web database programmer. Policies for what counts as a single user vary from vendor to vendor; some vendors count by the number of UNIX IDs that are in use, which means that the single Web user can take care of hundreds of transactions at once. Some vendors count it as the number of people who access the program, which would make the database program unusable in a general access Internet environment, but might work for an in-house local Intranet application. Finally, other vendors count it as the number of simultaneous server processes running, in which case care must be taken not to exceed this number during peak or busy periods on the Web server. When setting up your server, it is important that you find out very clearly from your vendor how your database server handles such legal and technical issues.

Commercial products are available that will control the number of simultaneous connections, and allow users to wait in line for the next available open license. This not only allows you to keep under your licensed user limit, but also allows the server hardware to be shared with other applications so that the Web usage cannot overwhelm the machine.

Commercial Products

The field for commercial plug-ins to the Web that will make database integration easier and more effective is exploding. All major database companies have announced upcoming products which will make it easier to access databases over the Web. The best place to find up-to-date information is on those vendor's home pages on the Web or in the **comp.databases.*** newsgroups.

Some third-party packages that may help you with your development are:

- ■ *gensearch/genquery* Leepfrog Technologies (**http://www.leepfrog.com**) distributes these two simple programs that allow for fairly easy query-by-example of Informix databases. They also offer other products for Web database development.

- ■ *w3spider* Spider Technologies (**http://www.w3spider.com**) distributes programs that help database programmers visually design Web pages using data from a variety of commercial databases, such as Informix (On-Line engine only, which isn't mentioned anywhere in their documentation), Sybase, and Oracle. Their run-time support manages open database connections to prevent exceeding user licenses and to improve performance on heavily loaded systems.

This market is exploding, but if you have extensive technical experience programming with your database package in your environment, rolling your own solution using your existing database tools is frequently just as easy as some of the more complex packages, and allows you to customize the system to meet your particular needs.

Connecting databases live to the Web is one of the most interesting and useful applications of Web technology, and frequently lifts up a popular and well-visited site from the other static and unchanging sites that might be in the same field. ❖

CHAPTER 18
Financial Transactions

Many of the Web sites in development today are a result of the dreams and hard work of the entrepreneurs of the Internet, *infopreneurs*. If you're interested in conducting commerce via your Web site, this chapter is a must read.

This chapter covers one of the most important and quickly developing areas of Internet technology: Adding secure financial transactions to your Web site. There are a number of different approaches and the chapter reviews the current high profile systems: eCash, First Virtual, CyberCash, Secure Pay and Web900. It would be an understatement to say that security plays an important role when discussing finances and personal information. You take a look at how you can provide your customers the security they desire when transacting business with you. Some Web servers have built-in security and this chapter covers them briefly. Finally, this chapter offers you some alternative methods of transacting commerce.

In this chapter, you learn about:

- A brief history of online commerce
- Network security measures
- Electronic Cash/Credit equivalents
- How to become an electronic merchant
- Software commerce systems for your Web site

When reviewing and discussing secure financial transactions, you need a basic familiarity with the concepts of Internet security implementations; so that is this chapter's first topic.

Development of Financial Transactions on the Internet

Internet Financial transactions began with the market for commercial online services such as Prodigy, CompuServe and America Online. Early on, the concept of an "Electronic Mall" was introduced first by Prodigy and later implemented by the other commercial online services. In fact, Prodigy was envisioned initially to be little more than a convenient place to shop! The Prodigy Electronic Mall was the result of a joint effort involving CBS, Sears, and IBM. It allowed Prodigy customers to order a wide variety of products, ranging from groceries and flowers to automobiles and other high ticket items. Transactions were done by credit card and the purchases were delivered to the buyer. In this transaction, Prodigy acted as a broker between the vendor and buyer. Each vendor's orders were sent to them by Prodigy at regular intervals. Prodigy received a percentage of the sales and garnered additional profits by selling advertising space.

An entirely new business concept was created! The Prodigy system is a considerable success and is a credible model for infopreneurs around the globe. However, there is a key difference between Prodigy and your Web site on the Internet. Prodigy is a closed service that its users connect directly to via modem. This means that the security of the connection is guaranteed.

The strength of the Internet (and its weakness where commerce is concerned) is that it is an open system. This means that your connection can be "listened to" by snooping ears. But because the lure of online commerce is so powerful, many large companies are working hard to implement a secure system for their own version of the Electronic Mall. The main forces driving the development of Secure Internet Protocols are the companies striving to reduce costs and increase profits by selling their products and services through the Internet. You will probably begin to hear many people talk of the "frictionless economy" where Internet technology removes all barriers to commerce regardless of time or space.

Another force is the promise to banks and merchants of cheaper, Electronic Data Interchange (EDI), the system currently used for credit card validation and commerce between large companies. EDI has been in use for years and generally requires dedicated communication lines and equipment. The Internet strategy is inherently simpler and less expensive to use. When banks accept and begin using an Internet version of EDI, their operating costs, and the costs to merchants for credit card validation will drop.

Currencies

The Internet is an international phenomenon; it's not nationally specific to the United States. Someone anywhere in the world can reach anywhere else in the world easily and seamlessly. Not so in the "real world" where there are borders, nationalities, languages, and currencies. When selling products or services on the Internet, you may have to contend with different currencies and exchange rates. Most Web sites specify in US currency (US$45) the prices of their merchandise; this is a good strategy. The buyer then must deal with the trouble of differing currencies. Many e-cash systems will eliminate this burden as well by converting currencies when funds are transferred into a special e-cash account.

Online Purchasing

The Internet, in general, and the World Wide Web, in particular, offer a convenient outlet for selling products and services. As the Web matures, more and more merchants are including some way for visitors to purchase from them. A number of strategies are in use, from some version of an electronic money, secure transmission of credit card numbers, taking orders and shipping them COD, to requiring visitors to establish an "account" with the merchant prior to purchasing a product or service. Only using electronic money or secure transmission of credit card numbers require any new implementation of technology; this chapter focuses on those strategies.

The introduction of electronic, virtual money has raised some serious concerns for everyone involved. The nature of this electronic money is digital, ones and zeros, and instantly simple to reproduce and defraud. The companies involved in creating digital money have created elaborate systems to prevent fraud.

The transmission of secure financial information raises more concerns. How do you prevent the information from being picked up by the wrong person and unencrypted? Technically, most of the systems currently in place are as secure as the current credit card validation system used in almost every store in the western world. The robustness of the security system is not enough, the customer needs to feel that it is secure. It becomes a marketing issue.

Security Concerns

The Internet is an inherently insecure system. Data is available to anyone with the will to retrieve it. Every week, you hear or read about someone breaking into—hacking—a "secure" computer system, like the Department of Defense. It is worthwhile to remain cautious when dealing with secure information and computers. Commonly accepted "secure" systems will eventually be exposed with weaknesses, and will then be enforced or retired in favor of the next "secure" system. The best security is not a powerful encryption, it is diligence. If you keep careful track of your transactions, maintain adequate security within your company, follow common secure practices, (like using passwords), you will be less likely to be the victim of some kind of fraud.

As a transactor of electronic commerce, you must be concerned with two areas of computer security:

- You must provide a way for your users to exchange information with you in a secure manner.
- The data you receive from your customers must be protected from falling into the wrong hands.

Your data can become vulnerable through sociological hacking, Brute Force hacking, Keyboard readers, and the ever popular "Packet sniffing."

Sociological Hacking

If you know a lot about somebody, it is often fairly easy to figure out passwords. A favorite pet, a child's name, or activity are all commonly used as passwords. You may have given passwords and private keys to coworkers and friends or you may leave that kind of information near the computer. Many instances of people breaking in to "secure" systems wasn't through some marvel of computer hacking, it was the result of being observant and nosy. All administrative personnel at your site must have proper account names and passwords.

Brute Force

It's possible to decipher any encrypted message given enough time. Computers are wonderful tools for deciphering. They can scan through every possible combination of an encryption until they find the code that unlocks the message. This process is referred to as a *Brute Force*. For many years, a 40-bit RSA encryption was considered invulnerable. With the increased power of computers and the advancements in mathematical algorithms, it was broken. Computers will keep getting more powerful and mathematicians will keep coming up with new ways of code breaking.

Keyboard Readers

While not common, it is possible to "read" the keystrokes entered into a keyboard using a simple program that attaches to the keyboard driver. This program reads unencoded keystrokes and saves them into a file for later reference thus defeating any encryption placed on the inputted information.

Packet Sniffing

Packet sniffing is the process of attaching a piece of hardware or software to an existing network and watching the packets flow through. Data transmitted across the Internet is broken into packets. Each of these packets is vulnerable to sniffing. Packet sniffing is not illegal; it is used to diagnose network problems. Misuse of the information is illegal but it is extremely difficult to detect a packet sniffer.

Public Network Security

There are two general kinds of networks, private and public. The Internet is a public network and this chapter covers only security systems for a public network. Network security spans three concerns: privacy, message authentication, and signatures.

- Privacy in transmission over public networks is accomplished by encrypting the sensitive data with one of three private key algorithms: RC4, IDEA, or DES.

- Message authentication proves the data was not tampered with. The message is encoded with a one-way hash (an irreversible encoding) and the hash is encrypted with the sender's private key. The result is a message digest. The message digest can be opened with the sender's public key and compared to the hash of the received message. Current message digests include MD4, MD5 and SHS.

- A signature is proof of origin of the message. A signature is a bunch of information about the sender encrypted with a private key. The matching public key can be used to unlock the signature. Associated with signatures are certificates. Certificates are messages signed by a trusted central authority's private key that validate the sender and the public key of the sender for the current message. Certificates can be opened with the central authority's well-known public key.

An online reference for Internet security is the World Wide Web Consortium. Visit their security area at **http://www.w3.org/pub/WWW/Security/**.

Session Negotiation Protocols

Session Negotiation protocols allow two parties engaged in a secure transaction to negotiate and establish the encryption algorithm and protocol that will be used for the session. For example Client A has SSL and SHTTP available and Client B has SHTTP and PCT available. Within the negotiation, they will establish SHTTP as the session protocol. All this negotiation exists within the client/server software; users do not need to worry about how to negotiate for session protocols. Three session negotiation protocols are used: SSL version 3.0 supported by Netscape and Microsoft; S-HTTP supported by Spry & NCSA; and PCT supported by Microsoft. These three protocols all function basically in the same way: they provide for negotiating what security protocols and algorithms will be used for the session. They all depend on a public key algorithm, of which there are three to choose: RSA, Diffie-Hellman, and DSS.

- *SSL version 3.0 (Secure Socket Layer)* Netscape Communications Corporation has introduced and implemented SSL into their ubiquitous browser and Commerce Server. SSL provides privacy and a secure connection between the client and server. For online information about SSL, visit **http://proto.netscape.com/newsref/ref/netscape-security.html**.

- *S-HTTP (Secure HyperText Transport Protocol)* Verifone Inc. based in Menlo Park, CA has created and proposed the S-HTTP standard. S-HTTP uses the RSA public key cryptography and features end-to-end secure transactions. S-HTTP is an extension to the existing standard HTTP. For online information about S-HTTP, visit **http://www.ncsa.uiuc.edu/InformationServers/WebSecurity/index.html**.

- *PCT (Private Communication Technology)* Microsoft developed PCT as an enhancement and replacement of Netscape's SSL. It is designed for general purpose business and personal communications. PCT supports privacy, authentication and mutual identification. For more information about PCT, visit **http://pct.microsoft.com/**.

Encryption Algorithms

Encryption has been around for a long time. It involves taking a piece of data and making it unreadable. Encryption algorithms actually garble the data. They are used instead of public key encryption because they are much faster. Once the data is encrypted, it will appear as digital garbage to anyone that doesn't have the proper "key" to unlock or decode the data. Over a public network, encryption allows the transmission of secure information. The security of the data is only as good as the encryption algorithm. Three robust encryption algorithms are available for use: DES, RC4, and IDEA. For online information about encryption and cryptography, visit **http://axion. physics.ubc.ca/crypt.html**.

- *DES (Digital Encryption Standard)*   Developed in the 1950's by IBM, this is the standard used in ATM "PIN" numbers. DES uses only 56 bits in the encryption so is more susceptible to a brute force attack than RSA. DES is the standard accepted by the US government.

- *RC4 (Ron's Code 4)*   Ron Rivest of RSA developed RC4. It is marketed by RSA Inc. RSA claims that RC4 is 10 times faster than DES and it uses a variable key size in the algorithm.

- *IDEA (International Data Encryption Algorithm)*   Xuejia Lai and James L. Massey of ETH Zuria created IDEA. It uses a 128-bit key algorithm.

Public Key Algorithms

The implementation of Public Key Algorithms resolves the problem of encryption key management. When a piece of data is encrypted, a key is created to unencrypt the information. As long as you have the key, you can read the file. If you have multiple encrypted files it would be possible to have a number of "keys" that you would have to keep associated with the appropriate data. One way around this is to create two keys. One key is used to encrypt the data and the other is used to decrypt it. The key that encrypted the data cannot decrypt it. One key is called your private key, the other your public key. If someone wants to send you an encrypted message, they need to use your public key to encrypt it. Your public key is by nature, public, and therefore available to anyone who wants it. Any data encrypted with your public key can only be decrypted by your private key. This way, you only ever need one key.

Digital signatures ensure that the data is from the sender that the data says it is from and that the data has not been changed or modified en route. To create a digital signature, you encrypt information about yourself with your private key. Anyone with your public key can decrypt and thus check your signature. A one-way hash is created by sending the sensitive message through a function that results in some 'number', and then encrypting that number with your private key. Anyone with your public key can decrypt and thus check the enclosed hash against the hash of message received. The following may be used in the creation of public signature algorithms; RSA, Diffie-Hellman, DSS.

■ *RSA (Rivet-Shamir-Adleman)* This algorithm was developed by three mathematicians: Rivet, Shamir, and Adleman. RSA is the most commonly used public encryption algorithm. RSA is online at **http:// www.rsa.com/**.

■ *Diffie-Hellman* This is the first public key based encryption algorithm. Proposed by Whitfield Diffe and Martin Hellman. Diffe-Hellman is the basis of a number of implementations such as Pretty Good Privacy (PGP).

■ *DSS (Digital Signature Standard)* National Institute of Standards and Technology created this standard. DSS employs Digital Signature Algorithm (DSA) as the algorithm. DSA is much slower than RSA and it uses between 512 to 1024 bits for the encryption key.

eCash

eCash uses the concept of an electronic "coin." The coin retains its value before, during, and after a transaction. Each coin is actually a registered serial number with an associated value. The bank that created the coin maintains a database of their serial numbers to ensure no duplicates are created. Part of the serial number points to the specific minting bank. To make a purchase, the buyer sends sufficient electronic coins to the vendor. The vendor either deposits them into a bank account, or stores them for later use. Currently, the only bank to support eCash by exchanging it for "real money" is Mark Twain Bank. eCash requires that proprietary software be installed on both the customers' and merchants' computers. eCash uses a simple graphic interface that stays resident on the client's computer and acts as a kind of virtual Automatic Teller Machine (ATM). When the client asks to buy something, the merchant's eCash software will send a request to the client to confirm the purchase (see fig. 18.1).

When the client agrees to the payment by clinking on Yes, the payment amount, in this case, $0.02 is transferred from the client to the server. The display for the client will decrease to $34.98 and the server's balance will increase by the same amount.

This is a very simple, clean strategy for providing online shopping. However, there are some disadvantages:

■ The client must be running Windows 95 or Windows NT.

■ The sellers choice of Web server is limited to roughly one dozen servers.

■ eCash only supports two national currencies, US dollars and Finnish Markars.

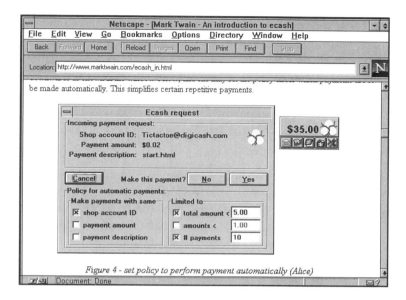

Fig. 18.1
Example of the
eCash interface.

Mark Twain Bank

Currently, Mark Twain bank is the only bank that will convert eCash in to real money. Mark Twain Bank is in partnership with DigiCash providing eCash for financial transactions. Mark Twain bank is located in St. Louis, Missouri. They are listed with the FDIC and they offer online services beyond eCash.

Mark Twain Bank maintains a Web space with information about eCash. We recommend their online tutorial located at **http:// www.marktwain.com/ecash_in.html**.

Who Uses eCash

A number of companies are currently using eCash to enable online shopping from their Web site. The following is a partial list of these merchants.

- AUTO-NET is an online forum to buy and sell used vehicles.
- Royal Copenhagen sells fine Jewelry from Denmark.
- Products from Zale sells steel framed homes, water filtration systems, books, food, and jewelry.
- BioNet offers herbs, homeopathies, vitamins, natural cosmetics and other healthful products.

Setting Up Shop-Server on Windows

Enabling someone to purchase from your Web site using eCash requires the server component of eCash called "shop-server." eCash has set up a server with the shop-server software, so a merchant can have their Web site hosted on the eCash server.

eCash works with the shop-server in the same way Netscape works with a Web server. eCash can only interact with a Web site that has the shop-server software installed and running.

If you have set up and are managing your own Web server. If you're leasing Web hosting from an Internet Service Provider, you may have problems setting up shop-server. Shop-server requires a CGI bin be set up and available. eCash has a set of CGI files created that once installed allows a customer with the installed client software to purchase products from you. The shop-server works very simply: When the client requests a hyperlink that you have designated as one that costs money, the shop-server sends a request to the client for payment. When the client accepts the request, the transaction takes place and the client receives or will receive the product. DigiCash has posted complete instructions for installing and setting up the shop-server on a number of different servers. Currently there are a limited number of servers that are known to be able to run shop-server.

DigiCash has a well-designed and informative Web site that describes eCash and offers all the component pieces needed to add eCash to your Web site (see fig. 18.2). Go to **http://www.digicash.com/**.

Fig. 18.2
DigiCash home
page.

These are the Web servers that can implement eCash:

EMWAC HTTPS server

WebSite

WebHub

Netscape Communications Server

Netscape Commerce Server

Netscape FastTrack Server

Microsoft Internet Information Server

Process Software Corporation Purveyor

Internet Factory Commerce Builder

Apache

NCSA

Microsoft Merchant Server is a Web server that will soon be able to implement eCash.

First Virtual

First Virtual is a small company that acts as a transaction broker. No custom software is required, unlike with eCash and CyberCash. All transactions are done through e-mail and then through regularly accepted channels. Neither the buyer nor the seller need worry about data encryption, key management, or other security concerns. First Virtual bills the merchant a fee for every processed transaction, similar to credit card companies.

How First Virtual Works

First Virtual acts as a transaction broker, when someone completes the process of buying a product from you, First Virtual will bill the buyer's credit card for the purchase. Generally these billings are every ten days and are a part of the regular credit card billing. If a buyer makes a series of small purchases that total less than US$10, First Virtual will wait ten days before posting them. After the buyer has paid his or her credit card bill and First Virtual has received the money from the credit card company (Visa or Mastercard), the money is held by First Virtual for 91 days before it is deposited into the seller's account. This holding period is designed to protect First Virtual from buyers who might contest the purchases and from the credit card company who might bill First Virtual for reimbursement.

The First Virtual based transactions are fairly straightforward, but time consuming. The buyer requests an item for purchase by entering a VirtualPIN; the seller tells First Virtual, who then sends an e-mail to the buyer to confirm the transaction. Once confirmed by the buyer, the transaction is processed by First Virtual.

All buyers must have a VirtualPIN to make purchases with the First Virtual system. The VirtualPIN is a buyer identifier. It does not contain any sensitive information such as credit card numbers. With First Virtual, no financial information is sent across the Internet.

To become a seller using First Virtual, you will need each of the following:

> A private e-mail account
>
> A Visa or Mastercard
>
> A checking account that accepts direct deposits through the United States ACH system
>
> A VirtualPIN, (supplied by First Virtual)

To use InfoHaus a buyer must have a VirtualPIN.

To make a purchase using First Virtual:

1. The buyer selects the product or item to purchase.

2. The server asks for and optionally confirms the validity of the buyers VirtualPIN.

3. The server notifies First Virtual of the transaction.

4. An e-mail is sent by First Virtual to the buyer to confirm the transaction

5. The buyer then does one of three things: replies "Yes" to confirm the purchase; replies "No" to decline to the purchase; or replies "Fraud" if they did not make the original purchase request.

6. When the buyer, replies with a Yes, his or her credit card is debited the amount of the purchase and the funds are directly deposited in to the seller's bank account.

Encryption System

First Virtual doesn't require any new or Internet-based encryption systems. First Virtual uses already established transactions systems for the transactions. Money changes hands through credit card billing, and direct deposits between the credit card companies, First Virtual and the seller. The only information needed is the VirtualPIN, which carries no financial information.

Who Uses First Virtual

There are a lot of companies using First Virtual. The following is a partial list of these merchants.

- *Reuters New Media*   Download detailed investor reports on a wide variety of publicly traded companies.

- *The Autoseller*   Buy/sell cars, trucks, motorcycles, RVs boats, and parts. The ads stay online until the vehicle sells.

- *The Washington Weekly*   The US national politics electronic news magazine.

- *Internet Society*   The Internet Society is the nongovernmental International Organization for global cooperation and coordination for the Internet and its internetworking technologies and applications.

Setting Up a First Virtual Account

To set up a account as a seller, you will need to get a VirtualPIN. To make it easy for a seller to get one, First Virtual maintains an online application form, at **http://www.fvcom/newacct/index.html**. Fill out this form and First Virtual will send you an e-mail with a 12-digit application number and instructions on mailing your bank information to First Virtual. You will receive an e-mail with your new sellers VirtualPIN when your account is set up. This application costs US$10. This process will work anywhere in the world, but all payments between you and First Virtual will be in US dollars. Once you have received your VirtualPIN, you can sign up with the InfoHaus, an online shopping mall (see fig. 18.3 and the next section). First Virtual offers a FV-API for adding this system to a Web server. An API is an "application programming interface" that allows a programmer to build applications using the technology built into the specific API. In this case, the FV-API is First Virtual's technology bundled to allow creation of more applications using First Virtual. But the FV-API is currently only available to UNIX servers. They do include source code, so it is possible to port over Windows NT, though there is no reference that this has been done by anyone.

> **Note**
>
> There are two types of VirtualPIN numbers, one for buyers and one for sellers. The buyer's VirtualPIN costs US$2, the seller's VirtualPIN costs US$10. To be a seller you must have a seller's VirtualPIN.

For more information about becoming a seller with First Virtual, visit **http://www.firstvirtual.com/info/sellerindex.html**.

Fig. 18.3
The First Virtual logo indicates a Web site that accepts payments using First Virtual.

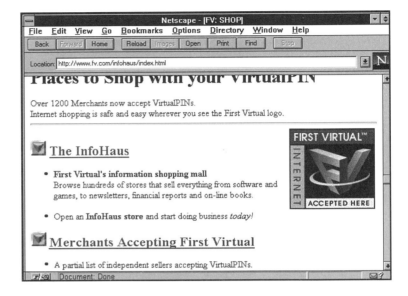

Welcome to the InfoHaus

The InfoHaus is First Virtual's shopping mall using their transaction system. You can sell anything legal through the InfoHaus: information, goods, and services. The InfoHaus supports both FTP and World Wide Web (HTTP) protocols.

Becoming an InfoHaus Merchant

Once you have your seller's VirtualPIN, you'll need to establish a commercial presence for yourself within the InfoHaus. You will need to send the InfoHaus a series of information including your business name, your VirtualPIN, the private e-mail account that is associated with your VirtualPIN, your preferred currency (currently your only choice is US dollars), your preferred language (currently English is your only choice), and a brief description of your business. This information can be sent to the InfoHaus either as a highly structured e-mail, (see their documentation located at**: http://www.fv.com/pubdocs/infohaus-guide-5.txt**) or it can be telnetted to them.

The InfoHaus maintains a structured directory of all the merchants who are set up with InfoHaus. Your listing can be a complete Web space with all the various HTML tricks or it can be a simple text listing of your services. The process for setting up a Web space with the InfoHaus is fairly involved and somewhat difficult given the choices of e-mailing or telnetting the information. It would be advisable to get a decent Telnet program for Windows NT if you want to set up and maintain a Web-based commercial presence within the InfoHaus. The InfoHaus bills for hosting your Web pages at a rate of $1.50 per megabyte of information per month. Additionally there is a $0.29 per transaction fee plus 2 percent of the transaction amount. There is a huge amount of information about the InfoHaus in the form of FAQs (Frequently Asked Questions). While it is not very structured, all the information is available for viewing. Navigating through FAQs is not a simple process. For more information about becoming an InfoHaus merchant, visit their Web site at: **http://www.infohaus.com/infohaus.html**.

Resources Available within the InfoHaus

There are already a large number of businesses who have signed up within the InfoHaus and that number is growing. While lacking a real search engine, the InfoHaus has divided up the listings into four different listings. A potential buyer can search by Topic, Business Name, Keyword, or Date. In addition to the FAQs mentioned above, the InfoHaus has created a Seller's guide, the InfoHaus Helpmeister, and a Newsletter. All of these are available from the InfoHaus home page: **http://www.infohaus.com/**.

Who Uses InfoHaus

There are hundreds of merchants using the InfoHaus. The following is a sample of some of them.

- *LandWare Inc.* Publisher of high-quality Mac, Newton, and Windows software.
- *PSYCHIC FRIENDS OF THE WEB* This business offers live 24-hour professional psychic consultation.
- 1ST INFOHAUS CONSULTING This business can help get a InfoHaus page started.

For more information about the InfoHaus, visit **http://www.infohaus. com/index.html**.

CyberCash

CyberCash is short for the CyberCash Wallet, which is the result of a cooperative agreement between CyberCash and VeriSign. The CyberCash Wallet gives a buyer the ability to purchase goods and services over the Web, and using a world-wide license of a 768-bit RSA encryption algorithm, CyberCash provides a secure channel for the transaction. The Wallet is a free software program, like eCash, that when installed on a computer allows CyberCash transactions.

How CyberCash Works

CyberCash works with the same basic structure as eCash and First Virtual. Figure 18.4 shows the six steps of this process. The process starts with a buyer requesting some product or service (step 1). The merchant's server sends a confirmation message to the buyer (step 2). When the buyer confirms the purchase, the merchant's server sends the transaction to CyberCash (step 3). CyberCash reformats the transaction data and sends it via regular dedicated lines to the merchant's bank (step 4). The Merchant's bank then sends an authorization request to the credit card company for the transaction authorization. When the approval (or denial) is complete, it is sent back to CyberCash with the approval code (step 5). CyberCash then sends the approval code to the Merchant who then forwards it to the buyer (step 6). This entire process takes between 15 and 20 seconds.

Fig. 18.4

The CyberCash transaction diagram.

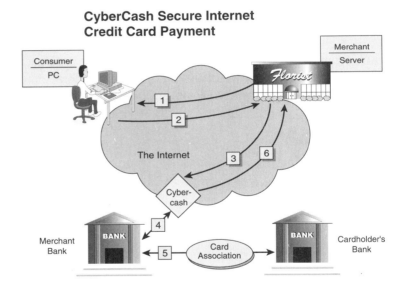

Requirements

CyberCash, like eCash and First Virtual, requires both the buyer and seller to set themselves up for using it. The following are the requirements for both buyers and sellers wishing to use CyberCash.

- Buyers will need the CyberCash Wallet, available for Windows 3.1, 95 and NT, Macintosh and PowerPC
- Merchants will need a merchant credit card account with their existing bank,
- A Terminal ID from the merchants bank for accepting Internet transactions
- CyberCash Wallet

CyberCash Wallet is compatible with the following Web browsers:

> FTP & Spyglass Enhanced NCSA Mosaic Version 1.15.111.0
>
> FTP & Spyglass Enhanced NCSA Mosaic Version 2.0
>
> Internet In A Box—Spry AirMosaic Version 03.0A.01.04
>
> InternetWorks Version 1.0.3
>
> NCSA Mosaic Version 2.0.0b4
>
> Netscape Version 1.1b3 and Version 1.1
>
> O'Reilly And Associates Enhanced NCSA Mosaic Release 1
>
> QuarterDeck Mosaic Prerelease 4

Setting Up a CyberCash Account

Setting yourself up as a merchant using CyberCash is relatively easy; there are explicit instructions online (see fig. 18.5 or go to **http://www.cybercash.com/cybercash/how/merch_setup.html**). There is an online application form at **http://www.cybercash.com/cybercash/how/merchantapplform.html** that you will need to fill out. After your application has been processed, CyberCash will contact you and begin setting up your online storefront, either on their or your server.

If your Web browser is not on the list of supported browsers, you will have to manually configure it to work with the CyberCash Wallet. CyberCash has instructions for doing this manual configuration.

Fig. 18.5
You can get
detailed informa-
tion online.

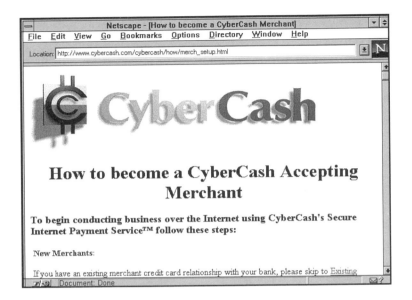

Who Uses CyberCash

CyberCash is being used by some fairly large Internet players, the following is a partial list of companies using CyberCash.

- *ElectroWeb*   A reseller of CD-ROM software, hardware, computer peripherals, consumer electronics, music and video games
- *Novell*   Novell's BrainShare '96 Web site. Learn about the latest Novell technologies.
- *Oracle*   Database development software
- *Price Online*   Price Club online

For more information about CyberCash, see **http://www.cybercash.com**.

Also, CyberCash has submitted RFC1898, a technical review of CyberCash Credit Card Protocol Version 0.8. This document describes in complete detail the workings of CyberCash. This and other RFCs are available on line at: **http://ds.internic.net/ds/dspg1intdoc.html**.

Type the RFC number (**RFC1898**) into the searchable field, and it will retrieve your requested RFC. An RFC is an Internet term meaning Request For Comments. When a new protocol is introduced to the Internet community, generally, an RFC is submitted.

Secure Pay

Secure Pay allows for purchasing products through checks. This system has been created by Redi-Check, based in Salt Lake City, Utah. Both CyberCash and First Virtual require the buyer or client to have a credit card. Secure Pay doesn't have this requirement. The buyer sets up an account with Secure Pay, giving them their checking account information, at Secure Pay's secure Web site and then chooses an account name and password. When the buyer wants to buy something, they enter their unique account name and password, which Secure Pay then validates. The buyer does not need any additional software. With Secure Pay, no financial information is transmitted over the Internet, so no security system is needed, (other than the initial sign up, which is secure).

Requirements

Secure Pay requires both the buyer and merchant to have bank accounts that will accept checks paid in US funds. No additional hardware or software is required.

How Secure Pay Works

Secure Pay is a fairly simple structure. A buyer purchases a product or service from your Secure Pay enabled site. The buyer will have entered their account name and password to make the purchase. This information along with the transaction re-sent to Redi-Check for verification. When verified, Redi-Check sends back a confirmation and then prints a check drawn against the buyers checking account and sends the check to the merchant via regular mail. The funds are available 24 hours after the purchase was made because Secure Pay cuts checks daily.

How To Set Up a Secure Pay Account

The first step to enabling Secure Pay as a merchant is to create a merchant account with Secure Pay (see fig. 18.6). They have set up an online order form at **http://www.redi-check.com/merchant/online.html**.

You will need to complete this form. The form allows Redi-Check to withdraw US$250 from your checking account as a one-time application and setup fee. Thereafter, there is a processing fee per transaction of 2 percent. After you have completed the application, Secure Pay will contact you to complete the process. Your account will be set up within two working days of submitting the application. Currently, Secure Pay can only handle US and Canadian funds; this affects the buyer more than the merchant.

Fig. 18.6
Fill out this form
to set up a Secure
Pay account.

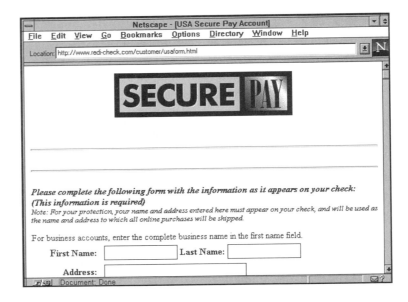

Visit the Secure Pay home page for information and applications at **http://www.redi-check.com**.

The following is a sample of the merchants using Redi-Check's services.

- Access Market Square Internet Shopping Mall
- Icentral's ShopSite
- Mentor and Associates
- Windows95.com

Web900

Web900 is a unique approach to online purchasing. Using the existing 900 number phenomenon for billing, the merchant can easily charge for online products. This strategy is designed more for selling "digital information" than durable goods. If you have a piece of software, you could sell it online very easily with this system.

Requirements

There are no special requirements for the buyer with Web900. The merchant needs to have a server that can run CGI scripts with either PERL version 4.0 or Visual Basic.

How Web900 Works

When a buyer wants to purchase something from you, he or she are shown a page that requests a redemption code. This code is available by calling a 900 number. When the buyer calls the number, the body of the message could simply be the redemption code. The buyer then enters that code into a CGI form which validates the code against an already existing block of codes the merchant has on their server. The buyer will be billed for the 900 number call on their phone bill in increments of US$10 and US$25. When Web900 receives payment from the phone company, they will forward 80 percent of the total to the merchant, keeping 20 percent as a transaction fee. See figure 18.7.

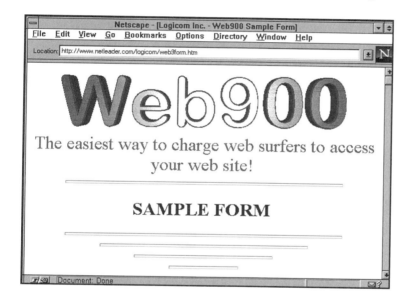

Fig. 18.7
Web900 sample form.

How To Set Up a Web900 Account

You will need to fill out the service agreement and fax it to Web900. The form is located at **http://www.netleader.com/logicom/webagree. htm**. While you're getting the form, follow the links to "Sample CGI Script" and download the CGI scripts for your system. Use the Visual Basic-based CGI script if you are using a WINS directory, use the other PERL-based CGI scripts if you are using a CGI-Bin directory. Web900 has created the form to use for requesting the redemption code. Follow the links to and download a copy of this form. Make sure you keep their information intact on the form because Web900 requires it.

After they have received your agreement, Web900 will send redemption codes to you as an e-mail attachment. Also they will have created your account. With the codes copied to the appropriate directory, the CGI script will work. If you have problems setting up the CGI script or placing the code file, you can contact Web900, they will walk you through the setup.

Web900 processes checks on the 15th of every month for 45 days prior. For example, the transactions that occurred in February will be processed on April 15th.

You can find Web900 online at **http://www.netleader.com/logicom/ web900.htm.**

Secure Web Servers

Many infopreneurs simply accept credit cards over the Internet by utilizing a secure Web server. No e-cash, virtual checks, or cyber-dollars are needed. Your customers will likely demand that you protect their financial details by implementing a secure Web server. Most credible Web server software companies have either delivered a secure server or are about to.

This chapter discusses a few of the high profile secure Web servers.

Netscape Commerce Server

Netscape has implemented a complete commerce strategy based on its Commerce server and browser. Additionally, Netscape has created the following resources for commercial transactions on the Internet:

> Merchant System
>
> Publishing System
>
> Community System
>
> IStore

Each of these software packages is based on the Netscape Commerce server. Each streamlines the creation of an online business. These are all complete solutions tailored for different business needs. The Merchant system is designed to provide all the necessary tools and support structures for large business to create online shopping malls or large online retail stores. The Publishing system allows for online subscription-based publications.

The Community system allows for the integration of bulletin boards, real-time chat services, and private groups. IStore is the basic package that allows merchants to create an online store with sample templates.

The Commerce Server is designed to allow secure commercial transactions. All of the security features are built into the server and are available through the administration utilities. The Commerce Server uses the Secure Socket Layer (SSL) protocol to provide security. SSL sits between the TCP/IP stack and the HTTP protocol. There SSL can provide a number of security features including: server authentication, data encryption and verifiable data integrity.

Who Uses Netscape Commerce Server

The following organizations are using some or all of Netscape's Merchant System:

- *Cybersuperstores* **http://www.cybersuperstores.com/cyber.html**
- *ISN (Internet Shopping Network)* **http://www.internet.net/**
- *Bank of America* **http://www.bankamerica.com**
- *Disney.com* **http://www2.disney.com/**
- *The Wall Street Journal on the Web* **http://www.wsj.com**

Client Software

The Netscape Commerce strategy relies on the client's use of Netscape's Web browser version 2.0. No additional software is required for the customer.

You can find more information about Netscape's support of commercial transactions on the Internet at **http://home.netscape.com/comprod/products/iapps/index.html**.

WebQuest Secure Server

The WebQuest server by Questar Microsystems will have a secure Web server available to the public by the end of the first quarter 1996. This server will support Microsoft's security protocol PCT. Some of the advantages of the WebQuest server are price, roughly a tenth the price of the Netscape package, ease of use and installation, and its support of additional Internet protocols.

Client Software

WebQuest's secure server supports both Netscape 2.0 and Internet Explorer 2.0. It will also support NCSA Mosaic's secure client (version 3.0) when it is released.

For more information on how Questar's WebQuest has implemented PCT and to download a copy of the server, visit the WebQuest home page at **http://www.questar.com/webquest.htm**.

Microsoft Internet Information Server

Microsoft's Internet Information Server supports secure transactions over the Internet through SSL and RSA encryption. Currently, Microsoft's IIS SSL only works with Microsoft's Internet Explorer 2.0.

Microsoft is working on a suite of applications similar to Netscape's Merchant System. This suite will be a combination of: Microsoft's Merchant server, a server linked to databases, which will allow secure financial transactions; the Merchant workbench, similar to Netscape's IStore and a client "shopping utility" which will make online shopping easier and more consistent for the buyer. All these products will be available from Microsoft some time in mid-1996. Microsoft has not established pricing for these software packages, though they will probably be significantly less expensive than Netscape's current prices.

Visit Microsoft's home page at **http://www.microsoft.com** and follow the link to "Search" and there search for "Electronic Retailing" and "Internet Information Server."

Shopping Carts/Shopping Malls

In addition to the online shopping malls discussed above, InfoHaus and the IStore, there are number of online shopping malls. The following is a short list found by using Yahoo:

> **http://www.opse.com/mallistings/**
>
> **http://malls.com/**
>
> **http://www.hummsoft.com/hummsoft/shopper.html**
>
> **http://worldshopping.com/**

As a merchant, you have the choice of using an existing "shopping mall" for hosting your Web site or hosting your Web site. If you choose the first, the above listing will give you a place to start. Look for a "shopping mall" that supports a search engine and is easy to navigate.

CGI Scripts

Some companies have built their own CGI scripts that allow them to sell online. Buyers are asked to post their credit card information when buying products. This strategy is fairly easy to implement and also fairly easy to break. The best way to implement this strategy is with a secure server like Netscape's Commerce Server. That way the connection between the client and server is encrypted and secure, making fraud very difficult. The actual implementation of the CGI will depend on what resources are available with your system, PERL, C++, Visual Basic, and on the abilities of the CGI programmer.

There is a large body of information online about CGI scripts. A good place to start is **http://the-inter.net/www/future21/cgia.html**.

Alternatives

In addition to the strategies reviewed above, there are other, in some ways simpler, ways of handling online commerce. Some companies allow people to place orders over the Internet and then deal with billing through common interfaces.

Taking Orders (COD)

One of the most common ways of offering products for sale over Internet is to take orders and then deliver products COD. This approach has some very distinct advantages. The interface is very simple to create. A basic HTML form that posts the order information to your e-mail account or some sort of database is easy and quick to create. Sending product COD resolves all concerns about security and fraud, by using an existing "secure" system. The other obvious benefit is that customers without checks can purchase products from you. A twist on this is to send customers a "bill" before sending out the merchandise. When the customer has paid the bill, you send out the product. These implementations are simply a carry over from mail-order catalogs.

Establishing Accounts

Another strategy commonly used is to require customers to establish an account with the merchant. Anyone can order over the Internet, again from a Web page form, but only those customers with an account will receive the products or services. You can require a potential customer to call you with their credit card number to establish an account, or require that they send you a check for a set amount and require them to maintain a minimum balance. A merchant using this strategy would ship only to people with established accounts. One advantage to this is existing systems are used to process transactions. People are used to giving out their credit card number over the phone. And depending on the implementation, creating an "account" is not unfamiliar to the general public.

Summary

The frictionless economy is on it's way. There are clearly many companies racing to develop a clean and secure interface for buying on the Internet. A standard has yet to be set, but many opportunities are available to the resourceful infopreneur.

Merchants who opt for setting up on the Internet will likely reap many benefits in both the savings they will see and the volume of business they will transact. It can certainly be much cheaper to set up a virtual store than a real one. Your virtual store will have many of the same challenges as a "real" store. You will need to market and promote to attract customers and assure them of a safe, secure place to shop. This chapter covered a lot of material; from here, use the Net to continue your explorations and craft a solution that is appropriate for your business and vision. ❖

## CHAPTER 19

Interactive and Live Applications

In previous chapters, you have explored Web interaction on the most basic of levels: HTML file transfer, forms, usage counters, and other elemental forms of information exchange. This chapter is devoted to the exploration of the next generation of interactivity and the advent of the *live* application—an application that integrates aural and visual response or information exchange.

The first section of this chapter examines the state-of-the-art for audio and video usage in interactive and live applications and advanced interactive concepts, such as live video conferencing. Commercial and noncommercial applications, tools and peripherals, and sites for both resources and interaction are described or provided.

The second section of this chapter presents techniques for expanding the interactivity of the Web. This section includes discussions of the proposed methods for implementing new interactive concepts, such as Auralview, W3Vision, and WebStage sessions. It also covers the fast growing area of virtual reality interactivity.

Your vision of this new interactivity is not limited to only existing technology. You do turn outward and examine where you can go and what the near and not-too-distant future may have in store for those who travel the Information Superhighway.

In this chapter, you learn about:

- Live applications to add multimedia to your Web site
- Tools for implementing advanced interactive applications
- Virtual reality engines and applications
- Resource sites for sound bites, video clips, and more

Interactive and Live Application Concepts

This section examines state-of-the-art audio and video toolsets and development technology, interactive applications, and example sites. Some advanced interactive concepts under discussion are: audio and video servers and clients and real-time video conferencing. Commercial and noncommercial tools and peripherals, applications, and sites covering both resources and example interaction will be described and/or provided.

To enjoy a firm footing in the coming discussion, it is necessary to have an understanding of certain basic concepts. Within this section, the concept of *server* and *client* appears. It is not unlike the standard references to client/ server in use today.

A *server* is a system that consists of both hardware and software that can offer an exchange of information and access to the services, software, or supplies required by the server's Web site visitor. Because the information transactions that are described in this section are audio, video, or a combination of both, the amount of information that needs to be exchanged is usually quite large. Add to this the security issues involved and because some of the *servers* on the Net are actually companies or organizations that are in the business of supplying these information transactions for a fee, the necessity arises for a controlled method for accessing this information—the *client*.

The client is also a combination hardware and software system. The software application is responsible for any security or access issues, but must also provide an acceptable method for transferring large files across the Net in a timely manner. The problem is greatly enhanced for applications that transfer large amounts of information that must be delivered in real-time.

Hardware issues also determine the *lag* time encountered with these transactions. Even having the highest speed connection (ISDN or T1) doesn't ensure that a timely transaction can occur.

During the design phase of your Web site, it is imperative that you define what type of hardware and software you expect your users to have. This will aid you in developing the look, feel, and content of the information you supply.

The toolsets, resource sites, and information supplied in this section deal with these subjects as necessary.

Audio Tools/Applications and Example Sites

One of the most popular options that you can add to your developing Web site is *streaming* or *on-demand audio*. On-demand audio allows visitors to your site to have access to audio that is transferred across the Net at speeds that allow the visitor to listen to audio in real-time.

How do you supply audio in real time? The secret to transferring the vast amount of information required for real-time audio is to use data compression techniques. This is a fast developing area of Internet technology and there are several methods that can be used to accomplish compression.

However, prior to selecting a satisfactory compression technique, it is imperative to ensure the *quality* of the audio offered to your Web site visitor. Taking a simple series of steps can ensure that you develop a high level of quality for your audio.

The First Step to Quality Audio

There are a few simple rules that you should follow to achieve the highest quality sound. It is very important to achieve a high level of quality because, as you will read shortly, the method that you use to encode the audio permanently alters the quality.

Use a High-Quality Original Source and Quality Equipment. Perhaps the single greatest factor in determining the level of audio quality is the audio source. The source that you use is determined by the equipment available to you. Some of the best sources of quality audio are:

Source	Quality Level
Audio compact discs (CDs)	High
Digital audio tapes (DATs)	High
Analog cassettes (pre-mastered)	Medium
Vinyl records	Low

To develop quality sound from scratch, you can use:

Source	Quality Level
Professional high-quality microphones	Highest quality
Condenser microphones	Lowest quality

(continues)

(continued)

Source	Quality Level
Professional recording equipment or facilities (i.e., multichannel recorders, sound rooms, mixing boards)	Highest quality
Home variety recording equipment or facilities (i.e., cassette tape recorders, bathrooms, ironing boards)	Lowest quality

Tip

One of the best resource lists for professional audio equipment can be found at **http://www.magicnet.net/rz/world_of_audio/gear/gear1.html**.

Try to encode your audio from 16-bit source files that were digitized with a 22.05 kHz sampling rate. Most compression techniques accept multiple other forms of source files (such as 8-bit or µLaw).

When you're creating audio sources, keep in mind that you can use any production resource. However, the encoding done by the compression algorithm can cause hiss and distortion.

Source files that were recorded at either 8000 Hz or 11000 Hz are also acceptable, but, once again, remember the favorite saying of computer geeks everywhere—GIGO (pronounced guy go), which stands for Garbage In, Garbage Out. If you want quality, start with the optimum quality available.

Remember, high-quality equipment will produce high-quality results. This is true for every element in the recording chain, from the input source to the audio capture device to the software used for capturing and editing. A little forethought about your audio source file's origin can save you headaches down the road. If you intend to provide commercial audio services at your Web site, you ought to invest in professional audio equipment. This type and level of equipment doesn't have to break your piggy bank, but it is professional equipment that should be acquired from a professional recording equipment dealer, rather than from a fly-by-night Gadget Supply or your local computer/hi-fi/appliance store.

Control the Recording Level. Create an audio source file for use on your Web site by using an internal sound card. There are many manufacturers of sound cards on the market. One of the Creative Labs' SoundBlaster is the de facto standard for the industry. Selecting the type of sound card you use should be based on the criteria previously listed concerning the quality of the audio source file required and the type of computer system that performs the sound capture.

> **Tip**
>
> One of the best resource lists for audio equipment and other sources is located at **http://www.music.mcgill.ca**.

Regardless of which card you use, setting the correct level of input to your sound card is critical. When an input signal exceeds the full range of amplitude available to your sound card (or any other piece of audio equipment), the result is a level that *crowns* the input amplifier. Crowning the input amplifier causes a flattening of the input that results in a clipped signal. Clipping is audible in the resulting source file as a high frequency, crackling noise.

Digitizing with your sound card requires a simple but methodical approach to achieve the finest, quality results. Using your selected audio source, you should perform several *test runs* adjusting your input level until it approaches but doesn't exceed the maximum level for the sound card input amplifier.

> **Tip**
>
> Most sound card manufacturers supply a set of utilities that perform specific tasks on their card. The input level of the various sources of audio being supplied to the sound card can usually be adjusted using a mixer utility.

> **Note**
>
> Look for an adjustment labeled Input Level or Recording Level. Most mixer utilities use some sort of visual display to provide you with either the level of sound coming in or a paddle control that is used to adjust the sound level. Ensure that no peaks above maximum occur. Generally, these excursions are indicated by a red light or red band in the case of Visual VU Meters. Be conservative with your level adjustments; you never know when an unexpected volume increase can occur.

Audio source files that do not use the optimum range of input amplitude ultimately produce unsatisfactory compressed files.

Digital Audio Editors. Once you have either created a sound file or received a sound file, you can manipulate and edit this file using a Windows-based editor.

In addition to your sound card manufacturer's set of utilities, an Audio Editor can be used to correct for errors that may have crept into your audio source file. An amplitude range that is too low can be increased or normalized; hisses and pops and other forms of distortion can be erased and the overall time of the audio recording can be changed. You can also change the file to add sound effects and even merge multiple sound files together.

Transmission Bandwidth versus Audio Type. Live audio compression techniques optimize compressed files according to the type of audio recorded and being transmitted. Speech delivery can usually be performed adequately at a transmission rate of 14.4 Kbps. Delivering music at 14.4 is a much more difficult challenge.

Encoding music for transmission to users that are connected to the Internet at 14.4 Kbps requires forethought in your music selection. It is important to remember that when transmitting audio, or video for that matter, a certain amount of bandwidth is required to do the original source justice. Transmitting a live version of the Podunk International Symphony Orchestra's version of Rossini's Overture to William Tell might be a wonderful service your Web site could supply; however, if you attempt to transmit this harmonically complex signal over a 14.4 Kbps modem, you cannot do the piece justice. Applications where the ultimate fidelity of the music is not as important as other content, such as using music as a background for advertisements where the vocal message is the primary purpose of the audio source, result in a much more successful application.

As you can imagine, using a system that uses 28.8 Kbps analog modems or ISDN and T1 digital modems results in higher bandwidth and, therefore, in greater capabilities. Increasing your bandwidth allows for greatly improved frequency response, a greater dynamic audio range, and a decrease in the number of artifacts, those *holes* in a decompressed file that cause audio noise and video flutter.

The Second Step to Quality Audio

Creating compressed files that meet the requirements discussed in the previous section requires the use of quality software that can encode the files using algorithms that make guesses as to what is most important in the audio source file. The algorithm encoder contains a predefined list of elements within a sound stream. All elements are weighted against each other and then are used to modify the stream according to each element's weight. The common elements used by encoders consist of the following:

- Transmission Bandwidth—usually either 14.4 Kbps or 28.8 Kbps
- Audio Compression
- Audio Equalization
- Noise Gating
- Audio Normalization

Transmission Bandwidth. As previously discussed, the transmission bandwidth is selected when you are determining what type of audio sources you plan to offer as a service. The encoding software uses this information to determine how much time it has in which to put the preprocessed audio source information. The overall reproduction fidelity and quality of your decompressed [expanded] files will be determined by the bandwidth available for determining various audio signal qualities.

Audio Compression. Have you ever noticed a weird rumbling noise, low frequency hum, or other strange form of distortion in an audio file that you are playing? The cause of that sound is not faulty playback software or cheap hardware, rather it is due to a side effect of encoding/compressing an audio signal—an *artifact*. This is a sound that wasn't there before encoding or compressing.

The suppression of audio artifacts is one reason that you want to supply the loudest signal possible to your sound card. Audio artifact signals are relatively low volume sounds. It doesn't really matter whether the original sound file was loud or quiet. Louder files tend to mask artifacts. Although your desire is to supply the loudest source file possible to the compression algorithm, you are limited by the amplitude of the loudest sound in the source. It only stands to reason that if you could control the variation between the loudest and softest signals you were compressing, you could effectively turn up the overall volume of the source file. This is where audio compression techniques enter the picture.

Audio compression reduces the difference between the loudest and softest areas of an incoming source file. What the audio compressor does is to use a predefined threshold to determine which input signal levels should be turned down and which should be left alone. How much control there is for turning areas of the source signal file up or down depends on how much compression is used.

Compression guidelines are rough at best and algorithmic guesses are based on years of experience. There are general rules-of-thumb, however, that should be helpful in most situations:

- Speech compression ratios at 14.4 Kbps—moderate to extreme, 4:1 to 10:1. This guarantees that the signal is loud enough to mask artifacts that are more apparent at this transmission rate.

- Speech compression ratios at 28.8 Kbps—low to moderate, 2:1 to 4:1. With a transmission rate of 28.8 Kbps, the dynamic range is greatly increased and the artifacts greatly reduced.

- Music compression ratios at 14.4 Kbps—moderate to moderately high, 4:1 to 6:1. Again, determined by the increase in artifacts and also the limited dynamic range of the supported audio.

- Music compression ratios at 28.8 Kbps—extremely low to moderate, 1:1 to 3:1. With the greater dynamic range, even a symphony orchestra would reproduce excellently.

Noise Gating. Noise gating is a function of audio compression. Simply put, it is the act of eliminating unwanted background noise that becomes audible during gaps in an audio signal. As in audio compression, noise gating is determined by setting a specific volume level above which signal amplitude is left alone but below which the signal is turned down or off. Even the least expensive compressors usually have some form of noise gating built in.

Audio Equalization. Equalization is a bit of a mystery to most people. Even though their automobile and home audio systems usually have some form of equalization control, most people have no idea what equalization is meant for or how to determine what changes to make in the settings that came set from the factory.

Simply stated, equalization changes the frequency formula of an audio signal. This is accomplished by boosting (turning up) or cutting (turning down) certain frequencies or frequency ranges. Ultimately, equalization is meant to compensate for frequency variations in the surrounding space. The response characteristics of your apartment or your car can be compensated for by using equalization. In addition, using specialized equalization systems, you can also compensate for some slight variations in the flat response curve of your speakers.

Attempting to use equalization for its intended purpose with sound files that you intend to supply over the Net is ludicrous, at best. However, you can use equalization to control another aspect of an audio signal—clarifying the signal. Clarifying the signal is essentially suppressing or filtering unwanted background noise or annoying frequencies. Using equalization, you can boost frequencies where the important content is and cut frequencies where the noise or unwanted sound is.

Some simple equalization systems only define ranges that it offers equalization for (that is low-, mid-, and high- range). Some systems allow you to choose which frequency to boost, other systems are preset at the factory. If you can select the boost frequency, or if you are using a graphic equalizer or audio processing software, begin the mid-range boost at 2.5 kHz. This mid-range boost, coupled with cutting out the high- and low- range signals, provides the clarifying effect that you generally desire.

Advanced graphic equalizers offer far more range selections and control. Whatever system you have, remember that the amount for each range depends on your equipment and source file. Experiment.

Audio Normalization. The last process that you can use to create the ultimate audio source is normalization. This is normally a software process included in most audio recording and editing software. In this process, the computer calculates how much the volume of a sound file can be turned up without causing distortion. This allows you to be conservative with your recording input levels and lets your audio recording or editing software normalization function adjust the signal levels. Just remember the following:

- Don't normalize your sound file and then perform any other form of control on your file or you'll end up with distortion.

- Never normalize at 100 percent; it may cause compression algorithms to fail. Normalizing at 90 to 95 percent will work effectively in most cases.

The Final Step to Quality Live Audio

You can now focus on your task at hand. How do you add quality audio services to your Web site? Using the guidelines described previously, you can develop applications that provide live audio feeds to your Web site visitors or you can subscribe to one of the existing methodologies.

Luckily, developing interactive and live application sites on the Internet has become quite a bit easier. Several companies have stepped to the forefront to offer development technology to enable the Web site creator easily implemented methods for creating audio *servers* that provide on-demand audio services to new users, subscribers, and visitors. In addition, each of these *server* applications comes with multiple platform *client* pairs that can be downloaded from the server or from any number of similar sites on the Web.

The audio tools described below are three of the most popular *client-server* pairs currently available. As previously mentioned, new toolsets and development tools are appearing all the time.

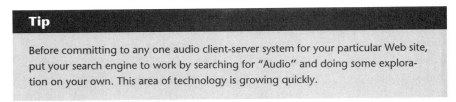

Tip

Before committing to any one audio client-server system for your particular Web site, put your search engine to work by searching for "Audio" and doing some exploration on your own. This area of technology is growing quickly.

RealAudio. RealAudio is currently the most popular *client-server* pair development tool available. RealAudio provides a complete set of on-demand audio software products including: audio servers, audio clients, and encoders.

RealAudio's home page is at **http://www.realaudio.com/** (see fig. 19.1). This home page provides download access for all RealAudio software products.

Fig. 19.1
The RealAudio home page where you can download software.

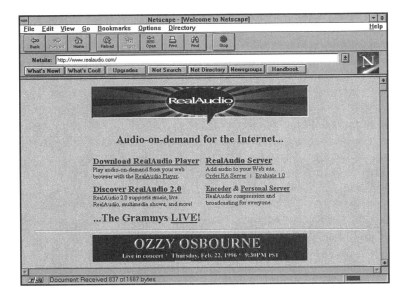

Selecting the RealAudio receiver download hypertext link opens another Web page that allows you to order the RealAudio Receiver software for several different operating systems: Windows 3.x, Windows 95/Windows NT, Mac, and a Japanese version.

Selecting the RealAudio server hypertext link opens another Web page that allows you to either order the RealAudio Server software or receive an evaluation copy that can be used to determine if the RealAudio Server system fits your specific Web site requirements.

Selecting the RealAudio Encoder hypertext link opens another Web page that lets you order the RealAudio Encoder software for several different operating systems: Windows 3.x, Windows 95/Windows NT, and several versions for the Mac.

TrueSpeech. TrueSpeech, available from DSP Group, Inc., is a new presence in the world of on-demand audio. The TrueSpeech system is being used by a growing number of live radio sites that are cropping up on the Net. An example of TrueSpeech being used for live radio and music sources is discussed later at the San Francisco Audio Network site. (Refer to the following section on example sites.) The DSP Group, Inc.'s home page is at **http://www.dspg.com/** (see fig. 19.2).

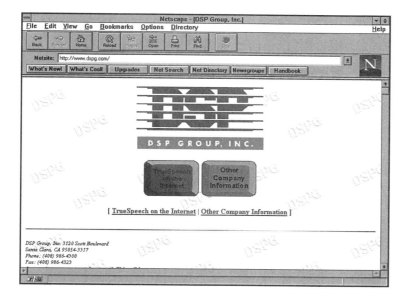

Fig. 19.2
The DSP Group, Inc.'s TrueSpeech home page.

This home page provides download access for their software products. To gain access to the download page, you double-click the TrueSpeech button, which opens another Web page where you can download the TrueSpeech Audio Receiver or view the TrueSpeech video across the Net.

Double-clicking the TrueSpeech logo opens an additional page where you can download the TrueSpeech Receiver for several versions of Windows, a couple of versions for the Mac, and a Japanese language version.

StreamWorks. StreamWorks, available from Xing Technology Corporation, is one of the fastest growing live audio programs. Part of the reason for this is, undoubtedly, their additional presence in the world of real-time video (refer to later in this chapter for a discussion of the real-time video sources) Xing Technology Corporation also provides a complete set of on-demand audio software products including audio servers and audio receivers. XingTechnology Corporation's home page is at **http://www.xingtech. com/** (see fig. 19.3). This page gives you download access for all of their software products. To gain access to the download page you double-click the StreamWorks logo.

Fig. 19.3
This is Xing
Technology
Corporation's
home page.

Once you have double-clicked the StreamWorks logo, you go to a page where you can download StreamWorks Audio Server information, order the StreamWorks on-demand audio client software for any version of Windows, MAC, or UNIX OSs, or test drive a StreamWorks audio server running at Xing Technology Corporation Headquarters.

Interactive Audio Sites

Having the desire to provide live audio across the Net, the next question should be, how do you present it to your visitor? There are a number of excellent sites that you can use as an example of interactive audio sites. These sites can provide methods that you can use to set up an audio server. These sites can be used as examples of ways for you to offer various services: the ability to explore new music; obtain sound bites, obtain freeware, shareware, and commercial demos of applications; and so on.

For an example of a site that uses the RealAudio Server visit Computer Express' home page at **http://www.dspg.com/allplyr.htm** (see fig. 19.4). Computer Express supplies computer hardware and software and uses audio on-demand for advertising purposes, one of the many applications for audio on the Net.

Fig. 19.4
Computer Express:
An example site
using RealAudio's
RealAudio Server

For an example of a site that uses the DSP Group's TrueSpeech Audio Server visit the San Francisco Audio Network home page at **http://www.sfaudio.net/sfan_logo.html**. The San Francisco Audio Network supplies a wide variety of audio services to their subscribers including the ability to sample new audio CDs and listen to live radio.

For an example of a site that uses the Xing Technologies StreamWorks Audio Server visit Xing Technology Corporation's Test Drive page at **http://www.xingtech.com/streams/streams.html**. The StreamWorks Test Drive offers visitors sample uses of their Audio Server: live radio broadcasts from KWBR FM 95.3 at 16 Kbps, classical music on ISDN's 112 Kbps, and a talk radio sports program from KKAL at 10 Kbps. These are prime examples of the types of functions that on-demand audio can offer over the Net.

Xing Technology's StreamWorks Test Drive page provides the perfect segue into the next subject: live video. The Test Drive page provides a sample of the StreamWorks audio/visual server.

Video Tools, Applications, and Sites

Auralview technologies are rapidly encroaching on the Internet's back country. Daily, you find that ASCII domination is being strongly challenged by Internet *auralview* capabilities. Live audio servers, video servers, and video conferencing systems are appearing almost daily. And while some may find it necessary to be running their Internet applications on a Sun SPARCstation with an MBONE feed, your average, run-of-the-mill, garden variety Windows NT machines certainly give them a run for their money.

Live video provides visitors to your Web site access to video information that can be transferred across the Net at speeds that are approaching real-time. The underlying technology for live video is developing rapidly, the hardware is becoming less expensive, and both are available to the business and home user. Before deciding to supply video resources to your Web site, however, there are several items that must be defined and certain resources acquired.

The following sections outline a series of steps that you can take to insure that you develop a high-quality suite of video information and provide that to your Web site visitor.

Use High-Quality Original Sources and Quality Equipment

One of the greatest factors in determining the level of video quality is using high-quality video sources. The source that you use is, of course, determined by your access to required equipment; however, here a few of the better sources of quality video:

Video CDs	Highest quality
Professional video cassette tapes	High quality tapes
Video Captured AVI Files	Unknown quality
Homemade video cassette tapes	Lowest quality

For developing quality video from scratch, you can use:

Professional video cameras	Highest quality
Computer video cameras	High quality
Home video cameras	Lowest quality
Professional recording equipment and facilities	Highest quality
Home variety recording equipment and facilities	Lowest quality

High-quality equipment will produce high-quality results. This is true for every element in the recording chain, from the input source to the video capture device to the software used for capturing and editing. Remember, a little forethought into your video source file's origin can save you headaches down the road. If you intend to add commercial video services to your Web site, you should invest in professional video equipment. Don't try to obtain professional equipment from anyone but a professional recording equipment dealer. Should your desire to provide video services outweigh your pocketbook, remember to get the highest-rated devices within your budget and put extra effort into acquiring quality source material.

Control the Color

Control of the color spectrum in your video source is of prime importance. The following are a few hints usually followed in the video production community:

- When selecting still backgrounds or color highlights always use color spectrums that are easily duplicable on an SVGA color monitor. You should attempt to preview your image through NTSC/PAL/HDTV output devices.

- Don't place saturated complementary (blue/yellow, black/white) colors next to each other since they may color-bleed.

- Don't use highly saturated colors, especially red, as they tend to color-bleed.

- Remember, the human eye is better at distinguishing differences in intensity than it is in distinguishing differences in hue. So use intensity as the primary variable and then hue, reserving saturation for more subtle differences.

- Control brightness and contrast.

- High saturation background colors should be especially avoided. Dark blue is a good background color.

Color differences are important within a single image or an animated image. Don't move the camera quickly, change from bright sunlight to shadow, or change between strikingly different subject matter. You must be sure not to change colors too quickly. This can result in a disturbing visual flickering.

Adding Textual Information

If you plan to edit your video and add textual information, make sure that your image and text are both contained within the expected screen size. In other words, don't let your text information get too close to the edge of your image. A good rule of thumb is don't place text closer than 1/10 of the overall screen size to any screen edge.

If you plan on changing the text displayed on the screen, allow for adequate delay time. This delay should be proportional to the text's complexity. Two to three seconds is fine for a word or two or a short sentence. Longer times are appropriate for more text; however, dense text should be avoided. Time yourself reading the text displayed and then add a few extra seconds. Also, text should not exceed twenty characters per line and you should use large font sizes (greater than 30 pt) for titles.

Applying Shapes and Frames

If you intend to add shapes such as circles, squares, frames, or other non-linear shapes, don't use single pixel-wide lines. If you do, you most likely will find that vertical lines lose their color and horizontal lines flicker. Both result in an annoying video. Most video editors allow you to set line width sizes; choose a line width of at least two pixels.

Motion Video, Animation, and Other Moving Bodies

Animated subjects are worthy of great detailed explanations. It is not within the scope of this book to approach that depth of discussion; however, a few hints certainly can't hurt.

If you plan on using a revolving or moving object, time your motion correctly. Rotating objects should complete a revolution within three to eight seconds, depending on the complexity of the rotating shape. You should test this on yourself and colleagues. If you make the motion too slow, the end result may be very boring; make it too fast and the motion won't seem realistic or might be difficult for the eye to follow. For moving objects, be sure that the speed of the motion is not too slow to put the viewer to sleep and is fast enough to hold the viewer's interest. Don't make your viewers' heads spin with excessive motion. Effective frame rate can be slowed down to achieve different visual effects. If you play a video at five to six frames per second (fps), the end result is a "slow motion" look. Increasing the speed to nine to ten fps results in a "jittery" video. Full motion for the human eye is 30 fps. Control your effects carefully because their results on your video can be immense.

Miscellaneous

The image aspect ratio of your finished video is also an important factor to remember. If you have ever tried to watch a movie that was shot in VistaVision on your standard television, you have run into the problem of improper aspect ration. Be sure that your final video image conforms to the aspect ratio of the viewing device—the SVGA monitor your visitors are using.

> **Note**
>
> The correct aspect ratios for NTSC, PAL, and HDTV are 4:3, 4:3, and 16:9, respectively. Computer displays, as a rule, do not conform to these ratios. As a result, video images with these aspect ratios appear distorted when viewed.

When recording your video masters, or when selecting masters that have been prerecorded, choose the highest resolution video format available. Any and all subsequent videos can then be dubbed from this master.

> **Note**
>
> When comparing the resolution of various video source standards, use the following guide. Resolution increases from left to right in the following formats:
>
> **VHS -> SVHS -> Hi8 -> BetaCam SP -> D2 Digital**

Video Transmission Bandwidth

Since you have already determined the transmission bandwidth of our video server, you need not concern yourself with the concept of fps transfer rates. Your only concern at this time should be with compression.

Compress or Don't Compress: Your Two Options

Taking a quick trip around the Internet and the World Wide Web in search of live video results in some startling revelations. If you attempt to run uncompressed video in a full motion mode, using a 14.4 Kbps modem, the time such running takes is incredibly long. This is certainly not full motion video. Choosing to use one of the available video servers or video conferencing servers that are available has to be a determining factor in both your equipment decisions (that is, going to an ISDN modem and supporting analog modems) and in your choice of Web site server. These are choices that you have to make based on need, funds, available equipment, and target audience.

A *video codec* is the device that physically performs the act of compressing and decompressing video images for transmission across a LAN or WAN. The current freeware CU-SeeMe application, offered by Cornell University, supports a codec that produces grayscale images compatible with the existing software.

Adding Quality Live Video to Your Web Site

With that little bit of video background behind you, you can now focus on your task at hand. How do you add quality video services to your Web site? Using the previously described guidelines, you can develop applications that provide live video feeds to your Web site visitors, or you can subscribe to one of the existing methodologies that are available today.

Just as in advanced audio techniques, there are also several companies that have stepped up to offer development technology to enable the Web site creator to add either a video *server* or *video conferencing* services to new users, subscribers, and visitors. Again, each of these video applications comes with multiple platform receiver pairs that can be downloaded from your Web site or from any number of similar sites on the Web.

The video tools described in the following sections are several of the more prominent Windows NT video applications currently available. Each of these applications serve as video teleconferencing servers. If you think about it, the step between a pure video service, such as the one offered by InterneTV (found at **http://www.crs4.it/~france/TV/** and where their viewers are allowed to watch Italian television with video and sound), to offer fully interactive video conferencing is a small one.

Tip

Before committing to any one video system, put your search engine (refer to Chapter 15, "Search Engines and Annotation Systems," for information on search engines) to work by looking for "Live Video" across the Net and then doing some exploration on your own.

FreeVue. FreeVue provides complete video teleconferencing products. The FreeVue home page is at **http://www.freevue.com/** (see fig. 19.5) and provides download access for their video conferencing software.

Selecting the FreeVue software hypertext link opens another Web page where you can download the FreeVue teleconferencing software for Windows NT.

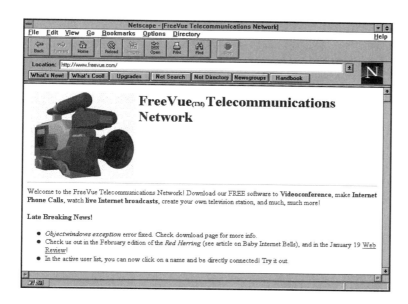

Fig. 19.5
This is the FreeVue
home page.

StreamWorks. StreamWorks, available from Xing Technology Corporation, supplies several products for the world of Internet real-time video services. They provide video conferencing software and MPEG players. The Xing Technology Corporation home page is at **http://www.xingtech.com/**. This page provides download access for all of their software products. To gain access to the download page you double-click the StreamWorks logo.

Double-clicking the Xing MPEG logo opens another Web page where you can download StreamWorks' MPEG player. Double-clicking the StreamWorks logo launches an additional selection screen where you can download StreamWorks' Video Conferencing software or test drive an example of the StreamWorks server that is running at Xing Technology Corporation headquarters.

CineVideo/Direct. CineVideo/Direct, a product of CineCom, is another popular video conferencing software product for the world of Internet real-time video services. The CineCom home page is at **http://www. cinecom.com/CineCom/cinvdrct.html** (see fig. 19.6). This page provides download access for CineVideo/Direct, a list of current connection sites, and a ListServer for easy access to these sites. They also provide a history of the product for those interested. Selecting the CineVideo/Direct Software hypertext link downloads the CineVideo//Direct software (currently available for Windows NT).

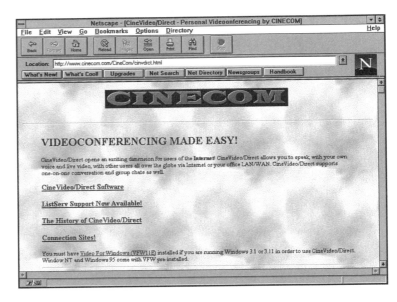

Fig. 19.6
This is CineCom's home page where you can download CineVideo/Direct.

Tip

Additional technical information about CineVideo/Direct is available at

http://www.cinecom.com/CineCom/directtech.html

CU-SeeMe. One of the more definitive video conferencing packages available is CU-SeeMe. This software package is a product of research being conducted at Cornell University and is available via anonymous FTP from their site at **ftp://gated.cornell.edu/pub/video**.

Note

There are no CU-SeeMe players for UNIX currently, but there are reflectors. This section is included anyway to give you general knowledge of the technology.

A commercial variation of CU-SeeMe, Enhanced CU-SeeMe, is available from White Pine Software, Inc. at **http://goliath.wpine.com/cudemown.htm**. Here, users can download a 30-day demo version of the Enhanced CU-SeeMe video conferencing software. They are first required to obtain a Registered DEMO Serial Number. The form for this registration can be found at **http://goliath.wpine.com/cuserial.htm.**

> **Note**
>
> White Pine Software, Inc. has been selected by Cornell Research Foundation as master licensee of Cornell's CU-SeeMe desktop video conferencing technology. White Pine's charter is to create low-cost, commercially enhanced and supported versions of CU-SeeMe and make it available to Internet users worldwide, bringing the advent of everyday video telecommunications one step closer.

> **Tip**
>
> White Pine Software, Inc. can be reached at **http://www.cu-seeme.com**.

CU-SeeMe provides Windows NT users with person-to person or group video teleconferencing. To provide the computing horsepower and equipment muscle necessary for video conferencing, CU-SeeMe connects each user in a group to a reflector site. A reflector site is usually a UNIX-based computer powerhouse, such as a Sun SPARCstation with an MBONE feed, that facilitates multi-participant conferencing.

> **Tip**
>
> If a user wants to be placed on the CU-SeeMe mailing list, he/she need only send an e-mail message with `subscribe cu-seeme-l` and his/her name to **listserv@cornell.edu.**

After installing the CU-SeeMe software and performing some relatively trivial configuration, the user can open a receive or send/receive connection to the numerical address of another participant on the reflector site. Once connected, a split screen appears that contains the live video of each person connected to the reflector. A user can never tell exactly what he might find when connecting to the reflectors. Connect and he might find himself in the middle of a multi-window conference—or staring at a test pattern or empty office.

Available Reflector Sites. The following is a list of the reflectors that are available for public use:

- www.cu-seeme.com (192.233.34.5)
- goliath.wpine.com (192.233.34.20)
- reflector.cit.cornell.edu (132.236.91.204)

- isis.dccs.upenn.edu (130.91.72.36)
- hilda.ncsc.org (128.109.178.103)
- NASA (139.88.27.43)

Hostname. A computer may need a hostname to talk on CU-SeeMe. If so, and the user doesn't already have a hostname, she must contact her network administrator. One quick way to provide a hostname is to make an entry into the hosts file, which is in the directory that contains the user's Windows Sockets stack.

A host file entry uses the following syntax:

<your IP address> <name for your PC>

If, for example, the user has selected a hostname of VIDconServer and his IP address is **228.232.6.4**, the host's file entry is

```
228.232.6.4 VIDconServer
```

Virtual Worlds: Tools, Applications, and Sites

The current state-of-the-art of virtual reality (VR) technology for the Internet community is Virtual Reality Modeling Language (VRML). This language is the basis of almost all VR participation on the Net today. The following paragraphs discuss both VRML and other variations on this theme and a VR site, and a site where you can obtain one of several VRML Browsers that are currently available.

While most VRML experiences are not truly "live"—it's coming quickly.

VRML (Virtual Reality Modeling Language)

VRML stands for Virtual Reality Modeling Language. It is a file format describing the geometry of network-aware 3D objects. A VRML file might describe a house, inside which one could find a door which is a hyperlink to another VRML file containing a library, in which one might find a book that is a hyperlink to an HTML page. Version "1.0" of the file format simply described the geometry of objects; VRML 2.0 will describe geometry with hooks for "behaviors" to be attached, using any number of programming languages, such as Java. The 2.0 specification is being finalized at the time of this writing, and an early implementation can be found in the "Live3D" plug-in for Netscape.

VRML has a support Web site, called the VRML Technical Forum, that is located at **http://vrml.wired.com/vrml.tech/**. This support site provides downloadable copies of the VRML Version 1.0 Specification and the VRML Programming Library Version 1.0 beta 1. These sites are also very helpful: **http://www.sdsc.edu/vrml/** and **http://vag.vrml.org/**.

> **Note**
>
> To properly serve VRML files off your site, you must map the file name extension to the right MIME type. For VRML 1.0 files, it is x-world/x-vrml. So, it should either be listed in your mime.types file, or added using an AddType directive in a configuration file.

VRML Browsers

There are several VRML browsers. The best listing of available browsers is at **http://www.sdsc.edu/SDSC/Partners/vrml/software/browsers.html**.

Live VR Worlds

There are a number of interactive world applications in development today. These worlds combine a 3-D experience with real-time person-to-person interaction. This section introduces you to three of the more advanced systems with the caveat that these sites are more than just Web site additions. These new worlds are a new technology on a par with Web technology; they represent the next generation of Internet technology.

Worlds Chat

Worlds Chat is the revolutionary 3-D, virtual chat, and entertainment environment. Worlds Chat allows users from all over cyberspace to meet and interact in a virtual space station. The chatting is done via keyboard, and the users create Avatars (digital actors) to represent themselves. Careful, it's addicting! To check it out, go to **www.worlds.net/products/wchat/**.

AlphaWorld

AlphaWorld is perhaps the first true online society. You can stake your claim and build your own site in this multiuser VR land. That's right, the users actually build the world! As of this writing, AlphaWorld is very much in beta, and very amazing. AlphaWorld is a creation of the same company as Worlds Chat. You will probably notice the visual similarities. Go to **www.worlds.net/products/alphaworld/**.

Traveler

OnLive! Technologies has developed software that allows real-time multi-point voice chat within 3-D virtual environments. What's that mean to you? It means you can talk—using your voice, not your fingers— to groups of people from all over the Internet. This is an interesting twist to the Chat scenario. The avatars have facial expressions and your avatar's mouth moves when you speak. This is certainly one of the most entertaining Internet technologies you will see anytime soon. Go to **www.onlive.com**.

The Not-Too-Distant Future: Auralview, W3Vision, and the WebStage

The not-to-distant future offers many possibilities—possibilities that are works-in-progress at this moment. As a finale to our discussion of Interactive and Live Applications, I would like to dance a bit in the dream world of the future. Here, I would like to define some of the future applications and concepts that I have introduced during our discussion.

Auralview

The world of *auralview* is only slightly different from where we are today. *Auralview* is really an extension of the concepts of video conferencing. In this future application area of Internet interaction, we not only have true, full motion video, either live, 3-D animated, or both, we also have 3-D sound and possibly even surround sound. The applications are endless: from Internet telephones, to interactive entertainment services; from distributed, industrial training 'films', to K-12 educational video shows. This is a world of interactive classroom-less colleges—a world in which talking to your computer is no longer a sign of impending visits to the little rubber rooms at some of our posh sanitariums.

W3Vision

World Wide Web [W3] Vision is a world of endless video and sound access from strategic places *around* the world, and *out* of this world. A place where, by simply 'dialing' in a requested location we can explore the ocean seas, floors, canyons, and volcanoes—where we can observe the Earth as it spins on its axis, in real-time and from any one of several hundreds or thousands of views and where a trip to the surface of the Moon, Mars, or Venus need not take leaving the planet, but could be enjoyed in the comfort of our living rooms.

WebStage

And finally, the intergalactic *WebStage*. The *WebStage* is a place where you can truly be a part of the action—where participation of world events, sporting events, plays, game shows, and training seminars takes place at your office desk, or in front of the home Multi-purpose AuralView Interface System [MAVIS]. This is our Internet future—a future you, as Web site developers, owners, and maintenance personnel, will help to define, refine, and direct. ❖

Index

A

H

S

X, Y, Z

QUE® has the right choice for every computer user

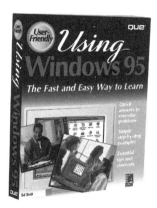

From the new computer user to the advanced programmer, we've got the right computer book for you. Our user-friendly *Using* series offers just the information you need to perform specific tasks quickly and move onto other things. And, for computer users ready to advance to new levels, QUE *Special Edition Using* books, the perfect all-in-one resource—and recognized authority on detailed reference information.

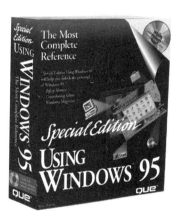

The *Using* series for casual users

Who should use this book?

Everyday users who:

- Work with computers in the office or at home
- Are familiar with computers but not in love with technology
- Just want to "get the job done"
- Don't want to read a lot of material

The user-friendly reference

- The fastest access to the one best way to get things done
- Bite-sized information for quick and easy reference
- Nontechnical approach in plain English
- Real-world analogies to explain new concepts
- Troubleshooting tips to help solve problems
- Visual elements and screen pictures that reinforce topics
- Expert authors who are experienced in training and instruction

Special Edition Using for accomplished users

Who should use this book?

Proficient computer users who:

- Have a more technical understanding of computers
- Are interested in technological trends
- Want in-depth reference information
- Prefer more detailed explanations and examples

The most complete reference

- Thorough explanations of various ways to perform tasks
- In-depth coverage of all topics
- Technical information cross-referenced for easy access
- Professional tips, tricks, and shortcuts for experienced users
- Advanced troubleshooting information with alternative approaches
- Visual elements and screen pictures that reinforce topics
- Technically qualified authors who are experts in their fields
- "Techniques form the Pros" sections with advice from well-known computer professionals

Complete and Return this Card for a *FREE* Computer Book Catalog

Thank you for purchasing this book! You have purchased a superior computer book written expressly for your needs. To continue to provide the kind of up-to-date, pertinent coverage you've come to expect from us, we need to hear from you. Please take a minute to complete and return this self-addressed, postage-paid form. In return, we'll send you a free catalog of all our computer books on topics ranging from word processing to programming and the internet.

☐   Mrs. ☐   Ms. ☐   Dr. ☐

me (first) ☐☐☐☐☐☐☐☐☐☐☐   (M.I.) ☐   (last) ☐☐☐☐☐☐☐☐☐☐☐☐

dress ☐☐☐☐☐☐☐☐☐☐☐☐☐☐☐☐☐☐☐☐☐☐☐☐☐

☐☐☐☐☐☐☐☐☐☐☐☐☐☐☐☐☐☐☐☐☐☐☐☐☐

y ☐☐☐☐☐☐☐☐☐☐☐   State ☐☐   Zip ☐☐☐☐☐ ☐☐☐☐

ne ☐☐☐ ☐☐☐ ☐☐☐☐   Fax ☐☐☐ ☐☐☐ ☐☐☐☐

mpany Name ☐☐☐☐☐☐☐☐☐☐☐☐☐☐☐☐☐☐☐☐☐

nail address ☐☐☐☐☐☐☐☐☐☐☐☐☐☐☐☐☐☐☐☐☐☐☐☐

Please check at least (3) influencing factors for purchasing this book.

nt or back cover information on book .... ☐
cial approach to the content .... ☐
npleteness of content .... ☐
hor's reputation .... ☐
lisher's reputation .... ☐
k cover design or layout .... ☐
x or table of contents of book .... ☐
e of book .... ☐
cial effects, graphics, illustrations .... ☐
r (Please specify): _____ ☐

low did you first learn about this book?

in Macmillan Computer Publishing catalog .... ☐
mmended by store personnel .... ☐
the book on bookshelf at store .... ☐
mmended by a friend .... ☐
ived advertisement in the mail .... ☐
an advertisement in: _____ ☐
book review in: _____ ☐
r (Please specify): _____ ☐

ow many computer books have you urchased in the last six months?

book only .... ☐   3 to 5 books .... ☐
ks .... ☐   More than 5 .... ☐

4. Where did you purchase this book?

Bookstore .... ☐
Computer Store .... ☐
Consumer Electronics Store .... ☐
Department Store .... ☐
Office Club .... ☐
Warehouse Club .... ☐
Mail Order .... ☐
Direct from Publisher .... ☐
Internet site .... ☐
Other (Please specify): _____ ☐

5. How long have you been using a computer?

☐ Less than 6 months   ☐ 6 months to a year
☐ 1 to 3 years   ☐ More than 3 years

6. What is your level of experience with personal computers and with the subject of this book?

	With PCs	With subject of book
New	☐	☐
Casual	☐	☐
Accomplished	☐	☐
Expert	☐	☐

Source Code ISBN: 0745-4

7. Which of the following best describes your job title?

Administrative Assistant .... ☐
Coordinator .... ☐
Manager/Supervisor .... ☐
Director .... ☐
Vice President .... ☐
President/CEO/COO .... ☐
Lawyer/Doctor/Medical Professional ...... ☐
Teacher/Educator/Trainer .... ☐
Engineer/Technician .... ☐
Consultant .... ☐
Not employed/Student/Retired .... ☐
Other (Please specify): _____ ☐

8. Which of the following best describes the area of the company your job title falls under?

Accounting .... ☐
Engineering .... ☐
Manufacturing .... ☐
Operations .... ☐
Marketing .... ☐
Sales .... ☐
Other (Please specify): _____ ☐

Comments: _____
_____
_____

Fold here and scotch-tape

9. What is your age?

Under 20 ....
21-29 ....
30-39 ....
40-49 ....
50-59 ....
60-over ....

10. Are you:

Male ....
Female ....

11. Which computer publications do you read regularly? (Please list)

_____
_____
_____
_____
_____
_____
_____
_____
_____
_____

The WebmasterCD has a simple HTML interface to point you to the right directories for the right software, hyperlinks to software companies, and more. Start your favorite Web browser and open the file INDEX.HTM right from the CD.